"A Gentleman and an Officer"

"A Gentleman and an Officer"

A Military
and Social History
of James B. Griffin's Civil War

Judith N. McArthur
Orville Vernon Burton

New York Oxford
Oxford University Press 1996

For Beatrice and Alice-Anne Burton

Oxford University Press

Oxford   New York
Athens   Auckland   Bangkok   Bogotá   Bombay
Buenos Aires   Calcutta   Cape Town   Dar es Salaam
Delhi   Florence   Hong Kong   Istanbul   Karachi
Kuala Lumpur   Madras   Madrid   Melbourne
Mexico City   Nairobi   Paris   Singapore
Taipei   Tokyo   Toronto

and associated companies in
Berlin   Ibadan

Copyright © 1996 by Judith N. McArthur and Orville Vernon Burton

Published by Oxford University Press, Inc.
198 Madison Avenue, New York, New York 10016

Oxford is a registered trademark of Oxford University Press

Library of Congress Cataloging-in-Publication Data
McArthur, Judith N.
A gentleman and an officer : a military and social history of
James B. Griffin's civil war / Judith N. McArthur and Orville Vernon
Burton.
p.   cm.   Includes a collection of letters from James B. Griffin to his wife
during his tenure in the Confederate Army.
Includes bibliographical references and index.
ISBN 0-19-509311-9   —   ISBN 0-19-509312-7 (pbk.)
1. Griffin, James B., b. 1825—Correspondence.
2. Soldiers—South Carolina—Edgefield—Correspondence.
3. Confederate States of America.   Army—Officers—Correspondence.
4. Confederate States of America.   Army.   Hampton Legion—Biography.
5. United States—History—Civil War, 1861–1865—Personal narratives, Confederate.
6. United States—History—Civil War, 1861–1865—Cavalry operations, Confederate.
7. Confederate States of America—Social conditions.
8. Edgefield (S.C.)—Biography.
I. Burton, Orville Vernon. II. Griffin, James B., b. 1825.   III. Title.
E547.H2G755   1996   973.7'42—dc20   96-32140

9 8 7 6 5 4 3 2 1

Printed in the United States of America
on acid-free paper

Foreword

When James B. Griffin went to war in 1861 he was in the prime of life, thirty-six years old, the owner of sixty-one slaves and fifteen hundred acres of prime South Carolina plantation land, full of confidence that the armies of the Confederacy would whip the Yankees in short order and establish the new nation's independence. Four years later he returned to a burned-out plantation without slaves, without capital, half of his land gone and the remainder mortgaged to the full amount of its diminished value. After a year of trying to make a go of it as a planter in the new order, Griffin gave up and moved to Texas, where he achieved success in a career as a brick manufacturer.

Griffin's story of agrarian grandeur and initial martial success followed by ruinous defeat and subsequent rebirth as a businessman is the story in microcosm of the South from 1860 to 1880. It is a story for the wartime years told with pathos and insight in Griffin's letters to his wife, skillfully edited and annotated by Judith N. McArthur and Orville Vernon Burton. As a field officer in the famous Hampton's Legion during the war's first year, Griffin was in a position to portray important operations in the Virginia theater. His letter describing the battle of Seven Pines, where he commanded the Legion after Hampton was wounded, is one of the best accounts of that battle from the Confederate side.

When the Legion was reorganized and Griffin failed to be elected as colonel of its infantry regiment, he resigned and returned to South Carolina. There he served intermittently in the defenses of Charleston and elsewhere until the end. His letters during these years offer glimpses of an important but neglected theater of war. They have considerable value to historians seeking to understand events in that theater.

But these are not merely military letters. They discuss matters concerning the running of the plantation and issues of family, kinship, and race back home in South Carolina. The letters constitute important documents in the social and cultural history of this plantation region of Piedmont South Carolina as well as the military history of a people at war. But Griffin would not have perceived a sharp line of demarcation between social and military history, and neither do the editors, for the Confederacy was a nation in arms to preserve a social order based on slavery.

Griffin did not put it that way. Like other Confederates of all classes from wealthy planter to dirt farmer, he professed to fight for liberty and *against* slavery. In a letter to his wife in February 1862 Griffin stated that he was "battling for Liberty and independence . . . rather than be a Slave, *Yea* worse than a slave to Yankee Master." He was using the word "slave" here in the same way that Americans in 1776 had used it to describe their subordination to the British. Like the secessionists of 1776, they too believed they were fighting for freedom. But unlike many Americans in Thomas Jefferson's time, who felt embarrassed by the paradox of fighting for their own freedom while holding other people in slavery, Griffin and his Confederate contemporaries recognized no paradox. Several weeks after declaring that he fought for Liberty and independence, Griffin wrote home in consternation that his faithful body servant had run away to the Yankees. "It is very singular," he lamented, "and I can't account for it."

These letters also offer important insights into gender relations and concepts of honor and masculinity in the South. Males of the planter class felt a patriarchal obligation as protectors of their dependents. At the same time, their honor and masculinity in time of war were bound up with defense of the state; to stay out of the army would dishonor their manhood. Yet to go to war would leave the plantation without its protector. Planters' wives, including Leila Griffin, coped well with their expanded responsibilities. Nevertheless, James Griffin and many others like him felt acutely the tension between their obligation to family and their honorable duty to the state. They reconciled this conflict by the rationalization that in fighting for the Confederacy they were protecting their families. Griffin's letters help us to understand this dilemma and its resolution.

McArthur and Burton have provided a context for these letters with an introductory chapter that is a superb piece of research and writing. Together, this introduction, the letters, and the annotations greatly enlarge our understanding of the social and military history of the South in the Civil War era.

James M. McPherson

Acknowledgments

We are deeply indebted to the descendants of James B. and Leila Griffin for sharing these letters for publication and for assistance in tracing family history. Linda Page provided essential genealogical information and documents, and Jack L. Gunter coordinated the search for photographs. For the reproductions we thank the families of Mary Dolorita and Jean Marie Cannon, Mary Elliott Gunter, Jim Griffin Gunter, and Jack L. Gunter.

We have worked on this book a long time, and, consequently, many friends and colleagues have contributed to this work in some way; we thank each and every one. A particular debt of gratitude we owe to Norman D. Brown, who did more than anyone to help launch the project and was unfailingly generous with time, expertise, and encouragement. We extend special thanks to John Hammond Moore, Robert Krick, and O. Lee Sturkey. Robert Krick undertook a time-consuming search in the National Archives, and O. Lee Sturkey shared his unpublished research on the Hampton Legion infantry and pointed out relevant sources. Both also read part of an early draft. Dr. Moore commented on the manuscript, researched some archival sources for us, and provided good company, friendship, and even a place to stay while researching in Columbia, South Carolina. Ann Malone read the entire manuscript, including the letters, and provided valuable insights on family and Southern History. Many scholars commented astutely on the first chapter, which is much the better for their critiques. We are fortunate that colleagues and friends are not mutually exclusive; J. Leonard Bates, Sonya Michel, Richard Jensen, Mark Leff, and James Barrett all took time to read parts of the manuscript. Jane Turner Censer, Bertram Wyatt-Brown, Ron Field, and David Moltke-Hensen provided insightful critiques.

John Slate at the Center for American History, University of Texas at Austin, arranged for the reproductions from the Wilmot Walter Curry Diary. Librarians and archivists at the Perkins Library at Duke

University, the Southern Historical Collection at the University of North Carolina at Chapel Hill, Rice University, Furman University, United Daughters of the Confederacy Relic Room, the South Caroliniana Library (SCL), the South Carolina Department of Archives and History (SCDAH), the Library of Congress, and the National Archives were exceptionally knowledgeable and generous in their time, tracking down minutia and checking details. As always Dr. Allen Stokes and his staff at the SCL made working there a pleasure, and the staff at the SCDAH were very helpful in figuring out military personnel; special thanks to Robert H. Mackintosh, Jr., Patrick McCawley, Alexia J. Helsley, Marion Chandler, and Bryan F. McKown. In an attempt to find where James B. Griffin attended school, we wrote or called nearly every possible school, and many friends searched their universities' alumni records for us. Professor Edmund Lee Drago spent much time looking for Griffin in the records of various Charleston schools. In Edgefield, we particularly appreciate the efforts of the archivists at the Courtesy Center and members of the Edgefield County Historical Society, especially Lynn Allen Booraem, Hendrik Booraem V, Diane Timmerman, Julian Mims, David Parket, and Bettis Rainsford. Vera Human Burton represents the best in what "community" is all about and provided lodging and love.

We are grateful for the support provided by the University of Illinois at Urbana-Champaign (UIUC). Student assistants included Shamsul Huda, Bruce Tap, Don Litteau, Julia Walsh, Brian Garrett, Thomas Ritz, Miller Karnes, and Rose Stremlau; Frank Freemon researched questions about medicine during the Civil War. Student contributions were made possible by generous funding from the UIUC Research Board. At the UIUC Library, we have depended on the Interlibrary Loan services and the Reference Department, where Carol Penka was a scholar's guardian angel. The staff of the UIUC History Department have helped in numerous ways, and we particularly appreciate the word processing efforts of Pat Prothe and Jan Langendorf. We appreciate the privilege of working with the people at the National Center for Supercomputing Applications at UIUC. For their work with databases and geographic information systems to help us produce the maps, we thank David Herr, Dr. Terence Finnegan, and Charles Herring; for her proficiency and good cheer in accomplishing multitudinous tasks, we thank Shirley Shore.

Fellowships at the Woodrow Wilson International Center for Schol-

ars in Washington, D.C., and at the National Humanities Center in
Research Triangle, N.C., allowed time to work on this book.

Hal Smith took time from his own work to proofread transcriptions
and to facilitate electronic communications between Texas, Illinois,
and New York. Georgeanne Burton read the entire manuscript several
times, improved both content and style immeasurably, and provided
inspiration.

We appreciate Sheldon Meyer's support of this book project and
the efforts of Sheldon's assistants, editors Karen Wolny and Andrew
Albanese, as well as those of Oxford production editor Joellyn M.
Ausanka. All the help from friends, colleagues, and editors have added
coherence and depth to this book, and we thank you and credit your
input; we alone, of course, are responsible for any errors as well as for
the content and interpretation of "A *Gentleman and an Officer.*"

This book is dedicated with love to Beatrice Georgia Burton and
Carrah Alice-Anne Burton.

Editorial Note

The letters of James B. Griffin are a privately held family collection, now in the possession of J. B. Griffin's great-grandson Jack L. Gunter of Dallas, Texas; photocopies have been deposited at the Center for American History, University of Texas at Austin. They have been transcribed literally, with no editorial changes except where necessary to clarify meaning, and all such additions are enclosed in brackets. Inconsistent spellings, such as Connor/Conner and recieve/receive have been left unchanged. Griffin's capitalization and punctuation have been reproduced as accurately as possible, although distinctions between some lower- and uppercase letters and between periods and the tiny dashes that he used liberally are sometimes ambiguous. He sometimes began a sentence with a lower case letter; these have been capitalized for readability. Griffin added postscripts by turning the first page of a letter sideways and writing a column of tiny script down the top margin, a nineteenth-century convention not amenable to mechanical reproduction, and postscripts have been moved to the end of the text.

Biographical footnotes for general officers have been drawn from standard sources such as *Generals in Blue, Generals in Gray, Dictionary of American Biography, Confederate Military History,* and *Biographical Directory of the Confederacy;* only biographies and special studies have been cited. Biographical information on the Griffin and Burt families has been documented wherever possible. Unattributed birth and death dates have been supplied from family records in the possession of Griffin's great-great-granddaughter Linda Page of New York City.

Contents

Maps

Abbreviations Used in the Notes

B&L   *Battles and Leaders of the Civil War.* Edited by Robert Underwood Johnson and Clarence Clough Buel. 4 vols., 1887. Reprint, New York: Thomas Yoseloff, 1956.

CAH-UT   Center for American History, University of Texas at Austin

CMH   *Confederate Military History.* Edited by Clement A. Evans. 12 vols., 1889. Extended ed., Wilmington, N.C.: Broadfoot Publishing, 1987.

CSR   *Compiled Service Records of Confederate Soldiers Who Served in Organizations from the State of South Carolina.* National Archives, microfilm. Copy in South Carolina Department of Archives and History, Columbia.

DU   Duke University, William R. Perkins Library

ECC   Edgefield County Courthouse, Edgefield, S.C.

FU   Baptist Historical Collection, Furman University

LC   Library of Congress, Manuscript Division

NA   National Archives

OR   *War of the Rebellion: A Compilation of the Official Records of the Union and Confederate Armies.* 128 vols. Washington, D.C.: U.S. Government Printing Office, 1880–1901.

SCDAH   South Carolina Department of Archives and History, Columbia

SCHS   South Carolina Historical Society, Charleston

SCL   South Caroliniana Library, University of South Car-
             olina, Columbia

SHC   Southern Historical Collection, University of North
             Carolina at Chapel Hill

SHSP   *Southern Historical Society Papers*. 47 vols. Rich-
             mond, Va.: 1876–1930.

TSL   Texas State Library, Austin

"A Gentleman and an Officer"

It is needless to speak of General Griffin on this side of the State, where he is so well known as a gentleman and an officer. Suffice it to say that he is the very man for the place in every possible view of the arrangement.

—Edgefield *Advertiser*, 29 May 1861

1 *"Without Counting the Cost"*

> *Resolved*, That the legislature, without counting the cost, should immediately organize and arm the people of this State for defense.
>
> —Edgefield Committee of Twenty-Five, Edgefield *Advertiser*, 14 November 1860

James Benjamin Griffin rode off to Virginia in 1861 to serve under Joseph E. Johnston—"Old Joe" to his troops—in a style that befitted a southern gentleman: on a fine-blooded horse, with two slaves to wait on him, two trunks, and his favorite hunting dog. He was thirty-five years old, a wealthy planter, and the owner of sixty-one slaves when he joined Wade Hampton's elite Legion as a major of cavalry. He left behind seven children, the eldest only twelve, and a wife who was eight and a half months' pregnant; the baby arrived while the newly commissioned Major Griffin was not yet 100 miles from home. The Confederate army paid him $150 a month and required him to furnish his own horse, saber, and pair of matched pistols.[1] As a field officer in a prestigious unit, the opportunities for fame and glory seemed limitless.

---

1. OR, ser. 4, 1:304. According to regimental historian Ron Field, Hampton changed his mind about the cavalry arming themselves, and Major Griffin requested that South Carolina provide the cavalry with pistols. Governor Francis W. Pickens was irritated with yet another request for pistols in July. Griffin to Col. Edward Manigault, Chief of Ordnance, 13 June 1861 and Pickens to Manigault, 7 July 1861, Letters and petitions to the Ordnance Board and Ordnance Officer, Ordnance Bureau, 1861–1864, State Auditor, SCDAH; both also cited in Field, in collaboration with William B. Bynum and Howard Michael Madaus, *South Carolina Volunteers in the Civil War: The Hampton Legion, Part 1: Regimental History* (Lower Swell, Gloucestershire, England: Design Folio, 1994), 51.

Griffin's experiences in the war have been documented in eighty letters to his wife, Leila Burt Griffin, in Edgefield, South Carolina.[2] Three-fourths of the letters were written at the Virginia front. Extraordinary in their breadth and volume, the letters encompass the entire service of a Civil War participant, first as a Confederate officer on the Virginia front and then as a militia officer in South Carolina. They detail living conditions and military maneuvers, criticize South Carolina and Confederate war policies, and reveal anxieties about the electioneering resulting from the provision of the Conscription Act of 1862 that allowed reenlisting companies to elect their officers. They also comment on the Edgefield scene and news from Leila; although her letters have not survived, Griffin's responses mirror conditions on the homefront.[3]

This study assesses the value and import of Griffin's letters and also places them in the context of the times, explaining changes and experiences in the lives of the people of Edgefield as reflected in the letters. Griffin's letters offer a unique opportunity to frame the people that Griffin wrote about in the precise socio-economic structure of Edgefield District (see map); they are a valuable primary source on family, kinship, friendship, class, and status in a southern community. Griffin's letters also add another dimension to our view of some celebrated

---

2. In 1860 Edgefield District covered more than twice the area now known as Edgefield County. Its eastern boundary was the Saluda River, which separated it from Newberry District, while on the west the Savannah River marked the boundary with the state of Georgia. To the north was Abbeville District, and between it and Newberry lay the southeastern point of Laurens District. The southern border ran along Lexington, Orangeburg, and Barnwell districts. The district seat, Edgefield Village, also called Edgefield Court House, lay near the center of the district, sixty miles southwest of the state capital, Columbia, and twenty-five miles from the thriving hinterland river city of Augusta, Georgia. For detailed description of Edgefield, see Orville Vernon Burton, *In My Father's House Are Many Mansions: Family and Community in Edgefield, South Carolina* (Chapel Hill: Univ. of North Carolina Press, 1985).

3. In his history of the Hampton Legion, Field quoted a newspaper account wherein a soldier stated that before the battle at Manassas, they burned all their letters. This may have been standard procedure so letters would not fall into enemy hands. Field, *South Carolina Volunteers in the Civil War*, 5.

South Carolinians. Fellow Edgefieldians Matthew Calbraith Butler and Martin Witherspoon Gary are mentioned frequently; they were Griffin's closest friends among the field officers, as was James Conner of Charleston. Many of the soldiers named in the letters were Griffin's neighbors and relatives. (See Appendix.) Some of these men were serving in the Hampton Legion, while others were attached to nearby South Carolina regiments, especially the Seventh, commanded by Colonel Thomas Glascock Bacon and part of Joseph P. Kershaw's (formerly Bonham's) Brigade. Both Bacon and Milledge Luke Bonham were from Edgefield, and the latter was kin to the Butlers and the Griffins. Civilians on the homefront worried about the safety of friends and neighbors as well as husbands, fathers, and sons. After mentioning that Butler had lost four men in a dramatic cavalry skirmish near Williamsburg, Griffin added reassuringly to Leila, "you didn't know them."

J.B. Griffin reveals in these letters his perceptions of the Edgefield planter aristocracy, its strengths and weaknesses, its expectations and obligations, its myths and realities as its members functioned at home and at war; the letters reflect Griffin's expectations of himself and his judgments as a husband, father, friend, leader, businessman/planter, slave owner/master, officer, and gentleman with all that connoted in southern society. As source material, these letters represent a case study of a member of the southern male gentry seldom analyzed by historians. We have reminiscences and biographies of well-known Confederate generals. We have studies and edited collections of letters revealing much about the famed common southern fighting man. But we know little about the distinct type of southern leader, the mid-grade officer, who translated strategic planning into operational and tactical maneuvers. Not an extraordinary officer like Stonewall Jackson, Nathan Bedford Forrest, or his friend Matthew Calbraith Butler (who cavalierly rode into battle with only a silver tipped riding whip), J.B. Griffin performed no unusually daring acts; nor did he inspire great loyalty in his men. He was a competent field officer but never attained lasting glory. No large destiny awaited him, although he yearned for such. In other words, James B. Griffin was a man without great vices and without heroic stature. Like Griffin, most officers of the Confederacy never became household names and rarely received the adulation of their men or the public; yet these men provided the core of southern political, military, and business leadership.

First and foremost, these letters are a story of the Civil War, a penetrating commentary by a participant. Griffin recounted details of military action and recorded his impressions of combatants and of politics in the war. Griffin described to Leila secret troop movements that would certainly have been censored in more recent wars. Some of these letters have considerable significance in the military history of the Civil War. The Virginia letters describe the Hampton Legion's role in the Peninsula Campaign: the march from Manassas to Fredericksburg, the siege of Yorktown and the retreat toward Richmond, and the fighting at Eltham's Landing and Seven Pines, where Griffin commanded the Legion after Hampton was wounded. The Peninsula letters are especially significant because the official records of the Union and Confederate armies contain relatively few accounts by Confederate officers. None of the Confederate brigadiers filed a report on Seven Pines; Griffin's letter devotes three pages to a minute accounting of the action.[4]

After his year in Virginia, Griffin served two active enlistments as an officer in the South Carolina Reserves, first as a lieutenant colonel in the Fifth South Carolina Reserves and finally as colonel in the First South Carolina Militia. Letters became fewer and shorter because he spent longer periods at home. The last letter was written in February 1865 as the military situation in South Carolina crumbled. After the war the family left South Carolina behind and began a completely new life in Texas; chapter 9 follows the Griffin story west.

Although Griffin was well informed on military affairs, the scope of this correspondence transcends battles and leaders. We discover in those most extraordinary of times the most ordinary of day-to-day issues—health, weather, gossip. One might expect to find a Confederate

---

4. On Seven Pines see James M. McPherson, *Battle Cry of Freedom: The Civil War Era* (New York: Oxford Univ. Press, 1988), 461–62, 464, 477, 576. Compare Griffin's letter of 2 June 1862 with the short account published by Conner's daughter. Mary Conner Moffett, ed., *Letters of General James Conner, C.S.A.* (Columbia, S.C.: R.L. Bryan, 1950). Only a few of Hampton's letters have been published and none of Butler's (at DU) or Gary's (at SCL).

officer meditating on slavery, emancipation, Lincoln, and so on. Instead, we are confronted by simple humanity with simple concerns. Momentous historical events intruded on Griffin's life and sent him off to war, but his heartfelt considerations were about his family, his community, and his own personal pride. These letters capture variations in Griffin's mood and thus highlight the difference between consistent, engrained cultural values and more ephemeral attitudes. The Civil War was the refinery, the ordeal by fire, that tested and verified, or modified, southern upper-class values.

Griffin clearly enjoyed the structured life of military camp and the privileges and responsibilities of rank. Foreign to his character were the moroseness common to the highest rank of southern leadership and the bitter cynicism often found in the rank and file. In the army, as at home in Edgefield, he knew precisely what he owed to equals and what was due him from subordinates. He took pride in doing his duty and failed to see why enlisted men and slaves might want to avoid theirs. These letters reveal Griffin to be the epitomal man of duty, to his community, his district, his state, his section of the country, his family, friends, and even his dependents, including slaves. Devoted to his family, Griffin faithfully wrote Leila twice per week, usually on Wednesdays and Sundays. He took the time to write to his young sons. At times Griffin was torn between duty and devotion. Of special interest in his letters is a constant tension between his perceived responsibility to his family and his obligation to the newly formed Confederate government. The letters highlight Griffin's personal decision over whether to go home to his family or reenlist at the end of his twelve-month tour of duty; he worried more about this dilemma than about the military situation. His changes in attitude toward these conflicting responsibilities as the war continued demonstrate his fluctuating morale and determination to continue the fight.

Griffin, like most southerners of his station and age, struggled with a need for reassurance about his own valor and status; the war was his very personal quest for recognition and affirmation. These struggles, writ large in the crucible of battle, were reflected in his letters. Men like James B. Griffin felt a driving need to be "honored," to "prove" themselves in personal courage and leadership ability. To this sensitive man, the respect of his peers, family, kin, and even subordinates was all too important. He craved his soldiers' homage in spite of, or perhaps because of, his punctiliousness in discipline and precision in drilling. Griffin's letters vividly illustrate this aspect of "southern honor."[5]

James B. Griffin's Genealogy and Kinship Networks

J.B. Griffin was born on 10 October 1825. His ancestors, like so many upcountry settlers, had come from Virginia, arriving in South Carolina sometime before the Revolution. Two branches of the Griffin family settled in contiguous districts of what at one time had been the old Ninety Six District. One branch, James and William, probably brothers, settled in Newberry District; the other branch, Richard, Anthony, and another William (all brothers and probably cousins of James and William in Newberry) chose the adjoining Laurens District.[6] The James in Newberry had a son James, who became J.B. Griffin's grandfather. He established himself near the town of Ninety Six in the northeast corner of Edgefield District. He fought in the Revolutionary War and was said to have been killed near the Saluda River in a Tory ambush in 1781 during the bitter Whig-Tory warfare that disrupted life in that region. He left a widow, Frances, the daughter of William Beal, and three young sons—William, Vincent, and James.[7] The youngest, James,

---

5. Bertram Wyatt-Brown, "The Ideal Typology and Antebellum Southern History: A Testing of A New Approach," *Societas* 5 (Winter 1975): 1–29, and *Southern Honor: Ethics and Behavior in the Old South* (New York: Oxford Univ. Press, 1982); Edward Lynn Ayers, *Vengeance and Justice: Crime and Punishment in the 19th-Century American South* (New York: Oxford Univ. Press, 1984); Kenneth S. Greenberg, *Masters and Statemen: The Political Culture of American Slavery* (Baltimore: Johns Hopkins Univ. Press, 1985).

6. George Leland Summer, *Newberry County, South Carolina: Historical and Genealogical Annals* (Baltimore: Genealogical Publishing, 1980), 238; Margaret Watson, *Greenwood County Sketches: Old Roads and Early Families* (Greenwood, S.C.: Attic Press, 1970), 241–42, 247; Thomas H. Pope, *The History of Newberry County, South Carolina*, vol. 1: 1749–1860 (Columbia: Univ. of South Carolina Press, 1973), 41, 65, 106, 114, 130, 139, 160–161, 183, 186, 203–5, 216, 234, 264, 269, 274–76, 282; May Teague Cluck to Mrs. C.G. Young, 6 Nov. 1929, Lee Harriet Randle Papers, DU.

7. Beal is sometimes spelled Beall. James and Frances were married on 16 Jan. 1775. William was born on 11 Jan. 1776, and Vincent on 5 Oct. 1779. Watson, *Greenwood County Sketches*, 247, confuses James Griffin with his son James B. Griffin when she incorrectly states that this James Griffin moved to Texas.

born on 15 December 1782, would become the father of J.B. Griffin. William died a young man, but Vincent and James raised families and became large landowners in the Ninety Six area.[8]

James, the father of J.B., moved closer to the center of the district and established a plantation northwest of Edgefield Court House, on both sides of Long Cane Road.[9] Reputedly he was "quite wealthy" and left a "large estate" to his son.[10] In January 1848 he deeded his children 911 acres, leaving himself with 1200 acres valued at $8000.[11] The probate inventory of his estate in 1855 showed 29 slaves and $1,213 in cash and outstanding notes. Livestock, crops, and personal effects were valued at over $4000.[12]

James Griffin married twice, but all of his children—William, Eliza Ann, and J.B.—were born during his marriage to Frances Bunting, who died sometime between 1825 and 1827. He married Nancy Mims in 1829, when he was forty-seven and she was thirty-four years of age,

---

8. *Abstracts of Wills of Edgefield County, South Carolina* (Albany, Ga.: Delwyn Associates, 1973), 42; Summer, *Newberry County, South Carolina,* 239; N. Louise Bailey, Mary L. Morgan, and Carolyn R. Taylor, eds., *Biographical Directory of the South Carolina Senate, 1776–1985,* 3 vols. (Columbia: Univ. of South Carolina Press, 1986), 2:939–40. Vincent and Richard Griffin, Jr., from the Laurens branch, were probably cousins; they married sisters, daughters of Nathan Smith Lipscomb, an Abbeville planter who represented that district for two terms in the state house of representatives and four in the senate. Other Lipscomb children chose spouses from the distinguished Bonham and Brooks families of Edgefield, beginning a complex genealogical web that linked these four families and the aristocratic Butler clan. Genealogical charts constructed for the families discussed in these letters were originally intended as an appendix. These charts, both hand-drawn and organized into the database program "Brother's Keeper," have been placed in the SCL, where interested readers can attempt to unravel some of the complex relationships that encompass kin and family in the South. The genealogies include the Griffin, Miles, Burt, Bonham, Lipscomb, Butler, and Brooks families.

9. Now Highway 35.

10. John Chapman, *History of Edgefield County from the Earliest Settlements to 1897* (Newberry, S.C.: Elbert H. Aull, 1897), 266.

11. James Griffin and Nancy Griffin to Diomede F. Hollingsworth and Wife, 5 Jan. 1848, Deed Book EEE, 301, ECC.

12. Inventory of the Estate of James Griffin, 14 Feb. 1855, Box 72, Probate Records, ECC.

and it was she who reared the children. Nothing is known about William, the eldest, who died before reaching manhood, nor much about the youth of J.B. and his sister Eliza. Both J.B. and Eliza married suitably within the planter class. Eliza's marriage in 1840, just before her seventeenth birthday, linked the Griffins with the several nearby Hollingsworth families, all substantial planters. The groom, twenty-one-year-old Diomede F. Hollingsworth, owned 32 slaves and over 1000 acres of land; in 1849 his plantation produced 65 bales of cotton.[13]

J.B. Griffin courted Emma Rebecca Miller, whose father, B. H. Miller, was roughly as wealthy as J.B.'s father, just below the top decile.[14] The two were married late in the fall of 1847, when Griffin had just turned twenty-two and his bride was fifteen. In Edgefield, the average age for brides was twenty; for grooms it was twenty-five. Generally Edgefield men selected younger brides, and the older the husband, the greater the difference in spouses' ages. In 1850, men with wealth and age similar to Griffin's were, on average, four years older than their wives.[15]

Fifteen months after their marriage, J.B. and Rebecca had a son, James William, called Willie. The following year the couple was expecting another child, but in September 1850 eighteen-year-old Rebecca and their second son died in childbirth. The rate of maternal mortality was high in the South; 3.8 percent of the white women who died in South Carolina in 1850 died, like Rebecca Griffin, in child-

---

13. Carlee T. McClendon, *Edgefield Marriage Record* (Columbia, S.C.: R.L. Bryan, 1970), 64, 76; McClendon, *Edgefield Death Notices*, 63, 81, 217. In 1850 Hollingsworth's land was worth $13,000, which placed him nearly in the top 3 percent of wealthiest household heads. Burt Family, Leonardo Andrea Genealogical Collection, microfilm, roll 6, 45, SCL. A bale of cotton weighs approximately 400 pounds.

14. Miller ranked 88.7 percentile in land among household heads.

15. McClendon, *Edgefield Marriage Records*, 64. A bride of fifteen was not unusual. Marrying younger brides tended to reinforce patriarchy. Burton, *In My Father's House Are Many Mansions*, 118–20, Table 3-2. Because age at marriage was calculated from people who reported they were married that census year, ages will be higher than age at first marriage since it also includes those who are remarrying that year.

birth or as a direct consequence. J.B. found himself a widower with a nineteen-month-old son. The newspaper commented that "the devoted husband, it is hoped whilst suffering this severe bereavement, will evince a proper resignation to the Divine Will, and employ much of his time in training up her little boy, and as his faculties expand, impress upon them the mother's spirit."[16]

Like most young wealthy widowers, J.B. remarried quickly. His second courtship took place at Sunnyside, the plantation of Capt. Eugene Brenan Burt about five miles northwest of Edgefield Court House. Captain Burt, himself a widower since the death of his wife, Sarah Dozier, in 1847, was a planter whose slave and property ownership ranked him in the third decile of wealthiest landowners. In 1850 his 1000 acres were valued at $4200.[17] Griffin was undoubtedly one of numerous suitors calling at Sunnyside, since Captain Burt had five daughters still at home, three of whom were old enough to receive proposals of marriage. Griffin married Eliza Harwood Burt, who preferred to be called Leila, on 22 February 1853; she was twenty-three and Griffin twenty-seven.[18]

His marriage into the Burt clan connected Griffin to another network of old Edgefield families, kin to the households of Captain Burt and his four brothers and also to their cousins, the Miles and Dozier

---

16. Edgefield *Advertiser*, 25 Sept. 1850; McClendon, *Edgefield Death Notices*, 81, 217. Sally McMillen, *Motherhood in the Old South* (Baton Rouge: Lousiana State Univ. Press, 1990), table 3. With the exception of isolated Maine, most non-southern states reported childbirth as cause of between 1 and 2 percent of white female deaths. South Carolina's percentage was exceeded by Florida (5.4), Georgia (5.0), Texas (4.9), and Maine (4.8).

17. Burt's acreage was evenly divided between improved and unimproved land. His previous year's cotton crop—20 bales—was not large, but he had raised 80 hogs, 1200 bushels of corn and 1000 of oats. Of the eighty household heads who were fifty years of age in 1850, Burt was the eighth wealthiest. Burt Family, Leonardo Andrea Genealogical Collection, microfilm, roll 6, 45, SCL.

18. Edgefield *Advertiser*, 22 Feb. 1853; McClendon, *Edgefield Marriage Records*, 64. According to her gravestone in Calvary Cemetery, Fort Worth, Texas, Leila was born on 10 Oct. 1829, four years to the day later than Griffin.

families.[19] Leila's father was the eldest of five brothers and three sisters, but her two youngest uncles are the only ones mentioned in Griffin's letters. Major Moody Burt, who apparently never married, was the only brother who lived outside Edgefield District. His plantation lay across the Savannah River in Columbia County, Georgia, which he represented for some time in the state assembly.[20] Dr. William Miles Burt, the youngest brother, had "a fair practice" at Edgefield Court House and was "well spoken of."[21] Griffin and Leila seem to have been especially close to his family.

The new branch on the Griffin-Burt family tree bore abundant fruit. Although the national birthrate had dropped to an average of 5.4 children by 1850, southern families tended to be larger. A year and a half after her marriage Leila gave birth to her first child; in all, she bore eight children (including twins) in nine years. None of the first three births were more than fifteen months apart; the next two came at intervals of roughly seventeen months. Since nursing women tended to experience delayed ovulation and might have been expected to give birth about every two years, the close spacing of the Griffin children suggests that Leila may have weaned her infants within a few months of birth or used slave wet nurses. Only between the last two children is the birth interval as long as twenty-three months, and this occurred when Griffin was in Virginia with the Confederate Army for

---

19. Handwritten account of Burt family, Armistead Burt Papers, Box 33, DU. This version says that Mathew and Ann Burt arrived in South Carolina in 1792. Robert B. Mathis, *The Mathew Burt Family of Virginia and the Deep South* (n.p., 1976), 4, and Bailey et al., *Biographical Directory of the South Carolina Senate*, 1:235, both fix the date at around 1770, which seems more plausible. The Mathis book, however, should be used with great care as it contains some striking errors—the most egregious of which is the repeated claim that Eugene Burt married Leila Griffin.

20. Obituary of Major Moody Burt, unidentified newspaper clipping, Griffin Family Scrapbook and Account Book, in possession of Jack L. Gunter, Dallas, Texas. This is a ledger in which Griffin kept his plantation and business accounts from the late 1850s through the late 1870s, and which his daughter Fannie subsequently filled with obituaries, poems, and stories clipped from various newspapers. Many of the clippings were pasted over the plantation accounts as well as on blank pages.

21. Chapman, *History of Edgefield*, 349–50.

a year and had only one furlough at home.[22] His two marriages gave Griffin a total of six sons and three daughters, whom he loved dearly, as he did Leila. And Leila loved her stepson as her own, referring to him as "my Son William Griffin."[23]

Southern culture was deeply family-centered, and kin relationships were central to an individual's self-image and standing in the community.[24] Naming patterns indicated and mapped bloodlines. Given names of both males and females descended through generations, linking past and present, and mothers' maiden names were passed on to sons as first or middle names. Leila's cousin, Maria Burt, and Andrew Pickens Butler, Jr., christened their sons Burt Butler and Pickens Butler. Common ancestors showed up in the naming patterns of related branches on a family tree: Stanmore Butler, born before the Revolution, reappeared in the names of antebellum Lipscomb cousins, Stanmore Butler Brooks and Stanmore Butler Griffin.

Griffin, who was named for his father and maternal grandfather, followed tradition in christening his own children. Each child had at least one name of an ancestor, and most had two. James William (Willie) was given the names of his father, uncle, grandfather, and great uncle. Robert Henry Burt, born the year that Leila's younger brother died, carried on his name. Fannie Eugene bore the name of her Griffin grandmother and great-grandmother and her Burt grandfather. Annie Diomede, called "Meadie," honored Griffin's recently deceased brother-in-law, Diomede Hollingsworth. Moody Burt shared his name with a cousin, Leila's uncle, and a great-great uncle. The twins, Claude Eugene and Francis Calhoun (Callie), celebrated grandfather Eugene Burt (again), great uncle Francis Burt, and the Calhoun branch of the Burt family tree, as well as honoring South Carolina's great statesman, John C. Calhoun. James Hampton was named in honor of generations of James Griffins and his father's regimental commander, Wade Hampton. Minnie Leila, the baby, bore

---

22. See McMillen, *Motherhood in the Old South*, 32, 111–25.

23. Mrs. J.B. Griffin to Gen. A.C. Garlington, 28 Jan. 1865, Petitions for Exemption, 1864–1865, Administrative Records, Adjutant General, SCDAH.

24. John E. Crowley, "The Importance of Kinship: Testamentary Evidence from South Carolina," *Journal of Interdisciplinary History* 16, no. 4 (Spring 1986): 559–77; Burton, *In My Father's House Are Many Mansions*.

the names of her aunt and her mother. The preponderance of maternal lineage names among the Griffin children reflects the Burt clan's much larger size. Names such as Harwood, Armistead, and Moody, Mary Ann, Harriet, and Caroline had been passed on for generations.

Kinship communities in Edgefield District were linked at many junctures. Griffin was kin by blood or marriage to the Butler, Bonham, Lipscomb, and Nicholson families, to name some of the more notable ones. Two sisters, cousins of Leila Burt Griffin, married two of Matthew Calbraith Butler's cousins, both sons of the late Governor Pierce M. Butler; one of Leila's Burt uncles married the widow of another of Butler's uncles.

Intermarriage within families heightened the significance of kinship bonds. In many instances among all white social classes in Edgefield, brothers of one family married sisters of another family, a pattern called sibling exchange which is often confused with cousin marriage. Leila's paternal family, the Burts, began this tradition soon after their arrival in South Carolina, when three sons of Mathew and Ann Burt married three daughters of Aquilla and Harrietta Giroud Miles. These families and the Doziers continued to intermarry, and instances of consanguine marriages occurred. Leila's sister Mary Ann married her cousin, another Aquilla Miles, and two of Uncle Billy's younger daughters married two of Leila and J.B. Griffin's own sons in Texas after the war (see Chapter 9).[25]

Ties of blood also helped family members economically. Aquilla Miles, Leila's cousin and brother-in-law, spent his life trying to work his way up to the planter class, and kinship ties to the Burts and Griffins surely contributed as much as the high cotton prices of the 1850s to his

---

25. Randle Papers, Box 33; Burt Family, 1–8, Miles Family, roll 32, 1–9, Andrea Files, SCL. Harrietta Miles appears in transcription of Aquilla's will as Henrietta, which Andrea believed to be an error, based on his examination of her name in the marriage register of St. Helena Episcopal Church, dated 3 Sept. 1771. The popularity of the name Harriet with subsequent generations suggests that he was correct. Aquilla Miles was the brother of Lewis Miles of St. James Santee Parish, who served six terms in the lower house of the South Carolina Assembly and was a delegate to the state ratification convention, where he voted in favor of adopting the U.S. Constitution. See Faunt, ed., *Biographical Directory of the South Carolina House of Representatives*, 3:397–98.

moderate gains. In 1840, just two years before his marriage to Mary Ann, Aquilla Miles had 10 slaves, while his prospective father-in-law held 47. In 1850, when the census first provides figures on real estate, Aquilla held 7 slaves and property valued at $1600.[26] By 1860, even though his crops did not increase, he had 10 slaves and twice as much land, now worth $6500, almost as much as his father-in-law. Griffin's letters indicate that the two families were close despite great disparities in economic status. Griffin may have assisted his wife's cousin and brother-in-law in ways that a kinsman had a right to expect: the loan of slaves or money, signature on a note. Aquilla's son Charles was living in Griffin's house in 1860, probably in an arrangement similar to an apprenticeship in plantation management. Such arrangements were common among kin in the community of Edgefield.

The Community of Edgefield

Griffin's life and letters profile his community in Edgefield just as any soldier interpreted the Civil War through the values he brought from home. As South Carolina led the South—first in nullification, then in proslavery and prosouthern arguments, and later in secession—Edgefield led South Carolina, which James L. Petigru is reported to have declared "too small for a republic, but too large for an insane asylum."[27] Edgefield produced numerous fire-eating secessionists, two Civil War governors, and four Confederate generals, as well as its quota of draft dodgers and deserters. The oft-quoted Charleston editor, William Watts Ball, declared that Edgefield had "more dashing, brilliant, romantic figures, statesmen, orators, soldiers, adventurers and daredevils than any other county in South Carolina, if not of any rural county in America."[28] After Milledge Bonham succeeded fellow Edgefieldian Francis Pickens as governor, the South's most famous

---

26. Representing 80 improved and 120 unimproved acres.

27. Sally Edwards, *The Man Who Said No* (New York: Coward-McMann, 1970), 75. Petigru grew up in what is now McCormick County, which was formed from the old Abbeville and Edgefield Districts. Abbeville was a neighboring district; it was hard to separate from Edgefield culturally, and both had been created out of the old Ninety Six District.

28. William Watts Ball, *The State That Forgot: South Carolina's Surrender to Democracy* (Indianapolis: Bobbs-Merrill, 1932), 22.

Griffin's Neighbors, Edgefield District, 1860

diarist, Mary Chesnut, commented, "So far the world does not seem to think it can have more Edgefield than it can bear! . . . The governorship, or any high office in South Carolina, is like the kingdom of heaven in one respect: it can be taken by violence—and Edgefield has violence enough to take anything."[29]

Edgefield, with its long tradition of extremism and violence, produced men violent in rhetoric and action. In 1816 Parson Weems, perpetrator of many George Washington legends, wrote a pamphlet which opened with these words: "Old Edgefield again! Another murder in Edgefield! . . . For sure it must be Pandemonium itself, a very District of Devils." Violence in Edgefield had deep historical roots. In the eighteenth century the Cherokee War and the Regulator battles anticipated the bloody confrontations between Whigs and Tories in the eastern part of Edgefield District. When historian Richard Maxwell Brown chose Edgefield and the South Carolina backcountry as one of the regions to explore in his study of violence and vigilantism in the United States, he pointed out that "the Edgefield tradition in South Carolina has stood for the syndrome of violence and extremism that until recent times was thought to epitomize the South Carolina spirit."[30]

Apart from its reputation, nineteenth-century Edgefield was statisti-

---

29. C. Vann Woodward, ed., *Mary Chesnut's Civil War* (New Haven: Yale Univ. Press, 1981), 427–28. For information on Bonham, see Milledge Louis Bonham, "Life and Times of Milledge Luke Bonham," unpublished ms., Edgefield County Historical Society, Edgefield, and SCL, and *Confederate Military History*, extended ed. (1899; rpt., Wilmington, N.C.: Broadfoot Publishing, 1987), 6: 377–78.

30. Mason Locke Weems, *The Devil in Petticoats, or God's Revenge Against Husband Killing* (Edgefield: Edgefield *Advertiser* Press, 1978 reprint); also quoted in Richard Maxwell Brown, *Strain of Violence: Historical Studies of American Violence and Vigilantism* (New York: Oxford Univ. Press, 1975), 84. For descriptions of the Cherokee and Regulator wars, see 71–81, 83 for quotation. Brown credits the lingering violent tradition of the backcountry for South Carolina's political extremism. Various other explanations have been offered: economic decline in the antebellum years that made high tariffs onerous; the large black majority; the dominance of John C. Calhoun in state politics and his national role as a proslavery apologist; the elitist structure of state government. See James M. Banner, Jr., "The Problem of South Carolina," in Stanley Elkins and Eric McKitrick, eds., *The Hofstadter Aegis: A Memorial* (New York: Alfred A. Knopf, 1974), 60–93, and Orville Vernon

cally representative of rural South Carolina. The black population was proportional to that in most parts of the state. The majority of the residents, like most South Carolinians, made a living in agriculture, constrained by the shared problems of declining soil productivity, fluctuating crop and slave markets, and competition from the newer cotton lands of Alabama, Mississippi, and Texas. Birth and death rates, and the ratio of males to females, resembled demographic patterns for the state as a whole. By standard statistical measures that can be computed from the federal census—literacy rate, farm size, land ownership, proportion of improved acreage—Edgefield matched averages for rural districts in the state.[31] In size, Edgefield was surpassed only by Charleston's large coastal district. Edgefield's population of 40,000 was the fourth largest in South Carolina.

Part of the upcountry, or Piedmont, Edgefield was both geographically and culturally distinct from the lowcountry or coastal districts. The two regions were separated physically by the midlands, a belt of sandhills that extended across the state and reached into upland border districts like Edgefield; they were divided culturally by distinctive patterns of settlement and development. The lowcountry had been heavily settled by planters from the British West Indies, southwestern England, and France, and their descendants constituted the state's economic and cultural elite. The upcountry was settled by migrants—many of them Scots-Irish—following the line of the mountains down from the backcountry of Pennsylvania, Virginia, and North Carolina. While the lowcountry developed into a plantation society where slaves outnumbered whites, the upcountry remained thinly populated and overwhelmingly white until the 1800s. Political competition was fierce between upcountry districts and lowcountry parishes.[32]

Religion was central to culture in Edgefield, as in the rest of the rural South. Throughout the nineteenth century, both blacks and

---

Burton, "In My Father's House Are Many Leaders: Can the Extreme Be Typical?," *The Proceedings of the South Carolina Historical Association,* 1987 (Aiken: South Carolina Historical Association, 1988), 23–32.

31. Burton, "In My Father's House Are Many Leaders," and Burton, *In My Father's House Are Many Mansions,* 4–7.

32. Lacy K. Ford, *Origins of Southern Radicalism: The South Carolina Upcountry, 1800–1860* (New York: Oxford Univ. Press, 1988), 5–7; Burton, *In My Father's House Are Many Mansions,* 19.

whites lived in a narrow world of kin, neighbors, and fellow church members; religion helped shape their world view.[33] Neighborhoods within Edgefield often were centered around church buildings, and the boundaries of these settlements, or communities within the larger community, were areas served by the church. J.B. Griffin grew up in the area served by Antioch Baptist Church. Nearby were the sister Baptist congregations of Horns Creek (attended in 1860 by several of J.B.'s neighbors and associates), Red Hill, and Republican churches, which sometimes shared a pastor.

Edgefield was most heavily influenced by Baptists, and J.B. Griffin's family were all Baptists. Antioch Church had begun as part of the Separatist Baptist movement in 1804, but had reorganized in 1830. In that reorganization, James Sr. and Nancy Mims Griffin, J.B.'s father and stepmother, were charter members, transferring their memberships to Antioch in September 1830 when J.B. was five years old.[34] When his stepmother died in 1852, the paper reported that she had been a member of the Baptist Church for more than twenty-eight years. She had been ill for eighteen days and would not take medicine for the pain. A devout Christian, she was looking forward to heaven.[35] Griffin's father died a little over two years later, and a long, flowery obituary noted that he was a "planter and a Christian." The paper stressed his "high sense of honor" and his service to the Baptists, Antioch Church, and his community. On his death, the church clerk wrote that "for the space of twenty-four years and six months" Griffin Sr. was "an exemplary member."[36]

Antioch Church records concur that James Sr. was a stalwart of the congregation. As a deacon, he served on numerous committees, such as the 1838 committee to revise Antioch's constitution, and represented the church at Baptist Association meetings. He often investigated disputes and talked with members about their conduct. It was

33. For a discussion of religion in nineteenth-century Edgefield, see Burton, *In My Father's House Are Many Mansions*, 21–28.

34. Nancy Mims Griffin, J.B.'s stepmother, joined the Village Baptist Church in late 1827 and left in mid-1830 to join her husband at Antioch Baptist Church. Edgefield Village Baptist Church Records, Dec. 1827 and June 1830, FU.

35. Edgefield *Advertiser*, 19 Nov. 1852.

36. Edgefield *Advertiser*, 14 Feb. 1855.

the practical Brother James Griffin who "proposed having a signal for the purpose of calling the people into the House for worship," and thus the church "ruled that a hymn be used as the signal."[37]

J.B. Griffin's name never appears in Antioch Church records except as the owner of slaves.[38] His father and stepmother were members; his sister and each of her husbands attended. The minister of Antioch Church conducted the marriage of Leila Burt and J.B. Griffin. But, beyond this, J.B. Griffin's church affiliation remains a mystery. Yet it is inconceivable that J.B. was not involved in the life of a church, especially since he and Leila had children, and so much of the social life of the rural community revolved around the church. One possibility is that J.B. chose to attend Leila's church. This was not uncommon; J.B.'s sister's husband, Diomede Hollingsworth, joined his wife's church.

More probably, Griffin was uncomfortable with the evangelical culture of his father's Baptist faith. Baptists disapproved of drinking and dancing, whereas J.B. enjoyed the good life with fine wine and elegant dinners. For an aspiring young man like J.B. Griffin, the zealous culture of his father may have been too restrictive. Allowing for many exceptions, the Edgefield aristocrats preferred the Episcopal Church. J.B., however, was not a member of Trinity Episcopal Church either. Nevertheless, J.B. was a man of upright moral character, and he may have been reluctant to give up the faith of his father. (Later in life J.B. converted to Catholicism; see Chapter 9.)[39]

Within a particular church, members did not seem to be distinguished by economic status (except for enslaved African Americans). In both 1915 and 1922 a Confederate veteran, the son of a slaveowning Edgefield farmer, responded to a question about whether "slaveholders and nonslaveholders mingled on equal footing at church,

37. Antioch Baptist Church Records, 1830–1855, FU.

38. J.B. Griffin's first wife, Emma Rebecca Miller, was buried at Antioch Church with their infant son. Antioch Baptist Church Records, 1843, July 1848, March 1857; Edgefield *Advertiser*, 8 March 1857, tombstone at Antioch Church.

39. In the antebellum South, many people who considered themselves Christians did not formally "join the church." Griffin's letters contain scattered references to God. Burton, *In My Father's House Are Many Mansions*, 72.

school, and public gatherings." In 1915 he replied, "Generally they did. Of course the standing of the family socially had much to do with their recognition." In 1922, he remembered that the upper class did not mingle with others. "They considered themselves and families above the former classes socially. . . . There was not such distinction at churches as was manifest at other gatherings."[40] Edgefield gentry lived and worked beside those from other classes. Griffin's immediate neighbors, the Deans on one side and the Timmermans on the other, had families to feed and only a few hundred dollars in assets.

The Griffin Plantation

In 1850 J.B. Griffin, as a planter in possession of 340 acres of land worth $3000, was almost in the top quarter of all local property owners (about 40 percent of all census households held no property).[41] He owned 26 slaves, which placed him almost in the top decile of all slaveowners. Living next to his father, on acreage deeded two years earlier, J.B. Griffin was well off but not rich, a young member of the gentry not yet come into his inheritance. Most likely twenty-four-year-old J.B. was also helping his sixty-seven-year-old father farm. A striking disparity in the demography of the two slave populations supports the supposition that father and son pooled their labor and their agricultural resources. In 1850 the father had a much older slave population (average age 21.9 years to J.B.'s 13.6) with a low child to woman ratio (1.6, just over half of J.B.'s 3.0). J.B., starting a new farm, had virtually all younger slaves. J.B. and James were both growing the same kinds of crops, mostly corn, peas, beans, wheat, and oats. They also grew cotton, ten bales for J.B., twenty for James.

---

40. Thomas Jefferson Howard, Tennessee Civil War Veterans Questionnaires, (1915): 3, and (1922): 3, Tennessee State Library and Archives.

41. The acreage listed in Schedule 1 of the manuscript agricultural census was less than the amount that Griffin's father deeded to him in 1848, suggesting that either his father was still farming it or the remainder was rented. In 1850, J.B. was in the 73rd percentile of all property owners and in the 87th percentile of all slave owners. For all household heads he was in the 74.2 percentile. When compared by household heads and by men his age (24) in 1850 he was financially secure. Of all household heads 24 years and under, only 13 of the 239 were wealthier.

By 1860 J.B. had inherited his father's slaves and land; he owned 36 adults and 25 children and a total of 1500 acres, of which 700 were improved. Total reported wealth of $81,350 put him in the richest 3 percent of all household heads in Edgefield District listed in the 1860 census. His personal property was assessed at $56,000 (only 77 people in Edgefield had a greater personal estate), much of it accounted for by his 61 slaves. Griffin was in the top 4 percentile of slaveowners; only 47 people in Edgefield owned more slaves in 1860.[42] In Edgefield at this time 46.1 percent of household heads owned at least one slave, but less than one-fourth of them held the 20 or more necessary to qualify as part of the planter class. Only 5 percent of this planter class were, like Griffin, "large planters" who owned between 50 and 99 bondsmen. Only 12 individuals in Edgefield owned 100 or more slaves, which qualified them as "great planters."[43]

In 1860 the two farms together were producing much more cotton, 113 bales, and much less grain; the plantation was no longer self-sufficient in food. The standard bushel equivalent of food required for a working adult per year was 25 to 35 bushels, more than three times what J.B. Griffin grew for home consumption. Even though 1859 was a poor harvest year for corn in the Southeast, Griffin clearly was not planting enough grain to supply his needs. At the same time, only forty farms in Edgefield yielded more bales of cotton than Griffin's in 1860. Griffin was producing a cash crop almost entirely. The 113

---

42. Only one person in the county younger than J.B. Griffin had more slaves; S.L. Shepperd, 33 years old, owned 69 slaves. A.L. Dearing, one year older than Griffin, had 205, which is the most listed in the district for one person. Of course, Francis Pickens, James Henry Hammond, and others owned more, but their slaves were in other districts, or even in other states on different plantations and were not all enumerated in Edgefield.

43. In 1860, the mean for slave owners was 14 slaves, median 8, mode 1 for the 1,552 slave owners recorded in the manuscript slave census. Looking only at the number of slaveowners in Edgefield in 1860 (1,552) and the number of white households, one would assume that 54 percent of all households (or families) were slave owners in Edgefield, but 158 of the slave owners were non-household heads; thus in Edgefield at this time 46.1 percent of household heads held at least one slave. The 158 non-household heads who owned slaves made up more than a tenth of all slave owners. The academic categories of "large planters" and "great planters" were not terms used in the 1800s.

bales of cotton, selling at 10 cents a pound in 1859, would have been worth over $4500. The high cotton prices of the 1850s motivated both planters and yeomen throughout the upcountry to grow more cotton and less corn. In 1860 Edgefield was the leading cotton-producing district in South Carolina, and Griffin, like most planters there, concentrated on his cash crop and bought corn and pork for his slave labor force. His accounts for 1860 show expenditures for flour, corn, wheat, and bacon.[44]

---

44. Griffin Family Scrapbook and Account Book, in possession of Jack L. Gunter, Dallas, Texas. The 1000 bushels of corn and 400 combined bushels of wheat, oats, peas, and beans reported in the 1860 agricultural census did not come close to the grain necessary to feed the white and slave population on a plantation of between 500 and 999 improved acres. Robert E. Gallman, "Self-Sufficiency in the Cotton Economy of the Antebellum South," *Agricultural History* 43 (Jan. 1970): 7. A standard self-sufficiency index which measures food production in the equivalent of corn bushels divided by the number of adult equivalents suggests some insights into J.B. Griffin's farming. This calculation takes into account what it would take to feed people (differentiating between children and adults) and animals, and figures the amount of seed that would need to be put aside for the following year's crop. In 1850, J.B.'s corn-bushel equivalent ratio was 22.7 and his father's was 68.1. In 1860, Griffin produced an amazingly low 12.8 corn-bushels equivalent. Generally the larger the improved acres, the higher Edgefield farmers' self-sufficiency ratio. J. William Harris, *Plain Folk and Gentry in a Slave Society: White Liberty and Black Slavery in Augusta's Hinterlands* (Middletown, Conn.: Wesleyan Univ. Press, 1985), 29. We use the same formula that Harris uses, which is from Roger L. Ransom and Richard Sutch, "Debt Peonage in the Cotton South after the Civil War," *Journal of Economic History* 32 (Sept. 1972): 641–69, esp. 660, where their estimates are conservative; see also their *One Kind of Freedom: The Economic Consequences of Emancipation* (Cambridge: Cambridge Univ. Press, 1977), 159, 251; Burton, *In My Father's House Are Many Mansions,* 51. See also Rosser H. Taylor, *Ante-Bellum South Carolina: A Social and Cultural History* (Chapel Hill: Univ. of North Carolina Press, 1942), 8. In a three-county sample Ford, *Origins of Southern Radicalism,* 244–56, found that among all farms of 200 or more improved acres 72.5 percent were self-sufficient in grain, only 33.8 in meat. Jeremy Atack and Fred Bateman, "Self-Sufficiency and the Marketable Surplus in the Rural North, 1860," 296–313, and Louis Ferleger, "Self-Sufficiency and Rural Life on Southern Farms," 314–29, both in *Agricultural History* 58, no. 30 (July 1984).

Griffin's plantation was part of the economic and social system of both neighborhood and community. The records reveal that Griffin was more than a farmer; he was also a businessman. Plantation accounts for 1859–60 disclose that he regularly hired out slaves. Few of those for whom the work was done paid immediately; Griffin carried their accounts for periods that ranged from a few weeks to several years.[45] His business experience would enable him to refocus his life after the war.

By 1860 Griffin was well established. Highland House Plantation encompassed 1500 acres and was valued at $25,000. Only fifty-one persons in all Edgefield claimed land of greater value. There are no photographs of the house, but when it burned in 1864, the Edgefield *Advertiser* described it as "the largest and most elegant [mansion] in our vicinity" with ten rooms of "costly furniture" and "large quantities of handsome china, porcelain, and silver."[46] He valued his livestock— cattle, sheep, hogs, horses, mules, and oxen—at over $3000. He took particular pride in his horses, for racing was the sport of gentlemen. One of his colts won first prize at the district agricultural fair in 1860, and Griffin's letters regularly reminded his young sons and the overseer to take special care of the colts.[47]

Griffin the farmer and slaveowner fit quite naturally into the community of Edgefield. From the very beginning, Edgefield farmers grew foodstuffs for subsistence and marketed the surplus in Charleston and in Augusta, Georgia. The invention of the cotton gin in the United States and the textile revolution in England, however, together produced a boom in short-staple cotton that transformed the economy of the interior during the opening decades of the nineteenth century. With high profits, even fortunes, that could be made in upland cotton, cultivation of the fleecy staple spread across the Piedmont, expanding the plantation system upon the backs of the enslaved African Americans. At the turn of the century, only a quarter of white households in the upcountry owned slaves; by 1820 almost 40 percent did. In the lower Piedmont, which included Edgefield, the incidence of slaveholding was higher than in the region as a whole: it rose from 28

---

45. Griffin Family Scrapbook.
46. Edgefield *Advertiser*, 14 Dec. 1864.
47. Edgefield *Advertiser*, 14 Oct. 1860.

Table 1-1. Population of Edgefield District South Carolina, 1790–1870

Year	Edgefield Aggregate Population	Number White	Number African American	(% Black)
1790	13,289	9,605	3,684	27.7
1800	18,130	13,063	5,067	27.9
1810	23,160	14,433	8,727	37.7
1820	25,119	12,864	12,255	48.8
1830	30,509	14,957	15,522	50.8
1840	32,852	15,020	17,832	54.3
1850	39,262	16,252	23,010	57.7
1860	39,887	15,653	24,233	60.8
1870	42,486	17,040	25,417	59.8

SOURCE: U.S., Bureau of the Census, *8th (1860) Census*, vol. 1: *Population* (Washington: Government Printing Office), 449–52; U.S. Bureau of the Census, *9th (1870) Census*, vol. 1: *Population* (Washington: Government Printing Office), 60–61. Edgefield Data Base.

percent to almost 45 percent between 1800 and 1820. In Edgefield the black population was almost equal to the white by 1820; by 1830 whites were outnumbered, and the black majority grew proportionally larger with each successive decade.[48] By 1860, 61 percent of the population was African American (see table 1-1).

The Slave Community

Slaves were an important part of Griffin's world. They outnumbered the whites on his plantation by more than five to one. They provided Griffin with wealth and influenced his disposition toward the world and himself. Yet he may have been unconscious of their influence, unattentive as he was to this culture that existed around him. Griffin's letters, for the most part, ignore the dynamics of the slave community

48. Ford, *Origins of Southern Radicalism*, 7–12; Burton, *In My Father's House Are Many Mansions*, 5, 19, 44–46. See Table 1-1. When the total exceeds the sum of blacks and whites, Native Americans have been added. In 1860, there was one Native American; in 1870, twenty-nine Native Americans.

on his plantation. Nevertheless, his minimal discussion is a reflection of his attitude toward slavery as an institution.

Griffin's sixty-one slaves lived and worked together as a community. Quite likely, the Griffin slaves lived in family arrangements. Several things suggest that families with male heads were the norm. Griffin mentions in an 1865 letter that one of his former slaves had gone to Augusta, Georgia, to look for his teenage son. Furthermore, the sex ratios balance remarkably well, especially for slaves fifteen years and older. In 1850, J.B.'s father had nine male and nine female slaves fifteen years of age or older, and J.B. had five male and four females of that "marriagable" age. In 1860, there were twenty such males and nineteen females. J.B.'s workforce suggests a stable slave population. In 1860, forty-four slaves were ten years or older; a comparison of the 1850 and 1860 census schedules indicates that most of these could have been either J.B.'s or his father's slaves a decade earlier. He purchased few, if any, slaves, and the mortality census of 1859 shows three deaths among them that year. Henry Griffin, a thirty-year-old farm laborer, and Kissy Griffin, a four-year-old, died of typhoid, each after a month-long illness; Silva Griffin, fifty-seven, died of dropsy after being sick half a year. In 1860, the coroner inquired into the death of "Abram a man slave of the said Jas B. Griffin." Abram had been cutting the tops of corn when a poisonous snake bit him on the arm and leg.[49]

The stable work force with natural increase substantiates family arrangements on the plantation. Living accommodations also suggest families. In 1860, Griffin reported 12 slave houses as homes for his 61 slaves; that averaged out at about 5 slaves a house, probably a family.[50]

---

49. This persistence rate is speculative, based upon the age, gender, and color of slaves in the 1850 manuscript slave census compared with the 1860 slave census. In 1850 only three of James Sr.'s slaves were mulatto and none of J.B.'s, and in 1860 there are only two mulattoes listed among J.B.'s slaves. Naming patterns reflect both African heritage and biblical names. Coroner Book of Inquisition, 1844–1855, p. 27, SCDAH. This Abram was the father of Griffin's slave valet, Abram. Leila's uncle Dr. W.M. Burt was the investigating doctor. Two other Griffin slaves testified at the inquiry.

50. For the entire slave census of Edgefield in 1860, the mean number of slaves per slave house was 4.2, and in 1870 and 1880, the average African American household size was 4.9 persons.

Inferences from census data can be risky, but in the 1850 slave census many of the slaves appear to follow what would logically be a family order of a father, mother, children. Some of these listings, however, look like groupings of mother and children only.[51] Church records also substantiate family relationships; members were listed as father, mother, wife, brother, and so on.

Records at Antioch Baptist Church contain references to several Griffin slaves. Some of the church records suggest a hegemonic function of the law and planter paternalism. A slave is sometimes cited as one of somebody's "boys" or "girls." Masters often brought to the church charges against their slaves for lying, stealing, or disobedience. In January 1832, the senior "James Griffins [sic] Peter" joined the Antioch congregation. In August of that same year, James Sr. "informed against his servants Peter and Peggy for theft." In September an investigating committee found that Peter and his wife Peggy were guilty, and the church declared nonfellowship with the slaves; in 1839 the couple were restored to church membership. In March 1850 James Sr. again reported Peter for stealing and lying. Peter admitted his sins to the church and declared himself unfit for church membership; he was expelled. Yet the master's word did not hold absolute sway. Slaves were allowed to defend themselves before the church disciplinary committee; committee members (excluding the slaveowner) were sent to investigate the charges, and the slave's cause was sometimes upheld. For example, in June 1844 James Sr. charged "one of his boys," Bob, as "out of the way" (drunk). A church committee investigated the allegations and reported back favorably on Bob, who was restored to full membership in the church in July. In disciplinary matters both whites and blacks were charged with drunkenness and fighting, but at Antioch some blacks (but no whites) were charged with adultery (at other churches both whites and blacks were so charged).

Churches gave an air of legitimacy to slaveowners' paternalist ideology and allowed them to see themselves as rightful and righteous guardians. Since churches were supposed to inculcate Christian morality, charges brought to the church against slaves gained a moral sanction. This sense of obligation was important to the slaveowners' self-image.

---

51. The 1860 slaves were listed generally by age, and did not appear to follow any other groupings.

Physically segregated by seating arrangements, whites and blacks worshipped together in the same building. In September 1832, at the same time that J.B.'s sister was "received by experience into the church," James Sr.'s slave Bob was "received by experience into the church." In 1843, another slave, Kejiah, went before the church, related her conversion experience, and was baptized. After James Sr.'s death in 1853, these people were referred to as the slaves of J.B. Griffin. In September 1856, J.B.'s slave Olive joined the church, and in May 1857 Olive's brother, Charles, was received by experience into the church. In August of 1861, both Charles and Olive, "the property of Mr. James B. Griffin," asked for letters of transfer. Interestingly, beginning in 1860, the church clerks stopped referring to slaves in quasi-familial terms, that is, "James Griffins Bob" or "Griffins boy Peter," and used designations such as "Kizziah the property of Mrs. Eliza Harrington" (J.B.'s sister). The escalating sectional tension may have encouraged a more legalistic view of relationships between masters and slaves. [52]

A social and occupational hierarchy existed within the slave workforce. In June 1865 Griffin referred to "Jim who has been my *Foreman*." Jim was also a skilled carpenter. Griffin's slave carpenters fashioned plow stocks and shovel handles for neighboring farmers and planters, and his blacksmith shop made plow sweeps and shod horses. J.B.'s account ledger reveals that his slave artisans frequently built or repaired plows and tools for other farmers; he also hired slaves out at $1.25 a day. These slaves were probably skilled workmen, for the same few names recur. In 1860, for example, he hired out Jim to B. P. Tillman on five separate occasions at $1.25 a day (Tillman's account was "by settlement in full" in 1864 though in kind, not cash), to Philip Eichelberger two days (paid in cash in 1863), to Bennet Holland for two days (paid in cash that year), to M. B. Wever for four and a half days (paid in cash in 1863). [53] In 1859 J.B.'s slaves shod two of S. B. Ryan's horses. In 1860

---

52. In May 1851 the Edgefield *Advertiser* noted that Antioch Baptist's new church had a large gallery for slaves. J.B.'s sister inherited Kejiah from her father James Griffin. These references are all taken from the Records of the Antioch Baptist Church, Jan., Aug., Sept. 1832, Sept. 1838, Feb. 1839, April 1843, June and July 1844, March 1850, Sept. 1856, May 1857, May and Aug. 1861.

53. Currency was highly inflated in 1863.

he hired Smith to S.S. Tompkins at $1.25 a day for nine days in February and two days in June. In March he hired Smith to Daniel Holland for four days, and immediately afterward for three days to neighbor Benjamin F. Mays. He also sold Mays 243 lbs. of iron, suggesting that the slave, "Smith," was a blacksmith or ironworker.

The Griffin slaves also had some leeway to work for themselves. They were permitted to cultivate private garden plots, and in slack periods they had access to his unimproved acres of woodland to sell for their own money whatever they produced or manufactured. Some apparently had a regular enterprise of making charcoal from firewood and selling it in town.[54]

The war immediately affected the slave community on Griffin's plantation. Some slaves were impressed into Confederate service, and two, Ned and Abram, went with Griffin to the Virginia front. Like Griffin and numerous white males, these African Americans also left home and family. Union reports of the first South Carolina troops to move into Virginia noted the soldiers had "Negroes with them, as servants." Officers and privates alike brought slaves to camp to cook, wash, and tend their horses. Col. Thomas G. Bacon of the Seventh South Carolina Volunteers reported home to Edgefield that food prepared by some of these slave cooks was abominable (one wonders if this was done deliberately).[55] James Conner, however, wrote that his own slave, Edward, "cooks capitally." Conner was amused that Edward "stands up for my rights in the most glorious manner. He and the company are always quarreling about what belongs to 'Cap'n.'" Edward even politely refused Griffin's offer to deliver Conner's dinner when the latter was out of camp positioning men to meet an expected attack; despite the danger of anticipated fighting, he took it himself.[56] Griffin was equally pleased with Abram, his valet, and Abram's adjustment to military life.

The increased freedom that slaves experienced in camp worried masters. Private Charles Hutson of the Legion's Washington Light In-

54. J.B. Griffin to Capt. J.E. Bryant, 21 June 1865, Miscellaneous Griffin Papers, possession of Jack L. Gunter, Dallas.

55. Edgefield *Advertiser*, 15 Oct. 1862; Bonham, "Life and Times of Milledge Luke Bonham," 540.

56. Moffett, ed., *Letters of General James Conner, C.S.A.*, 52, 71.

fantry, for instance, declined his uncle's offer to send him a valet because "one who has not seen the workings of camp-life cannot conceive how thoroughly a servant is spoiled by camp service. The very best are necessarily injured."[57] When Edgefieldian Emmett Seibels wrote home from the Seventh South Carolina Volunteers to ask for a camp slave, he specified that he did not want Bob: "he would be in Lincoln's army before you could say Jack Robinson."[58] Some slaves obviously saw federal lines as an open invitation to freedom, a fact of which some masters were keenly aware, and others, like Griffin, chose to ignore. Griffin was totally disbelieving when his slave Abram ran away to enemy lines late in the spring of 1862. Although this occurred only a few weeks after what Griffin perceived as a "light flogging," he convinced himself that the Yankees had lured Abram away. Finally, like thousands of other slaveowners whose bondsmen ran away during the war, he dismissed the matter by concluding that the former slave would always regret having been foolish enough to leave.[59]

---

57. Hutson to Mother, 28 April 1862, Charles Woodward Hutson Papers, SHC. Hutson was from Charleston.

58. Emmett Seibels to Ed Seibels, 28 Nov. 1862, Seibels Family Papers, SCL.

59. Bell I. Wiley in *Southern Negroes, 1861–1865* (New Haven: Yale Univ. Press, 1953), 134–38, 142–43, has useful information on enslaved people at the front. According to Wiley, in 1861 numerous "elite" slaves went to the front with their masters, but as the war became more difficult in 1862–1863, many were sent home to assist with crops and farm work. The duties performed by these slaves included barbering, errand running, cooking, cleaning, procuring extra food, and generally anything the master did not want to do. Many slaves used this work as an opportunity to make money for themselves, and masters seemed to tolerate this. Wiley claims slaves begged milk and butter and then sold it to army personnel; camp slaves also performed errands or laundry for other soldiers besides their masters. Wiley believes camp life was soft for slaves and they had leisure time for card playing and amusements. He argues that the presence of camp slaves raised the morale of white Confederates and that usually personal servants had long been associated with the master's family; therefore they were loyal to the master and to the Confederacy. He argues that the majority of runaway slaves were hired and thus lacking personal attachment to the master. See also Wiley, *Plain People of the Confederacy* (1943; rpt., Gloucester, Mass.: Peter Smith, 1971), 99–100, for useful information pertaining to the intimate relations between master

Griffin's attitude toward slaves was classic paternalism, and he apparently was a model master. Whereas some slaveowners raped slave women, took slave mistresses, fathered mulatto children, and exploited or abused male and female slaves atrociously, J.B. lived up to a higher ideal.[60] He did not sell slaves. He had no mulatto children. He passed along messages through Leila to the slaves at home: "Tell the Negroes all Howdy for me." He wrote that he was pleased to hear of their good behavior, fully expecting that his distant approval would gratify them. He also sent greetings from Ned and Abram and reported on their health. Griffin regarded it his duty to train and direct slaves, to reward them for good performance and correct them—physically if necessary—for improper behavior. In return, he expected them to love and revere him, and the possibility that Abram would deliberately repudiate him was difficult for Griffin to accept.

Very near the end of the war, on 3 February 1865, Griffin wrote Leila with some advice "in case Sherman honors Edgefield with a visit." He directed her to have the slaves hide the provisions, drive off cattle and hogs, and "Tell the negroes they can go if they choose, of course—But to remember they will always regret it." He trusted his slaves to hide foodstuffs although slaves throughout the area were giving provisions to the Union army, and he still maintained that the slaves who chose freedom, as Abram had done, would rue it. Mary Chesnut wrote of slaves during the Civil War that "they go about in their black masks, not a ripple or an emotion showing." Griffin seems to have lacked the same awareness that his slaves might have secret inner lives and concealed aspirations; he truly believed African Americans were better off enslaved.[61]

---

and slave. Although Griffin's slave, Abram, contradicted the model set forth by Wiley, more recent literature suggests that Abram was not atypical. See for example, Randall C. Jimerson, *The Private Civil War* (Baton Rouge: Louisiana State Univ. Press, 1988), 50–87, for a more modern scholar's discussion of the loyalty of camp slaves.

60. See Burton, *In My Father's House Are Many Mansions*, 145–46, 168–80, 183–90.

61. Mary Boykin Chesnut, *A Diary from Dixie*, ed. Ben Ames Williams (Boston: Houghton Mifflin, 1949), 293; Woodward, ed., *Mary Chesnut's Civil War*, 464.

Griffin and the Edgefield Elite

Much of Griffin's experience in the Civil War related closely to the problems and opportunities he experienced as part of the second tier of community and military leadership; in both Edgefield District and the Confederate Army, he ranked just below the top. An old Edgefield family, the Griffins were part of the elite and just on the cusp of the local aristocracy in 1860. Men such as Griffin—sometimes admired, sometimes despised, often envied—nonetheless stood in the shadow of men in the highest echelons of the aristocracy.[62]

The elite was as difficult to define in the antebellum South as it is today. It was a continuum rather than a category, and one "felt" rather than articulated its meaning. The "wealthy" elite was comprised of families that may or may not have been included in the "aristocratic" elite or the "political" elite. Benjamin Nicholson, who read law with Milledge Luke Bonham, despaired of ever achieving elite status. This son of a wealthy slaveowner pondered moving west in the mid-1850s because "[i]n this state a greater regard is paid to family & wealth, & consequently without either a young man must possess great ability to succeed."[63]

Members of the elite usually measured their wealth in land and slaves, but more important was their line of descent and marriage alliances. The "aristocrats" of backcountry Edgefield claimed descent from settlers from Pennsylvania, Virginia, and North Carolina during the mid-eighteenth century. Their ancestors had participated in the Regulator Movement of 1767–69 and had fought as Whigs in the

---

62. For comparative and informative purposes, the reader is directed to published biographies and edited letters of other prominent Edgefieldians. See Carol Bleser, ed., *The Hammonds of Redcliffe* (New York: Oxford Univ. Press, 1981), and Bleser, ed., *Secret and Sacred: The Diaries of James Henry Hammond, a Southern Slaveholder* (New York: Oxford Univ. Press, 1988); Drew Gilpin Faust, *James Henry Hammond and the Old South: A Design for Mastery* (Baton Rouge: Louisiana State Univ. Press, 1982); John B. Edmunds, Jr., *Francis Pickens and the Politics of Destruction* (Chapel Hill: Univ. of North Carolina Press, 1986).

63. His father ranked 73rd of the wealthiest people in Edgefield. Benjamin Nicholson, notebook, 41, Hughes Papers, SHC. On the Edgefield elite and social classes see Burton, *In My Father's House Are Many Mansions*, 47–79.

American Revolution. Committed to farming and the acquisition of slaves and land even before cotton planting spread to the upcountry, most amassed their early fortunes in land speculation, surveying, merchandising, and trading with Native Americans. Patrick Calhoun, Andrew Pickens, and LeRoy Hammond (not related to James Henry Hammond) referred to themselves as planters and farmers, but, in truth, all had been merchants and surveyors as well. They generally were Baptists or Presbyterians or, after the formation of the new denomination, Methodists, and they married women with similar upcountry backgrounds. They became the magistrates, sheriffs, and legislative representatives. Within one generation, this group of backcountry planters rose to wealth and prominence and established the basis of their descendants' claim to aristocracy.

The second generation aligned itself through marriage with the coastal South Carolina and Charleston power establishment. Patriciate clans formed interlocking relationships through marriage. Family links, important factors in political alliances and allegiances, often led to leadership in the community and the state. By the time of the Civil War, the first families of Edgefield frequently had intermarried.

By this time also the leading families had become Episcopalians. The founding of the Trinity Episcopal Church in 1833 unofficially demarcated Edgefield's establishment of an "aristocracy." Griffin's best friends had all become members of the elite Trinity Episcopal Church. Martin Witherspoon Gary, reared a Methodist and schooled at the Methodist Cokesbury Academy, joined and became a vestryman in Trinity Church. Matthew Calbraith Butler also joined and served as a vestryman, along with his father-in-law, Francis Pickens. Thomas G. Bacon, Griffin's commanding colonel on the coast of South Carolina, also belonged to Trinity Church. Controversial senator and Confederate General Louis Wigfall belonged to Trinity Church and within that membership developed an intense enmity toward the Brooks family, whom he blamed for denying his older brother Arthur, an Episcopal preacher, a position in the Edgefield church.[64]

The Edgefield elite was not a unified community, but one composed of economic, denominational, and old- and new-rich factions.

---

64. Wade Hampton, though not an Edgefield resident, was also Episcopalian.

Their ranks included planters, attorneys, doctors, newspaper editors, and officeholders. Whereas a self-made man like Governor James Henry Hammond saw the established Edgefield aristocracy as weak, indecisive, snobbish, and effeminate, a member of the Old Guard felt only scorn for the crass behavior and low origins of newer members of the elite. Following Hammond's election to the Senate after Edgefieldian Andrew Pickens Butler's death in 1857, Francis Pickens, a future governor, wrote, "The line was drawn distinctly between virtue and honor on one side and open blagarddism [sic] on the other." Carolina aristocrats wanted to defeat Hammond, "who had no family of distinction, but was the son of a Massachusetts adventurer." Still, in 1842, when cotton prices were low, Pickens had felt no compunction in asking Hammond to help relieve his financial difficulties.[65]

Yet however one measures this elite, J.B. Griffin's father, eulogized as a father of Edgefield District, was not far from the top echelon.[66] The elder Griffin's own father had died in the Revolutionary War, and thus the family had been in no position to prosper from immediate postwar opportunities. James Griffin, Sr., did not benefit from the largesse in western land speculation that the Pickenses, Butlers, Brookses, and Bonhams claimed as their legacy from the Revolution. Moreover, Griffin, Sr., remained a devout Baptist, and married locally rather than linking with a lowcountry family. Nevertheless, during his lifetime he built the foundation for his son, J.B. Griffin, to move into the top elite.

The elite highly valued education; it became indispensable for people entering that rank. Elite military academies, emphasizing military science in their curricula, flourished in antebellum Edgefield. Local academies and colleges also included instruction in the social graces important to South Carolina's chivalric society. Oratorical ability, developed and polished through formal education, was generally a prerequisite for leadership in the antebellum South. Oratory that inspired respect and awe, that demonstrated one's honor and virtue, was one way to obtain and verify membership in the elite. In August 1859 "An Observer" described how, after a parade of the Second Cavalry Regi-

---

65. Francis W. Pickens to Lucy Holcombe, 6 Dec. 1857, F.W. Pickens Papers, SCL; Edmunds, *Francis Pickens*.
66. Edgefield *Advertiser*, 7 Feb. 1855.

ment, the Governor of South Carolina addressed the militia, and then J.B. Griffin, "in a speech remarkable for its beauty and spirit. . . . spoke feelingly and eloquently, and as he closed all were ready to say that the Cavalry had a 'trump' of a General." Praise for skill in public address ranked among the highest compliments a southern leader could receive.[67]

J.B.'s oratory, and, of course, his letters, reveal him as an educated man, but it remains unclear where he received his education. If he followed the common pattern of planters' sons, he would have attended one of the excellent local academies in or near Edgefield and then enrolled at South Carolina College (now the University of South Carolina), but he is not listed among its graduates. All the Hampton Legion field officers and all but two of the initial company commanders were college graduates. Butler, Conner, Hampton, and others graduated from South Carolina College. Gary had attended South Carolina College but was expelled along with others in the junior class for rebelling against an unpopular teacher. He graduated from Harvard in 1854. While Edgefieldian James Henry Hammond was governor, the South Carolina Military College (the Citadel) was founded to prepare young men from good families for military leadership. Griffin's eldest son, Willie, received an appointment to this military college while still a boy.[68]

---

67. Edgefield *Advertiser*, 10 Aug. 1859. See Douglas Greenberg, *Masters and Statesmen: The Political Culture of American Slavery* (Baltimore: Johns Hopkins Univ. Press, 1985), on oratory and honor.

68. All extant college records for South Carolina schools and several out-of-state alumni records were searched for Griffin. Daniel Walker Hollis, *University of South Carolina I: South Carolina College* (Columbia: Univ. of South Carolina Press, 1951), 155–56. Academic activity was considered a luxury in the early nineteenth century and indulged in only by well-to-do planter families or talented boys like George McDuffie or Joseph Abney recruited into the elite. College degrees were not considered essential, and students often attended college for part of a curriculum. Griffin's education could be a reflection of the superb academies in and around Edgefield. For example, Moses Waddel (who became president of the University of Georgia) and his Willington Academy (which produced graduates John C. Calhoun, A.P. Butler, Pierce Mason Butler) were in nearby Abbeville. One possibility is that Griffin attended college but left before graduation, which was not unusual; some of these academies listed graduates rather than enrolled students. Often

Military service provided yet an alternate route into the Edgefield elite. It was a means to become a hero and obtain public office. At election times newspapers regularly reminded voters of their obligations to the men who had fought for them in various conflicts and often linked the ideals of the Revolutionary War to later military encounters. They glorified wartime service and honored veterans. Griffin was only eleven when the Palmetto Regiment with Thomas Glascock Bacon and other Edgefield men departed in 1836 for the Seminole War in Florida. Twenty-six years later it was Bacon, a judge well connected with the first families of Edgefield, who was selected as colonel, while Griffin, many times more wealthy, was his second in command for the South Carolina Reserves.[69] Between these two conflicts, in 1846, Preston S. Brooks and Milledge Luke Bonham won fame in the Mexican War. At that time Griffin had been old enough to serve, but he had also been the only son of an aging father and just beginning his own family. For Griffin's generation the sectional conflict of 1860 was *the* war and *his* opportunity to march into the state's and his community's heart forever. Success as an officer in this conflict could assure Griffin's move into the top echelon of the elite.

Griffin's social status as slaveholder and wealthy planter entitled him to public office. William C. Preston, with whom Edgefield's James Henry Hammond had read law, candidly observed of South

---

students left voluntarily, and at other times they were expelled. A letter of 1838 mentioned that many of the students from Willington were expelled from South Carolina College with no opprobrium. See Ralph M. Lyon, "Moses Waddel and the Willington Academy," *North Carolina Historical Review* 8, no. 3 (July 1931): 284–99, and Burton, "Pauper and Patrician: Education in Antebellum Edgefield," unpublished paper available from Burton. Edgefield *Advertiser*, 8 Dec. 1858.

69. Thomas G. Bacon, descendant of one of the district's older distinguished families, was 48 years old in 1860 and a judge. He owned nine slaves, $2000 in personal estate, and $3000 in real estate. Bacon's family had resided in Georgia and Edgefield and had established themselves as lawyers and judges since the Revolution. It is Bacon's ancestor who is the Ned Brace of Augustus Baldwin Longstreet's *Georgia Scenes*. See letters of 11 Aug. 1861, note 5, and 28 April 1862, note 5. Emily Bellinger Reynolds and Joan Reynolds Faunt, *Biographical Directory of the Senate of the State of South Carolina, 1776–1964* (Columbia: Univ. of South Carolina Press), 86.

Carolinians, "The object of a Southern man's life is *politics* and sub-
sidiary to this end we all practice law."[70] Griffin had not prepared for
a public career by studying law, and his interests lay in managing the
plantation rather than politicking; nevertheless, he held two appointed
offices from the state legislature, and in 1860 was chosen one of the
Edgefield delegates to the state Democratic convention in Columbia.[71] In 1862 he ran and lost an election to the South Carolina General Assembly.[72] Griffin's obituary would claim that he had no political ambitions for himself but sought advancement for his friends
instead: "to his friendship and influence, more than one of the young
aspirants of that day were indebted for their first political preferment."[73]

Although not a member of the legislature, Griffin had influence,
and influence mattered a great deal in antebellum South Carolina,
where the aristocratic structure of government largely withheld power
from the electorate. While every white male could vote, the only offices put before the people were those of state representative, state senator, and U.S. Congressman, and often only one pre-selected candidate was on the ballot. Legislative cliques constitutionally determined
who would "run" for governor and which "candidates" would be
awarded state offices.[74] The legislature also played a role in local government, for it appointed the commissioners who governed the parishes and districts. The system that developed over time allowed each
legislative delegation to control the selection of commission members
in its own district, and the power at stake naturally resulted in vigorous
competition for seats in the legislature. It also created networks of pa-
tronage among local ruling elites who helped legislators win election,
and these successful candidates then dispensed local offices.[75]

---

70. William C. Preston to George Ticknor, 2 March 1864, Preston Papers,
SCL; Burton, *In My Father's House Are Many Mansions*, 21.

71. Edgefield *Advertiser*, 17 Sept. and 11 Oct. 1860.

72. He came in 13th in a field of 17 candidates. Edgefield *Advertiser*, 22
Oct. 1862. See introduction to Chapter 7.

73. James B. Griffin obituary, clipping from unidentified South Carolina
newspaper, Griffin Family Scrapbook, 1881.

74. See Banner, "The Problem of South Carolina," in Elkins and McKitrick, eds., *Hofstadter Aegis*, 76–80.

75. Ford, *Origins of Southern Radicalism*, 304.

J.B. Griffin, like his father before him, was one of the "local notables" who influenced politics. His father petitioned with other prominent citizens to the General Assembly over the years, was a regular
poll manager during elections, and served as a Commissioner of Public Buildings. At his death J.B.'s father was eulogized as "a most exemplary citizen" of the community. According to one contemporary,
James Griffin, Sr., "had the good of his District, his State, and his
country warmly at heart. We hold up his life, to those who are coming
on to fill his place, as a pattern worthy of imitation."[76] J.B. inherited
his father's place in the leadership of the community, holding similar,
and in some instances identical, positions. Considered an honest and
impartial man, he was selected as judge for the agricultural fair and
was treasurer of the Histronic Corps. He was chairman of the board
for the Commission of Roads and Bridges; in 1851 he was one of three
election managers at Edgefield Court House. The General Assembly
chose him as one of five Commissioners of Public Buildings for Edgefield District. Like the Commission of Roads and Bridges and the
Commission of the Poor, the Public Buildings Commission had the
authority to impose a pro rata share of the state tax, and these three
commissions, along with the Commission of Free Schools, were the
mainstay of local government in most districts.[77]

Griffin's truly prestigious office, however, was that of brigadier
general in the South Carolina militia. The Edgefield *Advertiser*
announced in the spring of 1859 that Capt. J.B. Griffin of the Edgefield Hussars had been elected brigadier general of the Second Regiment of Cavalry, attached to First Brigade, First Division, without
opposition. The Hussars were Edgefield's most celebrated volunteer
militia company, organized by Andrew Pickens Butler in 1833 during
the Nullification Controversy. Since militia captains were elected by
popular vote of the company, Griffin clearly had gained the respect
of others, such as his slightly younger friends Butler and Gary. The
state legislature elected brigadier generals; Griffin's generalship indi-

76. Edgefield *Advertiser*, 7 Feb. 1855. This article was outside the obituary
section and reserved for prominent citizens.
77. Ford, *Origins of Southern Radicalism*, 304–5, uses the term "local notables." Edgefield *Advertiser*, 19 Oct. 1859, 1 Feb. 1860; Griffin Scrapbook;
Papers of the General Assembly, SCDAH.

cated that his influence extended to his local Edgefield legislators as well.[78]

As a brigadier, Griffin's duties included reviewing and drilling each regiment of his brigade at least annually, which gave him an opportunity to travel around the state and meet other local notables. Announcements by "General Griffin" regarding militia elections and musters appeared frequently in the Edgefield paper. The militia in South Carolina also had absorbed the slave patrol. Patrol districts, the smallest military districts in the state, were policed by "beat" companies whose duty it was to apprehend slaves without passes and search slave cabins for concealed firearms.[79] Both patrols and drills were largely inactive in quiet times, but the militia system was an integral part of community life and another institution through which the elite derived prestige and exercised power.

A military ethos pervaded antebellum South Carolina's culture. Politically the state was divided into military "districts" such as Edgefield; subdivisions were "regiments" such as Saluda Regiment in Edgefield District. The militia was a training ground for future political leaders. Because Edgefield was so large, the militia and patrol systems required extensive participation, and troops required leaders at every level from squads to brigades. Drills, parades, and week-long bivouacs and maneuvers regularly occupied militia troops in Edgefield. South Carolinians reveled in military display and admired the martial arts, which showed off two skills that white southern males prized highly, riding and marksmanship.

Southerners also relied on military titles as the standard form of address, no matter how brief the individual's service had been. Newspaper editors and even census enumerators prefixed a man's name with his military rank. Leila's father and her Uncle Moody were always known as Captain and Major, and men who held public office

78. Edgefield *Advertiser*, 10 Aug. 1859; David J. McCord, ed., *The Statutes at Large of South Carolina* 8 (Columbia: A.S. Johnston, 1840), 485–86.

79. John Hope Franklin, *The Militant South, 1800–1861* (Cambridge, Mass.: Belknap Press of Harvard Univ. Press, 1956), 173, 177, 184. See also Michael E. Stauffer, *South Carolina's Antebellum Militia* (Columbia: SCDAH, 1991); Benjamin Elliot and Martin Strobel, *The Militia System of South Carolina* (Charleston: A.E. Miller, 1835); H.M. Henry, *The Police Control of the State of South Carolina* (Emory, Va.: H.M. Henry, 1914), 22.

were more likely to be known by their military rather than by their civil titles. Edgefield's James Henry Hammond, confiding his career ambitions to his diary in 1839, admitted that the three public honors he most desired from the legislature were brigadier general of militia, governor, and U.S. Senator. After having attained all three offices, he was "General" Hammond in preference to "Governor" or "Senator"; Francis W. Pickens was successively congressman, minister to Russia, and governor, but always "Colonel Pickens."[80]

Events connected with or sponsored by the militia accounted for a significant part of community social life in the South. Local militia officers always made public speeches at celebrations such as Fourth of July gatherings. Quarterly company musters gave men the opportunity to socialize and politick among themselves and to drill and maneuver before groups of admiring female onlookers. Militia companies sponsored picnics, balls, and other social events at which a young officer might wear a colorful uniform and glinting sword and play the cavalier for the ladies. Women also derived higher status from a beau or husband in uniform. Although entwined with social life, militia musters reminded the community, as the sectional tension worsened in the late 1850s, that war was possible.

Sectional Conflict

Sectional tensions had been straining the nation for more than a decade, and Griffin's Edgefield neighbors were major actors in the great drama. In 1856 Massachusetts Senator Charles Sumner called the elderly and ailing Senator Andrew Pickens Butler of Edgefield a pimp who attempted to introduce the whore, slavery, into Kansas. South Carolina was mortified at this insult, and Congressman Preston S. Brooks, Butler's cousin and a fellow Edgefieldian, caned Sumner like a craven dog. The North was appalled, the white South delighted. For avenging the honor of his family and his state, Brooks became a hero in the South. Southerners sent him canes to replace the one he had splintered beating Sumner, and a testimonial dinner given in support of Brooks near his plantation at Ninety Six at the northeastern corner

---

80. Faust, *James Henry Hammond*, 210. Edmunds, *Politics of Despair*, 17, 19, 23. References throughout the Edgefield *Advertiser*.

of Edgefield was reputed to be the largest gathering ever held in the upcountry.[81]

Edgefield's James Henry Hammond, who replaced Butler the next year, made a states' rights speech in the Senate chamber, taunting northerners that the South's political weakness was more than offset by its economic strength and issuing a defiant warning: "You dare not make war on cotton. Cotton is king."[82] After the death of Preston Brooks in 1857, Griffin's brother-in-law, Diomede Hollingsworth, was one of the "Committee of Escort" appointed to retrieve his body from Washington, D.C., and return him to his native state. Local lore maintained that twelve stout men were selected because white South Carolinians feared that the Yankees would steal or desecrate the body of Brooks. Griffin, as captain of the Edgefield Hussars, met the funeral procession on its way to Edgefield.[83]

Another Edgefieldian, Milledge Luke Bonham, succeeded Preston Brooks in Congress, and in 1858 advocated Kansas's admission to the Union under the proslavery Lecompton constitution. To celebrate Congressman Bonham's speech against resubmitting the issue to the people of Kansas, the Edgefield community organized a public dinner for 1500 people. A measure of J.B. Griffin's emerging influence and prominence was his appointment on the five-member Committee of Invitation.[84]

In the next two years, national events would dramatically change

---

81. Edgefield *Advertiser*, 18 July 1856, 6 Aug. 1857; *New York Times*, 8 Oct. 1856, pp. 1–2; Burton, *In My Father's House Are Many Mansions*, 93–95. According to the *New York Times*; Griffin's Ninety Six relatives helped organize the celebration. Preston Brooks's grandmother was the aunt of A.P. Butler. Hence, Preston Brooks's father, Whitfield Brooks, was A.P. Butler's first cousin.

82. Quoted in Faust, *James Henry Hammond*, 346.

83. Edgefield *Advertiser*, 11 Feb. 1857. Obituary of Hollingsworth, Edgefield *Advertiser*, 4 March 1857. Edgefield *Advertiser*, 18 Feb. 1857.

84. Edgefield *Advertiser*, 18 Aug. and 8, 15, 29 Sept. 1858. See also the historical drama by Miss Hortense Woodson, "A Scene at 'Darby' in 1858," in Edgefield County Historical Society, *Bonham, Griffin, Lipscomb, Smith Families as Featured at the Mid-Summer Meeting of the Edgefield County Historical Society, July 18, 1941* (Edgefield: Edgefield Advertiser Press, 1941). J. Strom Thurmond starred in the role of Hon. Milledge Luke Bonham.

the nature of Griffin's world. The year after Bonham's dinner, in October 1859, radical abolitionist John Brown seized Harpers Ferry, Virginia, and conjured up the worst nightmare of white southerners by trying to incite a slave insurrection; immediately General Griffin activated the Edgefield militia and slave patrol. In 1860, the Republican party, an organization formally committed to preventing the expansion of slavery, ran Abraham Lincoln as its presidential candidate. The South's former Whigs nominated their own candidate, and Democrats divided into northern and southern factions. With his opposition split three ways, Abraham Lincoln was the odds-on favorite to win a majority in the electoral college. Even though he had promised not to interfere with slavery where it already existed, most white South Carolinians saw no distinction between Lincoln, John Brown, and the radical abolitionists. Secession seemed the obvious response to the threat of Republican domination.[85]

In Edgefield, as always, political interest was keen and radicalism ascendant. The Edgefield *Advertiser* was full of political opinions and reports of speeches and meetings. That year the muster of a volunteer militia company, the Edgefield Riflemen, was combined with the Fourth of July celebration, which offered prominent citizens extra opportunities for oratory. Leila Griffin's uncle, Dr. William Miles Burt, addressing the Riflemen in the assembly hall of Edgefield Female College, praised South Carolina's reputation for chivalry and its defiant stand against federal authority during the Nullification Crisis over tariff rates nearly thirty years earlier. Commending the state's volunteers who fought in the Seminole and Mexican wars, he warned the militiamen that they might have to carry on that tradition, now that "a storm is gathering."[86]

That summer and fall new companies were raised and offered to the militia, and citizen subscribers, men and women, donated money to equip them. Fear that abolitionist infiltrators might incite a slave insurrection prompted the formation of "vigilant associations" in rural

---

85. Stephen A. Channing, *A Crisis of Fear: Secession in South Carolina* (New York: Oxford Univ. Press, 1970); see also Ford, *Origins of Southern Radicalism*, 183–214, for an excellent discussion of the upcountry in the first secession crisis and opposition by Leila's kinsman, Armistead Burt.

86. Edgefield *Advertiser*, 25 July 1860.

neighborhoods. The slave patrol, which was supposed to visit each plantation once a month, became more attentive to this oft ignored duty, and new vigilant associations surpassed even the statutory requirements for patrolling. The Shady Grove Association, formed on 27 September 1860, announced its intention to have companies of five or six men patrol each neighborhood at least weekly to "apprehend any suspicious characters and detect any thing that may be injurious to our slaves." It determined to outlaw all slave congregations, "for any purpose whatsoever," and prevent slaves from visiting or even associating with free blacks.[87]

Lincoln's victory in November resulted in political tumult in South Carolina. Country villages as well as the state assembly in Columbia debated the question of state secession. Griffin supported his younger Edgefield friend, freshman state representative Martin Witherspoon Gary, who denounced a proposed resolution to delay action until all the southern governors could be consulted and a cooperative plan agreed upon. "Since it fails to protect our property and persons," Gary proclaimed, "this Union must be deliberately, solemnly, fearlessly, and speedily dissolved." He urged South Carolina not to wait for other states to join her. "Do the patriots of the South object to our taking the lead? By the unanimous consent and voice of the South she has been assigned the post of honor and danger."[88] Companies of "Minute Men," emulating their Revolutionary ancestors, formed throughout Edgefield District, and on 10 November the Hamburg Minute Men concluded an evening of fireworks and speeches by burning Lincoln in effigy.[89]

Six or seven hundred citizens turned out at Edgefield Court House on 13 November to hear the report of the Committee of Fifty, citizens who had been chosen eight days earlier and charged with drawing up resolutions for public discussion. The text appeared in the next day's paper:

---

87. Edgefield *Advertiser*, 17 Oct. 1860.

88. Edgefield *Advertiser*, 28 Nov. 1860. This speech was published as a pamphlet, "Remarks of M. W. Gary, Esq., of Edgefield, in the House of Representatives, Nov. 9 on Mr. Trenholm's Resolutions," and circulated. Copies of the pamphlet are in SCL and at CAH-UT.

89. Edgefield *Advertiser*, 14 Nov. 1860.

Resolved, That in the opinion of the people of Edgefield, the election of Abraham Lincoln as President of the United States, and of Hannibal Hamlin as Vice President, upon doctrines destructive of the rights and interests, the equality and safety of the Southern States, by the factious and sectional votes of our Northern confederates, utterly perverts the spirit of the compact formed by the Federal Constitution; that it must be promptly and sternly resisted by the state of South Carolina; and that the secession of the state from the Federal Union is the proper mode of resistance.

Resolved, That we anxiously desire the co-operation in measures for redress and protection of all or some of the States alike aggrieved, and would prefer that South Carolina should follow the lead of Georgia, or some other Southern State, to placing herself in the front; yet as the action of each State must be necessarily separate and independent, and as all unnecessary delay is dangerous, this State must proceed at once toward redress.

Resolved, That the legislature, without counting the cost, should immediately organize and arm the people of this State for defense.

A Committee of Twenty-Five, which included Griffin, was then appointed to recommend delegates to the state convention that would meet on 17 December in Columbia. Four days later another public meeting appointed a committee to invite two of Edgefield's own, gubernatorial candidate Francis W. Pickens and James P. Carroll, chancellor of the state (and brother-in-law of the late Preston Brooks), to address the citizenry "on the great questions of the day." The meeting adjourned with a motion by Griffin to re-form as a committee of arrangements, and on Saturday, 24 November, the event came off. Pickens and Carroll gave resounding speeches in favor of secession. Edgefield's two assemblymen, Martin Witherspoon Gary and Matthew Calbraith Butler, reported on their activities in Columbia, prompting the *Advertiser* to observe approvingly that "they are fully up to the mark of separate-State action, and will march to independence, in double-quick time." Another legislator, James Lipscomb, who lived in adjoining Newberry District but had brothers and cousins among the Lipscombs and Griffins of Edgefield, admonished the company that Newberry had already seceded and Edgefield would have to hurry to catch up. [90]

---

90. Ibid., and 21 and 28 Nov. 1861.

Within a month South Carolina was indeed out of the Union. On 17 December, delegates from all over the state met in Columbia at the opening session of the Convention of the People of South Carolina.[91] Judge Francis Hugh Wardlaw of Edgefield wrote the text of the Ordinance of Secession. Arthur Simkins, editor of the Edgefield *Advertiser*, expressed the hope that in next week's issue he might be able to publish the good news that South Carolina was "a free and independent republic."[92] On 20 December, the Secession Convention, as it was forever after known, fulfilled his wish.

Griffin's View on Causes of the War

In 1862, the Edgefield *Advertiser* editorialized, "We have felt convinced, from the commencement of this war, that negro slavery had much to do with it in the *All-seeing eye of Heaven*."[93] Griffin never discussed the system of slavery; yet slavery, the cornerstone of antebellum Edgefield society, was a critical ingredient in the Civil War. South Carolina society was built on slavery, and, ultimately, as some argued at the time, the state left the Union in 1860 to preserve slavery.

Griffin, however, like many white South Carolinians, never articulated this idea. His discourse fits neither the category of an apology for slavery nor of a rationalization to preserve a capitalist investment, nor again as a defense of an aristocratic, nonbourgeois way of life. He saw the war as a defense, not of slavery, but of "republican values," such as preached by forebears in the American Revolution, in which his own grandfather did fight (and die). Griffin described northerners as "black hearted wretches, who are doing all in their power, to subjugate a Noble race of people" (21 July 1861). He wrote not of the threat to African American slavery but of the danger of political and economic

---

91. Edgefield actually had seven delegates, but George Bosewell, who replaced Francis H. Wardlaw, did not arrive until 27 December. John Amasa May and Joan Reynolds Faunt, *South Carolina Secedes* (Columbia: Univ. of South Carolina Press, 1960), 102–4.

92. Edgefield *Advertiser*, 19 Dec. 1860. Another time in 1861, expanding on the community's active involvement in the Revolution of 1861, the Edgefield *Advertiser* ran the exuberant headline, "Edgefield Everywhere."

93. Edgefield *Advertiser*, 15 Oct. 1862.

slavery for whites if the South were defeated. "If the unprincipled North shall persist in her policy of Subjugating the South, . . . [those] able to resist them, will continue to . . . spend their lives, if necessary, in battling for Liberty and independence. . . . rather than, be a Slave, *Yea* worse than a slave to Yankee Masters," he assured Leila on 26 February 1862. He then expounded on the dire consequences of a northern victory.

Griffin clearly did not see the Civil War in terms of preserving slavery. Nor did it occur to him that his enslaved people might be hoping for an end to the old hierarchical and patriarchial order. He expected them to continue to carry out their "duties" just as he was performing his. Even when meat became so expensive in the spring of 1862 that he instructed Leila to cut rations, he assumed the slaves would identify with his interests and view war hardships as shared sacrifice: "Tell them to remember what I am going through. And what the country is now suffering" (2 April 1862). Acting the paternal role, he expected the slaves to respond as obedient children, the only capacity in which he could see them. ("Tell them it is very painful for me to have to shorten their allowances in this way—but I am forced to do so by the press of circumstances. Talk to them reasonably this way. And tell them I shall expect them to submit to it without a murmur. I will put them back on full allowance as soon as I can.")

A paradox throughout American history has been the rise of republican ideology amidst a slaveholding society; the tradition of liberty grew alongside African slavery.[94] Griffin failed to see any contradiction, and

---

94. The classic discussion of liberty and slavery is Edmund Morgan, *American Slavery American Freedom: The Ordeal of Colonial Virginia* (New York: W.W. Norton, 1975); also on the paradox of Revolutionary slaveholders, see John C. Miller, *Wolf by the Ears: Thomas Jefferson and Slavery* (New York: Free Press, 1977). On republicanism in South Carolina, see Ford, *Origins of Southern Radicalism*, and on Edgefield, see Harris, *Plain Folk and Gentry in a Planter Society*, and Burton, *In My Father's House Are Many Mansions*, 37–38; on the sectional conflict, see Michael F. Holt, *The Political Crisis of the 1850s* (New York: John Wiley and Sons, 1978). A good review of the literature on republicanism is Daniel T. Rodgers, "Republicanism: The Career of a Concept," *Journal of American History* 79, no. 1 (June 1992): 11–38, esp. 31 on the South.

his remarks do not indicate any guilt over slavery.[95] These letters show him to be perfectly serious in his conception that a struggle for liberty was the basis of the Civil War. Nevertheless, Griffin's way of life depended upon unfree labor, and his assertion of "battling for Liberty and independence" meant the liberty to own slaves.

War

South Carolina, considering itself a free and independent republic, nevertheless had a United States Army garrison at Fort Sumter controlling the harbor of its major city, Charleston. Militia companies from all over the state poured into Charleston, but neither South Carolina nor the federal government wanted to initiate hostilities; no shots were exchanged. Governor Pickens authorized fire-eater Maxcy Gregg, who had signed the secession ordinance, to raise a regiment, the First South Carolina Volunteers, for a state army. The Edgefield Riflemen reached Charleston on 7 January, joined Gregg's regiment, and were present for the excitement when, on 9 January, South Carolina batteries fired on *Star of the West*, a merchant steamer attempting to bring reinforcements and supplies to the garrison at Fort Sumter. The ship prudently turned and headed back to sea.[96]

For the next three months an uneasy military stand-off prevailed. South Carolina's agents in Washington tried to persuade outgoing President James Buchanan and the new chief executive, Abraham Lincoln, to relinquish Sumter. The remaining states in the lower South seceded one after the other to join the Confederate States of America. Lincoln notified Confederate President Jefferson Davis that supply boats would be sent to Fort Sumter, backed by warships that would not be deployed if the supply vessels were permitted to pass. The Confederates then made the first move. On 12 April 1861 the

---

95. See the essay by Gaines M. Foster for a summary of the literature on slavery and guilt: "Guilt over Slavery: A Historiographical Analysis," *Journal of Southern History* 56, no. 4 (Nov. 1990): 665–94. However, one still cannot ignore the influential essay by Charles Grier Sellers, Jr., "The Travail of Slavery," in *The Southerner as American*, ed. Charles Grier Sellers, Jr. (Chapel Hill: Univ. of North Carolina Press, 1960), 40–71.

96. Edgefield *Advertiser*, 16 and 30 Jan. 1861.

batteries opened fire on Sumter, which surrendered on the 14th.[97]
Upon news of the shelling on Fort Sumter, a celebration broke out in
Hamburg in Edgefield District in which "All pitched in, Jew and Gentile, negroes and all."[98]

Southerners expected a short war, and men rushed to volunteer lest
they miss out on the adventure and glory. After years of drill and
practice in the militia, men were anxious to prove themselves in war;
fighting confirmed their worth. The white South believed its men
were more honorable and brave than their cowardly northern opponents. The Civil War, then, became a test, not only of the region's
political and military might, but of southern white manhood as well.
Leila Griffin and other women, excluded from such tests—and all
that they implied about citizenship—demonstrated their patriotism by
sewing company and regimental flags that were presented in formal
ceremonies and acknowledged with elaborate oratory.

In Edgefield, old militia companies like the Edgefield Hussars were
brought up to full strength, and prominent citizens who aspired to
captain's bars recruited friends, neighbors, and kinsmen into new
companies. Local historians calculate that 59 percent of the eligible
men in the district—2,137 enlistments—fought for the Confederacy,
and 613 died. This number, however, is an underestimate. Martin
W. Gary's company was entirely omitted from the compiled list, possibly because one local historian so disliked Gary. Moreover, Edgefieldians fought in companies raised either outside of Edgefield or outside
the state. By November of 1861, the *Advertiser* claimed that Edgefield
had already contributed 1400 men to the Confederate army, three
times the number that Charleston had sent. Early in 1862, the news-

---

97. See W.A. Swanberg, *First Blood: The Story of Fort Sumter* (New York:
Charles Scribner's Sons, 1957), for details of the negotiations and military
action. Ft. Pickens in Florida was basically a sideshow to Ft. Sumter.

98. Edgefield *Advertiser*, 24 April 1861. The next day Lincoln called for
75,000 volunteers to serve for the three months that it would take to subdue
the "rebellion." The governors in the upper South refused to comply; Virginia, North Carolina, Tennessee, and Arkansas voted to leave the Union.
On 27 April Virginia invited the Confederate government to move its headquarters from Montgomery to Richmond.

paper pointed out that the village had almost no adult white males left: 27 married men and seven or eight bachelors.[99]

Roughly one-half of the enlistments were volunteers who came forward in the first few months after secession and formed whole companies—three in Gregg's First South Carolina Volunteers, six in the Seventh South Carolina Volunteers raised in March and April under Edgefield's own Thomas G. Bacon (the remaining initial four companies were from neighboring Abbeville), and two in the Hampton Legion.[100]

The Hampton Legion was one of the Confederate army's more celebrated units. The commander, Wade Hampton III of Richland District, was a southern aristocrat, and six of the Legion's officers became generals. Although, as was true for many planters in 1860, Hampton had mortgaged much of his property, he was considered the richest man in the South if not the United States, and his family was estimated to own 3000 slaves, probably more than any other. On his way back from Mississippi to accept his command, he visited President Jefferson Davis at Montgomery and offered the Confederacy the unsold portion of his previous fall's cotton crop, 4700 bales worth a million dollars, to sell in Europe for arms. The government ineptly failed to act on the offer, but it did commission Hampton as a colonel and authorized him in late April to raise a special regiment.

---

99. Edgefield *Advertiser*, 11 Nov. 1861, Jan. 1862. This is possible since Edgefield Court House had a town population of only 800, and many of those were attorney/would-be politicians who initially saw the war as an opportunity for glory. We do not know who sacrificed what, who fought, who stayed the entire four years, who deserted, who used political connections in the relatively safe state home guards. Even southern casualty rates are estimates based upon Union casualty estimates. Omitting those who were blind, deaf, paralyzed, or mentally incompetent, according to the 1860 manuscript population census, there were 3,746 men between the ages of 15 and 50—4,131 if one includes those up to 60 years of age. Another 691 boys were aged 12 to 14 in 1860. Burton is attempting to construct a database of Edgefield Civil War participants. For some estimates see Burton, "From Community to Nation: The Transformation of Local Values in Edgefield, South Carolina," unpublished paper presented at the Woodrow Wilson International Center for Scholars, May 1989.

100. Edgefield *Advertiser*, 30 Jan. 1861; D. Augustus Dickert, *A History of Kershaw's Brigade* (Newberry, S.C.: Elbert H. Aull, 1899), 37.

Wade Hampton was then forty-three years old with no military training or experience. He was six feet tall with a powerful build and a sportsman's experience in riding, shooting, and tracking. Ultimately his natural ability would make him one of the South's most effective cavalry commanders, but in the spring of 1861 Hampton had something different in mind, a special regiment that would combine under one command all three arms of the military. His proposed Hampton Legion would serve for twelve months and would have six companies of infantry, four of cavalry, and one of artillery—a total of 1,095 men. Hampton received twice as many volunteers as he expected; his own sons, Wade IV and Preston, enrolled in the cavalry as privates at twelve dollars a month. After the battle of First Manassas, he was permitted to increase the infantry to eight companies and the artillery to two. Hampton paid for the artillery himself, sending to England for rifled cannon.[101]

Hampton apparently took care to balance the legion with officers from various regions of South Carolina. As his second in command he selected Benjamin Jenkins Johnson, a planter from the Carolina lowcountry who had narrowly lost the gubernatorial contest to Edgefield's Pickens the previous fall. The position of major of cavalry went to an upcountry citizen, James B. Griffin. "It is with pride," the Edgefield *Advertiser* reported, "that Edgefield has given, in the person of Gen. J.B. Griffin, the third field officer to the Legion. It is needless to speak of General Griffin on this side of the State, where he is so

---

101. Virginia G. Meynard, *The Venturers: The Hampton, Harrison, and Earle Families of Virginia, South Carolina, and Texas* (Easley, S.C.: Southern Historical Press, 1981), 140, 194, 204, 211, 216, 976–79, 82; Edward L. Wells, *Hampton and Reconstruction* (Columbia: State Co., 1907), 40; OR, ser. 4, 1:305. OR, ser. 4, 1:296, 303–6; CSR microcopy 267, roll 364, "Hampton Legion—Captions and Record of Events." Infantry Company H, recruited from German-American volunteers in Charleston, was not mustered in until 22 August and did not reach Virginia until September. It was subsequently converted into the second artillery company and known as Bachman's Battery. Accounts of the raising of the artillery can be found in U.R. Brooks, ed., *Stories of the Confederacy* (Columbia, S.C.: State Co., 1912), 246–72, 276–83. The only general study of Hampton, Manly Wade Wellman's *Giant in Gray: A Biography of Wade Hampton* (New York: Charles Scribner's Sons, 1949), is inadequate.

well known as a gentleman and an officer. Suffice it to say that he is the very man for the place in every possible view of the arrangement."[102]

The Hampton Legion accepted two companies of Edgefield men, the Hussars and the Watson Guards. The Edgefield Hussars, led by twenty-five-year-old Matthew Calbraith Butler, nephew of founder A. P. Butler, became Company A of the cavalry battalion. M.C. Butler, a lawyer, was a member of one of Edgefield's most distinguished families and related by birth or marriage to many others. Butler and Griffin shared a cavalryman's camaraderie and a complex set of family ties of which only kin-conscious southerners could keep track.[103]

The second Edgefield company in the Hampton Legion was Martin Witherspoon Gary's Watson Guards, which became Company B of the infantry battalion. Named for the wealthy Edgefield planter Tilman Watson, who outfitted it, the company included as its youngest member Watson's grandson, David Myers, only fourteen years old. Gary, a thirty-year-old lawyer, was originally from Cokesbury in neighboring Abbeville District, where his father, Dr. Thomas Reeder Gary, practiced medicine and farmed. He was the brother-in-law of Maj. N.G. "Shanks" Evans; both he and Evans were to become brigadier generals. Another of Gary's sisters, Elizabeth, was married to Bluford F. Griffin of the Newberry branch of the Griffin family.[104]

---

102. Edgefield *Advertiser*, 29 May 1861. Augusta *Chronicle*, 25 and 26 May 1861, and the *Charleston Courier*, 25 and 29 May 1861, also report the formation of the Legion.

103. There is no biography of Butler, but sketches can be found in CMH 6:380–82; *Dictionary of American Biography* (New York: Charles Scribner's Sons, 1929), 2:363–64; and U.R. Brooks, *Butler and His Calvary in the War of Secession, 1861–1865* (Columbia, S.C.: State Co., 1909). His uncle Pierce Mason Butler had been governor; his uncle Andrew Pickens Butler, U.S. Senator. The late Preston Brooks was his cousin; Brig. Gen. Milledge L. Bonham was his father's cousin; and Gov. Francis Pickens was his father-in-law. See letter of 2 July 1861, note 3.

104. For biographical information on Gary, see CMH, 6:395–97; *Dictionary of American Biography*, 4:177: Reynolds and Faunt, *Biographical Directory of the South Carolina Senate*, 1:552–54; Brooks, *Stories of the Confederacy*, 368–70; Watson, *Greenwood County Sketches*, 235. William Arthur Shepard, D.D. Wallace, and most recently Dr. Lewis P. Jones have written unpublished biographies of Gary. See letter of 4 July 1861, note 8.

Gary, like Butler, had served under General Griffin in the militia, and in 1859 he had been elected colonel of the Second Cavalry Regiment. Gary had also been an aide-de-camp for Edgefield's militia General R.G.M. Dunovant at Sullivan's Island after the attack on Fort Sumter.[105] Gary would have preferred the greater prestige of a cavalry command in the Hampton Legion, but the lack of such an opportunity put him in the infantry. The *Advertiser* reported on 8 May that the Hussars had been accepted into the Legion, but did not mention Gary's company until 22 May.

The two companies left for training camp in Columbia early in June. Gary's company, planning to pick up some members along the way, departed on the fifth, and Butler's the following day. A large crowd turned out to see the Hussars off. Flanked by two other former captains, one of whom was Griffin, Andrew J. Hammond, signer of the Secession Ordinance and a former captain of the troop, gave the farewell speech. The rituals of community were played out again and again as women presented flags to their menfolk with stirring rhetoric that harkened back to the tradition of the Revolutionary War and, more recently, the Mexican War. Music played and women cheered and waved a sea of handkerchiefs. A free black woman sold beer during the jubilant festivities. Edgefield *Advertiser* editor Arthur Simkins lauded those who went to fight but paid an equal tribute to the "workers at home." They do their service, he said, "a service too that is none the less beneficial from being discharged without a flourish of trumpets or implied professions of superior loyalty."[106]

In the Griffin-Burt family, all males of military age volunteered except Leila's dentist brother-in-law. Her two nephews, Charles and Albert Miles, and two cousins, Augustus and Giroud Burt, left for Virginia with Bacon's Regiment.

---

105. Order signed by Brigadier General [R.G.M.] Dunovant, 16 April 1861, Martin W. Gary Papers, SCL. Dunovant was the brother-in-law of Preston Brooks.

106. Edgefield *Advertiser*, 12 and 19 June 1861. Andrew J. Hammond was not related to James Henry Hammond, but to the Hammonds of the Revolutionary era in Edgefield.

Lieutenant Colonel Griffin

Griffin's progress to join the Hampton Legion at the front was delayed because of the lack of troop trains to carry the cavalry forward. While the infantry battalion of the Hampton Legion left for Manassas Junction on 19 July 1861, the cavalry battalion remained behind. Under Major Griffin's command the men trained horses and "practiced with the broad sword."[107] This delay caused Griffin to miss the battle at Manassas. Nonetheless, when Lt. Col. B. J. Johnson was killed in that battle, Griffin was promoted to take his place.[108] Although it meant transferring to the less glamorous infantry, Griffin would be the commanding officer whenever Hampton was absent or incapacitated.

This episode, completely outside Griffin's control, set the stage for discontent. Gary and his Watson Guards emerged from the thick of the fighting at Manassas as heroes. Gary, albeit a remarkable soldier, was somewhat of a loose cannon and sometimes ignored standard army procedures. According to a recent regimental history, at Manassas Gary ordered a charge which was successful in its advance but put his men beyond their own lines, laying them open to deadly enemy fire, and even briefly bringing them under fire from their own troops.[109]

Since the cavalry had not been on the field at Manassas, some of the infantry (with Gary's instigation and encouragement) believed that Captain Gary rather than the absent Major Griffin should have been rewarded with promotion. An anti-Hampton and pro-Gary biographer put it bluntly: "The infantry had won the contest, and their reward was service under a man who had not seen the fight."[110] Griffin's

---

107. *Daily Dispatch* (Richmond), 20 July 1861; *Charleston Mercury*, 29 July 1861; Field, *South Carolina Volunteers*, 31–32.

108. Lieutenant Colonel Johnson died when a minie ball went "through his temple and out the back of his head." *Charleston Mercury*, 5 Aug. 1861; Field, *South Carolina Volunteers*, 5.

109. *Charleston Mercury*, 30 July and 5 Aug. 1861; Field, *South Carolina Volunteers*, 6. See letter of 24 July 1861, esp. note 3.

110. William Arthur Shepard, manuscript, Edgefield County Historical Society, (n.p.), 12.

letters revealed how much he regretted missing the battle, "more than almost any event of my life." Proud of Edgefield's and his friend Gary's performance, he was unaware that events had been unleashed that ultimately would change his and South Carolina's destiny.

Upon Griffin's promotion to lieutenant colonel, Matthew Calbraith Butler replaced him as major of cavalry, and the senior infantry captain, James Conner of Charleston, was promoted to major of infantry. Griffin and Conner became good friends, which helped relieve the tedium of camp life. In August the infantry set up "Camp Griffin" near Bacon Race Church.[111]

Having escaped injury on the battlefield, Griffin, like thousands of his fellows from the countryside, fell to an inglorious attack of measles.[112] His closest brush with death that autumn came when lightning struck his tent. Having little other action to report, newspaper corre-

---

111. OR, ser. 1, vol. 5, pp. 778–79.

112. Measles were usually the first epidemics to visit Civil War military camps. As people from rural areas, less likely to have encountered the disease as children, gathered into one regiment, they remained healthy until one of them contracted measles. His fellow soldiers would then come down with it simultaneously. The disease was characterized by high fever and extreme discomfort, sometimes progressing to dehydration and delirium. With rest and nursing care, recovery was likely, but some individuals developed pneumonia or other complications. During the summer of 1861, one of every seven Confederates serving in Northern Virginia contracted measles; more than 8000 cases were reported in three months. In the Union army, 76,318 cases of measles were recorded, and 5,177 of these men died with the cause listed as measles (others could have died with the cause listed as pneumonia or some other complication). Many ideas of measles causation were bandied about in this period, but Joseph J. Woodward is generally credited with recognizing that each person will have one and only one attack of measles. Woodward, *Outline of the Chief Camp Diseases of the United States Armies as Observed during the Present War* (Philadelphia: Lippincott, 1863). See Samuel L. Katz, "Measles," 835–38, in Wolfgang K. Joklik, Hilda P. Willett, D. Bernard Amos, and Catherine M. Wilfert, eds., *Zinsser Microbiology*, 19th ed. (Norwalk, Conn.: Appleton and Lange, 1988); Jonathan R. Buist, "Some Items of My Medical and Surgical Experience in the Confederate Army,' *Southern Practitioner* 25 (1903): 574–81; Bell I. Wiley, *The Life of Johnny Reb: The Common Soldier of the Confederacy* (Indianapolis: Bobbs-Merrill, 1943), 251. On exposure to diseases see letter of 2 Feb. 1862, note 2.

spondents wrote it up in detail. (See letter of 17 September 1861 and pages 124–25.

In November 1861 Hampton became acting brigade commander, and much of the daily responsibility of administering the regiment devolved on Griffin and Conner. The role came naturally to Griffin, accustomed to command in his previous roles as militia brigadier and slavemaster. In both capacities he took pride in being firm but fair, and he expected reciprocity: obedience in return for good leadership. Both the plantation and the army assumed hierarchy to be the natural order; slaves and soldiers were expected to endure discipline, submit to authority, and follow orders. "I find that Soldiers have to be watched very closely and some of them have to be punished to make them do their duty," he wrote on 11 August 1861, just as he might have described the difficulties of managing his enslaved people on the plantation.

Many civilian soldiers found it difficult to accept such loss of autonomy. Even the poorest of them was entitled to deference from slaves at home and was accustomed to at least surface respect from wealthier whites; in the army they were summarily ordered to drill and work, sometimes by their former neighbors.[113] Men in the Legion, who, in civilian life, commanded the labor of others and even brought their slave valets to camp, took offense when officers attempted to make them ditch diggers or teamsters. Pvt. John Bauskett, Jr., whose father was one of the wealthiest men in Edgefield, was sent to the guardhouse for refusing to drive a wagon.[114] Fifth Sgt. Pierce Butler spent more than one sojourn there by order of his captain and cousin, M.C. Butler, with the result that he became "very respectful and correct in his deportment."[115]

Because locally raised companies contained so many neighbors and

---

113. A delightful vignette of southern aristocrats paying homage to a muddied, barefoot well-digger described in Mary Boykin Chesnut's diary concludes Ford, *Origins of Southern Radicalism*, 372–73. Woodward, ed., *Mary Chesnut's Civil War*, 205.

114. Alifaire Gaston Walden, *Confederate War Diary of John Thomas Gaston* (Columbia, S.C.: Vogue Press, 1960), 6.

115. Matthew Calbraith Butler to Wife, 16 Aug. 1861, Matthew Calbraith Butler Papers, DU.

kinfolk, army discipline problems were compounded. There were six Butlers in the Edgefield Hussars: Matthew Calbraith Butler commanded his brother, Thomas Lowndes Butler, three of his first cousins—Pierce, A.P., and Edward—another cousin's son, William Henry Harrison Butler, and his second cousin, Pvt. Nathan Lipscomb Griffin, Jr. One quarter of the original Hussars—20 of 80—shared the surname of one or more other members of the company. The Watson Guards presented a similar situation. The roster of the 163 men who served in that unit indicates that 67 shared surnames. Company K from Edgefield of the Fourteenth South Carolina had sixteen Ouzts and eleven Timmermans, almost all of whom were related to one another. Company I of the Twentieth South Carolina Volunteers, raised in 1862 from districts bordering Edgefield but including Edgefieldians, had thirty-four men whose surnames were "Gunter," and most of the others were nephews, uncles, and cousins.[116]

During furloughs and convalescent leaves at home, these citizen soldiers freely aired their opinions of their neighbors-turned-officers.[117] Apparently their complaints reached Leila Griffin and caused her husband to lament his "pretended friends." He knew why he was not well liked—he strictly enforced army regulations and expected his men to come up to the mark in doing their duty. After spending time in encampments in Columbia and Richmond that fell short of his standards, Griffin was pleased to find that the cavalry camp at Ashland, Virginia, was run by regular army officers; he wrote with satisfaction that "every thing is conducted strictly according to army regulations."

---

116. Augustus Dickert, *History of Kershaw's Brigade*, 581; O. Lee Sturkey to Vernon Burton, 4 April 1990; D.A. Tompkins and A.S. Tompkins, *Company K: Fourteenth South Carolina* (Charlotte, N.C.: Observer Printing and Publishing, 1897), 5–7, 28–29. Nine of the Ouzts and six of the Timmermans died in the war. Hussars calculated from the roster printed in Chapman, *A History of Edgefield County*, 423–24; Watson Guards calculated from the unpublished company roster compiled by O. Lee Sturkey. Sturkey is preparing complete rosters of the Hampton Legion infantry which contain service records and biographical data for each man, as well as a history of the infantry campaigns. Gunter from Dickert, *History of Kershaw's Brigade*, 581.

117. These letters are typical from Union as well as Confederate soldiers. James I. Robertson, Jr., *Soldiers in Blue and Gray* (Columbia: Univ. of South Carolina Press, 1988), 122.

Griffin's relations with his men were typical; complaints about officers are one of the most common refrains in the letters of men once called "the worst soldiers and the best fighters that America has ever produced." Pvt. Richard Habersham of the Legion's infantry company C, the Manning Guards, described himself as one of the few men in his company who did not hate Captain Manning, but even he was irritated when Manning failed to fulfill a promise to appoint him to a noncommissioned office.[118] Pvt. Samuel Mays of cavalry company B, equally forthright about his dislike for Capt. John Lanneau, noted that most of the men were dissatisfied with the company officers.[119]

The Confederate Congress exacerbated these tensions between officers and enlisted men when it authorized the draft in April 1862. Twelve-month troops willing to reenlist for three years or the duration of the war were permitted the privilege of choosing their own companies and electing officers. Pvt. Charles Hutson observed that "the elections developed, if they did not create, all the ill-will of pre-existing cliques, and sowed discord and dissatisfaction in every corps, of which I have any knowledge."[120]

Griffin worried endlessly about these elections and the conscription policy itself. Significantly, he did not object to or express doubts about the principle of conscription, which was causing an outcry among many who claimed the Confederate government was becoming as dangerous to states' rights as the U.S. government.[121] Griffin's attitude

---

118. Richard Habersham to Mother, 6 April 1862, to Gather, 26 April 1862, Habersham Family Papers, LC.

119. Samuel Elias Mays, Jr., *Genealogical Notes on the Family of Mays and Reminiscences of the War Between the States* (Plant City, Fla.: Plant City Enterprise, 1927), 52. Mays's family was from Edgefield and he had born in the District. However, he moved out of the District and toward the Greenville area.

120. Charles W. Hutson to Mother, 28 April 1962, Hutson Papers, SHC.

121. Charles Hutson protested at "so gross an usurpation of authority" and was certain that the act was unconstitutional. "The despotism of the Richmond government has made slaves of us," he fumed, and expressed the hope that after the war the Gulf states would stand alone. Not until reassured by his father, who had been a member of the Secession Convention, did Hutson reconcile himself to the legality of conscription, and even then he feared the consequences of surrendering state power to Richmond. Charles W. Hutson to Father, 12, 25, 26 April and 13 May 1862, Hutson Papers.

was the pragmatic one of an officer who needed bodies to fill the ranks. The real problem, he believed, was the government's poor management in permitting short enlistments without having replacement troops drilled and ready. His concerns were also personal; were he voted out of office, he would be subject to the new draft as a private. He was very annoyed at the government for not offering more options to men like himself who had volunteered at the first call, while less committed Confederates stayed comfortably at home until forced to enlist.

Griffin's discussion of the reorganization of the army sheds light on a little studied episode; only one or two passing references to it appear in the correspondence of Butler, Gary, and Hampton. Griffin spent more time speculating about the proposed conscription bill than about the movements of the enemy—who seemed disinclined to make any. The Conscription Act cost him months of worry and uncertainty and the loss of a close friend. The text of the act left some doubt about whether field officers like Griffin were to be elected along with company officers. On 19 August 1861 Griffin wrote to Leroy P. Walker, Confederate Secretary of War, requesting "a copy of the act organizing the Hampton Legion." Walker forwarded the request to President Jefferson Davis, whose handwritten response stated that there was "no such act." [122]

In this widespread ambiguity, ambitious captains like Martin Witherspoon Gary saw an opportunity for advancement. Gary came from a wealthy upcountry slaveowning family, and his father represented Abbeville in the state legislature, yet Gary felt aggrieved that he was not fully accepted as one of the Edgefield elite. He was a man on the make, tough and ambitious for the promotion that he felt he should have gotten after First Manassas. Politicking for military office, he led some dissatisfied captains in petitioning for field officer elections. Specifically, Gary electioneered for the coveted position of lieutenant colonel of the Infantry, the position held by his friend J.B. Griffin.

Hampton, too, wrote the War Department for clarification on the elections policy, and weeks went by while Griffin and others waited

---

122. J.B. Griffin to Leroy P. Walker, 19 Aug. 1861, letters received by the Secretary of War, Record Group 109, War Department Collection of Confederate Records, NA, reel 7, no. 3446.

for the Secretary of War to reply. Griffin alternated between confidence and pessimism about his chances of victory if forced to stand for election. He pretended not to care about rumors reaching Edgefield that he would lose, but the lack of public esteem, so essential to the southern male's personal honor, hurt deeply. Proving himself on the battlefield at Eltham's Landing and Seven Pines restored his pride, and after being appointed acting brigadier general during Hampton's convalescence from a foot wound, Griffin's optimism about his chances for reelection grew. But his confidence turned out to be unfounded. On 16 June 1862, he lost the election contest to Gary, resigned from the army, and departed for Edgefield.

Only a part of this story of the reorganization of the Legion can be reconstructed from the surviving evidence. The only known account is a paragraph in one of John Coxe's reminiscences for *Confederate Veteran* written sixty years after the fact. Coxe, a member of Company F, remembered:

> When Hampton left us on the battlefield of Seven Pines, Lieutenant Colonel Griffin became our commander for the time being. Soon after getting settled down at Mechanicsville again, an agitation, headed by Captain Gary, began for a reorganization. Our year's service was more than up, and as it was known that Hampton would not return to us, it was argued by Gary and his partisans that it was high time to reorganize by electing new officers. The truth was that Gary wanted and expected to be elected colonel. On the other hand, Lieutenant Colonel Griffin and Major Conner resisted and took the position that the time was highly inopportune; that having just emerged from one bloody battle and while other and perhaps bloodier battles were closely impending, it would be quite inexpedient to reorganize at that time. The Legion was assembled several times and finally speeches [were] made by both parties. Finally the matter came to a vote and Gary carried for reorganization by a small majority, and immediately after this he, Martin W. Gary, was elected [lieutenant] colonel of the Hampton Legion.[123]

Coxe's rather matter-of-fact account only hints at tensions evident in Griffin's letters. In May, Butler had described to his wife the agita-

---

123. John Coxe, "Seven Days' Battles Around Richmond," *Confederate Veteran* 30 (March 1922): 91.

tion for an election: "It is all done by some of the captains who have been scheming, electioneering & plotting to get position. . . . Gary is to oppose Col. Griffin and it will be the most faithless breach of friendship and social obligation that I have ever known."[124] Thirty-six years later, Adjt. Theodore Barker still smoldered over Gary's behavior. Replying to a letter from Edward L. Wells, who was soliciting information for *Hampton and his Cavalry in '64*, Barker said flatly that the Hampton Legion infantry "was stolen by Gary."[125]

Major Conner's letters say nothing about Griffin's situation, and very little about his own, but one written in late May could have come from Griffin's own pen and reveals them as likeminded in their aristocratic belief that popularity was less important than respect as a principled political virtue. Commenting on the electioneering of the company officers, Conner wrote: "I care very little for what they do and have told them so. . . . They all say that they would rather trust me to take them in and out of a fight than anybody they know, but then I am so strict. They have the most unbounded faith in my coolness and judgment, but I will have discipline and things done right."[126]

Conner was probably more popular than Griffin, as Griffin implied to Leila when he repeated Gary's claim that the men preferred Conner to him and liked Gary better than either of them. In his letter of 26 May, Griffin mentioned that Conner had "long ago" said that, in the event of a reorganization, he would not go against Griffin and would be willing to serve under him. At some point Conner may have been urged to run against Griffin, perhaps by men who opposed Gary and thought Conner would have a better chance than Griffin of defeating him. Conner's daughter implied that such a scheme was afoot when she described her father's second promotion: "Unwilling to be used in the defeat of a worthy officer who would not by popular vote secure his re-election when the Legion was to be reorganized, Major Conner

124. M. C. Butler to Wife, 24 May 1862, Butler Papers, DU.

125. Theodore G. Barker to Edward L. Wells, 16 March 1898, Edward L. Wells Collection, SCHS.

126. The best discussion of these attitudes is Greenberg, *Masters and Statesmen*, see esp. 19. James Conner to Mother, 24 May 1862, in Moffett, *Letters of General James Conner, C.S.A.*, 98.

accepted an offer, which he had previously refused, and became Colonel of the 22nd North Carolina."[127] The "worthy officer" was evidently Griffin, whose letter of 14 June indicates that Conner had not made up his mind about the invitation. He may have declined with the intention of standing for election and withdrawn his refusal when it became clear that the company officers had another candidate slated for his office.

In some companies all of the original officers were defeated, and others, knowing that they had no chance, declined to run. The total rout in Samuel Mays's unit caused "much bitter feeling among the beaten crowd," who contested the election but were able to change only one office.[128]

One Gary partisan interpreted the elections in terms of upcountry and lowcountry competition: "Hampton had done nothing to allay suspicion that South Carolina's parish system would be perpetuated in the army. Soldiers from the hills arrayed themselves against coastal lawyers, who accepted preferment as a birthright." Griffin, however, was neither a lawyer nor from the lowcountry, whereas Gary was a celebrated trial attorney in Edgefield. The elections can be interpreted more realistically as a democratic rejection of the southern aristocratic ideal. Griffin seems never to have grasped the fact that proving himself as capable under fire as Gary had been at Manassas was not really the issue; his style, personality, and relationship with the men were. Whereas Gary was a brilliant extravaganza, Griffin was an effective "by-the-book" team player. Gary was outgoing, personable, and given to intemperate outbursts of profanity that delighted many enlisted men; Griffin was a private person, reserved and cautious in his speech. He was too proud to electioneer and manifestly lacked the guile of an even average politician. He was no match for a man like Gary, who

---

127. Ibid., 100.
128. Mays, Jr., *Genealogical Notes on the Family of Mays and Reminiscenses of the War Between the States*, 52. J. Hervey Dingle won Conner's position. Neither Griffin nor Conner ever mentioned Dingle, the original second lieutenant of Company C, the Manning Guards; Dingle was elected first lieutenant when the company reorganized, and Captain Manning was voted out. There is no record of the vote, but Coxe's account implies a close contest. Gary and Dingle were elected lieutenant colonel and major, respectively, of the infantry battalion. The two were friends.

was calculating enough in his personal life to send copies of a poem written "for only you" to several female acquaintances.[129]

The election story parallels William Faulkner's rendering of the elevation of Thomas Sutpen over the aristocrat Sartoris during the Civil War in *Absalom! Absalom!* The southern aristocratic code stipulated that the southern leader be called upon rather than seek appointment. The leader, needful of making independent decisions for the good of a community, could not be beholden to special interest groups. Ambition was deemed bad; even the extraordinarily successful politico John C. Calhoun denied that he wanted office; he needed to be asked to serve. Griffin behaved according to the gentleman's code of honor; a gentleman did not advance himself, and certainly never at the expense of a friend. Griffin seems to have expected the company commanders, as officers, to acknowledge his conscientious discharge of duty and recent bravery under fire and, as gentlemen, to reject Gary's dishonorable violation of friendship. Griffin's continuing denial that the office was important to him, and his refusal to campaign, exemplified the southern aristocrat's "passive ideal."[130] Detachment and "blandness" were considered virtues; complimenting an editor of the Edgefield *Advertiser*, another newspaperman admired his "blandness and ease and grace of manner."[131]

The South's aristocrats, however, were increasingly out of step with developing democracy. At this time the southern ascriptive culture was giving way to one more oriented toward achievement. Men like Gary represented a modern type, harbingers of demagogues like his own Edgefield disciple, Benjamin Ryan "Pitchfork Ben" Tillman, of the postwar era. They appealed directly to the populace, presenting themselves as men of the people. Griffin and the old order held themselves aloof; they never would admit ambition or pander to the populace; yet they expected the people to select them for those very reasons. The Civil War accelerated democracy and, so, brought South Carolinians

---

129. William Arthur Shepard, manuscript, Edgefield County Historical Society, (n.p.), 12; M.W. Gary Papers, SCL; Burton, *In My Father's House Are Many Mansions*, 116.

130. Kenneth S. Greenberg, *Masters and Statesmen*, see esp. 9.

131. *Charleston Daily Courier*, 9 Aug. 1964.

more in line with the democratic age. The relationship of leaders and followers was changing in the old Palmetto State.

Griffin served in Virginia for one year, and during that time he seems to have thought almost constantly about his family. Letters of all Civil War soldiers beg for more news from home, and Griffin's are typical. He pleaded for letters from Leila, the children, relatives—anyone. He was hungry for news of the children and regretted missing the changes in the youngest ones. Claude and Callie, the twins, were nineteen months old when he left, and the baby, Jimmie, who was born while he was in camp at Columbia, he saw only during a fall furlough. The twins learned to talk while he was gone, and Claude (born with clubfeet) finally took his first long-anticipated steps. Griffin worried constantly about Claude and urged Leila to take him to a skilled Charleston surgeon who had temporarily taken refuge in neighboring Newberry. He even dreamed one night that he saw both little boys running at play and Claude was outrunning Callie.[132]

Leila's Life on the Homefront

Leila Griffin had supervised the plantation on numerous occasions when her husband was traveling about the state on militia reviews, but his extended absence on the Virginia front placed inordinate responsibility on her. The burden on Leila and the children was a special source of worry to Griffin. His three closest friends were spared similar anxiety. Gary and Conner were bachelors, and Butler's wife had given up housekeeping and gone into lodgings with her two-year-old son while Butler's brother Pierce managed the plantation. Neither Leila nor Griffin had brothers to assume such a responsibility. Since both of Griffin's parents and Leila's mother were dead, her younger sister, Sue, moved in to help with the children. The two women, raised in the tradition that revered upper-class women while it "protected" them from matters outside the domestic sphere, ran the planta-

---

132. See letter of 16 Feb. 1862 (esp. note 4). Historians have not systematically studied dreams; they were important to nineteenth-century Americans because the Bible often referred to dreams. Lincoln discussed the significance of his dreams. See Burton, *In My Father's House Are Many Mansions*, 144.

tion with the assistance of an overseer and advice from their father and uncle.[133]

Although slaves performed daily chores in well-to-do households, women from elite families still had formidable domestic responsibilities. One Edgefield soldier, from a less well-off household of eight, remembered that his mother had one slave to help her in the house, yet "it took [his] mother's whole time to cook, sew, and keep the house." A woman of Leila's rank, the mistress of a plantation, oversaw all household production.[134] Food, clothing, linens—anything intended for domestic consumption—was grown or made under her eye. She directed slave gardeners in raising vegetables and fruits, and kitchen slaves in canning and drying the surplus for winter. Preserves, relishes, and delicacies the mistress put up herself, and Leila did this skillfully enough to win prizes for her brandied peaches and melon preserves at the district agricultural fair.[135] The plantation mistress raised the poultry that put eggs and meat on her table, ensured that the cows were milked and butter churned, and every fall oversaw the processing of several dozen hogs into hams, bacon, sausage, and lard. Entrusting none of this produce to the slaves who cooked and served

---

133. Other women, too, relied on relatives for advice. While away at the front John Warren (Jack) Tompkins wrote his wife Lizzie to go to his father, James S. Tompkins, with any questions about the plantation. Tompkins Papers, SCL.

134. Thomas Jefferson Howard, Civil War Veterans Questionnaires, (1915): 6, and (1922): 6; see Anne Firor Scott, *The Southern Lady: From Pedestal to Politics, 1830–1930* (Chicago: Univ. of Chicago Press, 1970), 22–44; Catherine Clinton, *The Plantation Mistress: Woman's World in the Old South* (Chapel Hill: Univ. of North Carolina Press, 1982), 100–145, for descriptions of the responsibilities of planters' wives. Elizabeth Fox-Genovese, *Within the Plantation Household: Black and White Women of the Old South* (Chapel Hill: Univ. of North Carolina Press, 1988), departs significantly from Scott and Clinton in contending that, with the exception of sewing, white women have been credited with much work that was actually performed by female slaves under their supervision. An especially useful collection on southern marriage and women is Carol Bleser, ed., *In Joy and Sorrow: Women, Family, and Marriage in the Victorian South, 1830–1900* (New York: Oxford Univ. Press, 1991).

135. Edgefield *Advertiser*, 24 Oct. 1860.

food, the mistress carried keys to the smokehouse, pantry, and store-rooms, doling out supplies daily when she ordered meals.

An enormous amount of time went into the production of clothing and linens for large households. Because of the proximity of Horse Creek Valley and the other antebellum textile mills, Edgefieldians could buy cloth more easily than many in the South. A former soldier mentioned that his mother did not have to spin and weave: "we could buy our cotton good at the factory cheaper than we could make it at home."[136] On a plantation the size of the Griffins', most of the cloth for slave clothes would have been purchased rather than spun and woven, but a set of cotton garments for summer and woolen for winter still had to be cut and sewn for sixty-one slaves. In addition to ac-complishing part of this endless task, Leila had to make the everyday clothing for herself and her family and keep it in repair. Very few southern women had sewing machines at that time, and even if Leila had one, she probably never sat down without sewing, mending, or knitting in her hands.

War changed the easy availability of cloth; Edgefield mills had to produce for the army before selling to the public. During the war Leila set some of the slave women to spinning and weaving cotton and wool, from which she made clothing for the children and for J.B. at the Virginia front. In 1861–62 shortages were not as severe as they would later become, when dyes had to be made from bark and berries and buttons improvised from seeds, pieces of gourd, or any-thing that could be covered with cloth and attached. By winter 1864, the manager of Eloise and Johnson Hagood's plantation in Edgefield could not obtain any wool and was forced to have the cattle sheared and the hair carded and spun with cotton in order to make slave clothes.[137]

War multiplied Leila's administrative responsibilities and decreased the available resources for coping with them. Still the plantation's

---

136. Thomas Jefferson Howard, Civil War Veterans Questionnaires, (1915): 6, and (1922): 6.

137. Mrs. Thomas Taylor et al., eds., *South Carolina Women in the Con-federacy*, 2 vols. (Columbia, S.C.: State Co., 1903), 2:51. For Hagood, see letter of 26 Nov. 1862, note 2.

chief nurse, she would have found it harder to procure medicines. Meals had to be prepared without items such as sugar, salt, spices, coffee, and tea, which gradually disappeared as the Federal blockade of the southern coast squeezed off imports. Coffee made from parched grain and tea from blackberry leaves or sassafras were tasteless but patriotic; sugar and salt, however, were harder to forgo. They could be given up at the table, but were essential ingredients in preserving fruit and curing meat. Because of the Union blockade and the neutrality of Kentucky, salt became scarce and rose drastically in price. In May 1861, a sack weighing 210 pounds cost 65 cents; by October, the same sack cost between seven and eight dollars. Leila had to hoard her supply of salt as if it were gold dust.[138]

Other essential articles underwent similar radical increases in price— wheat, flour, cornmeal, meats, bacon, fabric, iron, tin, copper, and utensils. Since prices rose more quickly than the currency depreciated, some scholars argue that scarcity was a more important factor than monetary policy in causing inflation. As early as spring 1862, food prices were four to six times greater than they had been in 1860. Between October 1861 and March 1864, the commodities index rose by an average of 10 percent a month. Civil War historian James McPherson, however, links the problem of inflation in the Confederacy to the paper money issued to cover government debt; issues of notes rose from 119 million in 1861 to 400 million in 1862. The price index for commodities that equaled 100 in 1861 reached 763 by 1863. Real wages, on the other hand, fell 65 percent during the war. In spite of attempts at tax reform to alleviate it, inflation persisted and became even more acute after the Union victories at Gettysburg and Vicksburg in the summer of 1863. In

---

138. See, for example, Charleston News and Courier, "Our Women in the War": The Lives They Lived, the Deaths They Died (Charleston: News and Courier Book Presses, 1885), 10–17, 60–65, 399–43, 426–49, for examples of how women did without. Superb descriptions and analyses of white women in the Confederacy are George C. Rable, Civil Wars: Women and the Crisis of Southern Nationalism (Urbana: Univ. of Illinois Press, 1989), and Drew Gilpin Faust, "Mothers of Invention": Women of the Slaveholding South in the American Civil War (Chapel Hill: Univ. of North Carolina Press, 1996). See also LeeAnn Whites, The Civil War as a Crisis in Gender: Augusta, Georgia, 1860–1890 (Athens: Univ. of Georgia Press, 1995), for an analysis of the war's effect on gender hierarchy.

1864, $46 purchased what one dollar did in 1861.[139] Paper money was increasingly regarded as useless.

Reacting to an economy racked by inflation, Edgefieldians on the homefront preferred to make exchanges in kind. As the war dragged on, more and more ads appeared in the Edgefield *Advertiser* for bartering. On 5 October 1864 the Granite Manufacturing Company ran an advertisement offering to barter drills and skirting for commodities at the following prices: corn, 50 cents per bushel; fodder, 50 cents per hundredweight; flour, $7 per barrel; and bacon, 12½ cents per pound. A 20 October 1864 ad offered to barter salt for pork, sugar for bacon, homespun for flour, bacon, or wheat, and salt for corn, wheat, or flour. A 6 July 1864 advertisement offered yarn for flour and sugar for bacon, and a 20 July 1864 ad wanted to exchange salt for corn, wheat, flour, or bacon. Few of these ads mentioned prices.

Leila had to deal with this situation as she tried to feed some seventy people on the plantation. The responsibilities of food and clothing could have occupied 100 percent of her time, but she also became her husband's agent in directing the overseer and monitoring the crops. Griffin seems never to have written separately to B.F. Spradley, the overseer, who was literate; instead his letters are full of instructions for Leila to have carried out—where, when, and how much cotton and grain to plant, to be economical with the corn, to have the wheat sunned, and dozens of other agricultural matters. The unaccustomed hours outside gave her an embarrassingly unladylike suntan, which, Griffin assured her, made him only more proud of her for "this is not time for *fair faces* and *tender hands*."

A fair face and tender hands were the mark of elite womanhood on both sides of the Mason-Dixon line, but they had special significance

---

139. The commodity index increased by 28 times between January 1861 and January 1864. The money supply increased elevenfold. Eugene M. Lerner, "Inflation in the Confederacy, 1861–1865," in *Studies in the Quantity Theory of Money*, ed. Milton Friedman (Chicago: Univ. of Chicago Press, 1956), 173. James McPherson, *Ordeal by Fire: The Civil War and Reconstruction* (New York: Alfred A. Knopf, 1982), 199–200; Charles Ramsdell, *Behind the Lines in the Confederacy* (1944; rpt., New York: Greenwood Press, 1969), 20–21, 75; Eugene M. Lerner, "Inflation in the Confederacy, 1861–1865," 163–78, esp. 163, 167, 170; Richard Cecil Todd, *Confederate Finance* (Athens: Univ. of Georgia Press, 1954), esp. 110, 117.

in the South's caste society. Pale skin and soft palms implicitly distinguished the gentry from the dark faces and callused hands of the African Americans who toiled for them, and from the sunburned wives and daughters of yeomen and poor who worked in the fields by necessity. Griffin noted that his own face had acquired "a pretty good coat of black" from the exposure to the elements, and joked that he and Leila would be well-matched. (He continued, nevertheless, to judge the other women he encountered by conventional standards of beauty.) Ladies like Leila Griffin could regain their fair complexions; how easily they would relinquish the independence acquired during the war and slip back into antebellum gender roles was a matter for conjecture. Despite his praise for his wife's managerial abilities, Griffin clearly did not anticipate that their relationship would be permanently changed. He expected to return to his role as patriarch and protector, allowing her to "retire" to domestic concerns.

Leila's reaction to the unaccustomed responsibilities thrust upon her by the war we cannot know, for her letters to Griffin have not survived. Some planters' wives stepped hesitantly into the absent husbands' shoes and were at times almost overwhelmed by the frustrations of coping with recalcitrant slaves and unfamiliar routines. Others developed competence and confidence as they succeeded at new tasks and learned to make decisions. The tone of Griffin's letters suggests that Leila was among the latter.[140] He seems to have relied on her judgment and ability, frequently responding to queries by advising her to "do as you think best," or "do the best you can." In none of his letters did he voice any doubt about her ability to cope, even with a crisis. When it became difficult to get meat for the slaves, he did not advise her to turn the problem over to the overseer or her father. Instead he casually issued a complex directive: she was to halve the allowance, explain the necessity of it to the slaves, instruct them all to plant large gardens, buy the seed for them, and ensure that the over-

---

140. Rable, *Civil Wars*, ch. 6; Scott, *The Southern Lady*, ch. 4. Not all absent husbands were as supportive and confident as Griffin. See, for example, the Laurens County couple described in Joan Cashin, " 'Since the War Broke Out': The Marriage of Kate and William McClure," in *Divided Houses: Gender and the Civil War*, ed. Catherine Clinton and Nina Silber (New York: Oxford Univ. Press, 1992), 200–212.

seer allowed them time off to cultivate the plots. All of this she apparently accomplished without much trouble, for the matter did not come up again. Griffin never took issue with Leila's ability to look after the plantation; he praised her development into "a *first rate* manager" and teased that she would make a "right managing Widdow."

She was up before daylight to get everything done, and she still prepared special boxes of food and handmade clothing to send to her husband and wrote the letters that he expected to receive regularly even as he acknowledged her extra workload. Although Griffin lamented his absences from his family and inability to care for them, it seems clear that, despite homespun and high prices, Leila and the children were not in want. Indeed, when he was later stationed along the Carolina coast in the winter of 1862–63, he casually requested her to send him provisions and large sums of money.

Not until the last months of the war, when Sherman's troops were marching through Georgia, was his presence really essential at home. The plantation house burned to the ground, and, having no home, Leila and the younger children went to live off the plantation, leaving over fifty slaves under the supervision of fifteen-year-old Willie. Quite likely some of these slaves had taken care of Willie as a younger boy, hunting and fishing with him, and they might have wondered who was supervising whom. Although Griffin never expressed anxiety about race relations, other whites were desperately fearful about the freedom experienced by slaves on the homefront during the war. As early as September 1863, James Henry Hammond, in a petition requesting a magistrate for the southwestern section of Edgefield, wrote, "The country around there is without exaggeration in a desperate condition. Negroes are uppermost, openly keeping white, & some very pretty, girls, & getting children by them. They do not conceal that they steal corn, meat & everything they can to support the fathers & mothers of their Sweet heart. There is not a Magistrate any [where] in reach."[141] This startling postscript sounds like the ravings of a paranoid man, but many whites were worried about being so outnumbered by the slaves.

By the end of the war, when the Griffins were in pressing need, the

---

141. H. Howard et al. to M.L. Bonham, Sept. 1863, Materials 1863–64, Bonham Papers, SCDAH.

military situation was also desperate. Griffin was denied permission to go to his family and bore it stoically. True emergency now stripped away chivalrous rhetoric. "My Darling you are now thrown upon your own resources and you must do the best you can," he wrote matter-of-factly. At the end, when defeat closed in around South Carolina, Griffin would no longer be able to claim the role of patriarchal defender of women and children; "I will try to [take] care of myself, and you take care of yourself and the Children." [142]

Griffin in the South Carolina Reserves

Griffin ended his military service in the South Carolina militia, without ever again holding a commission in the Confederate army. After his defeat in the reorganization of the Hampton Legion, he resigned and returned to civilian life in Edgefield in mid-June 1862. The troops around Richmond acquired a new name, the Army of Northern Virginia, and a new commander, Robert E. Lee, to replace Joseph E. Johnston, who had been wounded at Seven Pines. While Griffin was inspecting his crops, Lee pushed the Federals away from Richmond and back across the Chickahominy River in the Seven Days Battles of 25 June to 1 July.

In the quiet interval between the end of the Seven Days campaign and the second battle of Manassas on 29–30 August, it appeared that Griffin's military career might be salvaged. On 2 August 1862, he apparently won in absentia an election for colonel of the Legion (Hampton having assumed a brigadier general's command). Sometime in the latter part of August 1862, Griffin, undoubtedly feeling justly vindicated, left for Virginia to assume his new command. He stopped in Richmond to visit James Conner, who was convalescing from a serious leg wound suffered at the battle of Mechanicsville during the Seven Days. Private Charles Hutson of Company A, who had been left behind to recover from illness, wrote home that, while visiting Conner in the hospital, he had seen Griffin, who was enroute to his com-

---

142. Drew Faust, "Altars of Sacrifice: Confederate Women and the Narratives of War," *Journal of American History* 76, no. 4 (March 1990): 1200–228 analyzes the reaction of planters' wives to the failure of their husbands to live up to the patriarchal ideal during the Civil War.

mand.[143] On 29 August Griffin wrote to Leila from Richmond that he had just learned of his commission at home as lieutenant colonel of the Fifth South Carolina Reserves (SCR). After deliberating which command to accept, he told her he had decided to rejoin the Legion.

His next letter, however, dated 26 November, was written from Charleston on the eve of his departure for the headquarters of the Fifth SCR. What happened in the meantime was probably a new troop reorganization that deprived Griffin of his command.[144] Although the Hampton Legion still existed on paper in the summer of 1862, it was not functioning as a unit. The four cavalry companies were serving with J.E.B. Stuart; the two artillery companies were temporarily with the divisions of D.R. Jones and A.P. Hill; and the infantry was assigned to John Bell Hood's celebrated Texas Brigade.[145] The order calling the 2 August election has not been found, but apparently it was countermanded by orders that formally disbanded the Legion. The cavalry battalion had been officially detached, and on 22 August by Special Orders No. 196 of the Adjutant and Inspector General's Office, it was assigned to the Second South Carolina Cavalry Regiment under M.C. Butler.[146] At some time before 25 August, the artillery also was separated; Company A was thereafter known as Hart's South Carolina Horse Artillery (assigned to J.E.B. Stuart's Cavalry Division); Company B was designated Bachman's Battery South Carolina Artillery.[147] The infantry battalion, entitled to a lieutenant colonel's command under existing War Department policies, continued under Gary at that rank until 12 December, when he was promoted to colonel retroactive from 26 August. By that time it had been increased to ten companies—full regimental strength. The formal disbanding of the Hampton Legion left Griffin with no choice. Hutson reported in a letter dated 1 October that Griffin had resigned "some time ago"; his military record says only that he "declined col."[148]

143. Charles W. Hutson to Emily Hutson, 27 Aug. 1862, Hutson Papers.
144. O. Lee Sturkey, extraordinarily knowledgeable historian of the Hampton Legion infantry, suggests this. Sturkey to Judith McArthur, 24 May 1988.
145. OR, ser. 1, 11, pt. 3: 652; B&L, 2:315–17.
146. OR, ser. 1, 11, pt. 3: 657; "Hampton Legion, Captions and Record of Events," CSR, M267, roll 364.
147. "Hampton Legion, Captions and Record of Events."
148. Charles W. Hutson to mother, 1 Oct. 1862, Hutson Papers.

Griffin returned to South Carolina and accepted the position of lieutenant colonel with the Fifth SCR. With an attack on Charleston considered imminent, South Carolina used "emergencies of service" to put the Reserves on guard along the coast for ninety days. Griffin was stationed on the lower Carolina coast from November 1862 to mid-February 1863, posted in the Second Military District of South Carolina, which began just below Charleston at the Stono River and Rantowles Creek and extended more than a third of the way down the coast to the Ashepoo River. The offshore islands, in Federal hands since the fall of Port Royal in November 1861, gave the Union a potential base from which to invade the coast and also attracted fugitive slaves who heard that freedom could be found near the mouth of the Savannah River, about 180 miles from Edgefield. The commander of the Second District, Johnson Hagood, wrote that "the country to be guarded was extensive and penetrated in every direction by water courses, giving facility for petty marauding incursions which were to be expected." Griffin's regiment was part of the force deployed to keep the Yankees from gaining a foothold on the mainland. The troops were a mixture of infantry, artillery, and cavalry, with a strength that ranged from 1000 to 4000, and "they were constantly shifting, too, regiments coming and going as the emergencies of service required." Griffin's service here was easy duty relieved by duck and deer hunting and dining with the local gentry.[149]

As lieutenant colonel of the Fifth SCR, Griffin served under Col. Thomas G. Bacon, whose health was too poor to permit him to continue in command of the Seventh South Carolina Volunteers with the Army of Northern Virginia. Bacon's frequent involuntary absences meant that during much of this time Griffin was in de facto command of the regiment, as he had been of the Hampton Legion in Virginia. Griffin remained a stickler for the rules, as Henry W. Ravenel of Aiken, on the southeastern border of Edgefield District, discovered. Ravenel, who was sick, had received a summons from Col. Bacon to attend a court-martial because he had "failed to appear at Camp Griffin before the 1st of January 1863." He wrote in his diary on 5 February 1863, "I soon saw Lieut Col. Griffin (Col Bacon being sick) &

---

149. OR, ser, 1, 14: 736; Johnson Hagood, *Memoirs of the War of Secession* (Columbia, S.C.: State Co., 1910), 100.

reported my presence. He stated that my case had gone to the Court Martial & it would be impossible for the col. to interfere, as there were so many cases & he could not deviate from the rule. He was very kind however, & requested the Court to take up my case out of its order that I might not be kept in camp longer than necessary." Not all of the rank and file were as willing as Ravenel to acknowledge such merits. Griffin's devotion to strict authority again made him unpopular with his command, and he once again faced the possibility of being turned out by an election. Colonel Bacon appealed to General Beauregard, the department commander, to order that all officers be retained for the duration. "I will lose Lieut. Col. Griffin an able and efficient officer, unless you interpose," he explained. "Quite probable I will get a Lieut Col not worth one cent."[150]

Such tensions dampened Griffin's enthusiasm for military service. On 26 February 1862 he had written from Virginia, "we, who are able to resist them, will continue to do so, until we grow old and worn out in the service. . . . I would be proud of the thought that our youngest Boy, yes darling little Jimmie, will after awhile be able and I trust willing to take his Father's place in the field, and fight until he dies. . . ." Ten months later, following the emotional drain of the reorganization, and facing a new election threat in the reserve unit, he wrote, on 26 December 1862, "If they elect me (which I dont expect) I will serve, but if they do not I will go home and quit the war—" This time, however, the election was suspended, and he finished the ninety-day stint without incident.

Other Edgefieldians already were quitting the war. While Griffin took charge of the militia troops on the coast of South Carolina, some of his neighbors had to be forcibly persuaded to report for reserve duty. On 1 Feb. 1863 Griffin listed some of the Edgefield men conscripted for duty with the Fifth SCR and informed Leila of "defaulters who had to be invited down *specially*." A court-martial was being called, he said, to look into their failure to report earlier. Griffin treated these "croakers" with a jovial sense of humor. "I wish you could see some of them also. Shimmey Nicholson especially, he is the picture of de-

150. Arney Robinson Childs, ed., *The Private Journal of Henry William Ravenel 1859–1887* (Columbia: Univ. of South Carolina Press, 1947), 169–70; CSR, M267, roll 201, p. 322.

spair. He offers five hundred dollars if we will turn him loose and let him go home. George Addison, Jim Mims and Butler are all here. I hear Sam Tompkins has got home. He is also invited down." All of these were men of wealth (or from very wealthy slaveowning families), and some were among the very wealthiest in Edgefield (see notes to letter of 1 Feb. 1863, and census profile and wealth tables in appendix). Griffin's brother-in-law, First Lieutenant Aquilla Miles, went to Edgefield to round up slackers and those who had failed to answer the conscription call. Miles, not nearly as wealthy as most of these other Edgefieldians, was responsible for bringing them to camp. "Quilla raised a good deal of excitement about old Edgefield. I wish he could have found Jim Hatcher. I hear he talked very large, but he took good care to keep out of the way of Quilla."[151]

That these defaulters from the reserves were not poor lends some credence to the proposition that the Civil War was a rich man's war and a poor man's fight. But deserters from the regular army were much poorer than those in Griffin's militia list, and they faced more dire consequences, including the possibility of being shot on sight. Beginning in mid-January 1863, advertisements similar to those for runaway slaves appeared in the local paper offering rewards for return of deserters. One such deserter was William S. Morris, a twenty-eight-

---

151. Miles was forty-four years old in 1860, owner of 10 slaves, personal estate worth $11,370, and land worth $6,555. He was in the top 11th percentile of all household heads financially. By contrast, Shemuel W. Nicholson owned $30,000 in real estate (top 2%) and $80,000 in personal estate (top 1%), including 68 slaves. George P. Addison declared $37,000 in real estate (top 1%), and $95,000 in personal estate (top 1%), including 68 slaves. James Mims was similar to Aquilla Miles in ownership of land—$6,000 (top 21%)—and $10,000 in personal estate (21st percentile), including 10 slaves. Eighteen-year-old Sampson W. Butler had no wealth and still lived in the home of his father, Robert J. Butler. He was his father's substitute for conscription. The elder Butler owned land valued at $27,000 (top 3%) and personal estate valued at $32,700 (top 6%). Samuel S. Tompkins owned $18,000 in real estate (top 13%) and $32,700 in personal estate (top 6%), including 41 slaves. James Hatcher's $15,000 land value (top 17%) and $13,145 in personal estate, with 11 slaves, situated him near Aquilla Miles financially. All wealth percentiles exclude the 40.6 percent who owned no land in 1860 and the 5 percent who reported no personal estate in 1860. Calculations are derived from the appended Census Profile and the wealth tables.

year-old tenant farmer in 1860. He owned no real estate and only
$500 in personal estate. Other lists reveal war-weary veterans who were
primarily yeomen, tenants, artisans, overseers, or the sons of poorer
folks of Edgefield, men who went home to help families unable to
survive without them.[152]

After the Fifth SCR was disbanded on 15 February 1863, Griffin
saw no further military service until autumn of 1864.[153] The infamous
"Twenty Negro Law," excusing from the draft one white man on each
plantation that worked twenty or more slaves, had been passed after
Griffin accepted his commission in the reserves. As soon as he finished
the ninety-day stint, he was thereafter exempt from Confederate conscription, though still subject, like all males between sixteen and sixty,
to militia service in South Carolina. Griffin did not take up arms
again for one and a half years. Certainly he had modified his initial
determination to fight without pause.

South Carolina in Jeopardy

While Griffin drilled with the home militia in Edgefield, resistance to
the Federal assault on the Carolina coast went on without him. Like
all South Carolinians, he and his Edgefield neighbors kept their attention on the defense of the vulnerable tidewater area, especially after
Union forces on 7 April 1863 launched a long-anticipated attack on

---

152. Edgefield *Advertiser*, 15 and 21 Jan. 1863, 25 April 1865. Many poor
families were desperate for relief. For a study of poor relief in Edgefield during
the Civil War, see Patricia Dora Bonnin, "The Problem of Relief for the
Families of Confederate Soldiers in South Carolina," *The Proceedings of the
South Carolina Historical Association*, 1994 (Aiken: South Carolina Historical
Association, 1994), 75–82, and " 'The Loved Ones at Home': The Problem
of Relief for the Families of Confederate Soldiers" (History Undergraduate
Honors Thesis, University of Illinois at Urbana-Champaign, 1993).

153. There is some confusion as to Griffin's whereabouts in early 1864.
Friend and neighbor Z.W. Carwile wrote the Confederate Secretary of War
on 13 Jan. 1864 asking that his overseer be released from service. Carwile
mentioned if "his friend Col. James B. Griffin" was in Virginia, he could
bring the Secretary's answer. Z.W. Carwile to James Seddon, 13 Jan. 1864,
letters received by the Secretary of War, Record Group 109, War Department
Collection of Confederate Records, NA, reel 140, number S20.

Charleston, important symbolically as the city where secession and war began. But as Charleston successfully resisted repeated bombardments and months of siege, another threat to Edgefield and South Carolina was developing in Georgia. On 1 September 1864 Joseph E. Johnston's army evacuated Atlanta; William Tecumseh Sherman took possession of the city the next day. The Confederate military situation was becoming desperate and the invasion of South Carolina only a matter of time. Between Sherman in Atlanta and Union forces on the coast lay Edgefield and Griffin.

Across the Savannah River from Edgefield District stood the hinterland city of Augusta with major Confederate gunpowder and munitions factories. As Sherman began his march to the sea, Augusta, where the railroad connected Charleston to Hamburg, just across the Savannah River, seemed likely to be one of his targets. In a desperate attempt to prevent Sherman from wreaking havoc in South Carolina as well as Georgia, Governor Milledge Bonham called up the state militia, and those liable for service outside their residential districts (men aged fifty and under and some of the Confederate exempts) formed companies. Bonham ordered these companies to rendezvous at Hamburg to be organized into regiments. This time Griffin finally received formal command of a regiment, colonel of the First South Carolina Militia.[154]

Lt. Gen. William Hardee, who commanded the Georgia and South Carolina troops, prepared to resist both Sherman and the Union coastal assaults with the few, poorly outfitted troops that could be mustered. On 19 October 1864 Hardee reported to the quartermaster general in Richmond that he was "greatly in need of shoes, clothing, and blankets for the use of this command. . . . Very many of my men are absolutely barefooted." His summary of departmental strength reported only 23,605 men, of whom hardly more than half—12,446—

---

154. Charleston *Daily Courier*, 30 Nov. and 8 Dec. 1864; OR, ser. 4, 3:904. Since state law permitted only one-third of the men liable for service beyond their home districts to leave the state, and that for a duration no longer than two months, Bonham also asked the legislature to amend the militia regulations. It obliged with a new statute requiring men 16 to 60 to service anywhere in the state, and making those 16 to 50 eligible for service outside South Carolina at the governor's discretion.

were combat-ready.[155] The Confederate War Department, having no reinforcements to send, advised Hardee to make up a force of "detachments from garrisons, convalescents from hospitals, reserves, militia, and volunteers."[156] Griffin's First South Carolina Militia became part of Hardee's force, the Confederacy's last reserves.

Instead of attacking Augusta and marching through Edgefield to Charleston, Sherman headed straight to the sea and Savannah, bent on destroying the southern will to make war. Northern soldiers, playing by different rules than those of a gentlemanly conflict, put the torch to civilian society and the southern homefront. Although common in fighting Native Americans, this was the first use of "total war" against a white population. Hardee was forced to abandon Savannah (Sherman offered it to Lincoln as a Christmas present) and ordered some of the militia, including Griffin's troops at Hamburg, to the coast to defend Charleston.

Sherman left Savannah for South Carolina on 1 February 1865 with an army of 65,000 lean, hard Union veterans—four corps of infantry and a troop of cavalry—determined to make South Carolina pay for instigating the rebellion. It was time to take off the velvet glove and reveal the mailed fist, Sherman told his troops. Confederates estimated that Sherman would proceed one of two ways. If he marched toward Charleston, he would encounter Hardee; if he marched back toward Augusta, part of the South Carolina Militia would defend that city. Sherman did neither: feinting toward both Charleston and Augusta, he actually drove through the middle of the state to Columbia, cutting the Charleston-Hamburg Railroad and leaving Charleston isolated.

As Sherman advanced, the troops in Augusta and those with Hardee, including Griffin's unit on the coast, headed north to confront him. M.C. Butler's Second South Carolina Cavalry and Wade Hampton, now commander of all Confederate cavalry, had earlier been dispatched from Virginia to help bolster South Carolina's morale. According to an Illinois officer, Major Charles W. Wills, a note from Hampton to Butler, intercepted by the Federals, ordered Butler not to hinder Sherman's progress in getting out of South Carolina:

155. OR, ser. 1, 35, pt. 2: 637, 640, 643.
156. OR, ser. 1, 44: 864.

"Do not attempt to delay Sherman's march by destroying bridges, or any other means. For God's sake let him get out of the country as quickly as possible." Wills added, "Were I one of the S.C. chivalry, I'd be in favor of turning out en masse and building up roads for him."[157]

To rally the spirits of the men in the ranks, Lee persuaded Jefferson Davis to overcome his dislike for Joseph E. Johnston and appoint him commander of all troops in the Carolinas. Once again under "Old Joe's" command and fighting near his old comrades Hampton and Butler, Griffin had come full circle as he rode toward North Carolina with Hardee's patchwork little "army."

Johnston knew that war-weariness was enveloping the South and defeat was inevitable. Griffin, satisfied again in a fitting position of command and authority, would have preferred continuing to fight; Sherman's total war tactics stiffened his resolve. Late in January he wrote Leila from the coast, "Our only chance for peace lyes in our rifles, that will bring it after awhile, if we will only remain true to ourselves." The expansive nationalism he had expressed in his early fighting days in Virginia had changed; after a lengthy hiatus at home he now had a particular Edgefield locus. He explained in early February 1865 to Leila that he was "thoroughly disgusted with men who are resorting to all kinds of pretexts to be exempt from service, now that our very homes are threatened. Our wives and children almost at the mercy of a cruel and heartless enemy—that I don't believe I would go home were it in my power. A man in South Carolina who is really able to bear arms, even for a short time, who is not now found in the front—unless Providentially kept away really does not deserve the name of Freeman and should be considered as such for all time to come, by good, honest citizens and more especially by the helpless women and Children."

Ironically, at this same time, on 28 January 1865, Leila was writing an application for an exemption for sixteen-year-old William Griffin as the "only white person" on the plantation with "over Fifty negroes." Noting that her husband was away serving the state, Leila explained that "we have had the misfortune to have our dwelling house destroyed

157. Charles W. Wills, *Army Life of an Illinois Soldier*, compiled and published by his sister (Washington: Globe Printing, 1906), 357.

by fire . . . & I am necessarily compelled to reside away from the place, as there is no building that I can occupy on the premises." Leila's petition, endorsed by sixteen prominent citizens, was granted.[158]

Griffin did not finish the campaign of the Carolinas. Governor McGrath ordered the 1100 South Carolina militiamen serving with Hardee in North Carolina to return home to counter an anticipated Union cavalry raid. On 11 March, while Hardee's army was resting five miles outside Fayetteville, North Carolina, Griffin took the First South Carolina Militia out of the ranks and headed back to the border.[159] The regiment was disbanded at Spartanburg, and Griffin must have been nearly home when Lee surrendered to Grant on 9 April 1865 at Appomattox Court House, Virginia. One of Matthew Calbraith Butler's discharged young cavalrymen, riding slowly home, encountered Griffin and some of his regiment—"a lot of college boys"—on a train headed for Columbia, and rode with them until demolished tracks brought the train to a halt.[160] It is not known how the First South Carolinians proceeded after that, but the Edgefield paper reported on 19 April that Griffin and his boys had been home "for the last week or so."[161] Just as he had missed the opening of the war at Manassas, he was absent from the surrender in North Carolina. The war was over for him a month before it formally ended. He would have been preoccupied with spring planting when Johnston and Sherman began preliminary peace negotiations at Bennett Place, Durham, North Carolina.

While Griffin was attending to his own affairs, President Davis and the cabinet were fleeing south from Richmond, and the military drama was not yet over for all of the former officers of the Hampton Legion. Wade Hampton offered by letter to collect a cavalry force, escort President Davis across the Mississippi River, and continue the

---

158. Mrs. J.B. Griffin to Gen. A.C. Garlington, 28 Jan. 1865, Petitions for Exemption, 1864–1865, Administrative Records, Adjutant General, SCDAH.

159. Joseph E. Johnston, *Narrative of Military Operations* (1874; rpt., Bloomington: Indiana Univ. Press, 1959), 382; Nathaniel J. Hughes, *General William J. Hardee: Old Reliable* (Baton Rouge: Louisiana State Univ. Press, 1965), 278.

160. Walden, *Confederate War Diary of John Thomas Gaston*, 19.

161. Edgefield *Advertiser*, 19 April 1865.

resistance from Texas.[162] When the President and Hampton finally met at Charlotte, Davis authorized the plan, urging the Confederacy to keep up the struggle as long as men were in the field. Davis then headed to South Carolina under the protection of General Martin W. Gary and a cavalry escort. The President's party reached the home of Leila Griffin's kinsman, former U.S. Congressman Armistead Burt, in Abbeville on 2 May, where Davis was reunited with his family and presided over the last meeting of the Confederate cabinet.[163] Hampton returned to his headquarters at Hillsboro on 26 April only to find that Johnston had surrendered the army. Since he had not been with his command at the time, Hampton initially refused to concede that he was included in the surrender. He set off again to look for Davis, but, unable to make contact with the President, finally acknowledged the futility of prolonging resistance and accepted a parole.

Martin W. Gary, however, never did. Throughout the war Gary continued in command of the Legion infantry, which had been mounted and included in the cavalry brigade assigned to him after his promotion to brigadier general in May 1864. At Appomattox, after Lee formally relinquished his army on 9 April 1865, Gary's brigade was still shooting. When a Union courier, under a flag of truce, was sent through the lines with news of capitulation, Gary retorted defiantly that South Carolinians never surrendered.[164] He broke through the Federal lines and caught up with President Davis at Greensboro, North Carolina. A young woman

---

162. See Edward L. Wells, *Hampton and Reconstruction* (Columbia, S.C.: State Co., 1907), 66–67 for excerpts from the correspondence.

163. M.H. Clark, "The Last Days of the Confederate Treasury and What Became of It," SHSP 9 (Oct.-Dec. 1881): 544; William H. Parker, "The Gold and Silver in the Confederate States Treasury: What Became of It," SHSP 21 (1892): 307–9; Francis de Sales Dundas, *The Calhoun Settlement, District of Abbeville, South Carolina*, 2nd ed. (n.p., 1949), 42.

164. The different accounts all vary Gary's words slightly, but both Union and Confederate observers agreed on the essence. See Frederick Cushman Newhall, *With General Sheridan in Lee's Last Campaign* (Philadelphia: J.B. Lippincott, 1866), 213–14; Edward L. Boykin, *The Falling Flag, Retreat and Surrender at Appomattox* (New York: E.T. Hale and Son, 1874), 59–60; W.G. Hinson, "General Sheridan's Reference to M.C. [*sic*] Gary of South Carolina," *Confederate Veteran* 2 (Sept. 1894): 278; J.H. Doyle, "With Gary's Brigade at Appomattox," *Confederate Veteran* 29 (Sept. 1921): 332.

from upcountry South Carolina captured some of the emotions of the moment. As she forlornly watched the former rebels trudge home, she romanticized in her diary, "Gary burst into tears and cried like child. Sticking spurs into his horse and exclaiming, 'I'll never surrender,' he made his way out with a few of his staff." She wrote of others going to Brazil, and her letters passed on rumors that Hampton would go to Mississippi or Texas, but Gary, she happily reported, had proclaimed he was coming home to South Carolina.[165] Many white Edgefieldians took great pride that their "Bald Eagle" apparently never did surrender.

Four years earlier, few in Edgefield or South Carolina would have predicted surrender as the outcome. When Griffin arrived in Charleston to celebrate the capitulation of Fort Sumter, defeat, surrender, and bankruptcy were inconceivable. His story opens there in the euphoric spring of 1861.

---

165. Journal, 24 April 1865, p. 19, and letters in the Harry L. Watson collection, SCL. Most likely the journal is that of Ella Townes (1845–1925) of Greenville, S.C. Ella Townes married Stanmore P. Brooks in 1866 and died in 1925 at the home of Harry L. Watson. The journal and letters are part of that collection.

2 Fort Sumter to Manassas

Letters 1 through 15
14 April through 17 September 1861

The fall of the federal garrison at Fort Sumter brought Griffin, a brigadier general in the state militia, to Charleston to share in the celebration and assess the military situation. Within weeks, he was commissioned major of cavalry in the Hampton Legion and was drilling recruits in Columbia, where his two oldest sons happily visited him in camp. While Leila awaited the imminent birth of their eighth child, Griffin prepared to move his squadron to Virginia. The new baby, christened James Hampton, was less than two weeks old when Griffin departed for Richmond, torn between regret at leaving his family and eagerness to be at the front.

His initial hopes were disappointed, however, when a shortage of troop trains kept the Hampton Legion cavalry from reaching Manassas in time to take part in the stunning Confederate victory on 21 July. Griffin lamented that "we of the Cavalry had hard luck" in missing the action, the more so because the Legion's infantry had been in the thick of the fight and had drawn praise from Gen. P.G.T. Beauregard. Lt. Col. B.J. Johnson's death in action left the infantry without a commanding officer and forced a reorganization of the Legion's field command: Griffin was transferred to the infantry and promoted to lieutenant colonel. By August he was preoccupied with the less glamorous side of military life: poor drinking water, inadequate forage, and an epidemic of measles.

Letter 1   JBG to Leila Griffin

Mills House[1]
Sunday 1/2 past 12
April 14th 1861

My Dearest Leila

I arrived safely here this morning at four oclock, and found, as you have doubtless heard that Fort Sumter[2] has surrendered *unconditionally*. And what is wonderful, without the loss of a single life on either side. The excitement of course has subsided to a great extent. But still enough to keep things pretty lively. Anderson[3] with his men has just left the fort and I presume about now the flag of the "Southern Confederacy" is being raised over its walls. The report is that one of Ander-

---

LETTER 1

1. An elite Charleston hotel, still in existence today.

2. Fort Sumter, in Charleston Harbor, and Fort Moultrie, on Sullivan's Island, were federal installations that posed a delicate military and diplomatic problem after South Carolina seceded from the Union on 20 December 1860. At the time, Fort Sumter, commanding the main ship channel, was unoccupied, and the garrison at Fort Moultrie was small; Major Robert Anderson, acting without instructions, transferred it to the more defensible Sumter on the night of 26 December 1860. On 5 January 1861, President James Buchanan dispatched the merchant steamer *Star of the West* to relieve Anderson, but it turned back when fired upon from Morris Island. The situation remained stalemated throughout the winter, while South Carolina insisted on the surrender of the fort to state authority and Lincoln and his advisors debated. Against the advice of his cabinet, Lincoln notified South Carolina officials on 8 April 1861 of his intention to send provisions to Sumter. South Carolina immediately presented Anderson with a formal demand of surrender and, finding his conditions unacceptable, fired the opening shots of the Civil War on 12 April; Fort Sumter surrendered the following day. W.A. Swanberg, *First Blood: The Story of Fort Sumter* (New York: Charles Scribner's Sons, 1957); Charles Edward Cauthen, *South Carolina Goes to War* (Chapel Hill, N.C.: Univ. of North Carolina Press, 1950), 117–32.

3. Major Robert Anderson (1805–1871) had been given charge of the Charleston harbor defenses early in November, in the hope that an officer of Kentucky birth and proslavery sentiments would be more acceptable to the South Carolinians. A month after he was forced to surrender the Federal garrison, Anderson was elevated to brigadier general.

son's men was wounded[4] and not one on our side which is wonderful.
I will remain here a few days until I can visit all the forts[5] which
cannot be done today. When I arrived here I found the City crowded.
All the Hotels full. Great difficulty in getting rooms. I havent yet seen
any of our Boys but hear all are well.[6] I hope you and the dear little
Children are better. Kiss them all for me and accept for yourself the
kindest wishes and best love of your

Jimmie

Letter 2   JBG to Leila Griffin

Camp Hampton[1]
Near Columbia
June 12th 1861

My Dear Wife
I arrived here as I expected on monday evening. Found the camp
in a good deal of confusion. Col Hampton is still sick in bed, he, is
however, better and the Doctors say will be out in a few days. Lt

---

4. Anderson reported one man killed, two seriously and three slightly
wounded, all during an accidental explosion while saluting the colors after
the surrender. The South Carolina contingent had no casualties. OR, ser. 1,
1:12–13, 30–34.

5. In addition to Sumter and Moultrie, there were two other forts in
Charleston Harbor. Castle Pinckney, a small fortress shaped like a half-moon,
was located on Shute's Folly Island less than a mile east of the docks. Fort
Johnson on James Island stood across the bay from Moultrie. It was a ruin
that dated back to Revolutionary War days and had long been abandoned as
a military post.

6. The Edgefield Riflemen militia company had arrived in Charleston on
7 January and subsequently was stationed on Sullivan's Island. Edgefield *Advertiser*, 16 Jan. 1861.

LETTER 2

1. Camp Hampton was three miles east of Columbia at Woodlands Plantation, established by Hampton's grandfather, Wade Hampton I. The old
racetrack served as a drill field. Pvt. John Coxe remembered that "severe
company drills were inaugurated under the eyes of Lieutenant Colonel Johnston [sic], Major Griffin, and Adjutant Barker," but the entire command,
officers as well as enlisted men, dined together on fresh beef prepared in great

Col Johnson,[2] I found at the camp. I am very much pleased with him indeed, I think he is an elegant gentleman, and a fine officer.

I am quartered with the Cavalry, and already begin to look like a Soldier. I hope, my Darling, I will get a letter from you to night or tomorrow, and I sincerely hope you and my dear little Children are doing well. I am very anxious to hear from you, and am already anxious to see you. I think we will be ordered to Vir. Well—I will start again—just as I wrote Vir. my whole tent fell right over me, but fortunately did no harm except to blot my paper as you perceive. I was going on to say that I expect we will soon be ordered to Virginia. I dont think we will stay here longer than next week. I, in company

---

kettles by slave cooks and baker's bread sent out from Columbia. Hampton's sisters at Millwood, the adjoining estate of Wade Hampton II, took a personal interest in the legionnaires' welfare: Capt. James Conner was sent word that washing for his company would be done at Millwood, and a champagne basket of food and books arrived for the sick. Virginia G. Meynard, *The Venturers: The Hampton, Harrison, and Earle Families of Virginia, South Carolina, and Texas* (Easley, S.C.: Southern Historical Press, 1981), 216; John Coxe, "The Battle of First Manassas," *Confederate Veteran* 23 (Jan. 1915): 24. James Conner to Mother, 13 June 1861, in Mary Conner Moffett, ed., *Letters of General James Conner, C.S.A.* (Columbia, S.C.: R. L. Bryan, 1950), 27–30.

2. Benjamin Jenkins Johnson (1817–1861) had brought the Washington Light Infantry of Charleston into the Legion. A native of Beaufort District, he was educated at William and Mary College and later admitted to the South Carolina bar. A "great" planter who owned 119 slaves, he was also prominent in state politics. After winning election to the South Carolina House of Representatives at the age of 21 and completing one term, he returned in 1844 and served until 1853. That year he was elected to the state senate, where he remained until the war broke out. Johnson lost a close contest for governor to Edgefield District's Francis W. Pickens in 1860. N. Louise Bailey, Mary L. Morgan, and Carolyn R. Taylor, eds., *Biographical Directory of the South Carolina Senate, 1776–1985*, 3 vols. (Columbia: Univ. of South Carolina Press, 1985), 2:825; Robert K. Krick, *Lee's Colonels: A Biographical Register of the Field Officers of the Army of Northern Virginia*, 2nd ed. rev. (Dayton, Ohio: Press of Morningside Bookshop, 1984), 179; Charles Gaston Davidson, *The Last Foray, The South Carolina Planters of 1860: A Sociological Study* (Columbia: Univ. of South Carolina Press, 1971), 43, 215 (which lists 145 slaves).

with most of the Commissioned Officers took tea last night with Mr Frank Hampton.[3] He is a very nice Gentleman. They are all exceedingly kind to us. I have just commenced to day, to take a bad cold. I feel rather badly this evening on account of it. I hope my Darling, to be able to go home next week—but know I can only stay with you a very short time, for I am kept very busy.

We drill a great deal. Our companies are doing very well. Have dress parrade every evening, when the ladies turn out to see us[.] I have no uniform yet but will get one soon.

Give my love to every body and kiss all the dear little ones for me. Do excuse me for this badly written letter. I have to write on my trunk. I will write again soon. Must close now as the drill is about to begin. Write soon to your

Jimmie

Letter 3   JBG to Leila Griffin

Camp Hampton
June 14th 1861

My Darling Wife

I have a few minutes to spare and I propose to devote them to my Darling wife. You must not expect long letters from me for my labours are heavy, and besides there is always such noise and confusion that a man scarcely knows what he is writing. I was extremely sorry to hear that you and poor little Cally[1] were so sick[.] I do hope and pray that you both and all the rest may be well before this time. I am, as you know, very anxious to see you and my darling little Children. But

---

3. Frank Hampton, Wade Hampton's younger brother, operated Woodlands Plantation and owned 210 slaves; he was also a director of the Bank of South Carolina. He joined the cavalry battalion and after the reorganization of the army was commissioned lieutenant colonel of the Second South Carolina Cavalry on 22 August 1862. He died of wounds sustained at Brandy Station in June 1863. Davidson, *The Last Foray*, 207; Meynard, *The Venturers*, 216; Krick, *Lee's Colonels*, 150.

LETTER 3

1. Francis Calhoun Griffin, known as Cally, and his twin brother Claude Eugene were Griffin's youngest children, born 30 October 1859.

cannot yet tell when I can go home. I hope I can get off by the latter part of next week. But dont expect me for I might disappoint you. I will go as soon as I can. Col Hampton is slowly improving. He rode out to the camp yesterday evening. Another Company the "Washington Artillery"[2] came into camp this morning. They are a fine looking set of men. We have as fine a lot of Soldiers in Camp as I ever saw. And if I am not much mistaken, all that will keep them from distinguishing themselves, will be the want of an opportunity. I hope I will get a letter from you to night, and oh my darling it keeps [me] so very uneasy. I hope my Darling you will exercise all the patience you can control. And my hourly prayer is that you may be blessed.[3] If Mrs Lanham comes down you may send your flag down by her. She speaks of presenting her flag, but if I was her I wouldnt do it.[4] Whenever you write me, please write something about the crop and how your garden and the watermelons come on. My best love to all the Children. Kiss them every day for me. Tell them to be good children. Tell Paddy[5] not to forget his promise[.] Write me if your Father has an

---

2. The Washington Artillery of Charleston became Company A, Hampton's Legion Artillery. It was under the temporary command of Lt. James F. Hart. Capt. Stephen D. Lee, a West Point graduate who had been born in Charleston and grown up in Abbeville District, arrived to take command on 25 July. Lee had been on Gen. P.G.T. Beauregard's personal staff during the Fort Sumter crisis. Like Hampton, Lee was destined for a lieutenant general's commission, but it would come sooner—on 23 June 1864—making Lee, at age 30, the youngest man in the Confederate Army to hold that rank. Herman Hattaway, *General Stephen D. Lee* (Jackson: Univ. Press of Mississippi, 1976).

3. This is apparently a delicate reference to Leila's pregnancy. She gave birth five days later to her seventh child and Griffin's eighth, James Hampton Griffin.

4. Mrs. Lanham was the wife of Lt. James Lanham (see letter of 29 June 1861) of Cavalry Company A, the Edgefield Hussars. Mrs. Lanham did present the company flag she had sewn, although by letter on 24 June rather than in person. Matthew Calbraith Butler, the company captain, replied from Richmond on 1 July, and the Edgefield *Advertiser* printed both letters on 31 July.

5. The Griffins had no child christened Paddy. Possibly this was a nickname for three-year-old Moody Burt Griffin.

overseer. Tell your Sister I love her more than ever for staying with you[.] Good bye my Darling—from your

Jimmie

Tell Willie and Bobbie[6] to study hard—and tell them to write me.

Letter 4 JBG to Leila Griffin

Camp Hampton
June 25th 1861

My Darling Wife

Abram[1] has just arrived here bringing me a letter from Mrs Lanham, requesting me to inform her when we will likely move to Virginia. Send her word as soon as you get this that the last company of Cavalry are expected to leave on Saturday next. One company will leave on thursday, one on friday, and the third on Saturday. So that, my Darling you percieve that I will be forced to go without seeing you and my Darling little Children again. I regret it very much, but it cant be helped. I hope and trust My Darling, that we may meet again *soon.*

I will come home the first opportunity that presents itself. So my Darling dont grieve about it. Just feel that you are making the sacrifice, like thousands of others for the good of Our Country. Thereby benefiting our dear little ones.

Col Johnson leaves tomorrow morning with four Infantry companies. I expect to leave on Saturday[.][2] The Boys[3] are very well and

---

6. Twelve-year-old James William Griffin, known as Willie, was Griffin's eldest son and the child of his first marriage. Willie was born on 8 Feb. 1849. Robert Henry Burt Griffin, not yet seven, was Griffin's second son, born 7 Sept. 1854.

LETTER 4

1. One of Griffin's slave valets.
2. Pvt. Samuel E. Mays of Brooks Troop wrote in his diary that the infantry and artillery companies left for Richmond before the cavalry, which was still waiting for recruits who had not yet obtained horses. Ultimately it was decided that the cavalry should leave for Virginia, and that the absent recruits could join it there. Samuel Elias Mays, Jr., comp., *Genealogical Notes on the Family of Mays and Reminiscences of the War Between the States* (Plant City, Fla.: Plant City Enterprise, 1927), 28.
3. Willie and Bobbie apparently joined Griffin in camp sometime after the previous letter was written.

perfectly delighted with the Camp. They both want to go with me to Virginia. I will send them home by some friend towards the last of the week. Bobbie has on his calicoe shirt and is perfectly delighted with it. Kiss all the Dear Children for me every day and tell them to be good Children and not forget their Pa. I have a great deal of work to do this week in order to get the Squadron ready to move. Good bye my Darling[.] I hope and pray that you may all do better than you expect. Do my Darling remember all the advice I gave you before I left— Write me by friday's mail[.][4]

Your Devoted Jimmie

P.S. If Mrs Lanham or any other person comes down by friday, send my military saddle cloth[;] you will find it in the bag with my horse trappings.

---

4. The task of organizing the Confederate Post Office was given to John H. Reagan, a lawyer and judge who had served Texas in Congress since 1857. Appointed Postmaster General by Jefferson Davis in March 1861, Reagan immediately set about organizing the new department. Through the services of fellow lawyer H.P. Brewster, Reagan wrote to several key postal officials in Washington offering appointments in a Confederate post office. The majority of those offered positions accepted and, besides offering Reagan their own expertise, provided him with many necessary postal forms. Reagan's next task was to procure the services of the proper number of postmasters and mail carriers. Generally, existing postmasters and mail carriers were offered jobs in the Confederate post office; if they refused, they were asked to remain on the job until replacements could be appointed. Until the Confederacy was ready to take full control of the postal operation, scrupulous care was taken to ensure that all obligations to the government of the United States were met. An act of the Confederate Congress gave Reagan the authority to determine the date when the Confederate post office would assume operation. Reagan announced on 13 May that the date would be 1 June and instructed all postmasters to square accounts with the United States postal service as of 31 May. John H. Reagan, *Memoirs with Special Reference to the Secession and the Civil War*, ed. Walter Flavius McCaleb (New York: Neale Publishing, 1906), 124–35; Walter Flavius McCaleb, "The Organization of the Post-Office Department of the Confederacy," *American Historical Review* 12 (Oct. 1906): 66–74; Ben H. Proctor, *Not Without Honor: The Life of John H. Reagan* (Austin: Univ. of Texas Press, 1962), 130–33.

Letter 5 JBG to Leila Griffin

Congaree House[1]
June 29th 1861

My Darling Wife

O how sorry my Darling, I am that you seem to be so disappointed. I would gladly have gone home again if I could. But my darling, whilst it would be a momentary pleasure to us both—yet it would be just as bad when we had to seperate. And O my Darling let us make the best of it. And hope that we may soon meet again. Mrs Lanham has just come. She seems very much dejected for her. Jim[2] went off on thursday.

Dr Harrington and Sister[3] went off just now[.]

LETTER 5

1. Congaree House was a hotel at the northwest corner of Lady and Richardson (Main) Streets in Columbia.

2. Bvt. 2nd Lt. James M. Lanham served in Company A, the Edgefield Hussars, of the cavalry battalion. He joined the company in Edgefield on 6 June and was mustered into Confederate service on 14 June in Columbia. CSR, M267. The departure of the Hussars on Thursday, the 27th, was mentioned in the Charleston *Mercury*, 29 June 1861.

3. Griffin's older sister, Eliza Ann, born 30 November 1823, and Dr. William H. Harrington of Newberry married in December 1858; both had been widowed in 1857. Eliza had married Diomede F. Hollingsworth in 1840 and by him had at least one child, John Griffin Hollingsworth, mentioned by name in the will of James Griffin, Sr. Harrington, whose first wife was Sara Strother O'Neall, was born on 17 (according to O'Neall and Chapman) or 19 (according to Pope) November 1816. He graduated from the Medical College of South Carolina at Charleston and later represented Newberry for one term in the state legislature. In the 1840s and 1850s he was active in railroad promotion and civic affairs, and by 1860 he was a full-time planter. After the Civil War Harrington and Eliza moved to Crawfordville (O'Neall and Chapman) or Crawford (Pope), Mississippi, where he resumed medical practice; he died there in 1889. Carlee T. McClendon, *Edgefield Marriage Records* (Columbia, S.C.: R.L. Bryan, 1970), 64; John Belton O'Neall, *The Annals of Newberry in Two Parts; Part First by John Belton O'Neall, Part Second by John A. Chapman* (1892; rpt., Baltimore: Genealogical Publishing, 1974), 606; Thomas H. Pope, *The History of Newberry County, South Carolina*, vol. 1 (Columbia: Univ. of South Carolina Press, 1973), 267–68; Edgefield *Advertiser*, 4 March 1857, p. 4, c. 7.

My Darling, I will write you a long letter when I get to Richmond—which will be in a day or two. I have been run nearly to death this week in getting my men off—and now have only time to write you a line.[4] But I know you will excuse me for you know I must be busy from this hurried letter.

My Darling Wife—Good Bye, I hope and believe we will meet again before long[.] Do kiss each one of the Children and tell them Good Bye for their Father who has to leave without seeing them.

I am now going to sit for my Ambrotype [;] it will be sent you by mail as it cant be finished up in time[.]

> Good Bye
> Your Husband

Letter 6   JBG to Leila Griffin

> Jarrat Hotel
> Petersburg Va
> July 2nd 1861

My Darling Leila

You perceive from the heading of my letter that I am really in the State of the "Old Commonwealth". And am happy to inform you, that I am quite well. I arrived here last night, having under my command the last company of Cavalry, of the Legion (Capt Screven).[1] Here however I overtook Capt Lanneau's company,[2] who started

---

4. The Brooks Troop (Company B) left Columbia on 28 June and the Beaufort District Troop (Company C) departed on 29 June. Charleston *Mercury*, 1 July 1861.

LETTER 6

1. Capt. Thomas E. Screven commanded the Beaufort District Troop, Company C of the cavalry battalion. He was mustered into service on 22 June by Lt. Col. Johnson. CSR, M267, roll 364; Rolls of South Carolina Volunteers in the Confederate States Provisional Army: State Troops and Miscellaneous Rolls, 5 vols., 3:353, SCDAH.

2. Capt. John F. Lanneau commanded the Brooks Troop, Company B of the cavalry battalion. He enlisted on June 6 in Greenville and was enrolled in Confederate service on 14 June in Columbia. Ibid.

twenty four hours ahead of me. Capt Butler[3] is now in Richmond, where I expect to join him late this evening. It is only twenty two miles from here to Richmond. The whole Legion will be encamped in that City, at least by day after tomorrow. I can form no idea how long we will remain there. The general impression here is, that, a big fight must come off very soon. It is said that Gen Beauregard has got near enough to Alexandria, with some of his troops, to hear the enemy's drums.[4] It is scarcely worth while for me to write you any news—for before a letter can reach you, the news will have been transmitted by Telegraph, and have become Stale. But notwithstanding this

---

3. Matthew Calbraith Butler (1836–1909), nephew of the late Senator Andrew Pickens Butler and son-in-law of Governor Francis W. Pickens, was a graduate of South Carolina College and a practicing attorney in Edgefield. He served in the South Carolina legislature in 1860–61 as a prosecession Democrat, resigning to lead the Edgefield Hussars into Hampton's Legion, where it became Company A of the cavalry battalion. Butler was promoted to major after First Manassas. He was made colonel of the Second South Carolina Cavalry after Second Manassas, and served with distinction as a brigade commander under Hampton and J.E.B. Stuart. After losing his right foot at Brandy Station in June 1863, Butler was commissioned brigadier general to rank from 1 September 1863; he was promoted to major general of cavalry in September 1864 and opposed Sherman in the Carolinas in the spring of 1865. After the war, he resumed law practice in Edgefield and launched a long career in politics. A leading "Straightout" Democrat, he served in the legislature in 1866, ran unsuccessfully for lieutenant governor in 1870, and served in the U.S. Senate from 1876 until he was defeated by another Edgefieldian, Benjamin Ryan "Pitchfork Ben" Tillman, in 1894. See Chapter 1, note 103.

4. Federal troops had crossed the Potomac and occupied Alexandria, Virginia, on 24 May; they were expected to move next against the railroad junction at Manassas, 25 miles away. On 31 May Brig. Gen. Pierre Gustave Toutant Beauregard (1818–1893), the "hero of Fort Sumter," had been assigned to take command at the Alexandria line. On 20 June he had begun moving his regiments forward over Bull Run to protect the Confederate positions at Centerville, Fairfax Court House, and Sangster's Cross-Roads. T. Harry Williams, *P.G.T. Beauregard, Napoleon in Gray* (Baton Rouge: Louisiana State Univ. Press, 1955), 67–72; Alfred E. Roman, *The Military Operations of General Beauregard*, 2 vols. (New York: Harper and Bros., 1884), 1:79–80.

I will give you an account of a dozen daring Baltimorians. They took passage in [a] boat, leaving Baltimore for Philadelphia. Some of them dressed as Ladies, all were well armed, but arms concealed. As soon as the boat cleared the City, they dropped their Hooped Skirts, drew their repeaters, and demanded a surrender—which was acceded to. They took charge of the Steamer, turned her about and made for Fredric[k]sburg. On their way they Captured three Schooners, one loaded with ice, one with Coffee and the other with coal—They landed them safely, and carried the Prisoners (thirty eight in number), to Richmond, yesterday.[5]

The Citizens of this City are exceedingly kind and hospitable to soldiers.

And indeed we have been very kindly received, at almost every stopping place on the road. We [were] especially well cared for, at Raleigh, NC. Indeed the train scarcely ever stopped but the good Ladies—(God bless a woman) would send it something nice to the Soldiers.

I very unexpectedly met John Cutliff yesterday at
[rest of letter destroyed]

---

5. Griffin refers to the steamer *St. Nicholas*, which ran between Baltimore and Washington, D.C., not Philadelphia. According to the Richmond *Enquirer*, the Marylanders boarded on Friday and took control on Saturday morning, 29 June; it does not mention that they disguised themselves as women. In other respects, Griffin's rendition closely approximates the newspaper report. The Confederates sailed the steamer down the Potomac, where they captured the *Monticello*, bound for Baltimore with 8500 bags of coffee; the *Mary Pierce*, headed for Washington, D.C., with 260 tons of ice; and the *Margaret*, en route to Staten Island with 270 tons of coal. The prizes were taken to Fredericksburg and the captain and crew of the *St. Nicholas* were jailed in Richmond. Richmond *Enquirer*, 2 and 4 July 1861. The incident also impressed Confederate War Department clerk John Beauchamp Jones, who summarized it in his famous diary. Jones reported that "Col. Thomas of Maryland" disguised himself as a French lady, and led his accomplices in the capturing the *St. Nicholas*. John B. Jones, *A Rebel War Clerk's Diary at the Confederate States Capital*, 2 vols. (New York: Old Hickory Bookshop, 1935), 1:58.

Letter 7 JBG to Leila Griffin

July 4th 1861
Camp Manning

My Darling Wife

I am now quartered in Camp near the City of Richmond. We are about two miles from the heart of the City. Richmond is quite a large City, and portions of it very pretty. The scenery, in the Suburbs, on the river, is most beautiful. There are a good many Soldiers in and around the City. But how many, I have no idea. We are expecting Col Hampton with the remaining three infantry companies to day. When he gets here the whole Legion will again be together.[1] I do not know how long we will remain here, but think not very long. When we leave here we will join the other South Carolina troops under Genl Beauregard. Our men all prefer to go under him. Col Gregg's Regiment[2] were expected in Richmond last night, on their way home.

LETTER 7

1. Hampton did arrive on 4 July as expected with the Watson Guards (Company B), Manning Guards (Company C), and Bozeman Guards (Company E). The Legion was encamped at the old Rocketts fairground, east of Richmond. A journalist described the Legion at this time: "In the early encampments around Richmond it was recognized as the elite of regiments, and obtained the best of the social honors that were then so profusely distributed among military men. Its associations were aristocratic; its dress-parades at Rocketts were the wonder and fashionable resort of Richmond; and as a corps of gentlemen soldiers, they were perfect in every appointment." E.A. Pollard, *The Early Life, Campaigns and Public Services of Robert E. Lee, with a Record of the Campaigns and Heroic Deeds of His Companions in Arms* (New York: E. B. Trent, 1871), 739.

2. Maxcy Gregg (1814–1862) of Columbia was a graduate of South Carolina College and a Mexican War veteran. A classical scholar, scientist, and noted lawyer, Gregg was also a leading states' rights radical; he favored reopening the slave trade and helped write the ordinance of secession. Gregg then organized the First South Carolina Volunteers, a six-month regiment that he commanded on Morris and Sullivan's islands in Charleston harbor and subsequently in Virginia. Promoted to brigadier general to rank from 14 December 1861, he was killed at Fredericksburg in December 1862. Robert K. Krick, "Maxcy Gregg: Political Extremist and Confederate General," *Civil War History* 19:4 (Dec. 1973): 293–313.

I don't know whether they came or not. I hear that about one hundred of them have Volunteered for the [duration of] war, and most of the ballance say they will go home and return soon.[3] Gregg, I hear has an appointment of Col—in the Confederate army.[4]

The opinions about the war are numerous and various. Some think we will have a long war, some, a short one, and some, none at all. Some think we will have severe fighting soon. And others again think not. The Newspapers here think there will be various attacks made to day. But as I said in my last letter to you, it is scarcely worth while to write you any news of this kind for if a fight occurs to day, why of course you will get it by Telegraph long before my letter will reach you. I haven't yet seen any of the big men. Wigfall[5] has been very

---

3. Gregg's First South Carolina Volunteers contained three companies from Edgefield. According to Douglas Southall Freeman, Gregg's regiment included 27 doctors, 30 lawyers, and "many of the most eminent young businessmen of Carolina." It had been organized as an auxiliary to the state militia under the authority of a resolution passed by a convention of the people of South Carolina on 1 January 1861. Since the regiment predated the Confederacy and its Provisional Army, some of the men considered themselves under military obligation only to the state of South Carolina and refused to leave Charleston when the regiment was asked to transfer to Confederate service in late April. In Virginia the First South Carolina was part of the brigade of Gen. Milledge L. Bonham of Edgefield and served only a few weeks before its term of enlistment ended on 1 July. In the meantime Governor Francis W. Pickens had issued a call for 8000 twelve-month volunteers—the call to which Hampton and his Legion had responded—and on 30 June President Jefferson Davis had requested an additional 3000 South Carolina volunteers to serve for the duration of the war. Gregg's six-month volunteers, most of whom ultimately proved willing to serve under Confederate authority, were reorganized and became the core around which one of the new regiments was formed. Edgefield *Advertiser*, 30 Jan., 1, 8, 15 May 1861; Douglas Southall Freeman, *Lee's Lieutenants: A Study in Command*, 3 vols. (New York: Charles Scribner's Sons, 1942–1944), 1:518; A.S. Salley, *South Carolina Troops in Confederate Service*, 3 vols. (Columbia: R.L. Bryan, 1913–1930), 1:211–15; Cauthen, *South Carolina Goes to War*, 135.

4. Gregg's original commission, issued 7 January 1861, was for the South Carolina Army and issued by the governor. Salley, *South Carolina Troops in Confederate Service*, 1:215.

5. Louis Trezevant Wigfall (1816–1874), a native of Edgefield and member of the Texas delegation in the Provisional Congress, had accompanied

kind to our men, in having them comfortably Quartered though I have not yet seen him. I saw the other day at Petersburg a Lt Todd[6] whom I understand was Abe. Lincoln's brother in law. He is a good looking fellow. I wrote to you from Petersburg, which letter I hope you have received before now. I forgot to inform you in either of my letters, having been so much hurried lately, about the presentation of your beautiful flag—Col Bauskett[7] presented it, and Gary[8] received it

President Jefferson Davis to Richmond as an aide. See Alvy L. King, *Louis T. Wigfall, Southern Fire-Eater* (Baton Rouge: Louisiana State Univ. Press, 1970).

6. Mary Todd Lincoln's youngest brother, George, and three half brothers, Samuel, David, and Alexander, served in the Confederate Army. Jean H. Baker, *Mary Todd Lincoln: A Biography* (New York: W. W. Norton, 1987), 222–23.

7. Col. John Bauskett, originally from Newberry, had moved to Edgefield in the 1820s. A member of the bar since 1817, he also had extensive planting and business interests. In Edgefield he owned more than 2300 acres, a ferry, and a bridge over Stevens Creek. He moved to Columbia in the mid-1850s, and the census of 1860 showed him as the owner of 68 slaves in Edgefield and 42 in Columbia. Bauskett served two terms in the South Carolina House of Representatives in the 1820s and 1830s, and was an Edgefield delegate to the Nullification Convention in 1832–33, where he supported the Ordinance. He subsequently represented Edgefield for two terms in the state senate and another term in the house. His 20-year-old son, John, was a private in Company A, the Edgefield Hussars, of the cavalry battalion. John A. Chapman, *History of Edgefield County from the Earliest Settlements to 1897* (Newberry, S.C.: Elbert H. Aull, 1897), 105; John Belton O'Neall, *Biographical Sketches of the Bench and Bar of South Carolina*, 2 vols. (Charleston: S.G. Courtenay, 1859) 2:605; *Biographical Directory of the South Carolina Senate*, 1:109–10. CSR, M267, roll 364.

8. Martin Witherspoon Gary (1831–1881) was born in Cokesbury, South Carolina, and educated at South Carolina College (from which he was expelled in 1852 as a ringleader of the "biscuit rebellion") and Harvard University. Gary maintained a highly successful criminal law practice in Edgefield and was a secessionist leader in the state legislature. He was captain of the Watson Guards, later Company B of Hampton's infantry, and he commanded part of the Legion temporarily after First Manassas, when Hampton was wounded and Lt. Col. Johnson killed. Gary was promoted to colonel in December 1862 and to brigadier general to rank from 19 May 1864; in 1865 he commanded the last Confederate troops to leave Richmond. After Lee's sur-

in a very handsome manner. Every body said it was a beautiful *[sic]*. I presume you have seen an account of it, for I hear that the remarks of both Gentlemen would be published[9]—I would like to see it. Do my Darling write to me very often. I havent heard from you but one time since I left you, and that was the mournful letter you sent me by Mrs Lanham. I felt very badly before but a great deal worse after reading your letter. You begged me so hard to come home, and I couldnt. I do hope my Darling that you and the dear Children are well, and getting along well. Do my Darling, your best. I like camp life pretty well[,] fully as well as I expected. I have enjoyed good health since I left home. The nights here are very cold. I sleep comfortably under two blankets. Tell Dr Muse[10] I am much obliged to him for his kind-

---

render, he broke through Federal lines and joined President Davis at Greensboro, escorting him south to Cokesbury, where one of the last meetings of the Confederate Cabinet convened at the home of Gary's mother. After the war Gary served four years in the state senate, and with Matthew Calbraith Butler, led the "Straightout" Democrats who restored native white elite rule. His extremist views led him to break ultimately with Butler and Hampton, whom he had helped elect governor, and he was twice defeated in races for U.S. Senator by his former allies. Cooper, *The Conservative Regime*. See Chapter 1, note 104.

9. The flag presentation ceremony took place on 27 June while the company was still at Camp Hampton. The Edgefield *Advertiser* on 10 July 1861 reported that "Col. John Bauskett on behalf of Mrs. J. B. Griffin presented the 'Watson Guard' with a stand of colors, in a patriotic and earnest address." The paper did not print Bauskett's speech, but it gave the full text of Gary's response. Accepting the "beautiful and elegant flag," he promised: "we will cherish it not only as an evidence of the patriotism and kind partiality of Mrs. Griffin, but as a sure and perpetual incentive to the performance of duty and deeds of valor. . . . Tell the fair lady that we will ever hold dear this inspiring motto; that around it will ever cluster the fond recollection of the spirited generosity of the true, beautiful and good." At the conclusion of the ceremony, the paper reported, "the company then marched to their quarters, gave three cheers for Mrs. Griffin and three more for old Edgefield." According to the 26 June *Advertiser*, one side of the flag replicated the Confederate national flag, while the other side bore the names of the state and the company and the motto "Brave Comrades, Advance."

10. Dr. Julius E. Muse, originally from Darlington, had maintained a dental surgery practice in Edgefield Court House since the beginning of the year. He married Minnie Burt, one of Leila's younger sisters, on 16 December

ness in making my camp chest. I got the key but the chest did not arrive in Columbia before I left. It will be forwarded to me at this place. Do, Darling, give my love to your Father and each one of your Sisters and also to Dr Muse—Quilla[11]—Your uncles and families— Kiss my Darling Children for me. Tell Willie and Bob to write to me. Tell me something about each one of them even down to little Jimmie[12]—Good Bye My Darling

Your Jimmie

Letter 8　JBG to Leila Griffin

Cavalry Camp—Ashland
July 11th 1861

My Darling Wife

It has been several days since I wrote you last, not because I have not wanted to write, but simply because I could not. You will percieve by the heading of my letter that I have left Richmond. I have been very busy all this week in making preparations to move, and in getting here.[1] I am now stationed, with all the Cavalry of the Legion, at this place which is about fifteen miles from Richmond. This is a small country village situated on the Richmond and Fredric[k]sburg rail road. There is a regular Cavalry Camp here, no infantry, under the direction of army Officers. Every thing is conducted here strictly according to army regulations. I am very well pleased with

---

1857. Edgefield *Advertiser*, 21 March 1861; McClendon, *Edgefield Marriage Records*, 115; Eliza Cowan Ervin and Horace Fraser Rudisill, eds., *Darlingtoniana: A History of People, Places, and Events in Darlington County, South Carolina* (Columbia: R.L. Bryan, 1964), 20, 334.

11. Aquilla Miles was the husband of Leila's older sister Mary Ann, whom he married on 6 September 1842; she was his second wife. McClendon, *Edgefield Marriage Records*, 108; Burt Family, Roll 6, Leonardo Andreas Genealogical Collection, SCL.

12. James Hampton Griffin, the baby, had been born two weeks earlier, on 19 June.

LETTER 8

1. The companies arrived the day before, 10 July. M.C. Butler to wife, 11 July 1861, Butler Family Papers, DU.

the place[2] and am delighted with the Officers. Col Field[3] who is in command here, is one of the finest gentlemen I ever had the good fortune to meet. He is courteous and affable to every one. But a strict disciplinarian. I expect he will not be so popular with some of our Boys, who do not like to come down, square to the rules. My men are very comfortably quartered. And I have a very nice room in the house used by the Col and other Officers, situated right in the midst of the camp. I am very comfortably situated, and think it will be a real good schooling for me as well as my men. We are all very well except one or two men who are not seriously sick. I havent been sick since I left home, except head ache once or twice. I like Camp life very well. And when I can keep my mind from dwelling too much on "my loved ones at home" I am very well contented.

I left Cols Hampton and Johnson, yesterday morning, at our camp near Richmond, where they will likely remain for some time, how long I do not know. My Darling since I have arrived here and am quartered in a very nice room, I have thought more about you and my Darling little Children than I have any time before. It does indeed seem to have been an age since I left you. Were it not for the concientious feeling, that I am doing my duty, by serving my Country, I could not stand it.[4] I sometimes ask myself the question[:] Am I sorry that I volunteered. And I cant say yes. For I know, if I were at home, I could not be satisfied. And here I feel that my sacrifice is great

---

2. Samuel Mays of Brooks Troop noted in his diary: "There never was a better situation for a camp than Ashland. . . . it has always been a summer resort for the rich of Richmond and there were a great many summer hotels which we used instead of tents." Mays, *Reminiscences of the War Between the States*, 32.

3. Charles W. Field, a native of Kentucky and a West Point graduate, was appointed colonel of the Sixth Virginia Cavalry after he resigned his commission in the U.S. Army in May 1861. On 6 July 1861, he assumed command of the camp of instruction at Ashland, Virginia.

4. Matthew Calbraith Butler wrote to his wife on the same day: "I would give ten years of my life to see you and the babies this morning. I have been more homesick for the last three or four days than since I left home. Maj Griffin & I have been consoling with each other, but it is a poor consolation and we must make the best of it." Butler to wife, 11 July 1861, Butler Family Papers, DU.

indeed. But it is made for my Country. And I earnestly hope and believe that the God of us all will take good care of my Family. Tell Willie and Bobbie I wish they were here with me. Poor little fellows how I regretted to part with them in Columbia. I was truly glad I carried them with me to Camp. They were a great deal of company for me and besides they were so much pleased. If they were here they could see plenty of Cavalry parrades. There are eight companies here now and two more expected. Tell my darling little Fannie[5] and Medie[6] and Paddie that they must think about me and talk about me and love me every day. Tell them I think about them a great deal and love them a heap. Do Darling, kiss them all for me and dont forget to kiss my three little Juveniles. Yes—little Jimmie too. And Claude[7] and Cally, bless their little hearts, what would I give to see them. I do wish I had an ambrotype of each one of them. Give my love to your Father, Carrie,[8] and Sue.[9] Also to your sister[10] and Sissie—and Dr Muse and Minnie.[11] Also Drs. Burt[12] and families, and every body

---

5. Fannie Eugene Griffin, age five, was born on 31 December 1855. She was the third of Griffin's children and his oldest daughter.

6. Four-year-old Annie Diomede Griffin, the fourth child, was born on 3 March 1857, and named in honor of Griffin's late brother-in-law, Diomede Hollingsworth. She was always called Medie or Meadie.

7. Claude Eugene Griffin was the twin brother of Cally (see letter of 14 June 1861, note 1). The twins were twenty months old but no longer the babies since the arrival of Jimmie the month before.

8. Caroline Burt was the second of Leila's four surviving sisters. There is no record of a marriage for her, and since the girls' mother was dead, she may have been keeping house for their father at Sunnyside.

9. Sue Burt, Leila's youngest sister, moved into Highland House to help Leila when Griffin left for the army. She is the sister to whom Griffin referred on 14 June when he wrote: "Tell your sister I love her more than ever for staying with you."

10. Mary Ann Burt Miles was Leila's oldest sister. She was married to Aquilla Miles (see previous letter, note 11).

11. Minnie Burt Muse, who came between Leila and Sue in the hierarchy of sisters, was the wife of Dr. Julius Muse (see previous letter, note 10). Like Sue, she was apparently very close to Leila, and the Griffins named their last child—born two and a half years later—for her.

12. Leila had two uncles in Edgefield District, both of them physician-planters. Dr. John Harwood Burt of Clearwater Plantation was the more pub-

else—I cant write all their names. Tell all the negroes howdy for me and tell them not to forget what I told them when I left. Tell Sue I will answer her letter in a day or two, tell her to write often. I think out of so many of you—I ought to get a letter every day or two. Tell Dr Muse I received the Camp chest and am delighted with [it]—am really much obliged to him for it. When I get home and he goes to the war I will loan it to him. I expect Jim Dozier[13] is at home by this time. I am sorry to hear his health is so bad. I hope he is better before this. All our friends stand the campaign, so far, finely. Write to me very often my Darling, and tell all the rest of them to write. You may still direct your letters to Richmond, they will be forwarded from there. I sent you several messages by members of Gregg's Regiment, and would have written but was too busy. I recd your and Sue's letters by Pierce Butler,[14] which is the last I have recd. Tell Willie to write to me. And now my Darling wife good bye for this time.

Your Jimmie

lic figure, a dabbler in politics and a proponent of scientific agriculture. He died that autumn. His younger brother, Dr. William Miles Burt, appears in succeeding letters as "Uncle Billy" and "Dr. Burt." Chapman, *History of Edgefield County*, 349–50; Edgefield *Advertiser*, 9 Oct. 1861.

13. James A. Dozier had been third lieutenant of the Ninety Six Riflemen, which entered Confederate service as Company H of the Seventh South Carolina Volunteers. The day before Griffin wrote, the newspaper reported that Dozier had reached home the previous week "after being compelled by a long and protracted illness to resign his command." The Doziers were kin to the Burt family: Leila's mother was a Dozier, and her cousin Emily married Dr. Allen Stokes Dozier, who served for a time as surgeon of the Seventh South Carolina Volunteers. Edgefield *Advertiser*, 10 July 1861; Burt Family, roll 6, Leonardo Andreas Genealogical Collection, SCL.

14. Pierce Mason Butler, Jr., age 23, was the son of the former governor (1836–38) of the same name and a cousin of Matthew Calbraith Butler. Years later, Leila's cousin Annie became his second wife. John Chapman shows him as a fifth sergeant of the Edgefield Hussars; his service record gives his status as a former first lieutenant who enlisted as a private when the Hussars joined the Legion as Company A of the cavalry battalion. Butler subsequently served as first lieutenant of Company I, Second South Carolina Cavalry. Theodore G. Jervey "The Butlers of South Carolina," *South Carolina Historical and Genealogical Magazine* 4 (Oct. 1903): 307; Chapman, *History of Edgefield*, 423; CSR, M267, roll 364; *Rolls of South Carolina Volunteers in the*

I havent seen but one pretty lady since I have been in Virginia. Tell Mrs Lanham that Jim is as fat as butter.

Letter 9   JBG to Leila Griffin

Exchange Hotel, Richmond
July 19th 1861

My Darling Wife

I came down to the city yesterday, from Ashland—will return this evening. Since my arrival here our Legion have received marching orders. Col Hampton will leave with the infantry this evening or tomorrow morning. I will go back to Ashland this evening and I will expect to move tomorrow with the cavalry. We all go to Manassas. The infantry go by rail road and the cavalry [have] to march. We will have about six days marching to get there. We are all in a high state of excitement here at the news from Manassas. It seems that the Federal troops attacked our forces yesterday under Gen Beauregard. The report is—we thrashed them handsomely. Our loss is reported to be light. That of the enemy—heavy.[1] We are hourly expecting news that we can rely on. There is now no doubt of the death of Gen Gar-

---

Confederate States Provisional Army, 4:26, SCL; Burt Family, Andreas Genealogical Collection, SCL.

LETTER 9

1. By 18 July 1861 Beauregard's forces at Manassas had formed an extended line along the south bank of Bull Run and Maj. Gen. Joseph E. Johnston's troops were moving from the Shenandoah Valley to join him. As the Federals advanced slowly from Fairfax Court House toward Centreville, Brig. Gen. Irvin McDowell dispatched a reconnaissance force that advanced farther than ordered and was repulsed by a Confederate force under James Longstreet at Blackburn's Ford. Longstreet based his estimate of 900 to 2000 Union casualties on reports from prisoners, but actual Federal losses proved to be 19 killed, 38 wounded, and 26 missing. The Confederates reported 15 dead and 53 wounded. The victory at Blackburn's Ford delayed the Federal advance, permitting Beauregard to increase his forces along Bull Run. OR, ser. 1, 2:461–63; E.B. Long, *The Civil War Day by Day, an Almanac, 1861–1865* (New York: Doubleday, 1971), 96.

nett[2]—his remains are expected here today. He was defeated at Rich Mountain. And the enemy killed and took prisoners in two engagements about eight hundred. The first engagement was on the 11th and the last on the 13th.[3] It is generally believed here that Gen Beauregard has got even with them. We go directly to Beauregard—and now my darling wife, prepare yourself for anything and everything. In a few days more I will be in the midst of the lines of the enemy, taking my chances with other noble and brave hearts who are disputing every inch of ground with the enemy. I trust I may be permitted to see the end of hostilities and witness the Independence of our noble country. But if the God of Battles wills it and I am to fall—why be it so. And if it is so I have confidence in him that he will care for you and my darling little children. Do not my darling, allow this letter to make you low spirited. I do not write it with any such intentions. But only to induce you to take a practical view of these things. I hope and believe that I will go through, but I have made up my mind to only one thing—and that is to go where ever duty calls me and take the consequences.

Now and then a man is killed, but very few considering the number of shots. I will keep you posted as to the result of things when I get

---

2. Robert Selden Garnett (1819–1861) of Virginia had been appointed brigadier general in the Provisional Army on 6 June and given command of northwestern Virginia. Garnett was the first general officer on either side to be killed in battle.

3. Two thousand Federals under the command of Brig. Gen. William Rosecrans surprised Lt. Col. John Pegram at Rich Mountain in western Virginia on 11 July; Pegram surrendered 555 of his 1300 men on the 13th. At Laurel Hill, to the north, Brig. Gen. T.A. Morris forced Garnett to evacuate his position and retreat into the Cheat River Valley. Morris pursued him, and on 13 July he engaged the retreating Confederates at Corrick's (or Carrick's) Ford, where Garnett was killed. Confederate defeats at Rich Mountain, Laurel Hill, and Corrick's Ford, combined with Maj. Gen. George B. McClellan's other operations in western Virginia, gave the Federals strategic control west of the Shenandoah Valley. They also gained protection for their east-west railroad lines, and a base from which to launch raids on the Virginia front. The total Confederate loss, including the men Pegram surrendered, was approximately 700; Federal casualties were negligible. Long, *The Civil War Day by Day*, 93.

up there. Of course I cannot get there to take a hand in this fight, for it will take the cavalry a week to march it. And I doubt not this fight will be settled before we can get there. But I begin to think we will have enough of it. I received your very kind letter a day or two ago enclosing Willie's. Tell Willie I felt quite proud of him and want him to write me every week. I will answer his letter if I have time before I leave Ashland but if I do not, I want him to write me anyway. It will improve him. So my darling, kiss all the children and tell them I do love them and am very anxious to see them. But cant hope for it now. But hope the time will come around soon when we shall meet. Write often my darling, and tell my friends to write. Direct your letters to Manassas Junction, until I change the direction. My love to all—good bye. This is written in a great hurry and hustle.

Your Jimmie

Letter 10   JBG to Leila Griffin

Cavalry Camp—Ashland Va
Sunday—July 21st 1861

My Darling

I leave here tomorrow morning for Manassas.[1] I expect to be four days on the road. Col Hampton left, with the infantry on friday evening. They went by rail, and I presume arrived there yesterday morning—in time I presume to get into the fight.[2] It is reported and be-

LETTER 10

1. Samuel Mays wrote in his diary on this date that the cavalry was ready to move, but that no orders to advance had reached camp. "Some of the men applied for permission to go up and be with the rest of the Legion," he wrote, "but the Major would not give it." Typically, Griffin went by the book. After the battle, however, Mays was granted permission to go to the field to tend some wounded acquaintances. There he heard the details of the battle and speculated that the cavalry had been held back to protect Johnston's rear from the force of Maj. Gen. Robert Patterson, which should have followed Johnston from the Shenandoah and prevented him from uniting with Beauregard. Mays, *Reminiscences of the War Between the States*, 34, 37–38.

2. It took 30 hours to move Hampton's infantry by train from Richmond to Manassas, a trip that ordinarily took seven hours and that Capt. James Conner estimated should have taken the troops no more than 12. John Coxe

lieved here that they, I mean the two Armies, were engaged yesterday.[3] I am exceedingly anxious to hear the particulars of the fight. And I am also very anxious to get there, So that I can assist them in driving back the black hearted wretches, who are doing all in their power, to subjugate a Noble race of people. I have no fears that we will whip them. It may be that we will be some time about it—but there can be no doubt as to the result. The fourth Company of my Squadron (Capt Taylor[4] from Columbia) joined us here to day. They are not at all drilled—and I will leave them here for a few days. I hope my darling you will hear a favourable account of us before long.

I hope at least to so conduct myself that you will not be ashamed of your Jimmie. I know full well—that whilst you will be exceedingly anxious as to my safety—you would be proud to hear that I had done my duty. At your request, My Darling, I sent you, the other day from Richmond, my Ambrotype—taken in my uniform. I hope you will be pleased with it. If you like it— give Sue one of those you had before. I would have had another taken but my funds are running low and I thought you could Spare one. I hope you are all prospering and en-

---

described the long waits while the engine was repaired and the train was side-tracked to meet one coming from Manassas Junction behind schedule. Hampton's infantry arrived with no time to spare at 7 a.m. Sunday morning, but some of Jackson's foot soldiers from the Shenandoah were delayed even longer. While the battle was raging, his adjutant was at the station dispatching troops from the cars and trying to get them into action. Coxe, "The First Battle of Manassas"; Moffet, *Letters of General James Conner*, 40; Robert C. Black, *The Railroads of the Confederacy* (Chapel Hill: Univ. of North Carolina Press, 1952), 60–62.

3. Reports of fighting at Manassas the preceding day were inaccurate, although battle was imminent. McDowell's army was advancing and reinforcements from the Shenandoah Valley continued to arrive for Beauregard. Thomas Jonathan Jackson, not yet known as "Stonewall," appeared with his brigade on the 19th; more of Johnston's men reported at sunrise on the 20th, and Johnston himself arrived later that day. He and Beauregard conferred that night on a battle plan. William C. Davis, *Battle at Bull Run: A History of the First Major Campaign of the Civil War* (New York: Doubleday, 1977), 133–44.

4. Capt. Thomas Taylor commanded the Congaree Troop of Richland District, Company D of the cavalry battalion. *Rolls of South Carolina Volunteers in the Confederate States Provisional Army*, 3:353; CSR, M267, roll 364.

joying yourselves as well as possible, all things considered. I some-times envy you those big watermelons that I know you are eating every day. I have seen only three yet and they were quite small, and the price was 65 cts. I bought two peaches the other day at 10 cts a piece. Write me often my Darling, to Manassas junction. I prize your letters very highly. Kiss my Darling Children. Oh what would I give to kiss them myself. My love to all and accept a large Share for your own Self
from your Husband

Letter 11   JBG to Leila Griffin

Frederic[k]sburg Va
July 24th 1861

My Darling Leila

It is now nine O Clock wednesday morning. I have just arrived at this place and hasten to pen you a few lines before my men come up. I doubt not My Darling you have heard of the terrible battle fought last sunday at Manassas and that we won a most Splendid Victory but we lost many gallant men.[1] I hope you recd my letter written last friday, from Rich-

---

LETTER 11

1. On 21 July 1861, Beauregard and Johnston routed McDowell's army at the first battle of Manassas or Bull Run. The 600 infantrymen of Hampton's Legion were the first reinforcements to arrive. Just off the train from Rich-mond, the Legionnaires had time to gulp only "a handful of crackers and cup of coffee" for breakfast, Pvt. Richard Habersham wrote. They were ordered to the exposed Confederate left flank at Stone Bridge to support Col. Francis Bartow and Generals Barnard Bee and Nathan ("Shanks") Evans. Hampton's troops fought stubbornly for six hours and held their line even when men from Bartow's, Bee's, and Evans's commands fell back in confusion. Hamp-ton's horse was shot out from under him, but he held his men in position until Bee and Bartow advised withdrawal to Henry Hill. The arrival of Jack-son's brigade to reinforce the embattled left encouraged the Confederate de-fenders to reorganize and resume the fight. (It was at this point that Bee shouted his famous words: "There is Jackson standing like a stone wall!" and urged the troops to rally around the Virginians.) Hampton's Legion formed on Jackson's right. Capt. James Conner, the most senior officer not wounded, took Hampton's place as the Confederates drove McDowell's forces back from Henry Hill and overran the Federal batteries. Bee and Bartow were killed. Manassas was a stunning victory for the Confederates; there was speculation

mond in time to keep you from feeling uneasy on my account. I, of course was in no danger, for I was not there. And My Darling, it looks like hard luck to me that I was not. For in my humble judgement that was *The battle* of the revolution. I would have been there with my command if they could have transported us on the cars. But having so many infantry forces to transport we were ordered to March. Which is very tedious. I expect to get to Manassas tomorrow. But will be too late for the fight. I feel like I am going up a day after the feast. The infantry portion of the Legion was in the fight and I understand suffered awfully. It is generally believed that Lt Col Johnson of the Legion is killed, and the papers say that we lost in killed and wounded from three hundred to three fifty.[2] It is also rumoured that many of our men were killed by our own forces, through mistake.[3] I trust in God that may not be true, for I can scarcely conceive of any thing So horrible as that. My Darling, let me advise you not to believe any statement you may hear until it is fully confirmed. For really it seems that the truth is never published at first, and sometimes not at all. I am now within forty miles of the scene of action and thousands of contradictory reports are circulated here. Nothing is positively known here—except that they had a hard Struggle and we routed them completely. Took four of their five batteries and any

---

that the South had won its independence and that the Federals would not dare renew the attack. Davis, *Battle at Bull Run*; John Coxe, "The Battle of First Manassas"; Richard Habersham to Mother, 26 July 1861, Habersham Family Papers, Library of Congress, LC. Hampton's report appears in OR, ser. 1, 2: 566–67.

2. Lt. Col. B.J. Johnson had been killed at the onset of the fighting, leaving Hampton without a field officer or any company officer with battle experience. Griffin apparently refers here to the Legion's supposed losses, since he gives another estimate of Confederate losses a few lines later (see note 5). The Legion's reported casualties were 19 killed, 100 wounded, and 2 missing. This casualty rate was the highest in Beauregard's army; only Johnston's Army of the Shenandoah suffered more heavily. O. Lee Sturkey, who has compiled the most extensive rolls of the Legion's infantry companies, has found the casualty rate to be higher than officially reported: 22 killed or died of wounds. B&L, 1:195; Sturkey to Judith N. McArthur, 11 Dec. 1989.

3. Hampton's report does not mention this, but a member of Company B wrote home that they were "briefly" under Confederate fire by mistake. "A Letter from Captain Gary's Company," Edgefield *Advertiser*, 7 Aug. 1861.

quantity of small arms and equipment.[4] You may hear that I am wounded or killed, but dont give yourself any uneasiness about it, at least until it may be confirmed. You shall hear reliably if any thing happens to me. I have no idea how many men were killed. It is variously estimated that the enemy lost from five to forty thousand, and our loss is equally indefinite—from fifteen hundred to five thousand.[5] When I get up there and find out the truth, I will write you immediately. I left Ashland on monday, in the rain, and traveled in it all day. It didnt cease a minute all day. We all got wet but "nobody was hurt." The citizens have been remarkably kind and hospitable to us, since we left Ashland. They almost burden us with their kindness. Every body wants to do something for us. Very different from the treatment we received about Richmond. The ladies are especially kind. And by the by some of them are very pretty. Dont feel jealous. For my Darling if you could only know how anxious I am to see you, you would never doubt me, under any circumstances. My Darling, I can sympathize, with wives and children of the poor Soldiers, who are kept in such Suspense after a battle is reported. But remember what I tell you—believe nothing until you get it from a source, that you can rely on. I am very much pleased with the appearance of this country. The atmosphere is light and bracing and the nights are cool and pleasant. I am very well. The only sickness in the Squadron is a few cases of measles, which I left at Ashland. We are all low Spirited at the news of our Legion's suffering, but I hope it is not true. Write to

---

4. Beauregard reported that the fleeing Federals abandoned "some twenty-eight field pieces of the best character of arm, with over one hundred rounds of ammunition for each gun, thirty seven caissons, six forges, four battery wagons, sixty-four artillery horses completely equipped, 500,000 rounds of small arms ammunition, 4500 sets of accouterments, over 500 muskets, some nine regimental and garrison flags, with a large number of pistols, knapsacks, swords, canteens, blankets, a large store of axes and intrenching tools, wagons, ambulances, horses, camp and garrison equipage, hospital stores, and some subsistence." OR, ser. 1, 2: 503.

5. Rumors that reached Griffin were wildly inflated, and the casualty rates of later battles would make the numbers at Manassas seem small by comparison. Federal losses totaled 2,896: 460 killed, 1,124 wounded, 1,312 missing. The Confederates lost 1,982: 387 killed, 1,582 wounded, 13 missing. B&L, 1:194–95.

me my Darling—often I hear from you very seldom. Write to Manassas Junction until I tell you not. Remember me kindly to all my friends, and give my love to all my darling Children. I have never recd that letter that you said Sissie and Sue were writing to me. This is the third letter I have written you in the last six days—I must now close as I have to leave with my Column. So my Darling, Good bye. Take good care of yourself and the children and keep in good spirits and hope for the best. I doubt not many of our Edgefield friends are killed but as yet I know nothing.

Good bye My Darling
Your Jimmie

Letter 12   JBG to Leila Griffin

Manassas Junction Va
July 27th 1861

My Darling Wife

I sincerely hope you recd my letters regularly, If so, you have not been uneasy about me, in relation to the battle of last sunday the 21st inst. Yes, My Darling, I can sympathize with a wife who has a Husband engaged in a battle, and who cannot hear how he has fared. Suspense is terrible. But as I said before if you recd my letters regularly, you were kept posted as to my whereabouts, and must have known that I was not in the fight. But my Darling, I regret it more, than, almost any event of my life. I would not have missed it for thousands—And if it had been caused by any neglect or mismanagement of my own, I never could forgive myself. But it was my misfortune and not my fault. We were (I mean the Cavalry of which I had command) ordered to march from Ashland to this place. I started as soon as possible and made as much haste as I could, and arrived here, night before last thursday night. I came over in a terrible state of suspense. I heard on the way that our Legion had been cut up horribly. It was published in the papers that we had lost between three and four hundred men out of six hundred. And I could find out nothing reliable until I arrived here. And I am happy to say that notwithstanding we suffered a great deal still it is not near so bad as it was represented. We have lost sixteen men killed and over one hundred and nineteen in killed and wounded. Several of the wounded it is thought will die.[1] But a great many of them will get well. The heaviest loss we sustained is in the death of our Lt Col Johnson. He was shot through the head, right at the commencement of the Legion's engagement. His was indeed, a sad destiny. To be killed before he could have the satisfaction of knowing how bravely his men met the enemy and how effectually they were instrumental in repelling them. For all concur in Saying that the Legion did distinguish itself. Gen Beauregard pays them the highest compliment. Says he never saw volunteer troops fight better— and for the first engagement never saw men fight so well.[2] Some companies have especially distinguished themselves, and I am proud to say Capt Gary's ranks among the first.[3] His and Capt Connor's[4] compa-

---

LETTER 12

1. This is very close to the officially published figure. See previous letter, note 2. Sixteen men were reported killed outright, and three more later died of wounds.

2. Beauregard's report mentions Hampton among the officers whom he cites for "gallant commands," and includes the Legion in his praise: "Veterans could have behaved better than these well-led regiments." OR, ser. 1, 2:500. When he recalled the battle years later, Beauregard credited the Hampton Legion with "helping materially to check the panic of Bee's routed forces." B&L, 1:210.

3. The Edgefield *Advertiser*, 31 July 1861, extracted reports from the Virginia and Charleston papers to print three columns on the Legion's performance at Manassas. After Lt. Col. Johnson was killed, Gary supposedly rallied the Legion by shouting, "Follow me, Hampton Guards [a misprint for either Hampton Legion or Watson Guards], follow to victory," and his own company led the advance. After Hampton was wounded, Gary led the left wing of the infantry, and Conner the right.

4. James Conner (1829–1883) of Charleston was a graduate of South Carolina College and the former United States district attorney for South Carolina. He joined the Hampton Legion as captain of the Washington Light Infantry of Charleston, which became Company A of the infantry battalion. As senior captain, he assumed command on the field at Manassas after Hampton was wounded and was promoted to major to rank from that date. Conner was promoted to brigadier general on 1 June 1864, and lost a leg at Cedar Creek during the Shenandoah Valley campaign in the fall of 1864. After the war he resumed his law practice, and in 1876 he chaired the state Democratic party during the campaign that made Hampton governor and ended Republican

nies ocupy distinguished positions. I have heard many handsome compliments paid the different companies, but these two in particular.
And my Darling they honestly deserve it. I do not envy any man, his
laurels. But I do feel that we of the Cavalry had hard luck in not being
permitted to have an equal showing for distinction. I am sure, had we
been there we could have sustained our infantry, and been of great
Service to them. And I'll bet my life we would have got a many a
one. My men are all keen for a chance. I went yesterday to the battle
ground, which is about six miles from here. And O my Darling—I
have often heard of the horrors of war. And have had pictured in my
mind the horrible appearance of a battle field after a battle. But never
before could I have the least conception of the scene. In the first
place, I stopped at a hospital where—Gen Beauregard, had the
wounded enemy carried. Some of them are pitiable looking objects—
many of them are badly wounded. Gen Beauregard has them well
cared for. Their Army ran off and left their dead and wounded on the
field, never pretended to bury their dead nor take care of their
wounded.[5] The Legion were interested in taking one of the enemy's
batteries—and Gary was the first man to mount one of the guns, and
in the name of the Hampton Legion claimed the battery.[6] Col Hamp-

---

rule in South Carolina. Conner was elected attorney general on the Hampton
ticket and served long enough to establish the legality of the conservative white
"redeemer" government before resigning because of poor health at the end
of 1877.

5. Beauregard reported of the Federals, "Their abandoned dead, as they
were buried by our people where they fell, unfortunately were not enumerated, but many parts of the field were thick with their corpses as but few
battlefields have ever been." OR, ser. 1, 2:502. M.C. Butler wrote home
almost a week after the battle that many "Federalist" corpses were still lying
unburied on the field, "but I presume they are of such a class that nobody
cares whether they are interred or not." Butler to wife, 27 July 1861, Butler
Family Papers, DU.

6. According to a published letter from his company, Gary led the charge
and took the battery in the name of the Legion, but neither Hampton in his
official report nor Conner in a long letter home mentioned Gary's role.
Hampton reported giving command to Conner, who formed the regiment,
advanced upon Ricketts's battery, and took the two guns. "A Letter from Captain Gary's Company," Edgefield Advertiser, 7 Aug. 1861; OR, ser. 1. 2:566–
67; Moffett, Letters of General James Conner, 40–43.

ton himself was slightly wounded—a ball struck him in the temple [but] it seems not to have gone in deep.[7] I hope it will not hurt him. He is up and about. I would like to give you an idea, if I could, how many men were killed, but I can find no one who seems to know. Our loss in killed and wounded is variously estimated at from five hundred to twenty five hundred and that of the enemy at from five to ten thousand.[8] The enemy's loss is tremendous. And they were the worst whipped rascals you ever heard of—They ran so fast it took pretty good Cavalry to catch them. Oh if I could have only been there with my Cavalry. Col Hampton says we could have taken ten thousand

[rest of letter destroyed]

Letter 13   JBG to Leila Griffin

Camp Johnson near Manassas, Va
August 3rd 1861

My Darling Wife
    I have the pleasure of again informing you that I am quite well although I am daily expecting to be attacked with measles. As there are quite a number of cases in our camp, and I am more or less exposed to them all the time.[1] They seem to be a mild form however, and do not make the patients very sick. I am not at all pleased with our camp, and fear if we do not get away soon, we will have a good deal of sickness. We are camped on the bank of Broad Run—a large muddy ugly stream. Our drinking water is scarce and very bad.[2] Cant

---

7. Hampton suffered a slight head wound as McDowell's troops were driven back from Henry Hill.

8. See previous letter, note 5.

LETTER 13

1. Conner wrote on 14 August that 300 legionnaires were down with measles. Moffett, *Letters of General James Conner*, 51.

2. Broad Run, about three miles east of Manassas Junction, flows into Bull Run from the southwest. Griffin's fears about the unhealthful water supply were well founded; Hampton shortly came down with an undiagnosed, protracted illness that he feared was typhoid and that summer and fall Johnston's army suffered an epidemic of typhoid (camp) fever. Like dysentery and non-

get any clear water to wash in or to drink. I hope we will be moved from here soon. This is a very poor country. And there have been so many troops about here, that the resources of the Country are well nigh exhausted. We have a good deal of sickness in Camp already, mostly measles. One man by the name of Gary (no kin to Capt Gary) died here this evening, very sudenly. I suppose he died of disease of the heart. He was from Greenville Dist.[3] Everything remains perfectly quiet, in the way of fighting. There were some guns heard yesterday in the direction of Washington. And there is a rumour afloat, that the enemy were fighting among themselves— But I dont believe a word of it. I think it will be some time before we will have any more fighting of importance. The Artillery of the Legion, arrived here to day. We now have the whole Legion together except one Cavalry Company, which I left at Ashland, and will be here in a few days.[4] Oh, if the Artillery (which is a superb company) and the Cavalry had only been in at the fight of the 21st—The Legion would have made a reputation indeed. I doubt if ever such another opportunity occurs in which all the arms can be so successfully used, as they could have been on that memorable day. A few of the wounded men, belonging to the Legion have died of their wounds, but I understand most of them are recovering. They are all, or nearly all in Richmond, where they are well cared for. I received your kind letter yesterday,[5] enclosing

---

specific diarrhea, typhoid is caused by fecal contamination of the water supply when the latrines are upstream from the drinking water. Typhoid was responsible for one-fourth of all deaths in southern armies. M.C. Butler to Wife, 24 Aug. 1861, Butler Family Papers, DU; Wiley, *Life of Johnny Reb*, 253. Jonathan R. Buist, in "Some Items of My Medical and Surgical Experience in the Confederate Army," *Southern Practicioner* 25 (1903): 574–81, noted that when a regiment began to experience high rates of diarrhea and typhoid, the best treatment was simply to move the camp.

3. William Dellie Gary, age 35, died of epilepsy on 3 August at Brentsville. Thanks to O. Lee Sturkey for this information from his Davis Guards Roll, Company F.

4. Taylor's company was ordered to march from Ashland on 16 August. OR, ser. 1, 51, pt. 2: 236.

5. In light of Griffin's repeated complaints about the infrequency of letters from home, it is ironic that his good friend Captain Butler considered him lucky indeed in this respect. He wrote to his young wife on the same day:

one from Willie. I do assure you My Darling, my heart leaps with
Joy, when in looking over the mail, I find a letter addressed to me. I
am sure from the number of letters you say you have written me that
I have not received more than half. And it is fair to presume that my
letters, to you have shared the same fate.[6] Except your sweet letters,
My Darling, and two from Willie I have received *four* others all put
together, and one of them this evening from Minnie. I received one
from Dr Muse a few days ago, and have recd two[,] yes two[,] from
Sue. An average of one per month. And yet She thinks So much of
her Dear "Bud Jimmie". I dont include those received from Sis—But
I am happy to say My Darling that you do write me. And I appreciate
your letters, as none could appreciate them, unless it be some one in
my condition. I would be *delighted*, to receive a letter every day. And

---

"Maj Griffin got a letter from his wife yesterday sixteen pages long. Why cant
you write me such. You know it would all interest me." M.C. Butler to Wife,
3 Aug. 1861, Butler Family Papers, DU.

6. An immediate concern for Postmaster Reagan was the cost of the postal
operation. In creating the Confederate Post Office, Congress had stipulated
that it be self-sufficient as of March 1863. Although Reagan had inherited a
substantial deficit, he employed a variety of measures to reduce cost, including
eliminating unnecessary routes, negotiating a decrease in railroad charges, and
breaking up long routes into shorter ones to encourage more bidding. While
Reagan was successful in making the Post Office a self-sustaining organization, much of this success was at the expense of mail service. In many respects, controlling costs and efficient mail service were at odds. There were
frequent interruptions in service due to the refusal of mail carriers to accept
the low bids that the Post office offered, and eliminating routes slowed service.
As the war progressed, numerous other problems emerged. Many postal workers left their jobs to join the army, leaving inexperienced people in their
places. The transportation of military supplies often diverted trains from established schedules, causing confusion in mail delivery. As a result, many soldiers and their relatives turned to alternative methods such as sending letters
with furloughed soldiers or traveling friends. Reagan, *Memoirs*, 133–34;
McCaleb, "The Confederate Post Office," 73–74; Ben H. Proctor, *Not Without Honor*, 134–40; Robert C. Black III, *The Railroads of the Confederacy*
(Chapel Hill: Univ. of North Carolina Press, 1952), 226–27; Bell I. Wiley
and Hirst D. Mihhollen, *Embattled Confederates: An Illustrated History of
Southerners at War* (New York: Bonanza Books, 1964), 141–42.

really expected to get them nearly that often from some of my kind friends & *relatives* who think *so much* of me. But some how or other they dont come. But it doesnt become me to complain. I know some of them would write, especially Sue and Sissie, if they only had *time*. But Poor things they havent. And if they had—why you know they have no news to write. They know it would be very uninteresting to me, to recieve a letter only informing me about the welfare of those precious ones who lie around my heart. And the image of whom are constantly in my mind. To say nothing of the welfare of my many friends, and matters generally—in and around my Dear home. But its all right[,] they will write *next week*. I suppose too, they think that I ought to reply to each one of their letters. But my Darling I really havent time. I spend nearly all my spare time in writing to you my Darling. And in writing to you I consider that I am writing to all the family. For I know you give them what news I may communicate to you. Please say to the Dr and Minnie and Sue that I will answer their letters in a few days. Tell Willie that I will also answer his soon. He must write oftener. Do Darling give my love to each one of the Dear little children. Tell them to be good and obedient children—love their Mother & Father and love each other. My kindest regards to your Father and all the family. How is my colt—and how much wheat did we make—Keep me posted about my crop. Gary thanks you for remembering him. Says since the battle he fears the Girls will marry him in spite of all he can do—

Good Bye
from your Jimmie

Letter 14   JBG to Leila Griffin

Head Quarters Hampton Legion
Camp Griffin Aug 11th 1861

My Darling Wife
   I am just now disengaged after having been very busy all the morning, and propose to devote my leisure moments to writing to my Darling— We are still, at the same place, that we were when I last wrote you[.] But expect we will move again in a few days. We are ordered to Wolf

Run.[1] Which is about eight or ten miles from here, towards the Potomac in the direction of Washington. Col Hampton has taken a detachment of Cavalry, and gone down to day to look at the Country and select a Camp ground. Our Legion is in a bad condition on account of sickness[.][2] We have a great many cases of Measles—Lost another man last night. His nurse went to sleep the night before, and the sick man got up, went out of doors, and got wet, which caused his death. The ballance of the cases are doing very well—but will necessarily be confined for some time. Lt Crafton[3] is Sick and I think taking the measles. I still continue to escape them. I am, however exposed to them daily. I ordered Capt Butler a few days ago to take a detachment of men and scour the Country around, to see what he could find of the plunder that was left by the Enemy, in their flight from Manassas.[4] They found a good many things, such as guns provisions &c. They were gone nearly three days. Were much pleased with their trip. Saw a good deal of country, and a great many Soldiers, amongst the rest they met up with Col Bacon's Regi-

---

LETTER 14

1. Wolf Run Shoals is on the Occoquan River, which flows east from its juncture with Bull Run into the Potomac. It is roughly twelve miles southeast of Manassas and twenty miles south of Washington, D.C.

2. Richard Habersham wrote almost two weeks later that in one company only eight men had turned out for dress parade that day—all the rest were sick. Habersham to Brother, 23 Aug. 1861. Habersham Family Papers, LC.

3. Joseph D. Crafton of Company A, the Edgefield Hussars, enrolled 14 June 1861, at Camp Hampton as second lieutenant. He was promoted to first lieutenant by election on 29 August. Crafton was reported sick on the January–February 1862 muster roll, and there is no further record for him. CSR, M267, roll 364.

4. Butler wrote to his wife that he had ridden over the battlefield three times. He reported that the articles abandoned included ambulances, wagons, mess kits "perfectly fitted out," and all kinds of stationery. The civilian spectators who had fled back to Washington left behind fine carriages, liquors, and cigars. From a cavalry captain who had taken part in the pursuit, Butler also learned that the Federals had lost several trunks filled with ball dresses ("I suppose they intended to celebrate their arrival in Richmond by a grand Ball") and 3000 pairs of handcuffs intended for their prospective Rebel prisoners. M.C. Bulter to Wife, 31 July 1861, Butler Family Papers, DU.

ment.[5] And saw all the Edgefield Boys. Capt Butler says he saw Charlie and Albert Miles.[6] They were well, but had both been sick. Which is all I have been able to hear of the boys since I have been here. He also heard that Giroud[7] had received a discharge and had gone home. My Darling I would give almost any thing on earth to see you and my Darling Children—But know that at present I cannot. How long it will be I cannot tell. But I hope not a great while. My own private opinion is, if we can be successful in the next large engagement, that it will not be

---

5. See Chapter 1, note 69, and letter of 28 April 1862, note 5. Col. Thomas Glascock Bacon (1812–1876), an attorney and longtime clerk of the Edgefield District Court, had helped organize the first volunteer company from Edgefield. He commanded the Seventh South Carolina Volunteers of Bonham's (later Kershaw's) Brigade. The Seventh South Carolina, which contained six companies from Edgefield, had been at Manassas but not engaged. Chapman, *History of Edgefield*, 218; Emily Bellinger Reynolds and Joan Reynolds Faunt, *Biographical Directory of the Senate of the State of South Carolina, 1776–1964* (Columbia: Univ. of South Carolina Press, 1964), 86–87; D. Augustus Dickert, *History of Kershaw's Brigade* (Newberry, S.C.: Elbert H. Aull, 1899), 101–2.

6. Charles L. Miles, 24, and Albert Miles, 22, were the sons of Aquilla Miles (letter of 4 July 1861, note 11) and the stepsons of Leila's older sister Mary Ann (11 July 1861, note 9). The census of 1860 shows that Charles Miles was residing with the Griffins that year, and Griffin's frequent references to Aquilla and "the boys" suggest close relations between the two families, who were related by blood as well as marriage. The Miles brothers enlisted as privates in Company H, Captain Elbert Bland's, of the Seventh South Carolina Volunteers on 1 June 1861, and were mustered into Confederate service on 4 June. Albert Miles was killed on 28 June 1862, during the Seven Days battles. Charlie Miles subsequently advanced to fifth sergeant; he was wounded at the Wilderness on 6 May 1864, and paroled at Greensboro, North Carolina, on 2 May 1865. CSR, M267, roll 216.

7. William Giroud Burt was Leila's cousin, the son of her uncle William Miles Burt by his first wife, Mary Atkinson. He enlisted in Company H, Seventh South Carolina Volunteers, as a private on 1 June 1861, and was discharged on 28 July because of a hernia. He rejoined Confederate service in December as sergeant of Company I, Twenty-Second South Carolina Volunteers, was promoted to lieutenant on 12 March 1863; to lieutenant colonel to rank from 18 August 1864; and to colonel to rank from 30 July 1864. He was paroled at Appomattox. CSR, M267, roll 216; Krick, *Lee's Colonels*, 65.

long then before we shall have peace. I have not yet received my Commission, but will soon be Lt Col of the Legion.[8] Capt. Connor will take my place & The President has permitted Col Hampton to have a Junior Majr. I think Capt Butler will receive that appointment. I will have to go to the infantry and Butler will have command of the Cavalry. I know you are anxious to know how I sustain myself. Of course every man in camp knows more about the standing of every officer in camp than himself. But I honestly think my standing is very fair. I am aware that some men dislike me because I make them do their duty. I understand they consider me a very strict Officer. I only try to discharge my duty, which I am determined to do let the consequences be what they may. I find that Soldiers have to be watched very closely and some of them have to be punished to make them do their duty. You said in your last letter that Col Hampton was severely censored, for assisting in carrying the body of Col Johnson off the field. I think that is not true. He did not assist in it. It seems however—that at one time Col Hampton was out of sight of the left wing of the Legion—being with the right wing, which was some distance from the left. And Some of the men Said "we have no leader" whereupon two of the Captains proposed that Capt Gary take command of that wing, which he did for a time. Every one say [sic] that Col Hampton acted very bravely and gallantly[.] I do not desire another battle particularly[.] But I do hope—if we are to have another that I may have an opportunity to do something. I assure you I am heartily tired of hearing men say what they did in the fight—and I have no showing[.] Dont be uneasy about Me My Darling, for there isnt half as much danger in a fight as you suppose. Very few Officers or men are killed when you come to think of the number engaged. If we should have a fight I will inform you of the result immediately—by Telegraph. Give my love to all the dear little Children and kiss them for me. Tell them I hope to see them again before a great while. I do hope Jim Dozier is better and will recover— My love to all the family and friends—I hope Dr Muse

---

8. The death of Lt. Col. Johnson left the infantry without a commanding officer. It also revealed the weakness of the original organization in not providing for a major of infantry; the next most senior officer, James Conner, was a captain. Griffin's appointment was confirmed on 15 August, and he took rank from 21 July. Conner was promoted to major of infantry and Butler to major of cavalry; both also took rank from 21 July.

and the rest of the sick have recovered. Tell the Dr and Minnie & Sue that they must not get out of patience[.] I will write to them as soon as I can—Write often to me My Darling[.] Continue to direct your letters to Manassas until I direct you to change—Abram is well and sends his love to all

Good Bye my Darling
Your Jimmie

Letter 15   JBG to Leila Griffin

Head Qrs Hampton Legion [1]
Camp Griffin Sept 17th 1861

My Darling Wife

I received yesterday a letter from you dated the 8th which was eight days on the road. And I hadnt heard a word from you in the mean time. The same day that you wrote that letter I recd one from you. I was getting uneasy about it, for I dont think so many days have elapsed at a time without hearing from you since I have been in this country.

It brought me, however the welcome intelligence of the general good health of my Dear family. One exception however which I was sorry for—the sickness of poor little Claude. I cant conceive what keeps him so sick. It must be his diet. Does he use his bottle yet? if so I would stop it at once. I would feed him on nothing but rice and butter, for a long time. My health is not so good as it was before I had the measles.[2] I have been suffering recently from dysentery, which

---

LETTER 15

1. In his diary artilleryman Wilmot W. Curry sketched the layout of the camp on the Occoquan River near Wolf Run Shoals (see photo gallery). His diagram shows Hampton and his staff headquartered at Bacon Race Church with the infantry camped in front of them; the cavalry was half a mile below the infantry. The artillery was positioned to the west, across the roads to the village of Occoquan and the Potomac, and separated from the infantry and cavalry by woods and pickets. Additional pickets were posted west of the artillery. Wilmot Walter Curry Diary, CAH-UT.

2. Griffin contracted measles sometime after the middle of August. Butler wrote home on 24 August that Griffin was ill with measles. Conner wrote to his mother on 29 August: "I have not been writing much lately, not having

keeps me weak. I keep up all the time, but dont feel strong and lively as I generally do—The Doctor says—that dysentery is almost a natural consequence of the measles—That it always deranges—My Darling I will cut short the sentence that I was writing for the present and tell you how very near I came to be killed a little while ago—Dont be alarmed for I am all right now. When I commenced writing this letter to my *precious Darling*, there was a thunder cloud gathering in the west. Just as I finished the other page, it began to rain. I stopped writing and began to fix my tent to shut out the rain—Just at this time there came a strong blow of wind which broke my ridge pole—(that is the long pole that runs along the whole length of my tent at the top)—That let the tent down in the centre—but both the upright poles stood. The wind was very heavy and blew down a tent next to mine, in which there was a sick man, Dr Buist.[3] He then ran into my tent, to

---

the time, Colonel Hampton being sick with some sort of Malarial fever, and the Lieutenant Colonel down with the infantile complaint of measles. He was very uneasy about having them. Said he had been exposed to them at home while his children had them, and yet never could take the blame things, and now he would catch them when he could not afford it, and sure enough he did catch them, so that left me with my hands full and I have been very busy ever since." M.C. Butler to Wife, 24 Aug. 1861, Butler Family Papers, DU; Moffett, *Letters of General James Conner*, 54.

3. Dr. John Somers Buist of Charleston, who graduated from the Medical College of South Carolina in 1861, was commissioned assistant surgeon in the South Carolina Army by Governor Pickens and subsequently served as medical officer at the Charleston Arsenal and Castle Pinckney. After being transferred to Confederate service, he did duty at Fort Moultrie before being sent to Virginia. He was assigned as assistant surgeon of the Hampton Legion on 19 July 1861, and was promoted to surgeon on 2 February 1864, to rank from 31 October 1863. Buist served at this rank in John C. Haskell's artillery battalion until the surrender at Appomattox. After the war he was one of the leaders of the medical community in Charleston, where he helped organize the city health department and was elected city health officer. He taught at South Carolina Medical College and served two terms as president of the Medical Society of South Carolina. CSR, M331; CMH, 6:490–91; Joseph Ioor Waring, *A History of Medicine in South Carolina, 1825–1900* (n.p.: South Carolina Medical Association, 1967), 209–10; William B. Atkinson, *The Physicians and Surgeons of the United States* (Philadelphia: Charles Robson, 1878), 275.

take shelter from the storm. His servant came with him in my tent. About this time Abram was in a tent just in rear of mine which blew down also—And he ran into my tent, and seized the upright pole in the back part of the tent, to keep it from falling. Dr Buist's boy held up the front pole. The Dr laid himself down on the straw about the centre of the tent, and I covered him with my overcoat. I then went to where Abram was, and assisted him in supporting the back pole. Just at this time there came a flash of Lightning which struck the front pole of my tent, where Dr Buist's boy was standing, and killed the boy instantly. The shock knocked down both myself and Abram in a pile. My left side from my shoulder to my foot was completely paralyzed. I suffered no pain but thought at first that my left arm and leg was all broken up. I was perfectly sensible and cool all the time wasnt frightened at all. As soon as I found that my head was not affected, and I recovered my breath, which was knocked out of me for a very short time, I looked around and saw that the whole party was floored. I called to Buist and asked if he was hurt—He said no, but he thought the boy who was then lying near him was killed—I told him to call for help as I had very little voice. He hollered very feeble, as he was quite weak, very soon the men came—The Drs came immediately—I was taken in another tent near by. Where they rubbed me for about half an hour with mustard & hartshorn, which restored the circulation: and I was all right— I then got up and put on my clothes and went about my business.[4] Abram was affected just about as I was, he is now all right—But the boy who held the other pole, never kicked, I have no idea that he knew anything at all after the shock. It was a

---

4. Griffin's paralysis was probably due to temporary dysfunction of the nervous system caused when the electrical discharge moved down his left arm, side, and leg before passing into the ground. The treatment he received was of no specific benefit. The slave who was "killed instantly" received the electrical discharge through both arms and his entire body; it interrupted the heart's regular electrical activity when it passed through it. Today, "Dr. Buist's boy" would receive cardiopulmonary resuscitation until the heart recovered its normal electrical rhythm and beating pattern. A complete recovery could be expected. The best medical reference for this type of injury is Friedrich Panse, "Electrical Injuries," in P.J. Vinken, G.W. Bruyn, and R. Braakman, eds., *Injuries of the Brain and Skull* (New York: American Elsevier, 1975), 683–729.

pretty close shave wasnt it? But then a miss is as good as a mile. But notwithstanding I came through[.] I think I would prefer to chance canon balls and bomb shells—to another scrape of that kind. My friends say, I neednt be uneasy, for if Lightning cant kill me, nothing else can. You will understand my Darling why this sheet of paper looks so badly when you remember—that it was lying on the table where the ink stand was upset. And the rain beating in. When I came to finish it I found it, looking so bad that I thought, I would write another. But after a moments reflection I determined to write it on the same sheet. Col Wigfall,[5] is spending the day in our camp. He came into my tent just before the storm commenced, and staid only a few minutes and walked out, had he staid in here a few minutes longer he in all probability would have been killed, for he was sitting near the front door.

I am now writing at night, and as the mail doesnt leave until morning—I will close and finish it in the morning. The storm came up between three and four oclock this evening.

Wednesday Morning 18th. Good morning my Darling—I feel quite well this morning, so far as my electric Shock is concerned—and I even feel better than I have for several days past.

My Darling I have just sit down to finish out this sheet and here comes the mail carrier—Who by the way is Coles[6]—son in law of the Governor. Tell Sue that Gary says he is greatly indebted to her for her compliment—Says he appreciates it the more because it was unexpected—and has done him more good than any thing that has been said to him. I was going on to tell you when I recd my wound that

5. Lewis Wigfall (see letter of 4 July 1861, note 5) had been commissioned colonel of the First Texas Infantry on 28 August. During September and October the First Texas was encamped at Camp Wigfall near Dumfries, about ten miles below the Legion on Quantico Creek. W.C. Nunn, ed., *Ten Texans in Gray* (Hillsboro, Tex.: Hill Junior College Press, 1968), 181.

6. J. Stricker Coles had married Eliza Simkins Pickens, the second of the four daughters of Gov. Francis W. Pickens, on 23 April 1853. Matthew Calbraith Butler, another son-in-law, wrote to his wife Maria of her brother-in-law's appointment: "Col. Johnson appointed Mr. Coles Post Master of the Legion this morning, a very pleasant birth [*sic*] as he will [have] nothing to do, but ride backwards & forward to the city." Butler to wife, 30 June 1861, Butler Family Papers, DU; McClendon, *Edgefield Marriage Records*, 38.

the Doctrs say that a man is almost sure to suffer, after measles with either his lungs or his bowels—I think mine are getting all right again. My Darling, as to Willie—I dont know what to say—If Sue would teach them at home—I expect they would learn about as much. But Darling do just what you think best. You had better send some good warm clothes for Abram. Send my heavy Shoes and one or two winter cravats. My love to all and especially to my children.

Good bye My Darling
Your Jimmie

3 *Guarding the Potomac Line*

Letters 16 through 27
2 January through 26 February 1862

The Hampton Legion spent the fall and winter along the Potomac, erecting batteries between the Occoquan River and Aquia Creek. Griffin, not fully recovered from his lightning strike, went home on a medical furlough. Major Conner wrote on 15 October, "The Lieutenant Colonel has gone home, sick. His arm is almost paralyzed by that lightning stroke." [1] *The Edgefield* Advertiser *reported that Griffin was home "for a couple of weeks" and would be receiving recruits for the Hampton Legion during that time. Butler and Gary also went home to visit their families during this hiatus.* [2]

Griffin's brush with death attracted the attention of the newspaper correspondents, who had little to report in the way of military action during the quiet autumn on the Virginia front. Accurate accounts were published in the South Carolina papers from the Richmond Dispatch *and* Examiner *correspondents; the Charleston* Daily Courier's *own correspondent submitted a garbled version.* [3] *The* Courier's *report was part of a longer article, filed on 28 Sep-*

1. Columbia *Tri Weekly Southern Guardian*, 24 Sept. 1861 (Richmond *Examiner*); Charleston *Daily Courier*, 26 Sept. 1861 (Richmond *Dispatch*); Charleston *Daily Courier*, 3 Oct. 1861. Thanks to O. Lee Sturkey for sharing these items from his files.
2. Edgefield *Advertiser*, 23 Oct. and 13 Nov. 1861.
3. Moffett, *Letters of General James Conner*, 61.

*tember, describing the troops in Virginia and the Hampton Legion.
It included a description of Griffin's tent in the officers' quarters
that is worth quoting in full:*

> Take a peep into one of the tents. Here for instance is that of
> Lieutenant-Colonel Griffin. The floor is of straw, the bed is a cot, the
> washstand is the body of a tree with a board nailed across the top, the
> dining table is a camp chest, the chairs are stools, valises turned on end,
> or anything you like. A camp table, with a pair of folding legs, is in one
> corner and just now upholds a field glass, one or two military works, a
> writing case, and a flask. The latter is an indispensable "article of war,"
> and go where you may you will find them as plentiful as prayer books
> on your family tables at home.[4] From end to end of the tent is a strong
> line, which acts in the capacity of a wardrobe, sustaining everything
> from a clean shirt to a soiled napkin. A peg or two in the posts supports
> sword and pistols, perhaps a dress coat and pants, while the trunk,
> which stands in the corner, contains the remainder of the catalogue of a
> soldier's fit out. You will smile when I tell you that Lieutenant-Colonel
> Griffin has a "pet" in the shape of a veritable Yankee chicken, which,
> morning, noon and night, is as much an occupant of the tent as the
> master himself. When the latter is present, ten chances to one that she
> is either on his table or roosting on his shoulder. As the bantling neither
> lays nor crows, the height of Miss Chicken's ambition is to do her setting
> on the head board of the Lieutenant-Colonel's bed, whither she retires
> with as much regularity and punctuality as he does himself. The ani-
> mal's bones are not to be picked this side of Washington city.

*While Griffin was home in South Carolina, the Hampton artillery
in Virginia manned batteries earlier constructed below the mouth of
the Occoquan at Freestone Point and Evansport and fired on Federal
ships attempting to pass up the Potomac to Washington.[5] The infan-*

---

4. The substitution of the liquor flask for the Bible suggests a gendered
comparison: the military as an all-male sphere contrasted with home as refined
through the influence of women.

5. Curry Diary, CAH-UT; Hampton to Thomas Jordan, Ass't Adjt. Gen.,
First Corps, Army of the Potomac, 24 Sept. 1861, Hampton Papers, SCL;
Lily Logan Morrill, *A Builder of the New South: Notes on the Career of
Thomas M. Logan* (Boston: Christopher Publishing, 1940), 41–44.

Eastern Virginia Theater, 1861–62

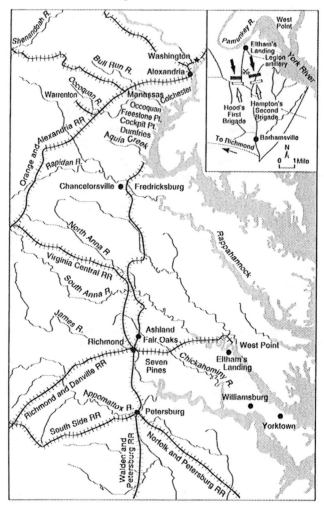

try moved ten miles down the coast to Dumfries, near what is now the site of Quantico Marine Base, to join Wigfall's Texas Brigade. (Wigfall had been promoted to brigadier on 21 October and given command of three Texas regiments and one from Georgia.) Samuel Mays recorded that they did picket duty there at Freestone Point, where they had "a most magnificent view of the Potomac River."[6]

Griffin rejoined his command in November 1861. A lengthy poem on the front page of the Edgefield Advertiser (6 Nov. 1861), written "To Our Soldiers," included best wishes for Griffin and the Legion as he departed Edgefield after his medical furlough.

> *. . . COL. GRIFFIN leaves to-morrow*
> *For his Legion on the border.*
> *Some recruits are going with him,*
> *And he carries num'rous boxes—*
> *Boxes, trunks, and bundles various*
> *For his brave and trusty Legion,—*
> *. . . With him go the warmest wishes*
> *Of a thousand glowing bosoms,*
> *For his safety and the Legion's*
> *For the weal of every soldier*
> *Edgefield claims along the border.*

About 1 December, the infantry and artillery reunited and went into winter quarters near the mouth of the Occoquan River, two miles below the village of the same name. Camp Wigfall lay opposite Colchester, which overlooked the Potomac some twenty miles below Washington, and five miles above the batteries at Freestone Point. The cavalry remained at Bacon Race Church until 11 December, when Butler moved it to Camp Wigfall.[7]

Camp life settled into a routine "so monotonous, so much of a sameness, that it is really quite trying to one's patience at times." Griffin devoured the local newspapers and passed the blustery days with chess games and conversation with his fellow officers. Skirmishing between

---

6. Mays, *Reminiscences of the War Between the States*, 41.

7. Morrill, *A Builder of the New South*, 43; Butler to Wife, 7 and 10 Dec. 1861, Butler Family Papers, DU.

cavalry pickets provided occasional drama. The most notable occurred one night in late January, when a group of scouts from Texas shot their way out of an ambush, deeply impressing Griffin with their cool bravado.

Hampton's absences as acting brigadier general left Griffin frequently in command of the Legion. He enjoyed the authority but was desperately homesick. In February 1862, as the companies debated whether to reenlist under the Furlough and Bounty Act, Griffin pondered his military future. He was strongly inclined to go home at the end of his tour of duty in June, he wrote to Leila; by then the war would probably be nearly over, or else it would "grow to be a monster."

Letter 16   JBG to Leila Griffin

Head Qrs Legion Camp Wigfall
Thursday night 2nd Jany 1862

My Darling Leila

Another mail, and no letter for me. My Darling I am getting quite uneasy. I havent received a letter from you in eight or ten days, and in the mean time I have written you three besides this one.[1] I hope it does not arise from indifference on your part. Is it possible that you are becoming tired of writing to your Husband so soon. I hope not— Nor will I believe it. I suppose you had a good deal of company about Christmass, which occupied all your time, and that I will hear from you soon. I wrote night before last to Sue, and last night to Willie— and to night I will write again to you notwithstanding I am quite tired. I have been riding all day—and notwithstanding it has been the coldest day we have had this winter, I rode all day without an overcoat. I rode with Col Hampton up towards our old Camp near Bacon Race Church, where he has stationed one of his regiments and a section of

---

LETTER 16

1. The irregularity of the mails was partly to blame for the lack of letters from home. Hampton expressed similar concern to his sister during this period. See Charles E. Cauthen, ed., *Family Letters of the Three Wade Hamptons, 1782–1901* (Columbia: Univ. of South Carolina Press, 1953), 80–81, 84. If Griffin's three previous letters reached Edgefield, they have not been located. See letter of 25 June 1861, note 4, on the Confederate postal service.

Artillery—With a view to guard Wolf run, and Davis' fords across the Occoquan.[2] He was informed to day that Genl Beauregard had ordered six more artillery guns to report to him. They seem, at last, to have awakened to the importance of properly guarding this section of country. They have sent some engineers down to lay off some works, and positions for the guns to guard these places. Strange to say they still expect an advance of the Enemy this week or next. Col Hampton had a little skirmish with the enemy yesterday,[3] a full account of which I gave in my letter to Willie. I am very sorry I didnt go with him, I would have gone, had I anticipated any thing of the kind—But he only went over to see about posting some pickets—and concluded after he had finished, to try this little project. I am closely tied down with my command drilling them every day. We have now a fine drilled Regiment. I am sorry to inform you that Maj Butler is sick—I fear he has the camp fever,[4] and if he has he will be sick a good while.

---

2. That winter Hampton commanded a provisional brigade consisting of the Legion, the Fourteenth and Nineteenth Georgia Infantry regiments, and the Sixteenth North Carolina Infantry. These forces were guarding the Potomac line between the Occoquan River and Aquia Creek. The Sixteenth North Carolina and Fourteenth Georgia regiments were posted at Wolf Run and Davis's Ford, respectively, three miles in front of Bacon Race Church. The Nineteenth Georgia was at the village of Occoquan, seven miles from the church, and the Legion was two miles farther down at Colchester. OR, ser. 1, 5:533, 1030, 1106.

3. This action does not appear in the OR, but Major Conner, who was with Hampton, described it in a letter to his mother, and Hampton himself recounted it to his sister. After checking the pickets near Pohick Church, where George Washington and his family had once worshiped, Conner and Hampton divided the cavalry. Conner and 20 men hid in a thicket and ambushed a party of 70 or 80 Union cavalrymen, and Hampton and the remainder of the force charged them as they rode up the hill. The Yankees broke and fled, carrying off three horses with empty saddles and an unknown number of wounded. Moffett, *Letters of General James Conner*, 74; Cauthen, *Family Letters of the Three Wade Hamptons*, 80. A full account appears in a letter from a member of the Legion printed in the Charleston *Daily Courier*, 30 Jan. 1862.

4. Camp fever is probably typhoid fever (see letter of 3 Aug. 1861, note 2). According to the unpublished research of O. Lee Sturkey on the Legion infantry, 45 men in the seven infantry companies died of disease between August and December 1861; nine more perished in the first three months of 1862. Sturkey to Judith McArthur, 11 Dec. 1989.

Some of the cases are in bed from six to eight weeks. You had better not tell this unless, you hear it from another source, as I dont know whether or not he has informed his wife of it. My Darling you have never said any thing about recieving my trunk which I sent by John Nicholson.[5] I presume however you must have recieved it. In it I sent all my thin socks home. I wish you to [send] some of them back to me, as I wish to wear them next to my feet, and the woolen ones over them—I am sure my feet will keep much warmer, as the wool socks, cause my feet to perspire and then when I am exposed to the cold my feet get very cold. Please send my boot hooks also. Darling do write me some long letters and give me all the news. Tell me how Spradley[6] gets along with his business—How do you like him—Tell him to [take] good care of every thing, the Stock especially. I want him to pay especial attention to the hogs, and raise all he can. Tell me every thing. I was greatly surprised at what you informed me about Mrs L— I know who gave her the book you alluded to—but maybe I better not tell it. Dr McKie—her brother in law gave her the book, I was in Augusta at the time and saw it.[7] But you had better not say any thing

---

5. There were two men named John Nicholson in the Legion and both went home to Edgefield during the fall because of illness. John Lake Nicholson was originally a member of Gary's Watson Guards but shortly transferred to Butler's Edgefield Hussars, with whom he enrolled for Confederate service on 6 June 1861. The newspaper reported his cavalry rank as fifth corporal, but his service record shows no rank other than private. He spent most of the summer on sick furlough in Richmond, and his record shows two hospital discharges: one in September and another in October or November. His cousin John Threewits Nicholson, fourth sergeant of the Watson Guards (Company B of the infantry), enlisted in Columbia on 12 June and was discharged on a surgeon's certificate on 22 November. It is probably this Nicholson to whom Griffin refers. The Nicholson and Griffin families were distantly linked through the branches of each that had intermarried with the Butlers. CSR, M267, roll 364; Edgefield *Advertiser*, 29 May and 5 June 1861; Edgefield County Historical Society, *Genealogy of Nicholson and Allied Families* (Edgefield: Society, 1944), 39, 41.

6. The plantation overseer, B.F. Spradley, was listed in the 1860 census as being 25 years old, with an 18-year-old wife, Missouri. He had $500 in personal property and no land.

7. Mrs. L. is Mrs. Lanham (see letters of 14 June 1861, note 4, and 25 and 29 June 1861). The McKies were an important Edgefield family with

about it— Let every body attend to their own difficulties. I would be
slow to believe such a slanderous report, unless there was better evidence than that given. My Darling I can scarcely hope to be able to
go home more than once more between this and the end of my term
of enlistment.[8] And as I couldnt be with you Christmass, I think I will
try to divide the time, and although it is a long time I hope to see you
about March. Dont say any thing about when I expect to go home for
I really cant tell when. And you had better not let the negroes know
when to expect me, or rather let them expect me at any time. I do
hope they will behave themselves and give you all no trouble.

Tell Willie and Bobbie they must take good care of Jeff, and not let
him run about. He must be kept in the yard. Tell them that Joe has
got fat and has grown to be a large dog—Col Hampton says he is a
very fine dog. He has hunted with him a little—I havent had time to
hunt any yet. We occasionally get some ducks, though not so many
as I expected. There are plenty of them on the river but we have no
chance to kill them. We had some very fine Canvass backs to day,
they are the finest ducks I ever eat[;] the flesh is exceedingly rich and
well flavoured. I believe I have given you about all the news of any
interest— And now after begging you to give my love to each one of
our dear Children, as well as to your Father and all his family and all
our relatives and friends I will wish you a happy new year and bid you
an affectionate good night from your

Husband

---

relatives in nearby Abbeville. McKie lived near Hamburg across the river from
Augusta, Georgia. Family correspondence is in the Thomas Jefferson McKie
Papers, DU. There is no way of knowing, of course, what book is referred to
here, but the reaction it provoked suggests Hinton R. Helper's inflammatory
The Impending Crisis of the South (1857). A descendant of North Carolina
yeoman farmers, Helper urged the non-slaveholding majority to use their
votes to liberate the region from the "oligarchial despotism" of the slavehold-
ing elite; his book was banned in several southern states. Another possibility is
Harriet Beecher Stowe's *A Key to Uncle Tom's Cabin*, in which she published
documentation for her controversial novel. David M. Potter, *The Impending
Crisis, 1848–1861* (New York: Harper and Row, 1976), 386–87; James Mc-
Pherson, *Battle Cry of Freedom: The Civil War Era* (New York: Oxford Univ.
Press, 1988), 199–201; John Hammond Moore to Vernon Burton, 22 Jan.
1993.

   8. Griffin's twelve-month enlistment would expire on 12 June.

Letter 17   JBG to Leila Griffin

Head Qrs. Legion Camp Wigfall
Sunday night January 5th 1862

My Darling Wife

My great anxiety and suspense was relieved yesterday evening, by recieving a kind and cheerful letter from you. I had really become quite uneasy, it having been nine or ten days since I had recieved one before. Your excuse, My Darling, was a perfectly good one. But I do sincerely hope that you may not again, during my absence, be surrounded by circumstances, which will conflict with your correspondence with me. O my Darling if you could only realize the real pleasure which it gives me, to receive, and the great disappointment it gives me not to receive, letters regularly—I know you would write often. Dont understand me as complaining or fault finding—Such is not my intention. For I really give you great credit, for writing as much as you do. I know the difficulties under which you labour, in the first place your great antipathy to writing at all, and then secondly, the vast amount of business, that is daily on your hands. I say, considering these things, I get letters from you even more frequently than one might expect. And then My Darling, I get very few letters from any person except yourself. If I were to estimate my friends by the letters I recieve—I wouldnt have many—I have been back in camps two long months, and let me tell you—I have recieved two letters from Sis, one from Sue, one from Maria,[1] and one yesterday from Doctr Muse. Those are the only letters I have had, from all my *many* good Friends, except yourself and one from Willie. My Darling, situated as I am here in one place for a long time, never seeing any person except the Soldiers of our command, and occasionally some Officers, who call here on business I cannot manufacture material to write you interesting letters. Camp life is so monotonous, so much of a sameness, that it is really trying to one's patience at times. This frequently accounts for the fact that Soldiers grow extremely eager for a fight. They want something to relieve the dull monotony of the camp life. This is the case, at this time with our troops. I believe they would,

---

LETTER 17

1. Maria Burt, Leila's cousin, was the daughter of Dr. William Miles Burt.

almost to a man, be delighted if the Enemy would come along. They have been told so many times, and for so long, that the enemy would move in a short time, that they have become perfectly incredulous. You cant convince them that the Enemy will not [sic] advance this winter. Notwithstanding our Generals are evidently of the opinion that they will advance, and that very soon. Col Hampton had another regiment sent to him to day, he now has under his command, besides the Legion, three Regiments and a field battery.[2] He will now be able to give the Yanks a warm reception, wherever they may choose to try to cross the Occoquan. It looked a little squally day before yesterday evening. There was a succession of fires apparently signal fires, from away up the lines near Alexandria, down the Potomac. I dont know what was the meaning of them—It may have been their signal for an advance, but if so they were deterred by a sleet which fell that night. The sleet was not heavy, but enough to make it dangerous to travel yesterday. To day has been a fair, still sunny day—but so cold, that the ice has not melted scarcely at all. This evening it clouded up again, and is now sleeting again. I fear we have got to the end of the good weather for this winter. It is now exceedingly cold, but I dont suffer from the cold. A good many of our men have been skating for the last day or two. One poor fellow from the Ga Regiment, was drowned yesterday. Two men were skating when the ice broke and they both went down. This Georgian jumped in and saved them— And afterwards went back to show how he saved them, when the ice broke with him, he went down and drowned before they could get him out.[3] I wrote to you in my last that Maj'r Butler was sick. I am happy to inform you that he is convalescent—I saw him to day—I hope soon to see him again in the saddle. We have a good many

---

2. See previous letter, note 1. The newly arrived regiment was the Fourteenth Georgia, which had marched from Manassas.

3. Richard Habersham recounted the same incident, but only mentioned one skater: "A young man from the W.L. Infantry came very near being drowned while skating on a mill-pond yesterday & was saved only by one of the Georgia Rgt throwing a plank to him. A short time after he was taken out, the young man who saved his life was drowned within a few steps of the same place. He was taken out with grappling-irons, but his breath was entirely gone." Habersham to Sister, 5 Jan. 1862, Habersham Family Papers, LC.

Commissioned Officers now sick— On that account we are in bad condition for a fight—So far as the men are concerned we are in very good fighting condition. I am satisfied that the condition of our army would not be improved, by going into winter quarters, without an engagement. I feel the army would be a good deal demoralized, by such an event. I dont know what to think, whether they will attack us or not. I am fully confident if they do come that we will *lick* them. And if we give them a thorough licking, in their present shattered condition, I think they will begin to think about giving it up. I wish they would quit their foolishness[.] For I tell you, I would much prefer being at home with my Wife and Children—I am delighted to hear that the citizens of old South Carolina, and old Edgefield especially, have come up to the mark—without being drafted. It would have been an everlasting disgrace to have drafted the men when the Enemy were on our own soil.[4] My Darling, do make Willie ask Mr G. L. Penn (if Ed has gone)[5] whether or not Ed ever sent me some medicine which I wrote to him to send me, for my horse's feet. It has never come and I am very much in need of it—And now my Darling, after sending

---

4. On 7 November 1861 the Union had won an important strategic victory at Port Royal, South Carolina. After a Federal naval squadron under Flag Officer Samuel F. DuPont invaded the sound and captured Forts Walker and Beauregard, a force of 12,000 commanded by Brig. Gen. Thomas W. Sherman occupied the area around Hilton Head and Port Royal. Port Royal remained under Federal control until the end of the war. It gave the Union a base between Savannah and Charleston from which to fuel and supply its blockade ships, and later became an important shelter for African American refugees. B&L, 1:671–91; Willie Lee Rose, *Rehearsal for Reconstruction: The Port Royal Experiment* (Indianapolis: Bobbs-Merrill, 1964).

5. George L. Penn was the founder of a drug and dry goods emporium operated by his son, Edmund M. Penn. Ed Penn had been a member of the Edgefield Riflemen (subsequently part of Gregg's First South Carolina Volunteers) and later was first lieutenant of the Confederate Light Guards, which became Company A of the Twenty-Second South Carolina Volunteers. He was mortally wounded at Boonesboro, Maryland, on 14 Sept. 1862. Chapman, *History of Edgefield*, 374; Edgefield *Advertiser*, 24 March, 11 April, and 25 July 1860, 15 May 1861; Mamie Norris Tillman and Hortense Woodson, *Inscriptions from the Edgefield Baptist Cemetery for the Edgefield County Historical Society* (Edgefield: The Society, 1958), 29.

my love to my children, and begging you to remember me to all my friends I will bid you an affectionate

Good night

Your Jimmie

Monday morning 6th. The snow is two or three inches deep—this morning. All well. Good Bye

Letter 18   JBG to Leila Griffin

Head Qrs Legion
Camp Near Occoquan Jany 10th
1862

My Darling Leila

Many thanks to you My Darling for another kind letter, dated the 3rd inst. received this evening. Also one from Willie in the same envellope. I am delighted to hear from you under any circumstances, and I am made doubly happy, when your letters bring me such cheerful and pleasant news. I feel truly thankful that kind Providence, has so far, answered my daily prayers, in caring for my Dear Wife and Children. Oh, My Darling what a comfort to me it is, to know that you and the dear Children although separated from me, are well, and appear to be getting along so well. I am also delighted to hear that the Negroes are behaving so well—Do say to them that I hear with pleasure of their good behaviour, and hope they will continue to behave well—tell them they shall not loose anything by keeping it up. I hope also from what you and Willie both write, that our new overseer may do well. Tell him, I have entire confidence in him although a Stranger, from what I have heard of him, and he must do his best. Do ask him if he has a good stand of wheat and oats, and how they look. Has he fed away all the pea vines yet, and how does he get along with his business generally. Tell him to be economical with the corn, I think there is no doubt but he will have plenty, but still it is safest to be economical. Do tell him to see himself to measuring the corn when they go to the mill, and see that no more is sent than is necessary, and that it all comes back. Dont forget sometimes to have the wheat sunned. My Darling I do think you are getting to be a *first rate* manager. And whilst I hope that the time is not near at hand for you,

Still, I believe you would make a right managing Widdow. But excuse me—My Darling that is too serious a subject to joke about just now. I am pleased to hear that you have your garden in such fine order. I hope to enjoy some of your nice vegetables this year. Dont forget the Watermelon patch when the proper time arrives. Tell your man Peter,[1] that he knows my plan for planting, and he must pursue it just as if I were there to attend to it. Tell him to make some hills next month, dig the holes deep and put the manure low down, that is the secret of success. If you have an early Spring he might plant a few hills as early as the 10th of March and then keep on planting all the time after that, every week or two. By the way you have never written me how much cotton you and Peter made last year. How has Laura[2] got—is she no better? Did she ever try the walnut root tea—if not do make her try it—drink it freely, and continue it for a long time. My Darling we have had very disagreeable weather for some days past— The first we have had with a slight exception this winter. We had a sleet and snow about a week ago, and the weather was quite cold. The Occoquan River froze entirely over, and the ice was so thick that men walked over it with impunity. We began to think that all our labour was lost, that the Enemy could walk across any where and of course would not be apt to cross under our rifle pits. Had they attempted, they could have thrown a heavy column across, at any point we were not guarding (for we can only guard the regular crossings) and they might have been quite troublesome. But fortunately for us, night before last we had a pretty heavy rain, and the weather moderated considerably. And now although the river is still frozen over, no one would dare to risque his weight on it. I really am at a loss to conjecture what is the programme of the Enemy. It was said when the weather was so fine that they were waiting for *hard* weather. Now we have had that and they still tarry. I am thoroughly satisfied, that McClelland [sic] doesnt want to come at all. It has been said by some that he has feigned sickness to give him an excuse for not advanc-

---

LETTER 18

1. A slave mentioned in Griffin's plantation journal.
2. No family members or relatives were named Laura; the reference may be to a house slave.

ing.[3] It seems that Public opinion would force him to move, as they are already speaking of one who is to supercede him. My opinion is that his reputation now hangs upon a rather slender thread. If he advances, and gets whipped, his reputation is gone—and if he does not advance, it appears as if they will call in another. I hear that he has pledged to advance by the 15th of this month. And I dont believe now he can do so if he wishes. The rains have made the roads so soft, that I dont believe Artillery can be carried over them. But as the Frenchman said, "we shall see what we shall see". My Darling I am really afraid that my letters are not very interesting to you but you must bear in mind that I have nothing else to write about. Tell Willie I am obliged to him for his letter, tell him he doesnt improve as much in writing as I would wish, but to keep trying, he will learn after awhile. Tell him to write to me every week. Give my love to all the Children and kiss them for me. Also remember me to all my friends and relatives. Abram and Ned[4] beg to be remembered to all. Good night, My Love—

Your Jimmie

You asked me if I would like to have a pair of pants. Why, certainly I would be proud to wear them—spun[,] wove and made by your own direction.

JBG

---

3. Maj. Gen. George Brinton McClellan (1826–1885), general-in-chief of the Union army and commander of the Division of the Potomac, was an exceptional organizer and administrator but conspiciously reluctant to take his well-drilled troops into action. With the help of detective Allen Pinkerton, he consistently estimated the strength of Confederate troops at far above their actual numbers and claimed the need to build up his own forces (actually three times the size of Johnston's army) as an excuse for repeatedly delaying an advance. In January he was in fact ill with typhoid fever. James M. McPherson, *Ordeal by Fire: The Civil War and Reconstruction* (New York: Alfred A. Knopf, 1982), 211–12; T. Harry Williams, *Lincoln and His Generals* (New York: Knopf, 1952), 49–57; Stephen W. Sears, *George B. McClellan, the Young Napoleon* (New York: Ticknor and Fields, 1988), 107–9, 135–49.

4. Ned was Griffin's second camp slave.

Letter 19   JBG to Leila Griffin

Camp of the Legion
Saturday night Jany 25th 1862

My Darling Leila

I am quietly seated in my tent. Maj Connor and Adjt Barker are si-
lently sitting on the other side of our comfortable fire, closely engaged
in a game of drafts.[1] And by the way My Darling let me tell you, that
yesterday, whilst we were all closely confined to our little cloth houses,
Col Hampton remembered for the first time that he had in his trunk a
board on which we can play backgammon, drafts and chess. Yes tell Dr
Muse I now have an opportunity to practice in playing chess and if he
doesnt look sharp I will be able to beat him when I go home. I assure
you we were delighted, when the Col produced the board[;] it will serve
to while away many a tedious hour. We have nothing in the wide world
to do, when the weather is so bad that we cant go out, as it has been most
of the time lately. We have only a few books in camp and those few we
have all read. We have plenty of tactics, but I think we are pretty well
versed in them, at least they have lost their novelty to us. Then we have
nothing to do but talk, talk, talk—until we are about run out of that article. True we get the papers[2] every day, but we devour every thing in

---

LETTER 19

1. Checkers.

2. According to Winifred Gregory ed., *American Newspapers 1821–1936*
(1937; rpt., New York: Kraus, 1967), 694–715, many towns in which Griffin
was stationed in the first half of 1862 had local newspapers. In Petersburg,
Virginia, he would have had access to the *Daily Express*. At Ashland, about
15 miles north of Richmond, there was no local publication; however, the
Richmond *Examiner* and *Enquirer* were no doubt available, and Griffin could
have easily sent his slave to run this type of errand. When stationed near
Fredericksburg, Griffin would have had his choice of four local newspapers.
The *Democratic Recorder* was a weekly publication; the *News* had both a daily
and a semi-weekly edition. There was also the *Weekly Recorder* and the *Virginia Herald*, which had a weekly and semi-weekly edition. Although there
were no local papers at Manassas Junction or Dumfries, he probably had
access to papers from Fredericksburg, only about 20 miles away. Richmond
papers could have reached him during the Peninsula Campaign. While at

them in a short time. So that you can readily understand what a relief it affords to have something new to divert our attention. It is really very trying to one's mind to be for a long time cooped up in camps. We have had a continuation of very disagreeable weather, through the most of this month. Night before last it rained[,] sleeted and snowed and yesterday—no—I am mistaken it was last night—(I declare I sometimes forget the day of the week)[.] This morning the ground was all covered with snow. About nine oclock the sun came out and the day overhead looked almost like a spring day. Most of the snow has melted and such a *slosh* and sloppy roads. To night the wind has sprung up from the North West and it is now turning very cold. I suppose there will be a good freeze by morning. I hope it will freeze hard for it would be far preferable to the mud. The cold I dont mind, but the mud is intolerable.

I am happy, My Darling, to inform you that our prospect for subsistence has very much brightened since I wrote you last. The Col represented our condition to Head Quarters and they very kindly and promptly, have come to our assistance[.] The Col wrote to Genl Johns[t]on,[3] that we must be removed our *[sic]* have additional transportation.[4] And asked for a number of mules and pack Saddles. Said that if he would furnish these we could stick it out—And indeed if any troops were to remain here we wished to do it. We have fortified, and are still fortifying this place, and desire to fight here, if any where.[5]

Williamsburg, he could have purchased the *Cavalier,* which had just begun publication in June 1862; he may also have read it while at nearby Yorktown, which did not yet have its own paper.

3. Maj. Gen. Joseph Eggleston Johnston (1807–1891) was commanding general of the Department of the Potomac.

4. Hampton's letter does not appear in the OR. A private in the First Texas infantry, however, described the barely passable roads: "One can see hundreds of dead horses, broken hacks, etc, lying along the roads in the mud holes." Robert W. Glover, ed., *Tyler to Sharpsburg: Robert H. and William H. Gaston, Their War Letters* (Waco, Tex.: W.M. Morrison, 1960), 13.

5. Hampton wrote to Johnston in December that he was "very busy" constructing defenses, but was so hampered by lack of tools that only a few rifle pits had yet been completed. He advised Johnston that his forces would be primarily dependent upon rifle power, since the heavy guns could not expect

The General and Qr Master Genl both wrote very handsome letters in reply.[6] The Genl said he did not want this post abandoned & that we should have all the transportation we wished[.] He turned the Col's letter over to the Qr Master Genl who wrote to the Col that he would give him a hundred mules and pack saddles if he wished them. We will now move the Cavalry near the rail road, and the ballance of the command will remain here, I suppose, the ballance of the winter. We will abandon the waggons and bring all our supplies on mules. I will really be glad when we get rid of the poor wagon horses. I am tired of seeing them. One old mule strayed up near my tent last night—and this morning he was reported dead—I ordered the Qr Master to have him hauled off. Soon the wagon came to take the old fellow away, when lo and behold they found he wasnt quite dead. Some of them told the wagoner to nock him in the head—but he said no—he had as soon kill a man. I told him to go and haul a load of wood and by that time he would be dead—I havent heard from him since.

Ned has been laid up a few days with a bad cold. I hope he will be up soon—Abram has a cold but is still up—He is a very fine boy, a general favourite with all the Staff. My darling I have just thought that here I have written you a great long letter and nothing much in it. But I know you will excuse it. You neednt mind about the cotton socks—I have got used to the woolen. Col Hampton left to day for Richmond to spend a few days with Mrs Hampton. Of course I am left in command of the Legion. But we are not doing much now except building more batteries for our canons. I will have a hundred men at work tomorrow sunday as it is. Do give my love to every body and especially is sent to My Darling Wife and Children[.]

Your Jimmie

Col Hampton and all the Staff, say, I write the longest letters they ever saw a man write, who writes so often. Maj Butler is better. I am quite well. I thank you.

---

to hold out long against the superior Federal artillery; his plan nevertheless was to "make this place as strong as possible and to hold it as long as I possibly can." OR, ser. 1, 5:987.

6. Neither letter appears in the OR.

Letter 20   JBG to Leila Griffin

Head Qrs of the Legion
Jany 30th 1862

My Dear Leila

I hope to get a letter from you this evening. I have not had one in a whole week. I hope you are not sick My Darling—you wrote me in your last about being unwell from a cold. Previous to the reception of your last letter I had received a letter almost every mail for several days in succession, which keeps up the average very well. I have just heard that Lt Tompkins[1] has arrived at Manassas, he will be here tomorrow. I understand he has a trunk for me, and I hope a letter. My Darling this is another gloomy day, been raining all day. Yesterday was a very pretty day, it seems as if we cant have more than one pretty day, and then pay for it by having three or four rainy ones. The sun hasnt shone, I dont think more than three or four days this whole month. I have been closely engaged to day, My Darling, examining the Commissary's quarterly report. It was an exceedingly tedious job. And consequently I feel rather tired. I should have written you last night, but for the fact that I didnt sleep much the night before, and was quite sleepy. I said, I didnt sleep much, night before last—It was quite an eventful night. Let me give you an account of it. In the first place a lot of young men from the "Washington Light Infantry" (Citizens of Charleston) took it into their heads to give a concert. They accordingly went to the village of Occoquan, distant from the camp about two miles, and about four from the camp of the Enemy. Just think of that, the idea of having an entertainment of that kind almost within gun shot of the Enemy's lines. But then we had the river Occo-

---

LETTER 20

1. Twenty-six-year-old Robert William Pinckney Tompkins was the son of James S. Tompkins, one of Edgefield District's large planters and a signer of the ordinance of secession. Tompkins was first lieutenant of the Watson Guards, Company B of the infantry battalion. He was slightly wounded at Seven Pines on 31 May 1862, and elected captain of the company on 12 June. Tompkins was killed at Sharpsburg on 17 September 1862. O. Lee Sturkey, Watson Guard Rolls, ms. in possession of Mr. Sturkey, McCormick, South Carolina; Sheila Fitsimmons Heath, "The James S. Tompkins Family of Edgefield, S.C.," ms. in possession of Ms. Heath, Warrenton, Virginia.

quan between us. I knew nothing of the affair until the arrangement was all completed. In the morning before the night of the concert— they asked through their Capt, permission to have it. I consented on condition that they would preserve good order, conduct themselves properly, and not report anything about it in the newspapers. They invited our Field and Staff and said it was gotten up for our express benefit. So that we all concluded to go. Col Hampton being in Richmond. I left the camp in charge of Capt Gary and went down. When I arrived, I found the audience already in attendance. The room was a very nice one, small, and pretty well filled. The crowd consisted mostly of Officers and about a dozen Ladies. I assure you I was surprised to see, in this country, such a collection of the "Fair Sex." True they were not so pretty but they were so dignified and Lady like. The Boys had erected a stage in one end of the house, and had one corner canvassed off for the performers to retire in. This canvass consisted of a very large and handsome quilt, which I suppose they had borrowed for the occasion, and a couple of Soldiers blankets. The curtain which was used to expose the Stage was made of the fly of a tent. They didnt have gas light, but good old *tallow candles*, with a wick about the size of your little finger. So you may imagine that the light wasnt very brilliant. The Performers were all blacked, and sung various songs, and performed beautifully on several instruments. They had the piano, two violins, a tamborine and one fellow played the banjo and another beat the bones. The music was really exquisite, and the whole affair passed off very pleasantly indeed. They closed about eleven oclock and we set out for camp—We had ridden about a mile when my ear caught the sound of a rifle, in the direction of Colchester. The very place we are guarding and where we always keep a picket.[2] In a few seconds I heard another, and then another, and then a volley. I was riding my fine mare "Belle Tucker". I gave her the spur and she soon carried me to the ferry where our Picket was stationed. I was accompanied by Adjt Barker. I found after seeing the Picket that the

---

2. The infantry was guarding the south bank of the Occoquan River from the town of Occoquan to the junction with the Potomac, about a mile below it. The nearly deserted town of Colchester was on the north bank, just below Occoquan. The Federals maintained outposts at Pohick Church, just north of Colchester.

firing was over the river, in an old house just across the ferry. It had by this time all ceased. But I could distinctly hear the moaning and groaning of some one who was undoubtedly wounded. I immediately suspected the cause. We have for a long time had eight or ten Texians over the river who have been acting as scouts for us. They have harrassed the Enemy a great deal and they the Enemy have made many fruitless attempts to catch them.[3] It turned out as I suspected[.] The Texians were all in this old house (there were eight of them in all[)], and had all gone to bed, leaving no watch at all. The Enemy were doubtless piloted to the house, and the first thing the Texians knew, the Enemy were trying to break the door down. The house was a two story one with several rooms in it—they separated some in each room, and the firing commenced. The night was exceedingly dark—and the Texians couldnt tell how many they were fighting. Certainly a pretty large crowd. The firing lasted only a few minutes, and the Cowardly rascals ran off—leaving two of their men dead and one badly wounded (died that night) in the yard. One of the Texians was wounded but not seriously.[4] I ordered more men down to the river, and awaited to

---

3. East of Colchester and Pohick Church a fork of the Occoquan and Potomac Rivers created a neck of neutral land where Union and Confederate cavalry scouted and skirmished. The "Texian" scouts were attached to the Texas Brigade, made up of the First, Fourth, and Fifth Texas Infantry regiments and the Eighteenth Georgia; it was still under the command of political brigadier Louis Wigfall but soon to be led by John Bell Hood. The spirited resistance that Griffin admires later in the letter foretold the fame that the entire unit would soon acquire in combat as "Hood's Texas Brigade." See Col. Harold B. Simpson's four-volume history, *Hood's Texas Brigade* (Hillsboro, Tex.: Hill Junior College Press, 1968–1972).

4. The chronology of events in OR, ser. 1, 5:4, refers to this incident as the affair at Lee's House, Virginia, on the Occoquan, but there are no reports. In the numerous unofficial accounts, details vary considerably, with the number of embattled Texans reported at various figures between five and a dozen and the Federal attackers at between 50 and 100. The most reliable versions agree that the fighting was brief, one Texan was mortally wounded, and a man upstairs helped put the attackers to flight by the stratagem of shouting to his comrades that Hampton was coming. The Federal force consisted of a detachment of the Thirty-Seventh New York Infantry and First New Jersey Cavalry led by Lt. Col. John Burke, who may have had the assistance of one or more Virginia spies in locating the Texans. Accounts of the incident that

see what would turn up—It wasnt long before I heard a whistle across the river—I answered, and the Texians asked for a boat—I sent over and had them brought over and the wounded man attended to—He is now doing very well. Those Texians are number one men, and their conduct on that occasion was as gallant and brave as any thing that has occurred in this war. Just think of their cool courage, to be suddenly surprised by an Enemy, from whom they had no reason to expect any quarter—Surrounded in the night by these rascals, in an old house, which was but a shell—and see them separating themselves each man with his rifle in hand slipping to a window and firing at their opponents—who were also pouring the bullets into the old House. Just think, I say of this conduct and compare it to the dastardly cowardice of the Enemy who had at last found the very men whom of all others they wanted to find—they had them completely surrounded and one would suppose just where they would like to have them. They also from the sign, next day, had a large force—And

----

approximate Griffin's are Richmond *Examiner*, 3 Feb. 1862; C.W. Hutson to Father, 29 Jan. 1862, Charles Woodward Hutson Papers, SHC; Donald E. Everett, ed., *Chaplain Davis and Hood's Texas Brigade* (San Antonio, Tex.: Principia Press of Trinity Univ., 1962), 51; Mrs. A.V. Winkler, *The Confederate Capital and Hood's Texas Brigade* (Austin: Von Boeckmann, 1894), 42–43; and Morrill, *A Builder of the New South*, 44. Samuel Mays in *Reminiscences of the War Between the States*, 48, and J.B. Polley, a member of the Texas Brigade but not one of the ambushed party, wrote that the Texans were being pursued by the Federals when they took refuge in the house. Polley's *A Soldier's Letters to Charming Nellie* (New York: Neale Publishing, 1908), 23, claims that the fight lasted several hours, and in *Hood's Texas Brigade* (1910; rpt., Dayton, Ohio: Morningside Bookshop, 1976), 17, he lengthens it to an all-day battle, with the Texans finally taking cover in the surrounding timber. John Coxe, a picket who had come off his first watch an hour or so before the incident, wrote the longest account in "Bloody Night Affair at Colchester, Va.," in *Confederate Veteran* 23 (April 1915): 168–69. He dates the fight several days too early and says it was nearly dawn when the boat brought the Texans across, while the rescue must have taken place several hours earlier in order for Griffin to have gotten to bed by 3 a.m. Coxe also wrote that the next morning "Lieutenant Colonel Griffin arrived in charge of an armed squad on its way to cross over to Colchester, and we joined it, the well scouts leading the way"; Griffin's letter suggests that the scouts alone went back and buried the Yankees. For the Union version of events see 5 February 1862, note 3.

notwithstanding all this as soon as their men began to fall they actually ran off—The Texians say they carried off several wounded, they could distinctly hear them complaining and groaning as they went off. But they left one wounded man on the ground who hallooed and begged them to come back after him. I suppose he was the one I heard crying after I got down. The Texians came out after the Enemy were gone, and found this wounded man and two dead ones—They carried the wounded man in the house—built up a fire for him, gave him some water—took the arms of the three men, and then brought their own wounded man down to the river—When I sent for them as I have already told you. The next morning they went over and decently buried them. I didnt get back to camp that night until near three O Clock—and that is the reason I was so sleepy last night. Dont you think it was quite an adventerous night? My Darling I have had to write you a pretty long letter to give you the history of the affair—and now as I have nothing more of interest to write—I will beg you to remember me to all my friends and accept for your own dear Self and each one of the Darling Children, the entire love of a Husband and a Father.

Sure enough the mail has come and brought me three letters—one from you[,] one from Doctr Muse and one from Maria. Many thanks to you all for your kind consideration. You say Mrs Thompson writes for three or four hundred dollars—Well I dont know where it is to come from. However I will write her a letter and send her what I have—I wrote you the other day that Ned was sick. He has got up again—My health is still very good—I dont think Willie would learn much at Mrs McClintocks[5]—I think he had better go to plowing—he is large enough to begin, and it would do him good—He must either go to school or go to work—And I prefer the work under the circumstances. If he works he must work steady—

Jimmie

---

5. Mrs. J. McClintock, 50 years old, was listed as a teacher in the 1860 census. See Rachel Bryan Stillman, "Education in the Confederate States of America, 1861–1865" (Ph.D. dissertation, University of Illinois, 1972), which argues that war distracted both students and teachers from the seriousness of studies (301–3). Enrollment dropped in all educational institutions, even those which were attended by males under the age of military service, because

Letter 21   JBG to Leila Griffin

> Head Quarters of the Legion
> Camp near Occoquan Feby 2nd
> 1862

My Dearest Wife

I recieved a short note from you this evening, from Lt Tompkins. He has had a very long and tedious trip. Been nearly two weeks on the road. He was four or five days in getting to camp from Manassas— on account of the quantity of baggage in his charge, and the awful condition of the roads.[1] He had finally to leave the trunks. So that I havent yet recieved mine. I will send for it tomorrow, and hope to enjoy the good things put up for me, by your own dear hands, in a day or two more. This is the *rainiest—snowiest—muddiest* and with all, the most disagreeable country I ever met up with. This has been a clear sunny day—and now, (ten O Clock at night) it is raining— Night before last it snowed—Yesterday it thawed, and it seems that every thing combines to keep the earth saturated with water. The roads, being traveled over every day by wagons, of course continue to grow worse. I havent travelled over them but from accounts, and from what I see around here, I know they are awful. I have been trying for the last two weeks—to have some new batteries built—but owing to the dreadful weather, get along very slowly. We never have two days in succession in which we can work. I never was so heartily tired of mud and water in my life. Col Hampton has not yet returned from Richmond—He has been gone a week—I am expecting him every day.

---

of the obvious effect of conscription and volunteering on colleges, the fear of some parents that Yankee victories might prevent children sent away to school from returning home, and the need to keep sons at home to help run the family farms as military volunteering created manpower shortages (304–6). Northern teachers left the South with the advent of war; southern ones were exempt from conscription, but many chose to serve in the army anyway, partially in response to public criticism of this exemption (308–12).

LETTER 21

1. The camp was 21 miles from Manassas (see letter of 2 January 1862, note 2).

My Darling, you have no idea how proud I felt, yesterday while reading one of your very dear letters to find that you felt that you had reason (as you thought) to be proud of your Husband. It done me a *power* of good. For while I dont expect much from the cold Charity of the world—And indeed ask for little, It is really charming and en-spiriting to feel that you are appreciated by one who loves you and one who is prompted by no deceitful motives, to bestow praise on you. But My Darling, let me say, while I thank you for the compliment, I have so far done nothing to merit it—Except perhaps, in showing a willingness to do, whenever an opportunity may offer. I have so far, never had the fortune (whether good or bad) to be engaged with the Enemy—I hope however, if it shall ever be my fortune to be engaged with them, that my conduct will be such, that if I do not merit your praise, will not cause you to feel ashamed— I, like every man, of course would not like the idea of being even wounded in battle—But I would dislike very much to go out of this Campaign without going through at least one battle—More especially as most of the officers of the Legion have had that good fortune. I assure you that the dangers of a battle, are not near so great as one, who is unacquainted, would suppose. I do not expect any fighting of consequence, in this army before Spring—But I think it will come then pretty heavy, if there is no change.

I honestly believe that the battle itself is about the least of dangers, to which the Soldier is exposed. Sickness is much more dangerous, caused from necessary exposure.[2] The health of our Command is very good, at this time considering the quantity of bad weather we have had. My own health continues very good— I wouldnt have believed that I could have gone through what I have. But it doesnt hurt me at all. I have entire command of the Legion, during the Col's absence

---

2. Griffin's observation was true both for soldiers suffering in Virginia from the wet, cold winter of 1861–62 (J.B. Polley of the Texas Brigade claimed that the Fifth Texas at one point had only 25 men fit for duty out of 800) and for the war as a whole. For every Civil War soldier killed in battle, two more died of disease. The Confederates suffered a disease mortality rate of 20 percent, twice that of the Union army. Poor sanitary practices were responsible for the two leading fatal diseases, diarrhea/dysentery and typhoid, but the third most common killer, pneumonia, preyed on men living in tents and exposed to changeable weather. McPherson, *Battle Cry of Freedom*, 487–88.

and flatter myself that we get along very well. I cant tell whether the men like me or not—they are very respectful to me, but that they are obliged to be— Military authority is the most powerful known to man. But doesnt do harm unless abused—I think the officers generally like me and most of the men two [*sic*] but some of them I reckon do not—An Officer, as a general rule, who does his duty is apt to make some Enemies.

My Darling I have written to Mrs Thom[p]son and sent her one hundred dollars, which I told her must do, for awhile. I will send her more as soon as I can. Have you money enough to get along with— Have you heard yet from the Molasses—Where is Bob Sullivan?[3] Do remember me to your Father and family and all Friends—Please say to Dr Muse I will answer his letter soon— Give my love to each one of the children—Bless their hearts how I do want to see them—I am so anxious to hear Claude & Callie talk—Tell Willie I will write to him in a few days—I think he had better go to ploughing—Good night—My Darling

from your Husband

Letter 22 JBG to Leila Griffin

Head Qrs of the Legion
Feby 5th 1862

My Darling Wife

Again I seat myself by my little table to write a few lines to you. I am happy to inform you that my health is still very good. We have at last had two consecutive days of sun shine, with a prospect at present of at least one more. But this climate is the most changeable of any, I ever experienced. I have seen here the sun set perfectly clear and in three or four hours it would be raining or snowing. This is the first time that I have seen the sun shine two days in succession this year. On sunday night and monday last a pretty heavy snow fell, about six inches deep—Most of it is still on the ground. The weather is quite cold, and although the sun shines in the day, the snow refuses to melt, except in places. Enough of it however has melted to keep the earth thoroughly drenched—And the roads you have no conception of

---

3. Sullivan was a merchant and trader.

them, it is really difficult to get over them on horseback. I saw, to day one of our wagons coming entirely *empty* and the driver said he had stalled several times. So far, we have made out to supply our men with provisions, but our horses have fared badly. We get no hay or fodder at all and often no corn from the Qr Master, owing to want of transportation. We have made out so far to buy and press enough in this country to keep our Staff horses—But the Cavalry and Artillery horses, (especially the cavalry) look badly. We have been trying for a week to get the Cavalry back to the rail road, but have not yet succeeded on account of the bad weather and roads. We have a lot of mules to *pack* with, but they are useless without pack saddles, and they havent yet arrived. Our prospects are pretty gloomy, but I hope we will get through some way. That we are ocupying [a] very responsible position is evident, by the manifestation of the Enemy. They continue to approach occasionally a little nearer to us, and then fall back again to their camp. I doubt not they would attempt to cross over and give us a fight if they thought they could succeed—but the fate of those who attacked our forces at Leesburg,[1] is still fresh in their minds, and they dont like the idea of crossing a river to fight. They came down, on monday, whilst the snow was falling, opposite the Village of Occoquan and fired into the houses, taking the chances of killing men women or children. We had two companies on picket there—they returned the fire and the rascals left. No damage was done to either side that we know of—certainly none, to our side. As soon as it was reported, I sent a party over to reconnoitre—they returned a little after dark and reported that they were about a mile [away] and coming

---

LETTER 22

1. The battle of Leesburg (Ball's Bluff) had been fought on 21 October at Ball's Bluff on the south bank of the Potomac. Although the battle was of little strategic importance, the Confederates acquitted themselves well and the Federals, trapped on the steep brushy slopes, were routed as badly as at Manassas. As they attempted to flee back across the river to safety, their overloaded boats overturned and many Federals were drowned. The Confederates lost only 155 men, while Federal casualties reached 921, many of them missing men presumed drowned. Brig. Gen. Charles P. Stone, who had directed the battle from farther downstream at Edwards's Ferry, was pilloried in the press, accused of ineptitude and collusion with the enemy, and briefly imprisoned. Long, *The Civil War Day by Day*, 129–30.

down towards Colchester, where we also have a picket—This news was reported to me about eight O Clock at night. I immediately ordered an additional company (Gary's) down to support the Picket, in case of an attack. I ordered my horse and went down myself, it was then Sleeting rapidly—I staid with the Picket until near midnight and returned—hearing nothing more of them. I suppose they concluded to go back. I am getting awfully tired of this defensive position—You are uncertain at what hour of the day or night you may be called up by their appearance. I have no idea that they will attempt to cross over to us, nor have I any idea that they could if they would. There only object is to come in pretty large parties to the river and harrass us as much as they can knowing that we have no means of crossing the river in force, and consequently, they are in but little danger. They are also all the time in search of the Texas Scouts. I am sorry to inform you that the poor Texian whom I wrote you was wounded, is dead.[2] He died yesterday. He was more seriously wounded than the Doctr thought—I am very sorry he died—he was a gallant, noble and brave man. By the way have you seen the Enemy's report of their fight with the Texians? They claim to have killed every one, but one, and took him prisoner.[3] Such a lie. My Darling I havent yet recieved my trunk, but have sent a wagon for it. Hope to get it soon. I also have an overcoat at Manassas, I will also get that—Would you believe it—I have gone through so much of this winter without an overcoat. And what is

---

2. The Richmond *Examiner*, 3 Feb. 1862, reported the wounded Texan as James Spaulding. Everett, *Chaplain Davis and Hood's Texas Brigade*, 51, identifies him as J.S. Spratling of the First Texas Infantry. Apparently, he was Pvt. J.B. Spratting of Company E, First Texas Infantry, who was reported killed in action on the Occoquan, 5 February 1862. Harold B. Simpson, *Hood's Texas Brigade: A Compendium* (Hillsboro, Tex.: Hill Junior College Press, 1977), 43.

3. According to the Union's account of the Affair at Lee's House, Burke and his men surrounded the house at 1 a.m. while a stag dance was in progress. They claim to have killed ten Texans—nine privates and a major—and one civilian. Another civilian, identified as the fiddler for the dance, supposedly surrendered. Burke's casualties were reported as one man killed and four wounded. Frank Moore, ed., *The Rebellion Record: A Documentary of American Events, with Documents, Narratives, Illustrative Incidents, Poetry, etc.*, 11 vols. (New York: G.P. Putman, 1861–68), 4:19–20.

more remarkable, I havent suffered for the want of one[.] I borrowed one
the other night when I went out in the Sleet—and I think once or twice
before. With those exceptions I have worn none this winter. I ordered
one immediately after mine was burned, from Charleston, and it has
just come—I have come to the conclusion that they are humbugs any
how. Do My Darling remember me kindly to all my friends—and give
my unchanging love to all our relatives and particularly to my Darling
Children. Tell Duck she had better send my boot hooks. I dreamed a
few nights ago I saw poor little unfortunate Claude [4] running about with
Callie—Lord Send I could see him as I saw him then. It is now within a
few minutes of 12 o clock at night, which is about my time for retiring—
What think you of that? Good night

Your devoted Husband

Letter 23   JBG to Willie Griffin

Head Qrs of the Legion
Camp near Occoquan Feby 10th
1862

My Dear Willie

I have received two letters from you recently, for which I am much
obliged to you. I wish you to write to me every week— It will be the
means of improving you as well as be a great comfort to me. I am
delighted to hear that Sue is going to teach you and the other Children. I hope you will be diligent and studious—Do my son practice a
great deal in writing—You do not improve as much in that as I would
like to see you. Your letters are pretty well composed, considering,
you have never written many—but your writing is not good, and I
discover several mistakes in your spelling. Both of these difficulties
you can overcome, only by perseverance and attention—I wish you to
study closely until the beginning of Spring, and then I wish you to get
Mr. Spradley to fix up a light plough for you, and try your hand at
that. It will do you good, devellope your muscles and give you
strength. And will also learn you some fundamental principles of
farming, which will be of great service to you when you grow older.
Do give my love to your Sis Sue and tell her she must be very strict

---

4. Claude had clubbed feet.

with her schollars—and if they do wrong, I would recommend a guard house as a corrective. It has a very happy effect on men, and I presume would have on children. Say to Sue that I received "Bill Arp's" production and had a good laugh over it, I am obliged to her for it.[1] I recieved this evening the first number of the Advertizer I have had since my return, and enjoyed Squigg's letter.[2] I hope I will recieve it,

---

LETTER 23

1. "Bill Arp" was the pseudonym of Charles Henry Smith (1826–1903), a Georgia humorist whose satirical letters to President Abraham "Linkhorn" were popular features in southern newspapers. An attorney who served with the commissary department of the Army of Northern Virginia, Smith was a southern partisan who articulated the pride and disgruntlement of the ordinary citizen through the ironic humor of a sharp-witted rustic. The Civil War letters were collected and published in 1866 as *Bill Arp, So Called*. The letter to which Griffin refers was published in the Edgefield *Advertiser* on 29 January 1862, and mocks the inability of the Federals to put down the "rebellion" and their ignominious flight at Manassas. In it he describes an unsuccessful attempt to get to Washington to ask "Mr. Abe Linkhorn" for an extension of the twenty days stipulated for the rebels to "dispurs." En route, "we got on a bust in old Virginia, about the 21st of July, and like to have got run over by a passel of fellers running a foot race from Bull run to your sity." Arp invited Lincoln and Secretary of State "Bill Suard" to a first anniversary celebration of Georgia's secession in order to "partake of our horswhipalities." On Arp, see David P. Parker, *Alias Bill Arp: Charles Henry Smith and the South's "Goodly Heritage"* (Athens: Univ. of Georgia Press, 1991), and James C. Austin, *Bill Arp* (New York: Twayne Publishers, 1969).

2. The letter was reprinted from the Huntsville, Alabama, *Advocate* on 5 Feb. 1862. "Elihu Squiggs," a private in camp on the Dog River below Mobile, described army life in the style of a southwestern humorist. All of the officers, he reported, have cocked hats and swords, and each one has six assistants and seven clerks. Some of the enlisted men are afflicted with "camp disease" characterized by a horror of the smell of gunpowder; the patient develops "a whiteness about the liver, and feels a strong inclination to advance backwards." In Alabama, "the trees are as green as any officer; and the weather is like summer; . . . The people down here are so used to being baked, no wonder they took to eating fire and got us all into hot water." Squiggs claimed that it was even hot enough to wash in the river on New Year's Day, "notwithstanding the Alligators are thick as gnats. Fact is, it is so sandy and smoky here we are obliged to do it. Why, one of our fellows, after scrubbing himself about an hour, found a shirt he had missed about three weeks before—washed down to it."

regularly from this time out. It is almost equal to a letter from home. By the way, speaking of papers—Do say to your Ma—that I had really forgotten, my promise to send her a Richmond paper, but hope she will excuse me. I have ordered the Richmond Examiner to be sent to my adress at home[;] she will get it soon—and then she will have plenty of news, as it is a daily paper. It is the best and most popular paper published in the City. Tell Mr Spradley to plant cotton in that field by his house, if he hears no more from me. I will now close and write a few lines to Bobbie—Good night my son[.] Give my love to all

Your Father

Letter 24   JBG to Leila Griffin

Head Qrs of the Legion
Feby 12th 1862

My Dearest Leila

This is the night of the week that I generally write to you— But will onlly write you a very short note, for I have a whitlow or what is called a bone fellon[1] on one of my fingers and I am suffering a great deal of pain from it. I know you will excuse me under the circumstances. It has been forming about three days—The Doctr says it will have to be opened tomorrow. It is very painful indeed, and as you may guess I am in no very pleasant mood. Except that my health is very good. I walked yesterday about ten miles on a stretch—Maj Connor and myself took a stroll up the Occoquan to take a little exercise, and we made about ten miles before we returned to camp.

We had a fine Dress Parrade this evening & the Legion made a better appearance than it has in a long time. Col Hampton made them a speech upon the subject of reenlisting.[2] His speech was very

---

LETTER 24

1. A whitlow or felon (called paronychia) is a small but bothersome abscess of the quick of a finger or toenail.

2. On 2 February 1862 Jefferson Davis had asked South Carolina to furnish an additional 12,000 enlistees to join the 6000 already in the Confederate army for the duration of the war. In order to meet this quota, the state needed to raise five new regiments and reenlist most of the twelve-month troops in Virginia, whose terms would expire in June. Hampton had also been author-

appropriate and well recieved, and I think will have a very happy effect on the command. I am inclined to think, now, that a majority of the Legion will reenlist for the war—that feeling seems to be increasing rapidly—More so since our recent defeats at Fort Henry[3] and Roanoke island.[4] Our People have no alternative but to fight the war through. I received a letter this evening from Sue, do present to her my thanks for it. Do present to your Uncle Billy and *Aunt* Helen[5] my congratulations on their *new born*.[6] Oh my Darling, how I wish you were here just at this time, to hear some splendid vocal music. A party of the men have just formed themselves quietly in rear of our quarters and are now serenading us. They sing beautifully, and I know you would enjoy it—for I really enjoy it myself although my finger is giving me

---

ized to increase the Legion to a brigade and had issued a call in South Carolina for enough men to fill two to four new regiments of infantry, each to have an artillery company and at least one cavalry company. Cauthen, *South Carolina Goes to War*, 144, and Cauthen, *Family Letters of the Three Wade Hamptons*, 83; OR, ser. 4, 1:902. Charleston *Daily Courier*, 10 Feb. 1862.

3. Fort Henry, poorly situated on the Tennessee River, was shelled by Federal ironclads and gunboats led by Flag Officer Andrew Foote on 6 February 1862 and forced to surrender while Ulysses S. Grant's infantry was still toiling through the mud to support the attack from the rear. Brig. Gen. Lloyd Tilghman temporarily saved the main garrison by dispatching it to the more defensible Fort Donelson on the Cumberland, but the fall of Fort Henry gave the Union forces an important water highway into Tennessee and opened the way for an advance southward. B&L, 1:368–72; Benjamin Franklin Cooling, *Forts Henry and Donelson: The Key to the Confederate Heartland* (Knoxville: Univ. of Tennessee Press, 1987), 101–21.

4. On 8 February 1862 Brig. Gen. Ambrose E. Burnside's 7500 men and an accompanying naval flotilla easily overcame the fewer than 2000 Confederates defending poorly fortified Roanoke Island, North Carolina. The Union thus gained control of the channels between Albermarle and Pamlico sounds and a strategic base from which to assault North Carolina. Even more important, the loss of Roanoke made a rear attack on Norfolk or Richmond a distinct and worrisome possibility. B&L, 1:660–70.

5. Dr. William M. Burt, Leila's uncle, had married Helen M. Eichelberger, his second wife, in 1858. According to the 1860 census, Helen was 22 years younger than William Burt and nine years younger than her new "niece," Leila. McClendon, *Edgefield Marriage Records*, 25.

6. Helen Harwood Burt was born in February and died ten months later on 5 December. McClendon, *Edgefield Death Notices*, 201.

[illegible]. They frequently give us a serenade. But My Darling you must really excuse me for my finger pains me so that I can write no more. They are now singing "They stole my child away"—Do give my love to all[.]

Your affectionate
Husband

Letter 25   JBG to Leila Griffin

Head Qrs of the Legion
February 16th 1862

My Darling

I recieved another one of your dear, kind, and affectionate letters, by yesterday's mail. I am happy to hear that you and the dear Children are well. And is it possible that our dear little Claude can walk all alone. I would be so delighted to see him. I dreamed one night, some time ago, before you wrote me he had commenced walking by a chair, that I saw him and Cally running about the house, and thought Claude could outrun Cally. I scarcely thought he would be able to walk so soon. I wish very much his feet could be operated on this Spring.[1] But I suspect you will not be willing to have it done during my absence. If it isnt done this spring, it must be done next fall. I was surprised my Darling, to find that you had been eight days without a letter from me. I assure you My Darling I average at least two letters a week, generally, I write on sunday and wednesday nights. I have lately recieved your letters very regularly. My Darling, I am *exceedingly* anxious to see you and my Dear Children, and hope to do so next month, if possible. But I wont set my heart on it too much for fear I may be disappointed. It is hard to tell what will be the condition

---

LETTER 25

1. Claude's affliction, clubfoot, is a congenital malformation of unknown cause; some experts think it has something to do with abnormal position of the fetus in the womb. About half of affected children have only one deformed foot and about half have the condition in both feet. Many children experience significant straightening of the foot with splinting and casting and are eventually able to walk. There are many surgical procedures based on the individual deformity.

of affairs, a month ahead. There is a great stir now among the Soldiers on the subject of reenlisting. Congress some time ago passed an act calling for the revolunteering of the twelve months troops, offering to give all who would revolunteer, fifty dollars bounty, and a furlough, so that each man might spend thirty days at home.[2] I understand that a great many are accepting the terms. And a good many have already gone home. I think all the companies in the Legion, except, perhaps one, will reorganize, and that one may too perhaps. The thing was working beautifully, until yesterday, when we recieved an order saying no more furloughs would be granted until further orders.[3] They had proposed to let twenty per cent of the whole force go home at a time, and when they returned, let others go. The order stopping the furloughs has somewhat stopped the volunteering, but I think it will be right again in a few days. One company in the Legion has already the number requisite for a reorganization, and several others are nearly full. I have no doubt that Gary's company will reenlist.[4] I think Gary

2. The Furlough and Bounty Act was passed on 11 December 1861, to take effect on 1 June 1862, and the reenlistment period was for three years or the duration of the war. In addition to the bounty and furlough, the act permitted companies to reorganize and elect their own company and field officers. After the reorganization, all vacated commissions were to be filled by promotion. James M. Matthews, ed., *Statutes at Large of the Provisional Government of the Confederate States of America from the Institution of the Government, February 8, 1861, to its Termination, February 18, 1862, Inclusive* (Richmond: S.M. Smith, 1864).

3. Johnston believed that granting enough leaves to stimulate heavy reenlistment would leave the army dangerously weakened just as the Federals would be launching a spring offensive, and he resented Secretary of War Judah P. Benjamin for sending recruiters among the troops and authorizing furloughs without consulting him. In order to keep the ranks from being depleted, Johnson instructed his generals to limit the number of furloughs granted in each command. On 12 February he told Brig. Gen. W.H.C. Whiting, who commanded the Occoquan Division in which Hampton's Legion was serving, to keep furloughs "as much below 20 percent as you please." Craig L. Symonds, *Joseph E. Johnston: A Civil War Biography* (New York: W.W. Norton, 1992), 136–37; OR, ser. 1, 5: 1057 (quotation), 1069.

4. Jack Tompkins, a member of Gary's company, wrote two days later that following the appeal of reenlistments, about 35 members of the Watson Guards had signed up for the duration of the war "if they could get the fur-

will be elected to a field office in the new organization. I believe I wrote you that Col Hampton is empowered by the President to organize a "Brigade Legion."[5] It will consist of four regiments of Infantry, of ten companies each, with one company of Artillery, and one of Cavalry attached to each regiment. The present Legion will doubtless be increased and form one of the four regiments. I know My Darling, you are very anxious to know what I, am going to do—And I'll tell you as well as I can. Of course, as I have said before, no one can see far enough in the future to tell what he will do four months hence. But I have looked at it from every side, and think now that, if I am alive, when my present term of enlistment expires I will go home, at least for a while. I feel that it is a duty I owe my wife and Children. I may be so situated that I cant go. But think now that I will. I may not be able to stay at home if I do go, but still my intention is to go and stay at least awhile. This you need not make public, but if you are asked what I am going to do—you may say that I want to go home if I can. I intend to do as I have always tried to do. Do what I conceive to be my duty, and care not for the consequences. My opinion is that by the time our term of enlistment is out, that the war will nearly if not quite be at an end. It will be either so, or it will by that time grow to be a *monster*. I wouldnt be surprised if we have some hard fighting to do before then. We have had several reverses lately—the last was

loughs forthwith." When the furloughs were cancelled, "a good many" of the signees said that they would not stay without the promised leave. Tompkins speculated that probably a third of the original company would reenlist and that the rest would be made up from new men. Lt. Benjamin Nicholson (see letter of 2 April 1862, note 1) was planning a trip to Edgefield during which he would sign up new recruits. Nearly all of Tompkins's fellow soldiers from the "Dark Corner" area of Edgefield District had so far declined to reenlist, even though they intended to stay in the army "for the war." They planned to serve out their twelve months and then return to Edgefield to reorganize and raise a Dark Corner company. The "Dark Corner" of Edgefield District was in the far northwest, bordering Georgia on the west and Abbeville District on the north. It began just above Scott's Ferry Road on the Savannah River and covered the area between the river and Stevens' Creek, extending on into Abbeville District to the Little River. J.W. Tompkins to Lizzie Tompkins, 18 Feb. 1862, Tompkins Family Papers, SCL. Chapman, *History of Edgefield*, 114–15.

5. The authorization appear in OR, ser 4, 1:902, 907.

the worst. But they are all except one, victories, which the Enemy cannot take much credit for, as they have been the result of their navy—and we have none.[6] Whenever they get out of reach of their gun boats we will thrash them again. My Darling, keep up your spirits—do the best you can, and be certain that I will go home to see you as soon as I can. Carry on every thing as best you can, and when I go home I will praise you a *heap,* or get Dr Muse to do it for me.

When I wrote you last I was suffering dreadfully with a bone felon. The next day the Doctr laid it open to the bone. And you ought to have seen what a Soldier I was. I laid my finger down on a table, and held it perfectly still—didnt move a muscle, until he had finished— Think you could have done that?[7] Do remember me to your Father,

---

6. Beginning in the middle of January 1862, the Confederates had suffered a series of setbacks in the West and off the North Carolina coast. On 19 January they lost a strategic battle at Logan's Cross Roads, Kentucky, the first Federal breakthrough across the line of defense for Kentucky. Fort Henry fell on 6 February and Roanoke Island on 8 February. On 10 February the Confederates lost another naval engagement at Elizabeth City, North Carolina, and the following day Union forces took control of Edisto Island, South Carolina. As Griffin was writing, Fort Donelson on the Cumberland River, the last defense against a full-fledged Federal invasion of Tennessee, was surrendering to Grant after a four-day siege. The Confederacy did have a small navy and an able secretary, Stephen R. Mallory. But of the ten existing naval yards in 1861, only two—Norfolk and Pensacola—were in the South, and the Confederacy could claim only ten ships, with a total of fifteen guns, when it organized in February 1861. Mallory initiated an innovative program of building ironclads, of which the *Merrimack/Virginia* was the celebrated prototype. However, the lack of raw materials, especially iron, compounded by the South's inadequate transportation system and a shortage of skilled labor, severely handicapped the shipbuilding program. Although the Confederacy managed to appropriate, build, and buy more than 130 ships during the course of the war, the Union amassed a fleet of 671 by 1865, and its superior naval strength contributed decisively to the outcome of the war. William N. Still, Jr., *Confederate Shipbuilding* (Athens: Univ. of Georgia Press, 1969), and *Iron Afloat: The Story of the Confederate Armorclads* (Nashville: Vanderbilt Univ. Press, 1971); McPherson, *Ordeal by Fire,* 173–75.

7. The longitudinal incision made to drain such an abscess is excruciatingly painful and today is performed under local anesthesia. This form of pain relief was not available in Griffin's time, and it is surprising that he was not given general anesthesia. See A.H. Crenshaw, ed., *Campbell's Operative Or-*

tell him I will write to him before long. Remember me to all our relatives and friends. Did your Uncle Billy ever recieve my letter? You ask me what was in the trunk that I sent home. I really dont remember what—not a great deal I think—All my summer socks, and those overshirts you made for me, and your little brush that I brought by mistake, and perhaps other little things—It is no great loss. Do give my love to all the Children and accept the same for yourself

from your Husband

Letter 26   JBG to Leila Griffin

Head Qrs of the Legion
February 19th 1862

My Dear Leila

Well, my Darling, I have at last recieved my trunk, it came to day—Just four weeks from the time you started it. My Darling you just tried yourself to see how many nice things you could send. I opened the trunk to day (it came about twelve O Clock) and had a regular party. Invited the whole mess and Capt Gary, Lieut Tompkins and Ball from Laurens,[1] a member of Gary's company. I cut one of the cakes, which was beautiful and very nice, and opened the apple cordial. All agreed in pronouncing it *splendid*. You were very highly complimented, while the cake & cordial was rapidly consumed. Every thing came perfectly safe and sound, notwithstanding the length of time it had been coming. The sausages were somewhat moulded, but I dont think are at all damaged, at least I hope not, for I am really *longing* for some. We also sampled the nice brandy peaches, I told the party that they were put up by your own fair hands, and four years ago at that. They were really very nice. Col Hampton is laid up in his

---

thopaedics, 4 vols. (St. Louis: C.V. Mosby, 1987), 496 (with drawings of the operation).

LETTER 26

1. Pvt. Beaufort Watts Ball, who came from a wealthy family in Laurens District, adjoining Edgefield on the east, enlisted at Richmond on 10 July 1861. He was on the sick list in August and discharged for rheumatism on 28 August 1862. He later became adjutant for the Legion. Sturkey, Watson Guard Rolls.

tent with the mumps.[2] (I tell him he is the largest case of mumps, I ever saw) So that he could not participate in the feast. I, sent him, however, a share of the good things. My darling every thing you sent is really a treat, but I believe I appreciate more than any thing else, the nice butter. I can eat it with a relish, and have the satisfaction of knowing it is *clean* and nice. We had such a nice lunch and enjoyed it so much, that we didnt have dinner until five O Clock, and it being a dark evening we had to have a candle lit. I suppose you will think that we are quite aristocratic. And so we are. Our usual meal hours are as follows, Breakfast from nine to ten (Dark rainy mornings from ten to eleven.[)] Dinner from three to four, *tea* from eight to nine. Dont you think that is rather aristocratic. We sampled, at dinner, your catsup—it is splendid. Every thing is nice *very nice*, ham[,] biscuit and all. For all of which my Darling will please accept the sincere thanks of her husband, and also of the whole mess. I am also obliged to you for the clothing you sent. I didnt need any thing except the towels and handkerchiefs, I have lost some that I had. The shirts you sent are very pretty, I will wear them after the cold weather is gone. I wear nothing now but the calicoe. The comfort is very fine but so far we have had plenty of cover, it will however be no drudge unless we have to retreat from the Yanks. In that case it might be in the way. The Majr. and I now have quite an extensive wardrobe, If the Yanks were to take our camp they would make money out of us. The Maj'r. recieved a box, from home a few days ago, and in it came our over-coats, at last—now that the winter is nearly over. But they are *stunners* I tell you, made of English cloth, Confederat grey—but such a price[—]how much do you suppose—Seventy dollars in cash, and then two dollars and a half, freight—So much for the fire. Do my Darling, give my love to Minnie and tell her I am greatly obliged to her for the nett cap—but see here, it looks to me like a baby's bonnet, hasnt she made some mistake, or does she suppose I have a baby out here to wear it. Whilst I am speaking of presents do let me tell you of one I recieved from Miss Carrie Connor, sister of the Maj'r. She sent me a very pretty, (I dont know what the name is) but I call it a dressing

2. Hampton's illness in February was considered serious enough that John-ston briefly considered transferring command of the Occoquan temporarily to John Bell Hood. OR, ser. 1, 5:1082.

case—It is a linen sack, to hang up in the tent, with pockets to hold a comb and brush, tooth brush, soap, &c—There was a nice cake of soap in one pocket and a box of tooth powder in an other. I acknowledged the reciept of it in a very *pretty* little note. My Darling, I would be pleased if you would reciprocate the favour, by making a little present to Maj'r C—This is a very pretty as well as a very useful present. She sent it in the Majr's box, and directed it to me with Miss Carrie Connor's compliments. My Darling the Mail has just come and the papers bring the unwelcome news of the capture of Fort Donnelson [sic] by the Federals.[3] Our reverses have been frequent of late—It seems that we fought gallantly at the Fort—but the full particulars I havent seen. Our defeat at Roanoke was really disgraceful.[4] Well, I

---

3. Although the defenders inflicted serious damage on Federal gunboats and Nathan Bedford Forrest's dismounted cavalry fought with distinction, Fort Donelson, on the Cumberland River in Tennessee, surrendered on 16 February, after a four-day amphibious siege directed by Ulysses S. Grant and Flag Officer Andrew Foote. Fort Donelson was only twelve miles from Fort Henry, which had been forced to capitulate ten days earlier; the combined loss was a serious blow to the Confederacy. Federal control of the Tennessee and Cumberland Rivers left the entire state of Tennessee vulnerable to a Federal drive southward and made the defense of Nashville impossible. On 23 February 1862, Nashville became the first Confederate capital to be occupied by the Yankees. (See also following letter, note 1.) B&L, 1:389–429; Cooling, *Forts Henry and Donelson*, 122–223.

4. Ambrose Burnside's troops had easily overrun hastily fortified Roanoke Island, overwhelming the small defending force and capturing most of it. (See letter of 12 February.) Brig. Gen. Henry A. Wise, a former Virginia governor who had been sent to secure the island, had repeatedly petitioned Maj. Gen. Benjamin Huger, district commander at Norfolk, for reinforcements and supplies; after his requests were denied, he appealed directly to Secretary of War Benjamin, who also failed to act. The shortage of munitions was not widely known outside the government, which feared the effect that such a disclosure would have on morale, so when Roanoke fell it appeared that the Confederates had lost because of War Department incompetence. Wise, whose dashing young son was among the casualties, was especially bitter; he and the press castigated Huger and Benjamin. A motion was introduced in the Confederate House of Representatives requesting Benjamin's resignation, and a congressional committee was formed to investigate the Roanoke fiasco. President Davis reluctantly removed Benjamin from the War Department on 17 March, and made him secretary of state. The committee's report concluded that

hope the day of triumph is not far distant. I have no other news to write—It has been raining all day as usual.

Do remember me kindly to your Father and family, also to all friends. Give my love to all the Children, and accept for yourself the warmest love of your devoted

Jimmie

Letter 27   JBG to Leila Griffin

Camp of the Legion
February 26th 1862

My Darling Leila

I am delighted, my Darling to learn by your last letter that Minnie has at last "Come through". And I am also pleased, and tender my congratulations that she has another Boy.[1] Notwithstanding you all were anxious for her to have a daughter. I really think she should be proud that she has another Boy. This is the time, above all others, that *men* should be raised. And this too, is the time above all others when females deserve sympathy. I assure you, I feel, far more anxiety about my dear little daughters, than I do about my Boys. For while men can manage to work for themselves, and can fight the battles of their Country if necessary, Females are very dependent. True, they too can do a great deal, and, 'tis true that our Southern Ladies have done and are still acting a conspicuous part in this war[.] In many instances (to the shame of our Sex be it said) a much bolder and more

---

Huger and Benjamin were negligent in handling operations at Roanoke; they should have reinforced Wise or ordered him to abandon the position in order to save his command. Craig M. Simpson, *A Good Southerner: The Life of Henry A. Wise of Virginia* (Chapel Hill: Univ. of North Carolina Press, 1985), 265–68, 270; Robert Douthat Meade, *Judah P. Benjamin, Confederate Statesman* (New York: Oxford Univ. Press, 1943), 219–29; Eli N. Evans, *Judah P. Benjamin: The Jewish Confederate* (New York: Free Press, 1988). Wise's report, with his correspondence to Huger and Benjamin, appears in OR, ser. 1, 9:122–70, followed by "Report of the Investigating Committee, Confederate House of Representatives," 183–90.

LETTER 27

1. J. Clarence Muse was Minnie and Julius Muse's second child.

manly part than many men. But still, when it comes to the physical test, of course, they are helpless. It is on this account, that I think the Parents should congratulate themselves on the birth of a son rather than a daughter. We cannot see, My Darling, into the future, but I trust & have confidance in our people to believe, that if the unprincipled North shall persist in her policy of Subjugating the South, that we, who are able to resist them, will continue to do so, until we grow old and worn out in the service, and that then, our Sons will take the arms from our hands, and spend their lives, if necessary, in battling for Liberty and independence. As for my part, If this trouble should not be settled satisfactorily to us sooner—I would be proud of the thought that our youngest Boy—Yes Darling little Jimmie, will after awhile be able and I trust willing to take his Father's place in the field, and fight until he dies, rather than, be a Slave, *Yea* worse than a Slave to Yankee Masters—Have you ever anticipated, My Darling, what would be our probable condition, if we should be conquered in this war? The picture is really too horrible to contemplate. In the first place, the tremendous war tax, which will have accumulated, on the northern Government, would be paid entirely and exclusively by the property belonging to the Southerners. And more than this we would be an humbled, down trodden and disgraced, people. Not entitled to the respect of any body, and have no respect for ourselves. In fact we would be the most wretched and abject people on the face of the Earth. Just be what our Northern Masters say we may be. Would you, My Darling, desire to live, if this was the case? would you be willing to leave your Children under such a government? No—I know you would sacrifice every comfort on earth, rather than submit to it. Excuse me, My Darling, I didnt intend to, run off in this strain. You might think, from my painting this horrid picture to you, that I had some doubts as to whether we might not have to experience it. But No, I havent the most remote idea that we will. I think our people will arouse themselves, shake off the lethargy, which seems now to have possession of them, and will meet the issue like *men*. We must see that we have *all*—Yes our all—staked upon the result—And we are obliged to succeed and we will do it. Just at this time the Enemy appears to have advantage of us. But this is no more than we have, all along, had of him, until lately. He did not succombe and give up for it—and shall we, Who have so much more to fight for than he has,

do so? I am completely surprised and mortified at the feeling manifested by our people at this time. But they will soon rally and come
with redoubled energy. Our Soldiers too, or rather our Generals have
got to learn to fight better. The idea, of a Genl surrendering with
12000 men under his command, is a species of bravery and Generalship, which I do not understand.[2] I wish Congress would pass a law
breaking an officer of his commission who surrenders. I recieved a
letter last night from your Uncle Billy—was very glad to hear from
him. If you havent sent my holsters and boot legs—you neednt send
them as I dont now need them. I also recieved a letter last night from
Sue, will write to her soon. My Darling tell Spradley, not to commence planting corn early[.] My land will not admit of early planting,
of either corn or cotton. I generally, commence planting corn from
the 15th to the 20th of March, and cotton about the same time in
april. I see that Congress is about passing a bill, to impose a heavy tax
on cotton raised this year[.][3] If they pass it—I wish no land planted in
cotton except the new ground, and the field next to the overseers
house, all the ballance planted in corn. I will write you, however in
time. My Darling, Now is the time to bring out all your courage—
Do not become despondent—Dont matter what *alarmists* and Croak-

---

2. At Fort Donelson Brig. Gen. Simon Bolivar Buckner surrendered the
entire garrison of approximately 12,000 men to Ulysses S. Grant, who had
refused him any terms except unconditional and immediate surrender. Delighted to have a military hero at last, northerners boasted that the Federal
commander's initials stood for "Unconditional Surrender" Grant.

3. On 28 February of the preceding year, the Confederate Congress had
passed an act levying a tax of ⅛ of a cent per pound export duty on all cotton
shipped after 1 August 1861. The revenue was intended to pay the interest on
a $15 million loan funded by an issue of 8 percent bonds. The Confederate
government hoped to raise $20 million through the export tax, but the tight-
ening Federal blockade so restricted shipments to Europe that only about
$30,000 was ever raised. Although treasury secretaries lobbied to have this
miniscule tax raised, opposition from the planter class kept Congress from
increasing it, even when the Confederacy's finances were desperate. Richard
Cecil Todd, *Confederate Finance* (Athens: Univ. of Georgia Press, 1954), 25–
30, 125; Stanley Lebergott, "Why the South Lost: Commercial Purpose in the
Confederacy, 1861–1865," *Journal of American History* 70 (June 1983): 58–
74. Lebergott argues that the Confederacy contributed to its own defeat by
refusing to disturb the interest of the planter class.

ers may say—take advice from him whom you *know* will advise you for the best. Keep up your spirits and your courage, and the clouds will soon pass away, and sun shine will return—My sheet is full—and I will close by begging to be remembered to all—My love to My Children and my Darling Leila

from your Husband

I enclose a few Virginia Cabbage seed—and a sprig of spruce pine. It grows here beautifully. G— Tell Willie to write often

4 *Retreat to the Rappahannock*

Letters 28 through 36
27 February through 6 April 1862

Late in February, Federal movements on the Maryland shore indicated that General George B. McClellan's army was at last preparing to take the offensive. The Confederate forces on the Occoquan were ordered to fall back forty miles to Fredericksburg. Although he disliked the idea of a retreat, Griffin assured Leila, who was "rather down hearted" after receiving the news, that the withdrawal was a sound strategic maneuver.

The new line of defense on the Rappahannock River forced McClellan to abandon his original design of outflanking Johnston's army. While Griffin waited and filled his letters with instructions on spring planting, Federal troops began massing for an amphibious landing farther down the Virginia coast, below Yorktown. By early April Griffin was again under marching orders as Johnston prepared a counter-movement.

Letter 28   JBG to Leila Griffin

[The left edge of this letter is badly frayed. Reconstructed words are bracketed.]

Head Qrs of the Legion
Feby 27th 1862

My Darling Wife
    I write to inform you that we are now under marching orders—We

will fall back to Frederic[k]sburg.[1] This is a *profound secret*, but it may be made public by the time you recieve this letter. If it is not, you must not say a word about it. For circumstances may change and the order may not be carried out. And in that event, of course it [ou]ght not to be made known, that it was contemplated. It is all important that every movement [of] an army should be secret, lest the Enemy should [k]now the contemplated move. The Soldiers are never [a]llowed to know when are *[sic]* where they are going. [I] dont know yet, what the programme is, but my [opin]ion is, that Burnside[2] is threatening to attack Richmond [a]nd so many of our troops are called to Tennessee [tha]t it is considered necessary to draw back the army of the Potomac to protect Richmond. If this conjecture is correct, we will abandon Centerville and Manassas and carry all the troops in the

---

LETTER 28

1. Johnston had advised Jefferson Davis as early as 22 November that if the Federals decided to advance toward Richmond the Confederates would not be able to hold the line on Bull Run and the Occoquan against them. He was also worried that his right would be outflanked if the large Federal force camped on the Maryland shore of the Potomac, opposite Dumfries, was secretly reinforced and ferried across to Virginia; such a move would put the Yankees two days' march closer to Richmond than the Army of Northern Virginia at Manassas. When reports of unusual Federal activity on the Maryland shore suggested that McClellan was finally getting ready to advance, Johnston had given Brig. Gen. William H.C. Whiting, commander of the Occoquan division, confidential orders to be ready to fall back to Fredericksburg at his signal. Whiting relayed the secret order to Hampton, and the army prepared to move to the south bank of the Rappahannock. There it could meet a Union advance from either Manassas or Fredericksburg, or be deployed against any alternative attack made via the lower Rappahannock or Fort Monroe on the peninsula. OR, ser. 1, 5:529, 1063; 51, pt. 2:1072–73; Joseph E. Johnston, *Narrative of Military Operations Directed during the Late War Between the States* (1879; rpt., Bloomington: Indiana Univ. Press, 1959), 101–2.

2. Brig. Gen. Ambrose Everett Burnside (1824–1881), whose famous sidewhiskers made his name immortal, was in charge of the highly successful amphibious expedition to secure a Union base of operations on the North Carolina coast. His victory at Roanoke Island had given the Federals control of the river outlets of every North Carolina port except Wilmington and had

direction of [that] place. All the troops on the South side of the [Occo-quan will go to Fredericsburg. When there we [will] be within three hours ride of Richmond on [the] rail road. We will have to march to Fred[ricksburg], a distance of about forty miles. This [letter torn] no doubt is very good policy, for if we [letter torn] have a fight here and conquer the Enemy, it would be almost a barren victory[.] We could not follow it up, for the Enemy would have but a short distance to travel before he would cover himself behind his fortifications and there the pursuit would end. While if he leaves his fortifications and marches down on Richmond, if we can lick him that far from home, we can pursue him and cut him to pieces. But notwithstanding all this I dont like, a bit to fall back from here. It looks so much like retreating from the Enemy. And then too—We have done so much work here, that I do hate to gi[ve] it up, without a fight— But the first and great[est] duty of a Soldier is to obey his officers without a [letter torn] and the same holds good for an officer with [letter torn] Superiors. So that I will try to retreat as gracef[ully] as I can. I have no idea that our Army fe[els] any apprehension of the foe in its front, if I [letter torn] that I would feel much worse, but I am su[re] this is not the case. My Darling, I am happy [letter torn] tell you that my health is still very good. I [letter torn] to day, and would you believe it, I weighed 16[?] [letter torn] That is more than I ever weighed before in [letter torn] life. So My Darling you see I am not Star[ving.] I have no other news of importance to [letter torn] and as I wrote you last night I will now [letter torn]. You may direct your letters to Fredericsburg [letter torn] you recieve this, unless I direct you otherwi[se.] [Letter torn] best love to you and My Children, and [letter torn] [re]-gards to all friends

Your Jimmie

---

opened up the possibility of a rear attack on Richmond, which the Confederates feared might be his next move. Instead, Burnside remained in North Carolina until July, when he left to join the Army of the Potomac. William Marvel, *Burnside* (Chapel Hill: Univ. of North Carolina Press, 1991).

Letter 29   JBG to Leila Griffin

Head Qrs of the Legion
Camp near Fredericsburg
March 12th 1862

My Darling Wife

I now propose to fulfill my promise to write you an account of our march to this place. I had written you before of the contemplated move, so that you, of course, were not surprised that it had taken place. Notwithstanding we had recieved orders more than a week beforehand to be ready to move at any time, and had been very busy all the time in making preparations, yet when the order came we were not very ready. I had no idea of the trouble to move a command. Col Hampton recieved the order about four oclock, on friday evening, to start his wagons that night, and his troops by day light the next morning.[1] We were scarce of transportation, and our Qr Mastr had been gone to Manassas, two days, for the purpose of getting wagons. About night we heard that he had returned without procuring any. So we began to make arrangements to move without wagons, at least with but few—that is we expected to carry what men could and destroy the remainder.[2] Some days before we had ordered our men to send all their surplus baggage to the rear

[remainder of letter lost]

LETTER 29

1. Whiting had received the marching order from Johnston at midday on 7 March and began preparing to move his troops out at daylight. OR, ser. 1, 5:529–33.

2. Scant forage and an entire winter of hauling supplies long distances over mired roads had taken a heavy toll on draft animals and wagons. The Legion had only seven wagons when Hampton received the order to move, and Whiting dispatched an additional 24 as soon as they reached his headquarters at 9 p.m. on 7 March. Due to the wretched condition of the roads, it took seven and a half hours for these wagons to reach Hampton, eight miles away. The inadequate transportation forced Hampton to destroy what could not be carried—a small quantity of ammunition, 59 tents, and all private baggage. Maj. Stephen D. Lee, appointed chief of staff a few days before, was in charge of evacuating the artillery at Bacon Race Church, the Sixteenth North Carolina regiment at Wolf Run, and the Fourteenth Georgia at Davis' Ford, Col. J.J. Archer oversaw the withdrawal of the Texas Brigade. All commanders were

Letter 30   JBG to Leila Griffin

> Head Qrs of the Legion
> Camp Bartow March 17th 1862
> [near Fredericksburg]

My Darling Leila

Again I take my seat to write a few lines to my Darling Wife. I miss your dear, kind letters very much indeed. I have no complaint to make to you for it. I am well satisfied that you have written me regularly as usual, but the letters havent yet found me. I am expecting every day to recieve a lot of them. Col Hampton telegraphed to Richmond the day after we came, that our Post Office, at present is Fredericksburg. I have no doubt that they will all find us after awhile. I shall expect to get a letter from you in a day or two, in answer to the first one I wrote you after my arrival here, as it ought not to take a letter more than three days to come through. I have been here a week nearly and have but once been outside of my own Camp. Yesterday being sunday and no Drills—I went into the Town. It is rather a pretty Town situated on the bank of the Rappahannock.[1] It has, I think about six thousand Inhabitants. We have in this vicinity a pretty large body of Troops—I understand about fifteen thousand. My own *private* opinion is, from the little examination I have made of this country, that we cannot hold this place, if we remain where we are. The hills on the other side of the river entirely command those on this side. I dont know whether it will be attempted to fight the Enemy here, or advance to meet them on the other side, or whether the Army will fall back still farther—My opinion is, between you and me—that we

---

forced to destroy military property for want of transportation. Their reports, including Whiting's defense of the property destruction, are printed in OR, ser. 1, 5:528–36.

LETTER 30

1. Pvt. John Coxe wrote that the Legion camped "on the lovely wooded heights some two miles beyond the city . . . We drilled much, but had a good time at Fredericksburg, as we were allowed to go into the city quite often and greatly enjoyed the plays at the theater, then known as Citizen's Hall. We visited all the interesting places, including the former home of George Washington's mother." John Coxe, "With Hampton in the Peninsular Campaign," *Confederate Veteran* 29 (Nov.–Dec. 1921): 414.

will do the latter. But this is only a conjecture of mine, and of course dont wish you to mention it. I presume we wont fight them until we get advantage of position. Genl Johns[t]on is at Rappahannock Station, with the main body of the Army.[2] Which is some twenty five miles above us. I thought My Darling when we fell back here, although I said nothing about it, that I would have an opportunity to run home, if it was only for a few days—But My Darling I am afraid I cant do it. I tell you this candidly, for I have always tried to deal with you in candour. It has always been my desire never to decieve or mislead you. And I have been well repaid for acting thus—for you have frequently complimented me for it. I have told you this, honestly because, from present appearances, I think so—If, however, I think I can do myself justice by leaving, I shall most certainly do so, if it is only for a very few days. But My Dearest, if I am deprived of that great pleasure, I hope I shall be rewarded for the privation. I can only console myself with the hope, that the good Lord will continue to preserve and protect me, until the end of my term of enlistment, as He has kindly done so far—and that He will then permit me to go *home* once more, to see those who lie so very near my heart. I have often thought My Darling, that I have been anxious to see my Dear Family—But my Darling I have never had that anxiety so fully developed before, as I have now. I count, not only the months but the weeks and even the days that separate me from those I love so much. My Darling there is nothing on this earth, (except inability) that could hold me away from you and our Dear little children, save the great cause, which now engages the mind of every Patriot in our Country. I feel My Darling that you, will give me credit for it, although I know it will be a painful suspense to you. But if God will, in His mercy spare my life—the time will soon roll round—It is now only a little more than two months—and then My Darling I hope to see you. Oh for the time to come. Let me beseech you My Darling, by the Love

---

2. Johnston's 23,000 troops were at Culpeper, west and slightly north of Fredericksburg, where Maj. Gen. Theophilus H. Holmes commanded the 12,000 troops of the right flank. On 17 March Johnston informed Jefferson Davis that he was moving the left wing of the army south of the Rapidan to be able to communicate with Fredericksburg, and that he expected the First and Second Divisions to cross the Rapidan the next day. OR, ser. 1, 5:1101–5; 11, pt. 3: 400–401; 51, pt. 2: 504; Freeman, *Lee's Lieutenants*, 2:142.

you bear to me and our dear little ones—not to become despondent and low spirited. Collect more and more fortitude. Times may grow a great deal worse than they now are—and still we can stand it—And even then not go through what our Grandparents went through, when they were struggling for the same thing—that we are now fighting for. Be calm My Darling, for if you allow yourself to become excited and despondent, you will only add to your troubles, without benefitting yourself in the least. Be prudent, cautious and learn to be courageous. Dont grieve at any thing—but school yourself to believe that everything happens for the best—And that no matter how bad any thing appears—that it might be a great deal worse—Learn My Darling to look on the brightest side of every picture. The prospect is doubtless gloomy at this time but I am sure the clouds will clear away before long—and all will again be sun shine. I will continue to write to you My Darling, as often as I can. But be not uneasy if you do not recieve my letters regularly—For we may be moved off at any time and then it may be so that I cannot write regularly—You can continue to direct your letters to this place until I direct you otherwise. Tell Spradley to plant corn in the new ground, and to be sure to plant every foot of land in peas. He will have no land in cotton except the Lindsay field—Tell him to put that in splendid order—and plant all the ballance of the land in corn and peas.[3] Tell your Man Peter to pay good attention to my watermelon patch. I hope to find you with a nice garden when I get home. I shall want a *heep* of vegetables. Give my love to Sue and tell her to write to me. Also tell Willie & Bobbie not to expect me to answer all their letters—Give my best love to all My Darling Children and Kiss them for me every day. My love to your Father and all the family—and my kindest regards to all my Friends—I send you twenty dollars more—If you need more money write me[.] Good night My Love

Your Jimmie

3. On 12 March Governor Francis Pickens had issued a proclamation calling on South Carolinians to reduce cotton acreage by four-fifths. He urged them to plant enough grain and other provisions to feed themselves and the army in the field. That spring southerners planted only one-half of the usual cotton acreage and devoted the rest to food crops. *Journals of the South Carolina Executive Councils of 1861 and 1862* (Columbia: South Carolina Department of Archives and History, 1956), 306; McPherson, *Battle Cry of Freedom*, 384.

Having more baggage than I can carry, I have sent the big trunk you
sent me back—You will find it in the Express Office in Augusta—It
may take some time to get there[.] I will send the key by private hands
or in a letter, soon.

Letter 31   JBG to Leila Griffin

Head Qrs of the Legion
Camp Bartow March 20th 1862

My Dearest Leila

About two weeks have elapsed since I have recieved a letter from
My Darling. I am expecting, every day to recieve my letters that were
sent to Manassas, but so far have been disappointed. I recieved a letter
yesterday from Sis—which was directed to Manassas. It was dated the
13 inst. and I doubt if it went there. But was directed here from Richmond. I was sorry to learn that she has been quite sick. She wrote me
that Doctr Harrington had gone to Mississippi. She also informed me
that Sallie Fair was to be married that night to Mr. Rutherford, her
old Beau.[1] Hers is the only letter I have recieved since I have been
here. It seems to have been a very long time since I heard from you
My Darling. I have been getting letters so regularly from you and Sue
for a long time that I miss them very much. I hope however, I wont
have to wait much longer now, before they will come to me regularly
again. I am quite uneasy about Minnie, as you informed me in the
last letter I recieved from you, that she was quite sick. I trust she may
be entirely recovered ere this. And that she and the Doctr and their
little Boys may be enjoying fine health, and all the comforts of a
happy and prosperous (Perhaps I should have said *prolifick*) family. Do
present my kindest regards to them and tell them that when they cant
employ themselves better, I would be happy to have them write to
me. I recieved a letter from Sue the day before we left our old camp—

LETTER 31

1. No notice of this wedding appeared in the Edgefield *Advertiser,* nor in
McClendon, *Edgefield Marriage Records,* nor in Barbara R. Langdon, *Edgefield County Marriages, 1769–1880, Implied in Edgefield County, S.C. Probate Records* (Barnwell, S.C.: Langdon & Langdon Genealogical Research,
1990).

in which she said your Father had been suffering a great deal lately with Rheumatism[.] I was very sorry to hear it, and hope that he has entirely recovered before this time—Wonder if he ever recieved the letter I wrote him? I wrote a letter, some time ago to your Uncle Moody,[2] but I never recieved an answer. I seldom get letters from anyone except Sue and your dear Self—yes, and my Sons, and occasionally one from Sis. But there is one consolation in it— I dont have them to answer. And besides My Darling, I had rather get a letter from you than half a dozen from any one else—Not that I "love them less, but yours more". I am anxious to hear My Darling if you have recieved all the money I have sent you in my letters. I have sent you one hundred dollars in all—Twenty dollars at a time—Four times to you and one twenty I enclosed in a letter to Sue. I fear one of them was lost, as it went to the office the day we fell back. I have never heard My Darling whether you have recieved your Richmond paper— I ordered it sent to you some time ago.

Every thing is as quiet now about here, as if we were hundreds of miles away from the Enemy—How long it will remain so, I cant tell. I assure you it is quite a relief to me to feel when I lie down at night, that there is no danger of being called up, by an alarm before day. This is a luxury that I did not enjoy for a long time before I left our old camp. We are doing nothing now but drilling. I suspect we will have to go to work again in a few days, in building batteries. I understand our Generals have decided to hold this line, and think they can do it successfully. I hope they can[;] they, of course are much more competent judges than I am. We have a fine body of troops here and they are in good fighting *trim*. The Legion is better drilled now than it has ever been. The change of water has produced some diarrhoea amongst them. But with this exception, which I think will not last long, the health is very good. My own health, I am happy to say is still very fine. I believe I am about as *tough* as any of them. But one

---

2. Moody Burt was the fourth of the five Burt brothers and the one about whom least is known. Although he is not listed in the 1860 census index for either South Carolina or Georgia, his obituary noted that he was a resident of Columbia County, Georgia, and had represented it in the state legislature. Obituary of Major Moody Burt [1874], clipping from unidentified newspaper, Griffin Scrapbook and Account Book.

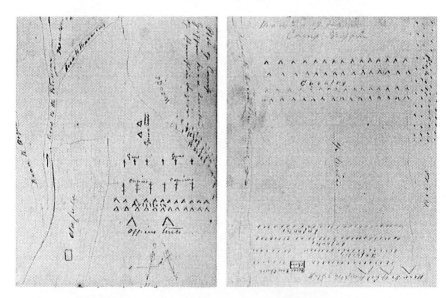

Sergeant Wilmot Walter Curry, a civil engineer serving in the Washington Mounted
Artillery, Hampton Legion, kept a diary from June through November 1861 that he illustrated with drawings of camp life and military activities. These and the following three
Curry drawings are reproduced from the Wilmot Walter Curry Diary with permission of
the Center for American History, University of Texas at Austin. Curry's 1861 sketches of
Camp Griffin, on the Occoquan River, Virginia, near Wolf Run Shoals, show the relative positions of the infantry, cavalry, and artillery and Hampton's staff headquarters.

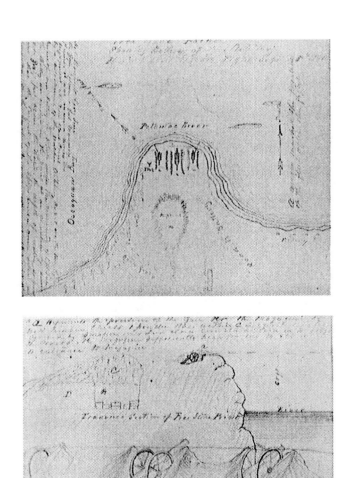

Hampton Legion batteries on the Potomac River, overlooking Freestone Point, erected to prevent Federal ships from passing up the river to Washington, D.C.

On October 2, 1861, Curry visited the batteries and "amused myself while there sketching the Lincolnite war vessels as they now stand."

Photo credits for the following family pictures: The families of Mary Dolorita and Jean Marie Cannon; Mary Elliott Gunter; Jim Griffin Gunter; and Jack L. Gunter.
James Benjamin Griffin, c. 1850.

James Benjamin Griffin, c. 1852.

James Benjamin Griffin, from a picture made at the time of his marriage to Leila Burt, February 22, 1853. This is a miniature mounted in a gold brooch. According to the Griffins' granddaughters, Mrs. Griffin wore it every day as long as she lived.

James Benjamin Griffin and Eliza "Leila" Griffin. This is their wedding picture of February 22, 1853. James was twenty-eight years old and Eliza twenty-four.

Captain Eugene Burt (1797-1881),
c. 1847

Fanny Eugene Griffin, oldest
daughter of Colonel James
Benjamin and Leila Griffin.
Born December 31, 1855;
died 1891. Photo c. 1873

Claude Eugene (right) and Francis Calhoun Griffin (below), twin sons of James Benjamin and Leila Griffin, born October 30, 1859, in Edgefield, South Carolina. Photos c. 1869.

Annie Diomede Griffin, born March 23, 1857. Daughter of Colonel James Benjamin and Leila Griffin. Photo c. 1900.

Moody Burt Griffin, born May 23, 1858. Son of James Benjamin and Leila Griffin. Photo c. 1878.

From left to right: boy standing with shotgun, Willie Griffin, son of
Robert Henry Burt Griffin and Etta Burt; man seated with big hat,
James Hampton Griffin; little girl touching shotgun, Bessie Burt
Griffin, and little girl seated by shotgun, Minnie Lee Griffin, two
daughters of James Hampton Griffin; woman with glasses, Ida Elliott
Griffin, wife of James H. Griffin; girl standing with white bonnet,
unknown; woman seated with hat, Mary Carlock, Penn Street neighbor; boy with apron, hat, and skillet, Roy Griffin, son of Bob and
Etta; woman holding child, Leila Rosalie Griffin, daughter of Bob
and Etta, child unknown; man with hat, sitting, Will Carlock, Penn
Street neighbor; boy with hat, standing, unknown; man seated in
front of tree with shotgun, unknown; boy seated by tree, unknown;
lady with hand on tree, Mary Mayless, cousin of Will and Mary; man
with black hat and vest, standing, Claude Griffin, son of Colonel J.
B. Griffin. Photo taken about 1898 near the old Colonel Griffin
house at 904 Penn Street, Fort Worth, Texas. The Trinity River is just
west of the old house, but the cliffs no longer exist due to road and
bridge construction.

Standing, left to right: (Little) Leila, daughter of Robert
Henry Burt Griffin and Etta Burt; Ida Elliott, wife of James
Hampton Griffin; Bessie Burt Griffin Gunter, daughter of
James Hampton Griffin and Ida Elliott Griffin; Helen Norris,
distant relative of the Griffin family; Minnie Lee Griffin Can-
non, daughter of James Hampton Griffin and Ida Elliott Grif-
fin; Francis Calhoun Griffin, son of James Benjamin Griffin,
twin brother of Claude. Seated, left to right: Annie Diomede
Griffin, daughter of James Benjamin Griffin; Eliza "Leila"
Burt Griffin, wife of Colonel James Benjamin Griffin; Rosie
Ferie, wife of Francis Calhoun Griffin. Photo was taken about
1905, on front porch of 904 Penn Street.

The Griffin family at their last home, 904 Penn Street, Fort
Worth, Texas, c. 1880.

thing My Darling, I am sorry for, entirely on your account, and that is, I am growing quite *grey*—At least so my friends *say*. And to tell you the truth I can see them shining in my head. This may be explained in one of two ways. Either that it is the result of trouble caused by being separated so long from those whom I love—or else it results from having no one to pull out the intruders as they make their appearance. Now which do you think it is? I suspect Sue would say the latter. My Darling if you were here, you would see the most magnificant sight in the way of Soldiers that you ever saw—Genl Whiting[3] had a brigade review yesterday. He reviewed four regiments and two batteries—It was a beautiful sight. He proposes to review Col Hampton's brigade in a few days—I wish you could witness it. Willie and Bobbie would nearly take *fits* over it—if they could see it. Genl Whiting is pretty strict—brings us down to oats. The men abuse him a good deal—but I think it is a good thing. Volunteers always abuse an Officer if he does his duty, and enforces discipline. But it amounts to nothing. Of one thing I am fully convinced, that an army undisciplined is very unreliable and almost worthless. Men must respect and fear their Officers, to be very effective. By the way have they drafted any one from Edgefield to fill out these five new regiments—I hope not[4]—I hope our District at least—will respond to every call, made upon her for troops, without a draft, even if it takes her last man who is able to bear arms to do it. However, I dont know if drafting isnt about the most equitable way after all—It places all on the same footing. I see *His Excellency*, The Governor and his Council[5] have de-

---

3. Brig. Gen. William Henry Chase Whiting (1824–1865) of Mississippi was second in command at Fredericksburg, under Maj. Gen. Theophilus H. Holmes.

4. See letter of 12 February, note 1.

5. Francis W. Pickens (1805–1869) was governor of South Carolina from 1860 to 1862. A cousin of John C. Calhoun, the son of Andrew Pickens, Jr. (the first governor elected from the upcountry), and the father-in-law of Matthew Calbraith Butler, Pickens was one of Edgefield's richest planters; his lavish Edgewood Plantation was a showplace of the district. Griffin may have shared the prevailing low opinion of the arrogant former Congressman and ambassador to Russia, who had been unpopular from the earliest months of his term. Pickens had been roundly criticized for failing to order the immediate seizure of the Charleston Harbor forts after South Carolina left the Union,

cided to supply all demands on our State, by Conscription, after to day. And to that end proposes to enroll all the troops now in service for a [no] less period than the war.[6] Hope he wont draft any of us before we get home. But I rather approve of the scheme. If our people wont volunteer to fight for their Liberty and their all—Why they ought to be made to do it. And it should bear equally on all, as near as can be. My Darling, it is now late at night—every body near me are asleep. It is a cold rainy stormy night—a Splendid night for sleeping— If I could only sleep with my Darling Wife. But that being impossible I must beg you to give my love to all my friends & relatives—and especially to Sue and all the children and also to your own dear self & bid you good night and turn into my humble bed with the Majr. Good night.

Jimmie

---

permitting Major Anderson to move from vulnerable Fort Moultrie to the Fort Sumter stronghold; the press then accused him of dishonoring the state by not beseiging Sumter. After the fall of Port Royal the previous November the secession convention reconvened on 27 December to deal with the military crisis and the lack of confidence in Pickens. On 7 January it curbed the governor's authority and restructured the executive by creating the five-member Second Executive Council. In addition to Pickens, the members were Lt. Governor W.W. Harllee, Attorney General Isaac Hayne, former governor William H. Girt, and former U.S. Senator James Chesnut, Jr., the husband of Mary Chesnut, whose acerbic observations about Pickens are preserved in her famous diary (C. Vann Woodward, ed., *Mary Chestnut's Civil War* (New Haven: Yale Univ. Press, 1981). The council exercised all the executive powers previously vested in the governor, plus vast new war powers that included complete control over military affairs. The Second Executive Council rapidly became as unpopular as Pickens had been; its firm governance and determined approach toward raising troops and requisitioning supplies led to public accusations that it was a five-headed dictator. John B. Edmunds, Jr., *Francis W. Pickens and the Politics of Destruction* (Chapel Hill: Univ. of North Carolina Press, 1986), 152–72, and Edwards, "South Carolina," in *The Confederate Governors*, ed. W. Buck Yearns (Athens: Univ. of Georgia Press, 1985), 162–75.

6. On 2 February the Confederate government had called on South Carolina to furnish troops enlisted for the duration of the war equal to 6 percent of the white male population, or about 18,000 men. James Chesnut Jr., the state's military chief, on 20 February reported 9,349 men enlisted for the war—3,000 more than the Confederate government had credited—and

Letter 32   JBG to Leila Griffin

Head Qrs of the Legion
Camp Bartow March 23rd 1862

My Dearest Leila

This is the thirteenth day since we arrived at this place, and I wrote you a note the very first evening of my arrival. A letter ought to reach you in three days, from this point, and it does seem to me my Darling that I ought to have had an answer before now. I received one from you day before yesterday written on the 15th, and you wrote as if you expected it to be brought by Lippie Griffin.[1] But it was mailed two

---

21,321 (including the Hampton Legion) enlisted for twelve months. A system of conscription was authorized in order to raise the additional regiments. The council on 5 March called for 5000 volunteers and declared that no one would be permitted to enlist in any organization then in service for less than the duration of the war until the five regiments were filled. Volunteering would end on 20 March and thereafter all men between 18 and 45 would be subject to conscription for the duration of the war. The hiring of substitutes was permitted, and the list of exemptions was slightly longer than it was for militia service. Commissioned officers were to be appointed by the council instead of elected by the troops. The conscription announcement stimulated the twelve-month troops to reenlist and brought out thousands of volunteers, including almost the entire student body of South Carolina College. The number of volunteers was so great that the draft was unnecessary, and by 28 April the state had exceeded its quota by more than 4000 men. James Chesnut, Jr., "Report of the Chief of the Department of the Military," *Journal of the Convention of the People of South Carolina Held in 1860, 1861 and 1862, Together with the Ordinances, Reports and Resolutions, Etc.* (Columbia: R.W. Gibbs, 1862), 587–613; *Journals of the South Carolina Executive Councils of 1861 and 1862,* 305.

LETTER 32

1. Eighteen-year-old Nathan Lipscomb Griffin, Jr., was a corporal in Company A, Butler's cavalry battalion. Lippy Griffin's father was the late N.L. Griffin, Sr., a prominent Edgefield attorney and the nephew of Griffin's aunt by marriage, Elizabeth Lipscomb Griffin. His mother, Ann Patience Butler Griffin, was a cousin of Matthew Calbraith Butler's father. Lippy Griffin was mortally wounded at Pohick Church, Virginia, in 1863. CSR, M267, roll 364; *Rolls of South Carolina Volunteers in the Confederate States Provisional Army,* 4:26, SCL.

days afterward. I would suggest to you My Darling, that the mail, is generally the most rapid and assuredly the most certain channel through which letters can be sent. And I would prefer that you send all your letters, to me by it. I can recall several occasions when I have been deprived of your kind letter on account of the uncertainty of men. So my Darling, dont trouble any one else with letters, at least whilst I am so convenient to a post office as I am at present. But when you have finished your letter send it to the office and then I will get it in due time. While if you send it by private hands, he will be delayed, in seven cases out of ten & I wont get it so soon. I have been here nearly two weeks and have recieved but one single letter from Edge-field—and in that you stated that you hadnt written me in several days before, on account of having a house full of company. Now My Darling, whilst I am pleased to hear that you are all having such jolly times, I submit that it works rather hard on me, to have to be deprived of the consolation drawn from your dear kind letters, informing me of the health and condition of My Dear Family from whom I have been separated so long. I am exceedingly obliged to the fair young Ladies who were so kind as to send their love to me, and beg leave to offer in return about the same quantity of that precious article, out of my own bosom. My Darling I suspect you will think I do little else than write to you, for if I mistake not this is the sixth time I have written you since I have been here. But most of them have been written late at night when almost every body else was asleep. It is now sunday and most of the Officers have gone to town to Church. But I chose to remain in camp and write to My Darling. I cant expect you to answer each of these letters, but I do hope you will have an opportunity to answer some of them. I saw West Burr [Barr?][2] yesterday who in-formed me that he saw you the day before he left home and that he had promised to let you know when he would leave, as you desired to

---

2. The surname appears to be Burr, but no West Burr appears on the Hampton Legion muster rolls or in the Index to Compiled Confederate Ser-vice Records; possibly Griffin intended the vowel to be a letter "a" and ne-glected to close the top. If so, he is referring to Edgefield Pvt. John Wesley Barr, also of Company A, Cavalry Battalion. Ibid.

send some things by him—He begs to be excused for not doing so, that he received notice to return to his company, and left immediately. I am very glad you didnt send me any thing as I have had to send back some of the things I had. I shipped the large trunk you sent me with what clothing I dont need, by Express to Augusta. You can find out when it gets there and have it brought up—I will enclose the key in this letter. Do give my love to Miss Helen and say to her I would have been pleased to send her some relic, as she desired from the banks of the Potomac—but it was impossible to transport any thing from up there except what was absolutely necessary. I intended to send you and her some small spruce pines, to plant, if I could have got them to the rail road—But Couldnt—They grow beautifully up there—Tell her she must take the will for the deed, and accept my thanks for the loan of the trunk. I would have sent the small black trunk home too but didnt think it was worth the expense. You will have to pay the freight on my trunk when you get it. Dont send me any other clothing, My Darling, unless I write for it—as I do not need it and it will be in my way. If you havent sent the scarf, dont send it[.] I dont need it now, as I hope the cold weather is pretty well over. I wrote you the other day, but will write it again, in case the letter should be miscarried. I want Spradley to plant the Lindsey field in cotton and all the ballance of the land in corn and peas—I want him to make a rousing crop of corn—tell him to clear up all the branches and get in every foot that he can. I want him to plant a large crop of potatoes also. Indeed all kind of provisions. I have no war news to communicate. The President and Genl Johnson were in Fredericsburg yesterday, came the night before and returned yesterday evening.[3] I presume they came up to decide upon a line of defence. I dont know the result of their deliberations. Do My Darling remember me kindly to your Father and family and all our relatives and friends. Give to each one of the Children the warmest love known to the heart of a Father and accept for yourself the whole heart of your devoted

Husband

---

3. There is no account of this meeting in either the OR or Johnston's *Narrative of Military Operations*.

Letter 33   JBG to Leila Griffin

Highland H
Head Qrs of the Legion
Camp Bartow March 26th 1862

My Dearest Leila

What a mistake! you percieve I commenced to head my letter High-land House. The very name is so dear to me that I wouldnt get an-other sheet of paper, but endeavour to delude myself into the idea of being there. I recieved, by to day's mail, two letters from you, My Darling, and one from Sue. I was delighted to get them although they were old letters directed to Manassas—They have been sent back, and have just reached us. I am sorry to hear that Minnie has been so sick. Lippie Griffin arrived here to day, I havent seen him yet, but have recieved the bundle you were kind enough to send me. Many, very many thanks to you, My precious Darling, for the beautiful scarf. Maj Conner is perfectly charmed with his smoking cap. And it is really beautiful. It is, as you said you feared it would be a very little too large but that can be easily remedied. He begs me to present his thanks to you for the beautiful present. You spoke of making one for me, if you do, please make it one size smaller—it is a little too large for me. My Darling, I have the pleasure to inform you that my health is still very good— Hard work seems to agree well with me[.] We are drilling very hard every day—I have the entire command of the Infantry of the Legion. This is the first time since I have been in service, that we have been thrown, for any length of time, near a large body of troops. But Soldiers are as thick about here as black birds. Genl Whiting, yesterday, reviewed eight regiments. It was the largest collection of Troops I ever saw, and presented a most magnificent appearance. Genl Ho[l]mes[1] has been in command of all the troops in this section, until a day or two ago. The President came up here, and ordered him

---

LETTER 33

1. Maj. Gen. Theophilus H. Holmes (1804–1880) commanded the Aquia District during the winter of 1861–62. Holmes, in the words of Douglas Southall Freeman, "a stiff and deaf representative of the 'Old Army,' " was as-signed to command the Department of North Carolina on 24 March 1862. Freeman, *Lee's Lieutenants*, 1:581; OR, ser. 1, 9:450–51; 11, pt. 3:392.

to North Carolina, and General G. W. Smith[2] is now in command
here. He is said, by those who know him, to be one of the very best
men in our Army—and I am glad he has command. I think Genl
Homes is a very good man too—but he is from North Carolina, and
I am glad they have sent him there. He says he thinks he can whip
Burnside, and I hope he will do it.[3] You ask me My Darling what is
the meaning, of our Army falling back? and you say there are various
conjectures for it. And you seem to be rather down hearted about it.
I expect by this time, you have seen by the papers that the Enemy are
very uneasy about this move. The New York Post says "it is the most
Masterly feat which has been performed in ages.["] There is no doubt
that the move has been a great strategic movement. After our Army
fell back—the Enemy came out in force, as if they proposed to advance on us, but from some cause, they have gone back. There are
no Troops of consequence, between this place and Alexandria,[4] So
one of our Scouts reports, who has just come in. It is thought, that
the Enemy have become alarmed for Burnside and are sending him
reinforcements. Our command are now under marching orders.[5]

---

2. Maj. Gen. Gustavus Woodson Smith (1822–1896), a confident and affable Kentuckian, was widely regarded as a superior officer; Johnston thought
him one of the best in the Confederacy. He had initially been assigned to
command the Second Corps of the Army of Northern Virginia, which consisted of all the troops not serving under Beauregard, and had been switched
to a division in October. Freeman, Lee's Lieutenants, 1: 162–64; OR, 5:
881, 1061.

3. After overcoming Roanoke Island on 8 February, Burnside, with a troop
strength of more than 11,000, moved on to New Bern, North Carolina, which
he captured after defeating a force of approximately 4000 under L. O'B.
Branch. He then advanced to Washington, North Carolina, which he took
on 21 March. Long, The Civil War Day by Day, 184–87.

4. The anticipated Federal advance had stopped at Manassas, where the
Army of the Potomac destroyed Confederate ordnance and occupied the abandoned camps only briefly before returning to Alexandria.

5. In fact, Burnside was moving aggressively in North Carolina (see note
3). However, on 11 March Lincoln had officially relieved the cautious and
contentious George B. McClellan as general-in-chief, permitting him to retain command only of the Army of the Potomac, which was preparing for a
major offensive in Virginia. By 24 March the Confederate War Department
was aware that Federal troops were embarking for the Virginia peninsula, and

Wherefor I do not know—and may be no where—We have often been ordered to be in readiness to march at a moments warning, and very seldom have moved. If we move I will notify you and keep you posted. The greatest objection I have to moving, is changing my Post Office. I have been here now going on three weeks and have only recieved one letter from you directed to me here. My Darling, it is only a little more than two months, until the time of enlistment, of the Legion will expire. I cant tell yet, whether they will reorganize or not. I am sure they would have done so some time ago, if they could have got furloughs. But they were stopped just as our men began to reenlist[6]— And the consequence was the reenlistment stopped too. I believe now that they would reenlist if they could get to go home. This idea of being drafted is any thing but agreeable to a Soldier who has been serving his country for twelve Months. But No one can tell what will be the condition of things two months to come. My Darling do write me if you need any money—have you paid our tax—I want to know, if Spradley will have plenty of corn—Give me the news generally. How does my colt look. Tell Spradley to turn him in the oat patch as soon as it will do. Give my love to all, and especially to each one of the dear Children & kiss them for me. I never recieved any thing you sent by Lanham except one letter—Tell the negroes all howdy for me & that I am glad to hear they are getting on so well. Good night My Darling

Your devoted Husband

Letter 34 JBG to Leila Griffin

Head Qrs of the Legion
Camp Bartow March 30th 1862

My Darling Wife
  I am quite sure there is something wrong with the mail arrangement, for I have been here nearly three weeks, and have recieved but one single letter, from you, directed to this place—And that one I

Robert E. Lee, who had recently been given general charge of military operations, was advising that part of Johnston's troops be sent to protect Richmond. OR, ser. 1, 11, pt. 3:392–94; Symonds, *Joseph E. Johnston*, 147–48.

  6. See letter of 16 February, note 2.

recieved a week ago. I *know* you have written frequently, but from some cause they do not reach me. And I fear too that you have not recieved all my letters—I have written you very often since we have been in this camp. I regret exceedingly, that I cant hear often from you. I assure you my Darling, my almost constant thoughts, when I am not specially engaged on duty, are about my much loved, Dear Wife and Children. It is indeed a great Sacrifice, to be for so long a time separated from all that is dear to one's heart. My Darling, I hope and pray that the Good Lord will protect my Darling family, and that he will also shield & protect your Devoted Husband, and in his chosen time will permit him to return to those whom he loves so devotedly. My Darling, I am perfectly aware of the uncertainty of human life at all times, rendered of course more so, by being engaged in a war—But notwithstanding all this, I have an abiding hope, that all will again be well, and that there are many days of happiness in store for us yet. I dont mean by this, to create an impression that we will not have great troubles for a time—Indeed I am well satisfied that we will. My opinion is, that the greatest events of this Revolution, will transpire within the next three months—I believe there will be a vast deal of hard fighting, and great privations endured—And my opinion is, that we will in the course of the time indicated, regain what we have lost within the past three months, and be revenged for the reverses we have sustained. Now My Darling such are my predictions— it remains to be seen how near right I may be. I believe we are going to have a fight on this line before a great while. If we do, you will doubtless hear thousands of rumours and reports, but my Darling my advice to you is, to give yourself no unnecessary uneasiness—believe nothing until it is fully confirmed. You remember the thousands of false reports that were circulated after the battle of Manassas. I know, that if you hear that we have had a fight that you will be uneasy about me—but My Darling as I said before, dont give yourself unnecessary uneasiness. There are a great many chances for me not to be hurt. In the first place in all battles there are a good many troops who are not engaged at all, and then there is only a small percent of the troops engaged, killed. Rest assured you shall recieve authentic information of the result, as soon as it can be forwarded to you, if we do have a fight. I dont write this, My Darling, to alarm you, on the contrary it is only, that in case a fight should occur you will not allow yourself to be alarmed by any reports—I remember that after the battle of Manassas the newspapers published accounts of men being wounded who were not in the fight. There is no indication of an early engagement in this direction. Indeed the news is, that the enemy are not moving in this direction—But in the direction of Genl Johns[t]on who is some thirty miles above us. I think that McClellan will only make a feint on Genl Johnson at present, while the main fight will take place in the direction of Norfolk.[1] My Darling, I wrote you the other day that Col Hampton's brigade would be reviewed soon—Well, it came off friday—I wish you could have been here to witness it. You would have seen your Jimmie riding at the head of the whole column conducting the Legion. The whole brigade, and especially the Legion, was very highly complimented by Genl Whiting. Col Hampton commanded the whole, and consequently I commanded the Legion, which had the Post of Honor, on the right. The Legion is now well drilled, and if they get a chance will do good fighting.

My Darling how do you come on farming and gardening. I hope you will have a good crop and a good garden, when I get home— remember I ate no vegetables last summer and am entitled to a double share this summer. And dont forget my watermelons. Do give my love to my Darling little children. Tell Willie and Bobbie it has been a long time since I recieved a letter from them. Remember me very kindly to your Father and family, Dr Burt and family, including

---

LETTER 34

1. McClellan's original plan had been to outflank Johnston's army by using superior Federal seapower to transport most of the Army of the Potomac to the small port town of Urbanna on the Rappahannock River below Fredericksburg. Such a move would have put his forces between the Confederate Army and Richmond and given him the advantage of position. Johnston's retreat from Manassas, however, had frustrated this design, and the new Confederate line of defense on the Rappahannock forced McClellan to choose a new landing site for his amphibious invasion. The revised plan called for transporting the army to Union-held Fort Monroe, which lay opposite Norfolk and below Yorktown, between the York and James Rivers. With his flanks and supply lines protected by the navy's gunboats, McClellan could then advance up the peninsula toward Richmond. Embarkation had begun from Alexandria on 17 March, and McClellan established his headquarters at Fort Monroe on 2 April. OR, ser. 1, 11, pt. 1: 5–6, pt. 3: 401, 405, 419; B&L, 2:166–69.

Auntie and Emily,[2] Jim Dozier and family, Dr Muse and family, Quilla Miles and family—and I might finish my sheet in names, but give you a "Carte blanche" to remember me to any and all you please—My love to Sue and tell her I havent had a letter from her lately—Tell Spradley not to draw too heavily on the cotton seed, for manure. For it might become necessary for him to have to replant his cotton.

And now My Darling, I beg that you will accept a heart full of love from your Devoted

Husband

Letter 35   JBG to Leila Griffin

Head Qrs of the Legion
Camp Bartow April 2nd 1862

My Darling Leila

I recieved to day, the letter you sent by the hand of Dr Burt. He gave it to Liet Nicholson[1] in Richmond, who brought it to me—but the trunk did not come—and what is worse, I doubt if it ever does. The rail roads are now transporting no private baggage by express. The roads are in the control of the Government, and they are kept busy in

---

2. Mary Ann Burt, Leila's aunt, was one of the eight children of Harwood and Susannah Miles Burt. She did not marry, and after her brother John Harwood was widowed for the second time she apparently helped care for his children, Emily and Gus; the census of 1860 shows her as part of the household. Dr. John Harwood Burt had died the previous fall, and, since Gus was in the army (see letter of 6 April 1862, note 1), the two women were probably living temporarily with Mary Burt's youngest brother, Dr. William Miles Burt.

LETTER 35

1. Twenty-year-old Benjamin Edwin Nicholson, first sergeant of Gary's Watson Guards, Company B of the Legion, was elected third lieutenant on 15 August 1861, and second lieutenant at the reorganization on 23 April. He was promoted to captain on 17 September 1862, after capturing a stand of colors at Second Manassas, and to major on 3 September 1864, for bravery at Deep Bottom. Benjamin Nicholson was a cousin of John L. Nicholson and the brother of John T. Nicholson (see letter of 2 Jan. 1862, note 4). Sturkey, Watson Guards Roll.

transporting troops. I am however, much pleased to get the letter, although a short one, even if I dont get the trunk. For I dont have that pleasure often these days. I have been here three weeks to day, and except the letter just alluded to, I have recieved only two letters, from you, directed to this place. I have written you very often, and hope you have recieved them all. I am happy to inform you that I am still very well, and have plenty of hard work to do in my official capacity. We had another beautiful review, this evening, of Col Hampton's "Brigade."[2] We had quite a number of Spectators to witness it—amongst them were a good many Ladies—did not know any of them, but I assure you they, at least some of them, looked very sweet and charming. It has been such a long time since I have been in company with Ladies, that I really fear I wouldnt know how to behave in their presence. We have again become very comfortably quartered, almost as well as we were before we moved. And as far as our appetites are concerned we are improved. We fare very well here, in that line. But it costs us a power of money—provisions are so very high, and our mess are very good feeders. It has now come to my turn to cater for the mess. We have seven in the mess, and we take it by turns—each one catering for two months. My turn commenced yesterday. The way I manage, is to give Abram money and he provides for us. He is a first rate Boy—I think more of him than I ever did. By the way, if those nice things you sent me should turn up, I assure you they will be thankfully recieved and properly appreciated and eaten. The cake you sent me before was about the best that I ever saw. To give you an idea of the price of provisions—Abram has just come in and reported that he paid $1.75 for half bushel of sweet potatoes and the same amount for a turkey here. Goblers sell for $2.50 to $3.00 a piece, butter .75 to $1.00—and other things accordin.[3] I am sorry to learn

---

2. See letter of 16 February, note 4.

3. By the end of 1861, inflation was running at 12 percent a month, and Confederate military setbacks in the spring of 1862 sent the price index up 100 percent in the first half of the year. John Beauchamp Jones, a clerk in the War Department, periodically noted in his diary the rising cost of provisions in Richmond. On 9 January 1862, he reported that butter sold for 50 cents a pound, bacon for 25 cents, and that beef had risen from 13 to 30 cents a pound. By 23 May 1862, he was writing indignantly: "Oh,the extortioners! Meats of all kinds are selling at fifty cents per pound; butter seventy-

by your letter that bacon is so awfully high. You must tell the negroes that it is perfectly impossible to give them but a very little meat while it is so high. They must have plenty of bread but very little meat— not more than half allowance. Tell them it is very painful for me to have to shorten their allowances in this way—but I am forced to do it—by the press of circumstances. Talk to them reasonably in this way. And tell them I shall expect them to submit to it without a murmur. I will put them back on full allowance as soon as I can. Tell them all to plant large gardens—and tell Spradley to give them time to work them—You buy the seed for them. Tell them to remember what I am going through. And what the country is now suffering. Many People havent enough bread to eat and doubtless some have no meat at all. If you can buy any beeves do so and feed them to them.[4] Make every possible effort to feed them as well as you can, and that ought to satisfy them. Take care of the salt, like it was gold dust.[5] You ought to have a great deal of it, as you bought so little pork. Economize it—

---

five cents; coffee $1.50; tea $10; . . . ." As the war dragged on, inflation and shortages caused prices to spiral uncontrollably. On 26 June 1864, Jones noted: "Flour fell yesterday from $500 to $300 dollars per barrel." McPherson, *Battle Cry of Freedom*, 338, 340, and McPherson, *Ordeal by Fire*, 199–200; Ramsdell, *Behind the Lines in the Southern Confederacy*, 5–6, 8–9, 11–12, 18–25, 28–30, 34–39, 49–50, 57–58, 62, 75; John B. Jones, *A Rebel War Clerk's Diary*, 1:104, 128; 2:396; Richard Cecil Todd, *Confederate Finance* (Athens: Univ. of Georgia Press, 1954), 110.

4. In the Edgefield area that spring, bacon cost 40 cents a pound, while beef on the hoof could be had for 30. Carol Bleser, ed., *Secret and Sacred: The Diaries of James Henry Hammond* (New York: Oxford Univ. Press, 1988), 286.

5. Griffin's analogy here is apt, for salt was becoming literally as valuable as gold dust. Before the Federal blockade ships returning from selling cotton had carried cargoes of salt as ballast. Planters bought it by the bushel to preserve meat, to keep butter fresh, and to preserve hides for tanning; it was also essential to the diets of both human beings and livestock. After the blockade scarcity resulted in enormous price increases and speculation. Salt that cost 50 cents a sack in 1860 was commanding $40 a sack by May 1862, according to a diary entry of former U.S. Senator James Henry Hammond of Edgefield. Having had the foresight to lay in large supplies before the shooting started, Hammond was able to sell salt from his reserves to his Edgefield neighbors for 30 times what it had cost him. The editor of the Edgefield *Advertiser*,

dont let the stock have any, or very little. I will send you all the money I can spare but if you need more, you will have to sell a little cotton to get it. Do ask Bob Sullivan to try to hunt up that sugar and molasses. Maj Butler arrived here yesterday—He is still somewhat complaining, but not sick. All our furloughed men are rapidly coming in. Our army is increasing rapidly every day. I think we will have a chance to try our luck, before very long. The Enemy are not far in front of us in large forces. But old Genl Joe[6] will thrash him out (that's my opinion). We have a fine body of troops here, and they seem anxious for the fight. You wrote me that Aunt Elize was in Edgefield. Do give her my very best love, and tell her I beg her forgiveness for not writing to her, in such a long time. It is not because I love her less—but only neglect and just got out of the habit of writing. I would give a great deal to see her. I am delighted to hear she has again got back to old Edgefield. Give my best love to Cousin Sue and Mr. Spencer. Also to all our dear relatives—including Sue and all the dear sweet children—and accept for your own dear self the devoted love of

Your husband

Letter 36 JBG to Leila Griffin

Head Qrs of the legion
Camp Bartow April 6th 1862

My Darling Leila

I am growing quite uneasy, for fear some of my Dear family are sick. The last letter I recieved from you, was the one you sent by Gus.

---

denouncing salt speculators, passed on to his readers a way to recover salt from smokehouse floors, a strategy that was widely prescribed in the Confederacy: householders were advised to alternate layers of smokehouse earth and straw in a barrel, pour water over them until the salt washed out, and then boil off the water. Ella Lonn, *Salt as a Factor in the Confederacy* (New York: Walter Neale, 1933), 16–18, 43; Bleser, *Secret and Sacred*, 286; Drew Gilpin Faust, *James Henry Hammond and the Old South: A Design for Mastery* (Baton Rouge: Louisiana State Univ. Press, 1982), 367–68; Edgefield *Advertiser*, 30 April 1862; Ramsdell, *Behind the Lines in the Southern Confederacy*, 20.

6. Gen. Joseph E. Johnston.

Burt.[1] and it was dated the 8th of march. I suspect, however, that was a mistake. But I think the one of the latest date, was the 22nd—that letter was written two weeks ago yesterday, and it was near a week in getting here. Since then I have heard nothing. What can be the reason? I would give a good deal to know. I have thought of various reasons for it—first I thought it was perhaps owing to an irregularity in the mails—but then, I see, every mail, brings letters and papers to my friends around me, both from Columbia and Charleston, and then I remember that my letters would come by the same rout. I cant attribute it to the mails—What then is it? If any of the Children were sick, I would suppose my darling would only write the oftener, even if it were only a line or two at a time. And if you were sick, so that you could not write, I presume you would get Sue or some one, to write to me. So that it would seem, to not be attributable to this cause. Well, then what can it be? I am at a loss to conjecture. It is also strange that Sue, who used to write so regularly, has all of a sudden dropped off—And then again My two Boys Willie & Bobbie, used sometimes to write—But they too have become silent. There must be a reason for all this—And as I feel, directly interested in the matter cant help but feel very anxious to know what it is.

Is it possible, that I have been so long away from home that the affections of those dear ones at home, has to a certain extent, weaned

---

LETTER 36

1. Augustus W. Burt, age 22, was Leila's cousin, the son of John Harwood Burt and Emily Elizabeth Roper. He enlisted in Company H of the Seventh South Carolina Volunteers on 15 April 1861 as second sergeant, was elected second lieutenant on 20 April 1862, and promoted to first lieutenant on 14 May 1862. Wounded in the right arm and both legs at Gettysburg (the left leg was later amputated), he was taken prisoner and spent the next year and a half in Federal hospitals and prison camps. While at Fort Delaware Gus Burt became one of the "Immortal 600" POWs chosen to be sent to Fort Wagner on Morris Island in Charleston harbor, which was under Confederate fire, in retaliation for the 600 Union prisoners that the Confederates moved from Andersonville to Charleston in an effort to force the Federals to stop shelling the city. He was so seriously ill, however, that while the ship was at Hilton Head, he was transferred to Beaufort. He was exchanged on 13 December 1864. SHSP 17 (1889): 46, 22 (1894): 127–46; Edgefield *Advertiser*, 21 Dec. 1864; CSR, M267, roll 216.

themselves from me. No—I know this is not the reason. But then, What is it?—Well I dont know what it is—but I know that's not it. For I know they love me still. But—but—but isnt it rather singular, that I get no letters, and especially when I have written so many, since I have been here. I think within the last four weeks, I must have written some ten or twelve letters, to my loving Leila, and have recieved from her, written within that time, three, *all told*. But then it will be all right someday.

This, My Darling, is a beautiful bright Sabbath Day—all nature seems to smile—The buds on the trees, even in this cold climate, are beginning to testify to the approach of spring. We have, within the last few days removed our camp a short distance—We are now out in an open field, and have the handsomest camp we have had in six months. I think two weeks of good open weather will bring up our men finely—A great many of them, who are on duty, have dreadful coughs, caused by the exposure to which they have been subjected, during the winter. All the sick have been sent back from here to Richmond. I have thought for the last week, that we were very near a fight, on this line. But I understand now that the Enemy who were threatening us in the front, have retired again, and it is supposed that they will go down the Potomac to Yorktown, and land there.[2] McClellan, evidently dreads to meet Johnson, and is trying to out General him. But he has got to be mighty sharp if he does it.

We are now under marching orders—I hear that some of the Troops have already been sent back to Richmond. The Enemy made a reconnoisance in force, down as far as Stafford C H. (which is twelve miles from here) a few days ago—I understand Sickles was in command.[3] Gen Smith sent out a brigade to meet them, as soon as he heard it— but before they could get there—Sickles left—Genl Johnson was down here at the time.

I think there will be certainly a great deal of fighting, here before

---

2. See letter of 30 March, note 1. On 4 April McClellan began advancing up the peninsula toward Yorktown.

3. Brig. Gen. Daniel E. Sickles (1819–1914), a Tammany Hall lawyer and former congressman, was a "political" general commissioned by virtue of his status as a War Democrat. He commanded New York's Second or Excelsior Brigade, which he had also helped raise.

long—and the result of these battles, in my opinion, will decide the war—that is, I mean, if we are successful as I believe we will be—I think the war will soon be over—but if on the contrary our Adversary should succeed—it will only tend to lengthen the war. The time of enlistment of the twelve months troops from our State, begins this week to expire. What they will do about reenlisting I do not know. I fear a great many of them will go home—And if they do, it is only attributable to the bad management (not to call it by a harsher name) of the Confederate Government, and more especially the State Government. The Confederate Government in the first place, for taking troops at all, for twelve months. And secondly, for not having other Troops ready drilled to take the place of these, for a short time at home. Almost every man would be willing to enlist for the war—if he could be allowed to spend a month at home. But this now cannot be granted, under the circumstances—and the men who reenlist, have to take their chances of getting home after awhile. And should these men, who have undergone for twelve months, privations and sufferings which can be appreciated only by a Soldier—decide to go home before again going into Service, the State says to him—you cant be allowed any more, the privileges of a Volunteer—but when troops are needed—you must take your chances with the men who havent been in the war at all—but have been quietly and comfortably at home— and if you should be drafted I will assign you a place—and appoint the officers, who are to lead you. This is the way the State expresses her obligations to her sons who have made the greater part of the reputation she has in this war so far. I dont know what the Legion will do—cant tell until the time comes—Cant tell what I will do my- self—Want very much to go home[,] am tired of *soldiering*. But wouldnt at all like to be drafted, as soon as I got home and put in as a private. There will be many changes though, before the 12th of June. I hope it will all be over by then. Gus, lost my trunk, but sent me word he would hunt it up and send it on—I never expect to see it. Have you heard of mine—did you get the key— Give my love to all as usual—Kiss my children for me—and do my Darling as often as you can write to your

Husband

5 *The Peninsula Campaign*

Letters 37 through 57
12 April through 14 June 1862

Griffin spent much of April on the move: to Ashland, fifteen miles above Richmond, and then down the peninsula between the James and York Rivers to Williamsburg and finally to Yorktown. He judged Yorktown "a pretty hard country to live in" and a difficult place to defend, and in May Johnston's army retreated slowly back toward Richmond, fighting several engagements along the way. Griffin was under fire for the first time at the battle of Eltham's Landing; he reported confidentially but proudly to Leila "that it is said I was very cool." At Seven Pines he commanded the Legion in a "short, but terribly hot fight" and was subsequently elevated to acting brigade commander while Hampton convalesced from a wound.

Interwoven in Griffin's accounts of mud marches and battles is an unusual look at the behind-the-scenes competition for election to company and field offices occasioned by the army reorganization that spring. After weeks of pretending not to care if he were voted out as lieutenant colonel, Griffin's tone changed to optimism. Since acquitting himself so well under fire at Seven Pines, he confided to Leila, he thought his chances of winning were good. Events were to prove otherwise.

Letter 37   JBG to Leila Griffin

Head Qrs of the Legion
Camp near Ashland
April 12th 1862
[Saturday]

My Darling Leila

You percieve that I am again at my old camp, where I was for a time last Summer—We have had a terrible march from Fredericks-burg—I received orders at two O Clock on monday night last to get my command ready to march *immediately.*[1] It was then and had been all night raining and was the coldest kind of a rain. I got up and went to work—We got off after breakfast—the rain was pouring down. We marched two days and bivouacked both nights in the worst weather I almost ever saw. The men had no tents and but one blanket each. I had no tent and until midnight the first night, *no blankets.* The ground was thoroughly wet—We took the rail road twenty five miles from here, and reached this place in the night—night before last—where we enjoyed the same comforts. The men had no provisions b[ut] hard bread (crackers) and fat bacon, which they carried in their haversacks—And the officers didnt even have that, only as they could get it from their men—I lived several days on it myself and thought it was mighty *good.* We have had a gay time I assure you. I was fully confident that it would make nearly every one sick but strange to say— very few are sick—

LETTER 37

1. Robert E. Lee, who had been receiving anxious dispatches from the small garrisons of Maj. Gen. John Bankhead Magruder at Yorktown and Maj. Gen. Benjamin Huger at Norfolk, had advised Johnston on 25 March that orders to move part of his army toward Richmond and the Peninsula would be forthcoming. Two days later, in response to instructions, Johnston dis-patched 7500 men from the Rapidan and 2500 from Fredericksburg. On 4 April, when it became certain that McClellan's destination was Yorktown, the divisions of D.H. Hill, D.R. Jones, and Jubal A. Early were sent forward. Subsequently, as evidence mounted that McClellan was massing almost the entire Army of the Potomac against the coast, James Longstreet's division and the remainder of G.W. Smith's, including the Hampton Legion, were ordered to Richmond. OR, ser. 1, 11, pt. 3: 397, 405–6, 420; Johnston, *Narrative of Military Operations,* 108–10; Symonds, *Joseph E. Johnston,* 147–48.

We have stopped here, I suppose, only for a few days—We will then go to Richmond and from there towards Yorktown—This is no *retreat*—The Enemy who were threatening us in front—quietly withdrew and have gone down the river to that place or somewhere on the paninsular. This is a Strategic move, of McClellan but will be promptly met by Genl Johns[t]on. I am going to send a man to Richmond for our mail, and will send this letter by him. I hope he will bring me a letter from my Darling—

I have no time to write more at present but will write again in a few days. Direct your letters to Richmond until I direct you otherwise. Remember me kindly to all & give my best love to all my Dear Children—I am happy to inform you that I have stood the trip well and [a]m very well—Accept the best love

your devoted Husband

Letter 38   JBG to Leila Griffin

Head Qrs of the Legion
Camp at Ashland
April 13th 1862

My Dearest Leila

I wrote you a short letter yesterday, and as I now have a little leisure I will write you again. I am compelled to write again with a pencil, as my trunk hasnt yet come up. Some of the tents have come and they are just in time—as it has just commenced raining again—We have had a pretty hard time this trip. We have never experienced any thing like hardships before, compared to what we have experienced on this march. It rained, sleeted[,] hailed and snowed—And the men had to march all the way through mud and water—had to wade several creeks. But they stood it like *men*. And strange to say very few have been made sick by it. I directed each man to carry one blanket, in addition to their knapsacks and haversacks—This was the only covering the men had at night to protect them from the awful weather. I had four tents from each company and more blankets for the men put on the wagons—but we have never seen the wagons, so that they did us no good. Every thing that I had was put on the wagons, and not a thing has yet come up. I have got on (I am almost ashamed to say it) the same underclothes that I left camp with. We all laugh at

each other about our dirty shirts—This is by no means our usual cus-
tom, for we are really a very neat set of officers. I generally keep about
as neat in camp as I do at home. It was funny to see us when we
would stop at night. The first night, we built up a big fire and stood
up around it, for we had nothing to sit upon and the ground was too
wet to sit on it. So we were were forced to stand. Abram was behind
with my wagon and [I] kept thinking he would come up with my
blankets—but he didnt come—We got some hard crackers and fat
bacon, broiled the bacon on a stick, and as we had ate nothing since
early in the morning—we made quite a hearty supper—We then began to discuss how we would sleep—There were four of us—Maj
Conner, Doctor's Darby[1] & Taylor[2] and myself. Col Hampton and

---

LETTER 38

1. Dr. John Thomas (or Thomson) Darby (1836–1879) of Orangeburg District studied at South Carolina College and the Medical College of South
Carolina before graduating from the University of Pennsylvania medical
school in 1858. He taught at the Philadelphia School of Anatomy until the
outbreak of the war, when he returned to South Carolina and was appointed
surgeon of the Hampton Legion. He subsequently advanced to become medical director of the Army of the West and in 1863 undertook a secret mission
in Europe. After the war he returned temporarily to serve on the medical staff
of the Prussian Army. Darby later taught at the University of South Carolina
and served a term as president of the South Carolina Medical Association
before accepting a position at City University of New York, where he rose to
hold the chair in surgery. Waring, *A History of Medicine in South Carolina,
1825–1900,* 216–17; William B. Atkinson, *The Physicians and Surgeons of
the United States* (Philadelphia: Charles Robson, 1978), 476; *Confederate
Veteran* 35 (1927): 141–42; *Rolls of South Carolina Volunteers in the Confederate States Provisional Army,* 3:351, SCDAH.
2. Dr. Benjamin Walter "Watt" Taylor (1834–1905) graduated from the
Medical College of South Carolina in 1858 and practiced in Columbia before
the war. He was appointed assistant surgeon in the South Carolina Army and
served in Fort Moultrie before transferring to Confederate service and the
Hampton Legion. He was promoted to surgeon in the fall of 1862, then to
surgeon for the Second South Carolina Cavalry, to division surgeon for
Hampton's Cavalry Division, and finally to medical director for the cavalry
corps of the Army of Northern Virginia. After the war Taylor resumed practice
in Columbia and was elected president of the South Carolina Medical Association, the State Board of Health, and the Board of Regents of the State Hospital for the Insane. Waring, *A History of Medicine in South Carolina, 1825–*

Adjt Barker[3] went to a house. We four made up our minds to stand it with the men. The Doctors had half a dozen *Stretchers* along— (These are pieces of canvas about six feet long and two and a half wide—they are used to carry sick & wounded men on). We got these, and with three of them made a pretty good shelter over us, and spread the other three on the ground to lie on—This was our bed[,] covering and all. We went to bed—wrapped in our overcoats, which were pretty wet—We remained in this condition until one of the Servants came up with a few blankets—We covered up with these and slept pretty well—next morning we had breakfast with a light bill of fare, and set out early. This was a worse Day than the one previous. We marched about twelve miles & took up again. I had one of my sick head aches & as the rain was pouring down so hard, I went to a house, where I had very comfortable quarters. I bathed my feet in hot water and went to *bed*, actually a *feather bed*—with nice clean *sheets* and a ruffled pillow case—I tell you it was a good feeling—This is the first bed I have slept on, in a house, since I rejoined the Legion last November. I slept delightfully, and woke up next morning perfectly well and as bright as a lark. I had a good warm breakfast prepared for the Majr and Dr Taylor, who had been out all night. The man who entertained me was exceedingly kind and wouldnt let me pay him a cent.

The next day we laid over all day, waiting for the cars—Got off

---

1900, 309–10; William B. Atkinson, *Physicians and Surgeons of the United States*, 211; *Rolls of South Carolina Volunteers in the Confederate States Provisional Army*, 3:351, SCDAH; CMH, 6:867–68; Ulysses R. Brooks, *Butler and His Cavalry in the War of Secession, 1861–1865* (Columbia, S.C.: State Co., 1909), 416.

3. Twenty-nine-year-old Lt. Theodore Gaillard Barker of Charleston, an attorney and graduate of South Carolina College, had served in the South Carolina Army as adjutant to Col. J.J. Pettigrew at Charleston Harbor before joining the Hampton Legion as adjutant. Following Hampton's promotion to brigadier general, Barker was advanced to captain and made assistant adjutant and inspector general. He served with Hampton throughout the war, advancing to major when Hampton was promoted to major general, and was twice wounded. After the war he resumed his law practice and during Reconstruction helped James Conner organize Democratic rifle clubs. Barker took an active part in Hampton's gubernatorial campaign in 1876 and served as one of the counsels for the Democratic Party. CMH, 6:445–46; *Rolls of South Carolina Volunteers in the Confederate States Provisional Army*, 3:351.

about dark, and reached this place about two hours afterward—We got out of the cars & were ordered to bivouack in the street immediately on the side of the rail road. This was in the mud. I looked around and found a vacant lot near by— Where I took my command. We then had to bring every stick of wood, we burned about half a mile—Here again, we had to wait on ourselves, as we sent our boys with the horses—The Maj, Dr Taylor, and myself put out and brought in a big turn of wood—and made a nice fire—ate our usual supper and retired—The next day we moved our camp to this place. Which is a very nice place about a mile from town[.] And we are again beginning to get comfortable. There isnt much here to eat—but I reckon we wont starve—I think, since I have got through with this trip, that I can stand *any thing*. I havent taken even the slightest cold, and felt very well all the time except the evening I had the head ache. Indeed, this is the first time, since my return (six months) that I have been for a moment unfit for duty—I really have cause to be very thankful. My Darling the mails are necessarily irregular now owing to transportation of troops. But you shall hear from me as often as possible—and do write to me the same. Direct your letters to Richmond—I dont think we will remain here long— & when we leave we will go first to Richmond—My love to all and especially and particularly to my Darling Wife and Children.

Your Devoted Husband

Letter 39   JBG to Leila Griffin

Head Qrs of the Legion
Camp near Ashland
April 14th 1862

My Darling Leila

Notwithstanding I wrote you a letter yesterday and one the day before—I will take occasion to write you again only a line or two to inform you that we are ordered to march to day in the direction of Yorktown. I dont know at what point we will stop, but will write you as soon as I do— We have to march about seventy miles and I suspect it will be several days before I will be able to write again. In the mean time you had better continue to direct your letters to Richmond as we will make arrangements to have our letters forwarded from there—My Darling you will have to sell some cotton to get what money you need—Tell Spradley to cross all the land he plants in cotton, and plant corn in the same way that I had it planted last year— Tell him to take good care of the colts and also to pay especial attention to the hogs[.] I wish him to raise every pound of Pork he possibly can—I havent time to write any more. My love to all especially My Dear family

Your Devoted Husband

Letter 40　JBG to Leila Griffin

Head Qrs of the Legion
Camp near Williamsburg
Friday night April 18th 1862

My Darling Leila

I am now seated under my little rustic bivouak, and will only drop you a line to inform you that I am quite well, and am thus far on our march to Yorktown. Which place is only ten miles from here—We expect to go there tomorrow—This is the fourth day of our march[.] The weather & roads have been delightful, which has made the march very pleasant, comparatively speaking—Our men are generally well and in fine spirits—I understand we are to be stationed near York-town[.] You may write me at that place for the present—I will write you again as soon as I get down there and sorter fixed up—Give my love to all and especially to my dear Children and accept the same for yourself—I hope soon I see you all

Your Jimmie

Letter 41　JBG to Leila Griffin

Head Qrs of the Legion
Camp near Yorktown
April 25th 1862

My Dearest Leila

I have just had the pleasure of reading a very dear letter from you, and one from Sue—I am delighted to hear that you are all well. As to your being sun burned, My Darling, So far from not owning, you, I will only be the more proud of you—This is no time for *fair faces* and *tender hands*. And besides, if you are some what burned, you will only be better mated with your Husband—The March winds and my great exposure, of late—has taken a good deal of the *red* from my cheeks, and in its stead has deposited a pretty good coat of black. I fear the danger is that you may be ashamed to own me, but then You can have a good time in *whitening* me—and fixing me up generally, according to your own liking. All this My Darling, is very pleasant to contemplate, but I wont allow my mind to dwell too fondly on it, for fear the pleasant cup may slip from my lips just at the time that I am ready to taste its contents. I suspect I will have to go through at least one battle before my time expires. But I candidly confess that I am beginning to doubt, about having a battle at this point soon—When we first arrived here, all thought that the fight would soon come off— but as yet there is no evidence of its commencement—There is more or less skirmishing every day between the Pickets, and shots are also exchanged every day between the Enemy's gun boats and our batteries. Occasionally a man is struck but not often. I wouldn't be surprised if a fight occurs between Richmond and Fredericsburg, before it does here—I wish very much they would send us back up there—I would much prefer to fight up there, than here. The *living* here is pretty tight. We get nothing but bread and meat, and occasionally coffee— Mostly *Sassafrass* tea. Butter and milk is unknown. This, though we can stand very well—Our men dont complain at all—although they are without tents, and living pretty hard—They seem to be willing to endure anything, and all they ask is to be in the fight. This is a great, and I fear I may add unfortunate day with us of the Legion—The Companies are reorganizing under the "Conscription law."[1] They are

LETTER 41

1. When it was evident that reenlistments under the Furlough and Bounty Act would not fill the ranks, and with the enlistments of the twelve-month troops—half of the Confederate Army—beginning to expire, the Confederate Congress on 16 April 1862 passed the first of several conscription bills. All able-bodied white male citizens between the ages of 18 and 35 became subject to the draft for three-year enlistments, and one-year volunteers already serving in the army were required to remain for an additional two years. The hiring of substitutes was permitted, and a supplementary law on 21 April established a list of exempted essential occupations. Albert Burton Moore, *Conscription and Conflict in the Confederacy* (1924; rpt., New York: Hilary House, 1963), 13–15, 53–56.

electing all their Company officers—and I am satisfied that a good many of the old officers will be turned out, and *worse* ones put in their stead. As a general rule—the officers who have discharged their duties propperly—are not popular with their men—and those who have allowed most privileges, and have been least efficient, are the men who will be elected. There are some exceptions to this rule— Gary will be reelected Capt in his company—Tompkins,[2] first Lieutenant and Nicholson,[3] second and it is thought Gus Tompkins[4] will be junior second. Bates[5] declined reelection— There will be fewer changes in the officers of this company than in any of the others— Several of the Capts will be turned out.[6] I think, this is quite an

---

2. Robert William Pinckney Tompkins (see letter of 30 Jan. 1862, note 1).

3. Benjamin Edward Nicholson (see letter of 2 April 1862, note 1).

4. Twenty-eight-year-old Richard Augustus (Gus) Tompkins was an older brother of Robert William Pinckney Tompkins. The original second sergeant of the company, he had been promoted to first sergeant on 15 August. He was elected third lieutenant on 23 April and promoted to second lieutenant on 16 June. He was severely wounded at Sharpsburg and promoted first lieutenant to take the place of his brother Bob, who was killed in that battle. Advanced to captain on 3 September 1864, he was paroled at Appomattox and after the war moved to Texas, where he died of yellow fever. The Tompkinses were evidently related to Leila: the oldest brother, Stephen Samuel Tompkins, named two of his children Henrietta Giroud and Daniel Holland, names that appear in the Burt and Miles genealogies. Sturkey, Watson Guards Roll; Heath, "The James S. Tompkins Family," 5–6.

5. Andrew David Bates, 37, was the original second lieutenant of the company. He was in poor health and was dropped from the rolls after 23 April. After the war he was a farmer, militia captain, and railroad promoter. In 1877 he became the first mayor of Batesburg, which had been named in his honor. Lindsey G. Hall, *Things and Incidents of Long Ago* (Columbia: State Printing, 1970), 201; Sturkey, Watson Guards Roll.

6. As it turned out, only two of the seven infantry captains were voted out: Brown Manning of Company C and James G. Spann of Company G. Both men were perceived as martinets; they were also large landowners who apparently adopted a patrician attitude. Companies C and G also had the second and third highest rates of death from disease, suggesting that the officers may have been lax in enforcing camp sanitation and attending to procurement. Four of the seven first lieutenants in the infantry were defeated: James Lowndes (Co. A), Reuben R. Hudgens (Co. D), George D. Hester (Co. F), and Ransom D. Spann (Co. G). Of the six victorious candidates, only James

unfortunate time for all these changes, inasmuch as we are in sight of the Enemy, and may be attacked at any moment. And it would be very hazardous to throw our Command into a fight under so many new officers. I suppose the Field Officers will be selected soon—My opinion is—that according to the bill—the Field Officers of the Legion will not be elected.[7] Our men are rather Clamorous for the election—and we (the Field Officers) are perfectly willing that they should have it. But it is not yet known whether they will have the privilege. And if they do it is uncertain who they will elect—Col Hampton will be appointed Brig-Genl[8]—And I think my chance would be very good for Col—but this is by no means certain—for, as I told you before, its hard for an officer to do his duty and remain popular with his men. I dont believe, however, that any man in the command could beat me—But My Darling I feel that I must go home, at least for awhile—and my intention is to do so if I am alive when I get through.

If I do, I think Conner or Gary will be elected Col and the other Lt Col—I look with great anxiety to the day when I shall have the extreme pleasure of seeing once more my Darling Wife and Children. But I would much rather see them after I had gone through a battle. It would be terrible to remain in service for twelve months without

---

J. Exum, who rose from senior sergeant to first lieutenant of Company G, had no previous service as an officer. O. Lee Sturkey to Judith McArthur, 11 Dec. 1989.

7. The conscription act allowed the twelve-month men then in service to reorganize under the conditions specified by the Furlough and Bounty Act, which allowed elections to continue wherever they had previously been permitted. Under militia tradition, company officers were elected and regimental officers (those above the rank of captain) were appointed. Since the field officers held commissions from President Davis, they appeared to be exempt from election. In practice, however, appointments often confirmed an election by the non-commissioned officers or the captains of the companies. Some company officers and enlisted men who were dissatisfied with the field officers took advantage of the reorganization to contend that all officers should be elected. When the Furlough and Bounty Act passed, James Conner had observed that "It is a horribly poor Bill, and will lead to more electioneering jealousies, and heartburnings and discontent among officers and men, than anything that could be devised," a prediction that proved entirely accurate. Moffett, *Letters of General James Conner*, 78.

8. Hampton's promotion to brigadier general took effect on 23 May 1862.

going through a single battle. My Darling I recieved a letter to day from Capt Ward[9] who informed me that there was a trunk in Hunt's Hotel in Columbia directed to me— This is the trunk you sent by Gus—You had better contrive to get it back home. By the way—did you ever get my other trunk[?] I sent the key in a letter. Give my love to all and accept for yourself and the dear Children a heart full of love

Your Jimmie

Letter 42   JBG to Leila Griffin

Head Qrs of the Legion
Camp near Yorktown
April 28th 1862

My Dearest Leila

Notwithstanding we were hurried to get here for fear we would be too late for the fight, We have been here ten days, and no fight yet.[1] And, what is more, I dont believe there will be, soon—I am inclined

---

9. Probably Richard Ward of Edgefield District, who had been wagonmaster for the Legion until his retirement in September 1861.

LETTER 42

1. While Johnston's army was on the march, Maj. Gen. John B. Magruder had used his small force in a skillful delaying action against the Federal invaders. On the north bank of the York River opposite Yorktown, he garrisoned Gloucester Point, which overlooked the narrowest part of the river and was the only point that could be commanded by the inferior Confederate artillery. To protect the line south of Yorktown from a rear attack, he constructed a series of dams along the Warwick River and garrisoned the Warwick line, stretching thirteen and a half miles across the neck of the peninsula, with 5000 men. This tiny force and the 6000 men at Gloucester Point halted the Union advance. On 5 April McClellan, with a paper force of 135,000, and 58,000 men ready to move, ordered simultaneous advances against Yorktown and at the Halfway House between Yorktown and Williamsburg. Both were easily checked, the latter by Magruder's line at Lee's Mill on the Warwick. After these tentative probes, the ever cautious McClellan concluded that the defenses were unassailable and settled in for a siege, giving the Confederates valuable time to bring up reinforcements. OR, ser. 1, 11, pt. 1: 1–18; William Allan, *The Army of Northern Virginia in 1862* (1892; rpt., Dayton, Ohio: Press of Morningside Bookshop, 1984), 79; B&L, 2: 168–71.

to think that McClellan has some other scheme than to attack us here. And between you and me, I dont care if he doesnt, for I dont think this is the place for us to fight. McClellan is steadily and slowly approaching our lines, and he *may*, attack after he entrenches up to us—but I am inclined to doubt it. I wouldn't be surprised if our army falls back from here, before we fight—This is only a conjecture of mine. I am very anxious to get away from here, for it is a pretty hard Country to live in. Our fare is rather rough I tell you.

The Legion was reorganized, and have turned out a good many Officers, as I told you they would. In the "Edgefield Hussa[r]s"—Clarke is elected Capt—Pierce Butler 1st Lieut—Markert 2nd Lieut—and an Abbeville man by name of Talbert—Jr 2nd Lieut—[2]

The Legion has sustained considerable loss in the reorganization. The question of Field Officers—has not yet been decided—My opinion is, that they will be appointed. But whether they are appointed or elected, I have decided, in my own mind, to decline the office. I am prompted to this only by my devotion to my family—It's a pretty hard trial, I assure you. I will decline a very high, honourable and proud position, and if I leave the service I will have to do so, when our Country needs the service of all her sons—This is why I say it is a severe trial—But in looking at the condition of those who are dearer to me than all the world besides, seeing how dependent and helpless they are—having no one to look to for protection in these troublesome times—I have concluded to sacrifice my position, and go home, at least for a time, Provided, that is, I am allowed—I look forward My

---

2. Tillman H. Clarke had joined the Hussars, which became Cavalry Company A, as a private and had been promoted to second lieutenant on 30 August 1861. His service record shows no further promotions, but the rolls for April–July 1862 are missing. He signed the company roll as captain commanding on 4 August 1862. Clarke defeated J.J. Bunch, who had been elevated from first lieutenant after M.C. Butler's promotion to major. Michael A. Markert had been bugler and corporal. The Edgefield *Advertiser* of 7 May 1862 reported the election of John Talbot of Abbeville as third lieutenant; the name may be a misprint for John Forsyth Talbert. Pierce Mason Butler, Jr. (see letter of 11 July 1861, note 13), had been fifth sergeant. The reorganization took place on 25 April. CSR, M267, roll 364; *Rolls of South Carolina Volunteers in the Confederate Provisional Army*, 4:26ff, SCDAH; Chapman, *History of Edgefield*, 423.

Darling, to the time when I shall see you all again with the most intense anxiety. This is perfectly natural, as I have been so long separated from you, and I suspect it is rendered more so, because there is a chance, that I may be denied that great pleasure. This is a risque, of course, at all times, but it is certainly a little more *risquey* in war than in peace times. But, My Darling I hope and pray that the good Lord, who has so far Shielded me from danger will, continue to take care of me, and will allow me to see My Darling Wife and Children once more. I cant say when I will be able to get off—but will do so as soon as I can—In the mean time I hope my Darling will keep up her Spirits and Courage. I congratulate you My Darling on your fine gardens—hope they will continue to prosper, and repay you for your industry. I am glad to hear that little Jimmie is getting on so finely— You must learn them all to rough it—for, judging from present appearances, We will have to undergo some of the hardships that our ancestors experienced—We have just heard the news of the fall of New Orleans, I hope it isnt so, but am afraid it is.[3]

I have been very fortunate, lately in recieving your precious letters. I recieved, to day, one from you and another from Sue—I wrote to Sue Yesterday—I have heard nothing of my trunk. It may be in Richmond. What did you send in it? Write me, so that I may know if it is much loss. Have you ever recieved the trunk that I sent home? and did you get the letter containing the key. I went down to Bacon's Regiment yesterday, but was sorry to find Capt Bland's company[4] ab-

---

3. The bombardment of the forts below New Orleans had begun on 18 April and continued for six days without forcing a surrender. Finally, in the early morning hours of 24 April Admiral David Farragut boldly led his fleet of 17 frigates and gunboats past the forts, losing only three vessels. After defeating the Confederate fleet upstream, he reached undefended New Orleans on the 25th and dropped anchor. The loss of New Orleans deprived the South of its largest city and most important port and gave the Federals a key base of operations for attacks against the Confederate heartland. Long, *The Civil War Day by Day*, 201–4.

4. Dr. Elbert Bland, aged 39, was captain of Company H (later renamed A) of the Seventh South Carolina Volunteers, the company in which Leila's nephews, Albert and Charlie Miles (see letter of 11 Aug. 1861, note 6), were serving. Bland was from a wealthy Edgefield family and was married to Emeline Rebecca Griffin, the sister of Lippy Griffin (see letter of 23 March 1862,

sent. They were off on picket, so I didnt have the pleasure of seeing the *boys*, as I anticipated. They were all well though. Col Bacon[5] looks badly—Seebles *[sic]* looks very well[6]—They are in a great stew, about being disbanded[7]—All who have not reenlisted are determined to *go home* if possible. They volunteered to remain until the 1st of

---

note 1). A graduate of the medical college of New York University, he served briefly as assistant surgeon of Maxcy Gregg's First South Carolina Volunteers before joining the Seventh SCV. He was elected lieutenant colonel of the regiment in the reorganization on 14 May. Bland was later wounded at Fredericksburg and killed while commanding the regiment at Chickamauga. Chapman, *History of Edgefield*, 345–47, 418; Krick, *Lee's Colonels*, 48; Dickert, *History of Kershaw's Brigade*, 558, 111.

5. Thomas Glascock Bacon (see letter of 11 Aug. 1861, note 5, and Chapter 1, note 69) declined to stand for reelection in the reorganization the following month because of poor health. He returned to Edgefield and served successively as colonel of the Fifth Regiment of state troops and as a member of the state senate in 1863–65. Reynolds and Faunt, *Biographical Dictionary of the Senate of South Carolina*, 1:86; D. Augustus Dickert, *History of Kershaw's Brigade*, 101–2; Chapman, *History of Edgefield*, 48.

6. Emmet Seibels, aged 40, an Edgefield attorney, was major of the Seventh SCV. He was promoted to lieutenant colonel on 9 May and dropped from the rolls at the reorganization a few days later, after losing the election for colonel to Bland. He then served as a volunteer aide to Matthew Calbraith Butler. In camp near Manassas the preceding fall Seibels and Bland, who were close friends, had fallen into a dispute over one of Seibels's moves during a chess game; heated words were exchanged and Bland ultimately demanded atisfaction. A three-man board of honor, which included the colonels of the Fifth South Carolina and Fifteenth Georgia regiments, failed to bring the matter to a resolution. When word of the proposed duel, which was strictly forbidden by army regulations, reached Brig. Gen. Milledge L. Bonham, he ordered both officers arrested, but they slipped away and faced each other on 26 November. Bland was unhurt; Seibels suffered a chest wound from which he soon recovered. Krick, *Lee's Colonels*, 290; Burton, *In My Father's House Are Many Mansions*, 91; Emmet Seibels to Ed Seibels, 15, 28 Nov. 1861; J.J. Seibels to Ed Seibels, 28 Dec. 1861, Seibels Family Papers, SCL. (Seibels signed his letters "Emmet," although his first name is often printed "Emmett.")

7. The Seventh South Carolina Volunteers, which contained six companies from Edgefield and four from neighboring Abbeville, was among the twelve-month regiments organized immediately after the firing on Fort Sumter and one of the first to reach Virginia. Their enlistment had expired in

May. I think they will then be disbanded— Though the question was not decided, when I was there. This is another objection I have to leaving the Service—South Carolina is doing herself very little credit, in this war—You asked me about the Legion—All twelve months troops whose term of service had not expired, when the conscription bill passed, are required to remain in service for two years longer, if the war lasts so long—And the only trouble about these other S-C regiments, is that their term of service expired a day or two before the bill passed—I think they ought to stay. Tell Spradley to take extra care of the *colts.* And to raise every pound of meat he can—and to look out he doesnt get in the *grass.* My Darling let me advise you to plant lots and cords of pepper—raise it to sell—You can sell all you make at a high price—Tomatoes too will sell high next winter—Plant lots of potatoes—look out for provisions.

It is late at night and I will close—My love to all as usual

Your Jimmie

Letter 43   JBG to Leila Griffin

Head Qrs of the Legion
May 6th 1862

My Dearest Leila

We have deserted the lines at Yorktown—left there saturday night[1]—The Enemy followed us up as far as Williamsburg—A body

---

mid-April. Dickert, *History of Kershaw's Brigade,* gives the date variously as 16 April (p. 37) and 14 April (p. 101), while Chapman, *History of Edgefield,* 218, reports 15 April. The officers' commissions are dated 15 April.

LETTER 43

1. Johnston had gone to the peninsula reluctantly, arguing that it would be only a matter of time before McClellan's superior artillery destroyed the batteries at Gloucester Point and Yorktown, opening the York River to the Federal fleet, which would then be able to land troops behind Confederate lines. He had advocated concentrating forces before Richmond instead of a delaying action on the peninsula. On 24 April Johnston advised Lee that he expected to be compelled to fall back soon, and on 30 April the first shots from McClellan's completed batteries made up his mind. On Saturday, 3 May, after delay and counterorders, Johnston ordered a withdrawal, and the retreat up the pen-

of Cavalry showed themselves there sunday evening & were charged upon by our Cavalry led by Maj Butler who were in the Rear—He ran them off, killing several, and taking eight Prisoners.[2] We left there next morning—leaving one Division behind—They were attacked yesterday, and had a good deal of skirmishing[3]—The result hasnt yet been reported—A portion of the army (We amongst the number) are moving towards West Point, on York River—How far we are to go I dont know. The mail facilities, are now very irregular[.] So you neednt be uneasy, if you dont hear from me regularly. It has been a week since I have had an opportunity of sending you a letter. Dont be un-

---

insula toward Richmond began at midnight. OR, ser. 1, 11, pt. 1:275–77, pt. 3:486–90; Freeman, *Lee's Lieutenants*, 1:148–55; Symonds, *Joseph E. Johnston*, 148–53.

2. All four divisions had reached the old colonial capital of Williamsburg by midday on Sunday, 4 May. Hampton's brigade was the rear guard, screened by Butler's cavalry. At Fort Magruder, situated in front of Williamsburg at the junction of the Hampton and Yorktown roads, the Confederate cavalry and the forward units of the pursuing Federals skirmished briefly, and the Union troops were driven into the woods. In his report to headquarters Brig. Gen. J.E.B. Stuart noted: "all join in praise of the brilliant dash of the Hampton Legion Cavalry upon the enemy's cavalry in front of Fort Magruder." Commanded by Butler, the Hampton cavalry took the lead, charging across an open field, where the Federals held ranks until Butler's men were within a hundred yards of them. The Richmond *Examiner* reported: "In a few minutes the Hampton boys reached their rear, and a hand to hand combat ensued—spirited but brief," and quoted Johnston as saying that the charge had saved Stuart's command, which was for a time cut off. OR, ser.1, 11, pt. 1: 445 (first quotation), 443; Richmond *Examiner*, 10 May 1862, p. 1 (second quotation), 21 May 1862, p. 1; Brooks, *Butler and his Cavalry*, 70–79.

3. Before daybreak on Monday, 5 May, the Legion and the other brigades of Smith's Division resumed the retreat, slogging through heavy rain and thick mud. Consequently, they were not engaged in the battle of Williamsburg, which broke out an hour or two after daylight when Joseph Hooker opened an attack on the rear guard. The Confederates, under James Longstreet, initially pushed the invaders back toward the woods, but by mid-afternoon Hooker had been reinforced by Phil Kearney's division and Winfield Scott Hancock had captured a line of redoubts on the Confederate left. Johnston's army got away safely, in part because of ineffective Federal pursuit. Allan, *Army of Northern Virginia in 1862*, 17–24; Freeman, *Lee's Lieutenants*, 1:174–200; B&L, 2:200–201.

easy about me, live on hope—It is only a month until my time is out—And then I hope to see you all—Butler had two men killed & four wounded[4] —You dont know any of them. I am glad we fell back from Yorktown, for I didnt want to fight there. We have entire confidence in our General (Johnson) And he will whip McClellan sure, in my opinion, whenever he sees proper to fight him.

I havent time to write you more, and I am afraid you wont get this—Direct your letters to Richmond. I will get them from there— Do give my love to all, especially my Darling Children and be always assured that you have the most sincere love of

Your Devoted
Husband

Letter 44   JBG to Leila Griffin

Head Qrs of the Legion
May 8th 1862

My Dearest Leila

We are now at New Kent Court House—about thirty miles from Richmond—We have had a pretty lively time on this retreat. The enemy followed us up to Williamsburg[.] I wrote you an account of Butler's gallant charge on sunday evening. Monday morning the Enemy came out again and Gen Longstreet's division met them and they had a severe fight—We had some 800 or 1000 Men killed & wounded—The Enemy's loss was heavy but number not known[1]—

---

4. The two fatalities were B.W. Boggs and Stephen D. Boynton. Orderly Sgt. James Shaw, Privates McGinnis, Newton M. Fowles, Richard Flannigan, and Gillespie Thornwell were wounded. Fourteen Federals were reported captured and 15 to 20 killed. Richmond *Examiner,* 21 May 1862, p. 1. Originally reported in Charleston *Mercury,* 12 May 1862, p. 2, and Charleston *Daily Courier,* 14 May 1862, p. 2.

LETTER 44

1. Losses were heavy for an essentially indecisive action fought only to cover a retreat. Longstreet reported 1,560 men killed and wounded and 133 missing out of a force of some 31,000; the Federals lost 2,239 out of roughly 40,000 engaged. McClellan's report appears in OR, ser. 1, 11, pt. 1:448–50, and Longstreet's on 564–68.

We drove them back—Genl Smith's division, of whom the Legion forms a part—was hurried up towards West Point to meet the Enemy there, who were sent up by the river, and hold them in check until the rear of our column could pass. We reached Barrhamville, [sic] near West Point on monday evening and found that the Enemy were landing in force—Gen Smith had his troops formed in line of battle, tuesday evening, expecting an attack early the next morning. The men lay on their arms all night. Wednesday morning came but the Enemy did not. So after breakfast We were ordered to attack him—I had the honor, My Darling of leading the Legion into action—we had heavy Skirmishing through most of the day—All the fighting was done in a thick woods. We succeeded in driving the Enemy from every position, drove him back to cover of his gun boats, when we had to stop—My men fought very gallantly—But the Texas Brigade under Gen Hood was most closely engaged—They lost some thirty men in killed and wounded, only five or six were killed[.] We had only one man seriously wounded—some five or six others were slightly wounded.[2] This is the first time, My Darling, that I may be said to have been directly under fire.

---

2. Griffin describes the Battle of Eltham's Landing (West Point). On the night of 5 May, Smith's Division camped at Barhamsville, eighteen miles from Williamsburg and twelve miles from New Kent Court House, on the New Kent Road. It remained there, covering the flank nearer the York and protecting the wagon trains from a possible attack from the river, until the rear divisions of Longstreet and Hill caught up the next day and moved ahead. On the afternoon of 6 May, cavalry scouts along the York reported that Federal transports protected by gunboats were putting troops ashore at Eltham's Landing opposite West Point. Smith decided to let the Federals—Brig. Gen. William B. Franklin's division—advance inland, out of range of the heavy ordnance on their gunboats, before confronting them. He positioned Whiting's command that night with orders to prevent the enemy from moving on Barhamsville until all of the wagons had passed. When the expected attack failed to materialize that night or the following morning, 7 May, Smith changed his strategy and ordered Whiting forward to clear the Federals out of the woods. In a battle that lasted about two hours, Brig. Gen. John Bell Hood's Texas Brigade, with the Hampton Legion on its right, drove Franklin a mile and a half through the dense woods and back to the river. They suffered only 48 casualties, while the Federals lost 186 killed and wounded. Griffin led the infantry and Conner commanded skirmishers composed of two

And I may venture to say to *you* that it is said I was very *cool*. Of Course this is for your ear only. We left last night and arrived here about Mid day to day. We have had a pretty rough trip from Yorktown[—]had very little sleep—and still less to eat. But we dont complain. I dont know yet our destination, But suppose we will stop not very far from Richmond. I will give you the particulars when I see you, which I hope will be soon.

I saw Charlie, Allie and Gus to day for the first time—they are all very well[,] Albert especially[;] he is fatter than I ever saw him. I am writing this on my knee and must close as it is getting dark and I have no candle—Give my love to all—the dear Children included—and accept for yourself the best love of

Your Jimmie

Letter 45   JBG to Leila Griffin

Head Qrs of the Legion
May 11th 1862

My Darling

I have an opportunity to send off a letter and only have time to write you a line. I am very well—We are within 25 miles of Richmond and the Yanks are close on our heels—I think Genl Johnson has gone about as far as he wants to—And if the Enemy chooses to come forward—I think he will give him battle and I am confident will whip him—Our troops are in good health and Spirits—We are now having

---

flank companies from the Nineteenth Georgia and two from the Legion. Hood's regiments, which bore the brunt of the attack, withdrew first after rout; and before Hampton could withdraw the Legion, Griffin repulsed a "strong attack" on his line, during which four men were wounded. The Legion was then withdrawn and the day belonged to the Confederates. Hampton, in his official report, wrote that "Colonel Griffin, in command of the Legion, handled them admirably." Freeman, *Lee's Lieutenants*, 1:193–200; Johnston, *Narrative of Military Operations*, 125–26; OR, ser. 1, 11, pt. 1: 225–26, 626–33; pt. 3:500. First person accounts include John Coxe, "With Hampton in the Peninsular Campaign," *Confederate Veteran* 29 (Nov.–Dec. 1921): 442–43, and Alifaire Gaston Walden, comp., *Confederate War Diary of John Thomas Gaston* (Columbia, S.C.: Vogue Press, 1960), 7–8, which mentions Griffin leading the infantry.

an active campaign—But all the better—If we whip McClellan I think
the war will soon be over— Tell Dr Burt to get Spradley excused from
Conscription—I think he can do it.[1] It is just one month My Darling
until My time is out—and then I hope to see you all again[.]

Give my love to all—the Darling Children especially[.] Dont be
alarmed if you dont hear from me regularly for I may not be able to
get letters off regularly—I recd two precious letters from you yesterday[.]

> Good Bye
> My Darling
> Your Jimmie

Letter 46   JBG to Leila Griffin

> Head Qrs of the Legion
> Bivouack May 13th 1862

My Dearest Leila

We are now within twenty miles of Richmond near the Richmond
and York River rail road. And about seven or eight miles from New
Kent Court House. I suppose we are about as far as we are going at
present.[1] We received orders to leave Yorktown on friday evening the
2nd inst. The movement to commence at dark. And our Division to
form the rear guard. We therefore, a little before sun set were formed

---

LETTER 45

1. Leila's uncle, Dr. William Miles Burt, was one of three examining physicians on the Edgefield District board of exemptions. Overseers were not yet
exempt under Confederate law, and while South Carolina allowed them to
petition for exemption, the board did not have the authority to excuse overseers; these cases were decided by the state adjutant and inspector general.
Spradley would have had to have been obviously medically unfit in order
for Dr. Burt to have excused him. Moore, *Conscription and Conflict in the
Confederacy*, 68–69; Edgefield *Advertiser*, 16 April 1862.

LETTER 46

1. On 9 May Smith's Division was ordered to Baltimore Cross Roads, eight
miles from New Kent Court House, and Longstreet's was moved near Long
Bridge on the Chickahominy River. Supplies were shipped from Richmond
via the Richmond and York River Railroad. OR, ser. 1, 11, pt. 3:503.

in line of battle in a field bordering on the road. There to await the passage of the Troops. This precaution was necessary in case the Enemy should have known of our movement and attacked us. Our men were permitted to lie on their arms in line of battle, (without fire) each man with one blanket and the night quite cool—Maj Conner & I took our position under a Holly bush—just in the rear of the Legion, without any blanket and nothing but my overcoat to lie on—here we remained until ten or eleven O Clock—When I recd intelligence, that on account of Gen Longstreet being unable to get his sick off in time—the movement would not begin until the next night.[2] I then went up to the wagon, and got my blankets[.] Here we remained all day saturday, and that evening again formed line of battle. About dark the movement began—All the Troops in and around Yorktown had to pass by us—The Cavalry were sent forward to report if there was any advance of the Enemy—The troops continued to pass by until about two o'clock at night. But we didnt get off until after day light. It is about twelve miles to Williamsburg, where we arrived about noon— We passed through the Town and traveled two or three miles farther. A good many Troops stopped in the Town—About two or three O Clock in the afternoon—the Enemy's Cavalry appeared in sight of the Town—We had a great deal of Cavalry there and amongst the rest was our own, under Maj Butler—as soon as the Maj saw the Enemy, he asked if he might be allowed to charge them—the reply was yes— when away he went—He only had eighty men—but he supposed he would be sustained by the Virginia Cavalry. He put the Enemy to flight—and pursued them until he came up with their reserves, when finding he was not sustained by the Virginia Cavalry he retired[3]—He

---

2. The army did not have enough wagons to transport the sick, and Johnston had to ask the navy to supply a gunboat for the purpose. More serious delay arose from confusion among subordinate officers, whose modifications of orders threw the march off schedule. Symonds, *Joseph E. Johnston*, 153.

3. The cavalry charged in two columns. Lt. Col. Williams C. Wickham led the Fourth Virginia, which rode to the right of Fort Magruder and met the enemy in the woods beyond. The other column was Butler's men and the Tenth Virginia under Col. James Lucius Davis; it rode left of the fort and charged across an open field. The official reports do not mention a failure to sustain Butler. General McLaws praised all three cavalry commanders and said that Davis charged "in gallant style, driving them back with but little loss

killed and wounded several and took eight Prisoners. Butler lost two men killed and several wounded. The charge was a very gallant one. That night the Troops were again put on the march, at two O Clock— Except Longstreet's command, who were ordered to remain and give the Enemy battle, if he chose to come out the next morning— Which he did—The fight was a hard one, and our loss was heavy, about a thousand killed and wounded. But we drove the Enemy back and his loss was much heavier—That night the ballance of the Troops were drawn—In the mean time Genl Smith's command was hurried up towards West Point, anticipating that the Enemy would send up a column by the river to that point, to attack our right flank—We arrived at Barrhamsville (five miles from West Pt[)] on Monday evening—When we arrived there, we found as was expected, that the Enemy were landing—Gen Smith reviewed the ground and on tuesday evening formed his Troops in line of battle, expecting an attack that night or early the next morning—But they failed to come. So, as I wrote you before, Col Hampton and Gen Hood were ordered out on Wednesday morning to attack him—We met the Enemy about eleven o'clock and after a fight of three or four hours drove him from every position, and forced him to take shelter under his gun boats—Hood had eight men killed and twenty eight wounded, two of whom have died since—We had four men wounded[,] only one severely. The loss of the Enemy supposed to be over a hundred[4]—That night we moved off toward New Kent Court House—Where we halted for the night— Since then we have moved only a few miles. The Enemy keeping close up with us—Now that we have stopped it seems that they are not so keen to fight us. We are just lying here waiting for him and ready to whip him when he comes. I am delighted that we have got out of the peninsula—It was no place for us to fight—and I consider our retreat from there the greatest Strategic movement of the

---

to us." Neither Davis nor Wickham, who was severely wounded, furnished a report. Richmond *Examiner*, 10 May 1862, p. 1; OR, ser. 1, 11, pt. 1:442, 445.

4. The Union regiments engaged were the Fifth Maine; First New Jersey; Sixteenth, Thirty-First, and Thirty-Second New York; Ninety-Fifth Pennsylvania; and Battery A of the New Jersey Light Artillery. The Federals reported 48 killed, 110 wounded, and 28 missing. OR, ser. 1, 11, pt. 1:618.

war—We had pretty tight living on the march— But no complaint—
The troops are in splendid Spirits—ready to fight or move in any direction that Genl Johnson may indicate. All are confident of success
whenver the fight comes off. I hope it may come off before I have to
leave—Do write me if Spradley has to leave and when—I think the
State laws exempts [sic] overseers[5]—The S.C. regiments who were
expected to be disbanded are ordered to reorganize—They are electing their Company Officers to day and tomorrow will elect their
Field Officers. I understand the seventh Regt will elect Aiken[6] Col—

5. Despite pressure from the planter class, the Confederate Congress had
not exempted overseers, but four states, including South Carolina, had passed
their own conscription laws before the first Confederate statute was enacted.
As a result the state and Confederate exemptions sometimes conflicted. The
South Carolina Secession Convention had exempted overseers from the draft
and from militia service (but not from patrol duty or alarm service) on plantations with more than 15 working hands if the owner was absent in state service, or over 60 years old, infirm, or female. Plantation owners had to apply
to the state adjutant and inspector general for the exemption. The Edgefield
Advertiser reported on 16 July 1862 that conscripts for the district would total
350 to 400 for the district and 6000 to 7000 for the state if the state exemptions
were overruled but "much smaller" if not. The main groups affected were
overseers and military cadets. The War Department instructed its agents
merely to file a protest in cases of conflict and agreed not to draft those claim-
ing exemptions until their cases had been decided. The matter was finally
resolved when the Confederate Congress on 11 October passed the "Twenty
Negro Law" exempting one white male on every plantation working 20 or
more slaves, a category that included the Griffins. Journals of the South Carolina Executive Councils of 1861 and 1862, 113; Moore, Conscription and
Conflict in the Confederacy, 68–69, 123; Cauthen, South Carolina Goes to
War, 166–67.
6. David Wyatt Aiken, an Abbeville planter and the cousin of former governor William Aiken, was originally adjutant of the Seventh SCV. He was
elected colonel at the reorganization and commanded until he was badly
wounded at Sharpsburg. Aiken rejoined the command in June 1863, but after
Gettysburg he transferred to Macon, Georgia, as commander of troops and
defenses. He was retired on medical grounds in April 1864 and after the war
devoted his energies to agrarian interests and politics. Aiken was a member of
the national Grange executive committee and owner and editor of the Rural
Carolinian, through which he urged crop diversification and scientific farming
methods. He was elected to Congress in 1876 on the Hampton "straightout"

Bland[7] Lt Col and Burriss[8] Majr—I have seen the boys several times[;] they are generally well—

Do my Darling write often to me and give me all the news—tell me all about the crop—also about the dear Children—God bless them how much I want to see them and you—Remember me very kindly to all and accept for your self the best love of your

Devoted Husband

Letter 47   JBG to Leila Griffin

Head Qrs of the Legion
May 17th 1862

My Darling

We have moved again since I wrote you last. We are now within six miles of Richmond—arrived here yesterday—[1] We left our camp about noon, day before yesterday, and had the most tedious march, for the length of it we have ever had. It was raining and had been for twenty four hours before—and the road which had been exceedingly dusty, became very muddy—It rained on us all the way—and we made eight miles by one oclock at night—*thirteen* hours, in travelling eight miles—It was perfectly awful—We were, as usual, near the rear,

---

ticket and served five terms. Dickert, *History of Kershaw's Brigade*, 558; Krick, *Lee's Colonels*, 26; Claudius Hornby Pritchard, Jr., *Colonel D. Wyatt Aiken, 1828–1887: South Carolina's Militant Agrarian* (n.p.: Claudius Hornby Pritchard, Jr., 1970).

7. Elbert Bland (see letter of 28 April, note 4).

8. The election took a different turn here. John L. Burris was elected captain of Company K, and William C. White of Edgefield was voted in as major. Burris was wounded at Sharpsburg and resigned; White was killed in the same battle. Dickert, *History of Kershaw's Brigade*, 111–13, 159.

LETTER 47

1. On 15 May Federal gunboats made an unsuccessful attempt to pass the Confederate obstructions at Drewry's Bluff, seven miles below Richmond on the James River. Although Richmond was temporarily saved, Johnston decided to draw still nearer to the capital. That day he abandoned the line along the lower and middle Chickahominy and took up a new position only six or seven miles from Richmond, where he could more easily meet an advance from either the James or the York. OR, ser. 1, 11, pt. 1:276.

and could have marched it in two hours and a half. So you can judge what a time we had—The men had to stand most of the time or sit down in the mud. When night came it was excessively dark and it was difficult for the men to see each other in the road. But we got through at last, and crossed the Chickahominy river, the point we were making for. When we stopped—I had the fly of my tent to keep the rain off me—Spread my blanket down in the mud and—without a mouthful of supper went to bed and slept as sweetly until sun rise, as if I had been on a feather bed—We were then ordered again to move, and came to this place. We are resting to day—I dont know how long we will remain here.

I suppose our Generals will examine the country around Richmond—and establish their lines. I think our whole army in Virginia will now be concentrated around Richmond, and make the fight here—That is if McClennan will come[.]

My Darling, the mail carrier is waiting on me & I will send this letter off and write you again by tomorrow's mail[.] I am very well— Do remember me to all. My love to the Children[.] Good Bye My Darling

Your Jimmie

Letter 48 JBG to Leila Griffin

Head Qrs of the Legion
May 17th 1862

My Dearest Leila

I had not time this morning to finish my letter to you in time to get it off by to day's mail—So I sent off a short note by the mail carrier— and will now write a longer one. I gave you a brief account of our tedious march to this place. I dont think we will remain here very long—at least I hope not—For it is an unpleasant camp—The ground is low, and flat, and the water scarce and bad. I suppose our Generals will look around and decide upon the position for our army. The retreat of our Army from the Peninsula is the grandest feat of the war. And I believe we are now about to adopt the proper course—Viz— concentrate the whole army around Richmond and defend it *"to the death"*. I believe we can do it successfully, provided the James river can be so obstructed as to prevent the Enemy's gun boats from runing up to the City. And the opinion is that this can be done. It seems that our Government has adopted a policy from the beginning to do nothing until they are forced to do it. They have had abundant time to effectually blockade the river—but they have postponed it until now—They are now very busy, in blockading the river and in building batteries to command the river. The Enemy sent up two gun boats day before yesterday to reconnoitre our obstructions—our batteries opened fire on them and ran them off—[1] I think the first fighting will be near these batteries—I presume the Enemy will attempt to take them and if we will successfully resist them there—I believe, we are safe—I am well satisfied we can whip any land attack they may make[.] Well My Darling here it is again—orders have just come to move in an hour—We go still nearer to Richmond—Such is the life of a Soldier. Subject to orders to move at all times—I hoped to be quiet to day, and I thought I would write My Darling a long letter—But I must be up and doing—I will finish this letter to night or as soon as I can—In the meantime *adieu.*

Sunday morning 18th

Good morning my Darling—and a bright and beautiful morning it is. Well my Darling, We are again in sight of Richmond. After a campaign of nearly eleven months we have got back within a stone's

---

LETTER 48

1. The James had been vulnerable ever since the Confederates had been forced to evacuate Norfolk on 9 May as a consequence of abandoning Yorktown. The best location at which to contest a Federal advance was Fort Darling, or Drewry's Bluff, where a cliff about 100 feet high overlooked the south bank of the river about seven miles below Richmond. The War Department had paid almost no attention to the fort until after the evacuation of Yorktown, and the preparations that were finally undertaken were hurried and makeshift. Nevertheless, when the Union ironclads *Monitor* and *Galena* led three wooden ships up the James on the 15th, they were unable to pass the weighted hulks that the Confederates had sunk as obstructions, and the Federal vessels could not elevate their guns high enough to damage the Confederate batteries, which fired directly down on them. The *Galena* was badly damaged, and, after almost four hours of shelling, the Federals gave up the attempt and panic subsided in Richmond. Long, *The Civil War Day by Day,* 211–12.

throw of the Camp we left when we were ordered to Manassas.[2] We will soon get comfortably fixed I hope—And I hope too that we have made our last march until we march out to meet the Enemy. I am better pleased with the appearance of the country here, for fighting purposes. Richmond is encircled with a belt of Soldiers—& I believe, are prepared to thrash any force that McClellan may bring forward.

As to my position and what I shall do—I am *kinder* bothered to know *what to do*. I see by the papers that the Governor & Council in their wisdom, have seen fit to conscript all men between the ages of 35 & 50 years of age, for State Service.[3] And for me to be forced into Service as a private, soon after I get home, would be pretty tight papers besides being rather an inglorious termination of my Military career. You can well understand the awkward position I am placed in—If I am to continue in Service, I would much prefer to remain attached to my present Corps than any other—And besides I have a beautiful position. But then on the other hand, I have been so long away from you and the dear Children that I am half crazy to see you—It is pretty hard—but I still think I must go home—You wrote me that Spradley was enrolled—I hope he hasnt had to leave— If he has write me immediately—My Darling, I recd a letter yesterday from Sis, and she informs me that there is a Surgeon from Charleston named Dr Osier[4]

---

2. The poor ground and scarce water motivated Johnston to move the camp again on the 17th. This time the army stopped about three miles in front of Richmond, before a line of redoubts built the previous year. Hill's division, along the Williamsburg Road, formed the center; Longstreet's, covering the river road, formed the right; and Magruder's, on the Nine Mile Road, formed the left. As part of Smith's reserve division, the Legion was behind Hill's left and Magruder's right. OR, ser. 1, 11, pt. 1:268; Johnston, *Narrative of Military Operations*, 128.

3. Confederate conscription (see letter of 25 April, note 1) disrupted South Carolina's military organization and prompted the Executive Council to organize two corps of reserves to defend the state. The first, which could be sent into active service anywhere in the state, was made up of men 35 to 50. The second was intended for patrol duty and internal defense and conscripted only men exempt from militia duty, resident aliens, young men 16 to 18, and older men 50 to 65. Cauthen, *South Carolina Goes to War*, 146.

4. In later letters Griffin writes this name as Dr. Ogier (see 29 November 1862). The Charleston city directories list only one Ogier, Dr. Thomas L., who was apparently in Newberry only temporarily; in later years he was listed

who is said to be superior to Dr. Geddings[5]— I think my Darling, it would be a good opportunity to have poor little Claude's feet operated on. I think you had better go up to Newberry and let him see him and if he thinks he can do it—Have it done—I think you had better do it at once—as this is the most favourable season of the year— Darling dont wait for me to come home—but go at once, it is a good chance and Dr Harrington[6] will be of great service[.]

Write me when you will go[.] My love to all—I must close as I have a great deal to do

Good Bye My Darling
Your devoted Husband

---

in joint practice with his son in Charleston. Thomas Ogier graduated from the Medical College of South Carolina in 1830 and resided for several years in Paris before returning to Charleston to practice. With Dr. Thomas M. Logan, the father of the Hampton Legion captain (and later brigadier general) of the same name, he coauthored A *Compendium of Operative Surgery Intended for the Use of Students* (1834–86). After serving as district surgeon in the Confederate Army, he became medical director of the Department of South Carolina, Georgia, and Florida in 1862. Following the war, Ogier lived for a short while in Newberry before returning to Charleston. *The Charleston Directory* (Charleston: Walker, Evans, 1859), 156; *Charleston City Directory for 1867–68* (Charleston: J. Orrin Lea, [1868]), 128; *Rolls of South Carolina Staff and Confederate Officers*, 1:101, SCL; Waring, A *History of Medicine in South Carolina, 1825–1900*, 280.

5. Dr. Eli Geddings, a native of Newberry, studied medicine privately in Abbeville and was licensed to practice in 1820; in 1825 he became the first graduate of the new Medical College of South Carolina. He taught anatomy at the college before opening his own school, the Charleston Academy of Medicine. From 1831 to 1837 he taught anatomy and physiology at the University of Maryland and edited the *Baltimore Medical and Surgical Journal and Review* before returning to the Medical College of South Carolina, where he had held every chair by the time he retired in 1858. During the war he served as a member of a Charleston medical board which consulted with army physicians on important surgical operations and as a consultant on the Medical Board of the Provisional Army. Waring, A *History of Medicine in South Carolina, 1825–1900*, 235–37; Atkinson, *The Physicians and Surgeons of the United States*, 694; *Boston Medical and Surgical Journal* 99 (1878): 742–43; *Transactions of the AMA* 30 (1879): 819–23; *Rolls of South Carolina Staff and Confederate Officers*, 1:101

6. Griffin's brother-in-law.

Letter 49   JBG to Leila Griffin

> Head Qrs of the Legion
> Camp near Richmond
> May 21st 1862

My Dearest Leila

I received day before yesterday, a letter from you dated 13th inst—saying you had not had a letter from me in a week. This must be owing to an irregularity in the mails—for I have written two or three letters a week—except for a few days after I left Yorktown—and if you dont get them it is the fault of the mails. I am sorry for this—for I can appreciate your feelings in not getting your letters regularly—Nothing worries me more than to fail to get my letters regularly. I am quite well—but am inclined to think, my *personal appearance* is not a great deal improved by the campaign. I have lost the ruddy complexion which I boasted of last winter and have put on in its stead a good coat of *dark brown*. And I am told I am getting quite grey— What do you think of this? If you could know what all I have gone through since you saw me last you wouldnt be surprised that I look older. We are pleasantly situated now, and [have] a great improvement in our fare. But nothing extra at that—And such prices for what we do get—you never heard any thing to equal it. I bought a sheep yesterday at 30 cts per lb, which will make it cost about fifteen dollars. Butter goes readily at $1.00 per lb and glad to get it at that—We are camped near a gardener—he has no vegetables yet except cabbage and asparagus—I never eat as much asparagus in all my life as I have in the last few days. It is the finest I ever saw. I have ate nothing but salt bacon and bread for so long, that I am greatly in want of vegetables. I hope you will have plenty when I get home.[1]

LETTER 49

1. Although they had no concept of vitamins, contemporary physicians knew that scurvy and night blindness were due to poor diet. A prolonged bread and salted meat diet will lead to a deficiency of vitamin C, producing the clinical syndrome of scurvy. The disease, which had plagued isolated garrisons in the West before the war, was a major problem for both Union and Confederate armies. When a significant percentage of the troops, perhaps 5 percent, was diagnosed with scurvy, the remainder were likely to be suffering from sub-clinical scurvy, called the "scorbutic taint." Fresh vegetables erased

My Darling I have a piece of bad news to write you—I fear I have lost Abram. He left me while I was at Yorktown, and I havent heard a word from him since. It is very singular and I cant account for it. He has been a good boy and a faithful one to me most of the time, since I have been in service. And only gave me cause of complaint a few times after he commenced to cater for our Mess, which was the 1st of April—I gave him money and made him buy provisions for us. He seemed to like it well at first. But grew tired before long, as provisions became scarcer. I had to scold him on two or three occasions, and once while at Ashland gave him a light flogging which was the only time I had struck him since he left home—He left me on the 28th of April[.] He went out as usual to buy provisions, and got a pass to cross the York river, said he saw negroes coming from over there, with poultry and such things as could not be bought where we were. This is the last I heard of him—I think he was decoyed off by some one, after he left—for I offered him a $20.00 bill that morning, but he declined, saying he had as much money as he would need for that day—I have never informed you of this before, because, I have always believed he would turn up again—and indeed I think so still—but he may not.

I am sorry he was such a fool—I'll bet he will always be sorry for it. I have been pretty hard up lately for a servant—for since he has been gone, Ned has had the Measles, another singular fact—and he isnt well of them yet.

I have had to hire a boy to attend to my horses—Ned will soon be well however. My Darling I am growing quite impatient for the time, when I am to see you and my dear Children. I hope it will not be much longer. I am anxious My Darling for you to go up to Newberry as soon as possible, and get the Surgeon from Charleston (Dr Osier) to operate on Claude's feet—I would like to be present when it is done, but if it is postponed until I go home it will be so warm—that I think you had better have it done at once. It will be a good chance

---

all signs of scurvy and the scorbutic taint within a few days or even hours. Kenneth J. Carpenter, *The History of Scurvy and Vitamin C* (New York: Cambridge University Press, 1986). John K. Stevens, "Hostages to Hunger: Nutritional Night Blindness in Confederate Armies," *Tennessee Historical Quarterly* 48 (1989): 131–43.

to have it done—better than going to Charleston at this time. If you go over, write me, and let me know what time and how long you will be there. For it may be that I might get home while you were there & if so, of Course I would meet you there.

Do remember me kindly to all friends and relatives—my love and a kiss to each one of the Children—

I have nothing more of interest except that Tom Lipscombe[2] has made up a company from Kershaw's brigade—and has come into the Legion—He is at present in the Infantry—but it is a Cavalry company—He will go home soon for equipment—and when he comes back will join Butler's command—Milledge Lipscombe[3] is a private in the Company—He has an ambrotype of his Lady love— She is quite pretty—He left her in Fla

Write often to

Your Jimmie

2. Thomas Jefferson Lipscomb and his brother Milledge Bonham Lipscomb (see note 3) were from a wealthy planter family originally based in Newberry County. As the sons of John Lipscomb and Sarah Bonham, they were related through their father's family to Griffin and through their mother's to Matthew Calbraith Butler. Their maternal uncles included James Butler Bonham, who had died in Texas at the Alamo, and Brig. Gen. Milledge Luke Bonham, the former commander of Kershaw's Brigade and later governor of South Carolina. Tom Lipscomb, age 29, was a graduate of both South Carolina Medical College and Jefferson Medical College. He enrolled in the Third South Carolina Volunteers on 14 April 1861, and served as second lieutenant of Company B and aide-de-camp to his uncle, General Bonham. When his twelve-month enlistment with the Third South Carolina expired, he had taken advantage of the Furlough and Bounty Act to raise a cavalry company and was commissioned a captain. The company subsequently became Company G of Butler's Second South Carolina Cavalry; Lipscomb attained the rank of colonel on 1 September 1863, and commanded the regiment after Butler became a brigadier general. Tom Lipscomb married Hattie Harrington, the daughter of Griffin's sister's second husband, Dr. William Harrington of Newberry. After the war he was elected mayor of Columbia. O'Neall, *Annals of Newberry*, 606, 649–50; Pope, *History of Newberry County* 1: 268–69; Krick, *Lee's Colonels*, 206; Salley, *South Carolina Troops in Confederate Service*, 2:322; Dickert, *History of Kershaw's Brigade*, 90; CMH, 6:107; Brooks, *Butler and His Cavalry*, 545–46.

3. Milledge Bonham Lipscomb, age 25, graduated from South Carolina College with Matthew Calbraith Butler in 1857, studied law briefly, and then

Letter 50   JBG to Leila Griffin

Head Qrs of the Legion Saturday
night 12 oclock May 24th 1862

My Darling

I intended to have written you a long letter to day. But while we were at the dinner table—we recd orders to move out at once to the support of a brigade in front of us who were attacked by the Enemy. We did so—And found that they had then had a Skirmish and all was again quiet.[1] We were then ordered back to camp—We will perhaps have to go out again tomorrow to relieve this Brigade, and hence my letter or rather my note to night. The mail leaves early in the morning and I only write a few lines to say I am well but quite tired. If I dont have to go out tomorrow I will write you a long letter—(for I have a good deal to write you about my position) and if I cant write tomorrow I will as soon as I can. I recd a dear letter from you to day—which by the way, was advertized, and the reason was you failed to put "Hampton Legion" in the direction. Look out for this in the future. It is late and I am tired & I know you will excuse this note—My love to all

Your devoted
Husband

Letter 51   JBG to Leila Griffin
[Written on reverse side of previous letter]

Sunday Morning—In bed—
May 25th

My Darling

I havent yet got up but I will write a line or two more before the Mail leaves—We had two Skirmishes yesterday (I mean our Troops

---

turned his attention to planting. He had been a captain and volunteer aide on General Bonham's staff in 1861. Lipscomb served as a private in his brother Tom's Company G, Second South Carolina Cavalry, until the end of the war and saw action at Sharpsburg, Brandy Station, and Gettysburg. CMH, 6:706–7; *Rolls of South Carolina Staff and Confederate Officers*, 1:17.

LETTER 50

1. On 24 May Union cavalry drove the Confederates out of the village of Mechanicsville, five miles above Richmond, and Federal troops skirmished

had) the entire results of which is not known yet—We are ready and waiting for McClellan to come on—I suppose that a long and bloody battle will be fought here, whenever Mc. chooses to advance—I have no doubt that he will make a desperate effort to take the City[.] But I dont believe he can come it.

My Darling Strange to say, I recd yesterday a letter from you and in the same envellope one from Willie—dated the 29th April[.] It has been written nearly a month[.] Give my love to Willie and tell him I am obliged to him for his letters[,] also the same to Bobbie but I very seldom get any letters from them—I will write to them soon—My Darling I sent My dog Joe home, by a Friend who lives in Columbia, John Kinnerly,[1] he promises to carry him to Mr Boatwright's on the Ridge,[2] and then drop you a note. Send for him and take good care of him—How is Jeff—

I must Close—

Your
Jimmie

Letter 52   JBG to Leila Griffin

Head Qrs of the Legion
May 26th 1862

My Darling Leila

I will again make an effort to write you a few lines, as the note I sent to you yesterday was quite a short one. Every thing remained very quiet all day yesterday along the lines. The Yanks seemed to be keeping the Sabbath. I am now writing about nine oclock am. and everything is still quiet. Most people are expecting a fight daily. But I con-

---

with Robert Hatton's Tennessee Brigade, of Smith's Division, near Seven Pines and were driven back. Johnston, *Narrative of Military Operations*, 130.

LETTER 51

1. Possibly John Kennerly, a private in Company A, cavalry. The Columbia city directory (1860) cites John Kennerly, clerk, boarding at the northwest corner of Washington and Sumter Streets in the residence of E. Kennerly. CSR, M267, roll 364.

2. The Ridge was in the southeast section of Edgefield District, between Edgefield and Columbia. B.T. Boatwright was a farmer.

fess, I do not believe it will come off so soon, unless Genl Johnson makes the attack. I have no doubt that McClellan is even now digging holes and throwing up breastworks.[1] The Chickahominy is the line at present between the two armies. The bulk of our army is nearer to Richmond but we picket out near the river, on all the roads leading from the City in that direction. It was in this direction that the Skirmishes occurred, about which I wrote you yesterday. I have no doubt that there will be more or less Skirmishing every day.

My Darling, I recieved your letter in which you stated what Lanham had heard about me. This I have no doubt worries you more than it does me. I have learned to disregard the slanderous rumours that are generally propagated by a certain class of people whose whole life is spent in gathering up and distributing false and slanderous reports on those who have in many cases been their best friends. This is particularly the case with Lanham, for if there ever was a man who acted the part of a friend to another, I have towards him. And since he acted so that he had to leave the Legion, he, it seems would be pleased to draw others down on a level with him.[2] But my Darling, dont give yourself any trouble about it, for whenever I get so low down, as to be injured by anything that Lanham might say of me— why then—I'll be pretty low down. The young gentleman (Hamilton) whom Lanham quotes is quite a Gentleman. He was a Lieutenant in one of our Artillery companies and was not reelected in the reorgani-

---

LETTER 52

1. The sarcastic reference is to McClellan's well-known reluctance to take the offensive; in fact, he was building bridges across the Chickahominy rather than breastworks. As usual, he believed himself to be facing superior numbers and had been bombarding Washington with requests to reinforce his 80,000 effectives. On 20 May the Federals had reached the left bank of the Chickahominy at Bottom's Bridge, which the Confederates had already destroyed. Finding the right bank lightly defended, McClellan sent a division to occupy the opposite heights, leaving the remainder of his forces on the left to guard his supply and communications lines and to protect the right rear while the bridges were being rebuilt across the rain-swollen river. OR, ser. 1, 11: 25–31.

2. Bvt. Second Lt. James M. Lanham (see letter of 29 June 1861, note 1) of Company A, cavalry, had been AWOL. He was allowed to tender his resignation, which took effect in January 1862. "Hampton Legion," CSR.

zation.[3] He is a high toned, and gallant young man. He has been home, to Charleston, but has again returned to the Legion. I asked him about what you wrote me. He said, that he had said, that in the reorganization of the Legion most of the good company officers were turned out, and that he wouldnt be surprised if they were to pursue the same course and turn out Maj Conner and Myself. But so far from saying any thing against us—he is a warm personal friend of both of us.

You asked me if Gary and myself are as good friends as we used to be. I answer—we are *not*. I have been a good friend to him up to within a few days ago—I have allways talked very freely and confidentially to him about my views. I told him that I expected to retire, after my term of service expired, and would be glad to see him promoted. He always said he would be satisfied with any [commission] so [long as] it was a field office. I told him not to express my views to any one, for I would not say positively what I would choose to do—but reserved to myself the right to act as I might choose, according to the circumstances. All this time Gary seems very anxious to impress me with the belief that the men didnt like me as well as they did Maj Conner— and that they liked him better than either of us. Maj Conner had taken the position long ago, that if the Legion reorganized he would not allow himself to be placed in opposition to me—but would be perfectly willing to serve under me.

Well, the Secretary was not heard from. Gary said the men were very anxious for an election and Col Hampton wrote again to the Sec. Still no answer comes. A petition signed by most of the company officers & addressed to the Sec. of War asking for an election was sent to Col Hampton. He forwarded it through Genl Whiting, who endorsed on the back of it—Positively and emphatically *Disapproved* saying that the Field Officers were *good officers* and *first rate men* and that this was a move to turn them out and fill their places themselves and that they were not competent for the positions, and a whole lot of other compliments to us—and in this way the paper went up. And no answer yet.

---

3. Second Lt. Paul Hamilton of Company A, artillery, enrolled in Charleston in June 1861. The muster roll shows that he was dropped on 15 April 1862. "Hampton Legion," CSR.

And now that the thing is so long being decided the *scheme* devel-
lopes itself. Gary is to be elected to my office, and one of the other
Captains to the Majr's. This can be done very easily, where the company officers combine together. They can turn out any Field Officer.
We were all willing for the men to elect their Officers, but since this
scheme has been discovered, it has given general dissatisfaction. I told
Gary the other day after I saw that the Gov. and Councill had conscripted all men between the ages of 35 & 50 that I dont feel like
giving up my handsome position and be a conscripted private as soon
as I get home. This evidently didnt suit him. He much preferred my
going home so that he wouldnt be brought in contact with me. He
seems to be quite uneasy. I dont know how the matter will end—but
my opinion is that the election will be refused, and the present officers
will be reappointed. Col Hampton was tendered the appointment of
Brig Genl a day or two ago. He however declined it on account of its
date. He has been discharging all the duties of that office for nearly
six months and he thinks it is unfair to date his commission at this
time.[4] I dont know if the President will date it back. If he does not
the Colonel says he would prefer to go back and devote all his time to
the Legion—provided the field officers be appointed. But that if the
other officers are to be turned out by these company officers that they
may take his office too, for he will give up his command.[5]

My Darling all these things together has given me a good deal of
trouble. The idea of your most intimate friend being instrumental in
removing you from a high and honorable position and taking that
place for himself looks rather badly, and all the time trying to make
you believe, that he wouldnt do anything against you for the world.
But the idea my darling, of being absent from my dear family any

---

4. See letter of 2 January, note 2. The date of the commission remained
23 May 1862, and Hampton ultimately accepted it.

5. Matthew Calbraith Butler quoted Hampton to the same effect in a letter
written two days earlier. Hampton had assessed the situation as early as January, when he wrote to his wife: "My men would, I think nearly all go in for
the war with me, but they would split up on some of the other officers. . . .
I am satisfied with my field and staff officers and should like to retain them."
M.C. Butler to Wife, 24 May 1862, Butler Papers, DU; Hampton to Catherine Hampton, 14 Jan. 1862, in Cauthen, *Family Letters of the Three Wade
Hamptons*, 82.

longer, is almost killing me. But if I go home now and give up my prospects here I may be forced into service without an office. This, I wouldnt like to stand and then what am I to do[?] If I could go home on furlough I wouldn't mind it. But that is out of the question at this time. Indeed, I dont want to go now—I will hang on at least till this storm blows over and see if there is to be a fight. If I should be so fortunate to get through it, I will decide what I will do. In the mean-time, I want My Darling to give me her views on the subject. Which would you prefer me to do—go home and take the chances of being a Conscripted Private—or be a full Colonel of the Legion. Tell me honestly which to do—that is if I can. Dont say anything about this yet for I dont know how it will work out. I must now close as I am ordered to go out on picket.

   Do, my Darling, remember me to all my friends and give my love to my darling Children. I will write to Willie and Bobbie soon. Good bye My Darling.

Your Jimmie

Letter 53   JBG to Leila Griffin

Head Qrs of the Legion
May 28th 1862

My Darling,

   Since I wrote you last, my command has had another very unpleas-ant trip on picket[.] We were ordered out to the front, late monday evening—We reached the ground about nine O Clock at night and the darkest night that you almost ever saw—Cloudy, cold and hit [sic] a raining—and within about a quarter of a mile of the Enemy. The ground was low and flat and a great portion of it covered with water. I got my pickets posted by 12 O Clock and without any shelter at all and what is more without fire, (for fires were prohibited), the Maj, Dr. Taylor and myself spread down our blanket—and went to bed, covering up head & ears with another. Here we remained, about two hours when I woke up and found that we were lying in a puddle of water. I got up and set up from then until day. We remained here all day and until 12 O Clock last night when we were relieved and had to march four miles back to camp through mud and water nearly half leg deep. We got to camp and I went to bed about 3 O Clock, and when I got up I find an order to have rations prepared for a March this evening. And now my Darling—I'll tell you a secret—We are going out to whip McClellan, if we can.[1] And I believe we can. Before this reaches you the thing will be over. If we succeed, which God grant we may, our prospects will brighten—and if we fail, (which God forbid) our prospects will be gloomy indeed—I of course hope to be one of the fortunate ones & will be spared to go through with it, and see my Country free once more. If I get wounded I will telegraph you immediately—And if it should be God's will that I shall fall, I hope to fall at the head of my men and leave the Legacy, to my Dear Dear very Dear family, that I died the most glorious and honorable death known to man—That of fighting for Liberty.

If we drive the Enemy before us, as we hope to, I have no doubt we will pursue him until we drive [him] from the Soil of Virginia. In this case I may be unable to write you regularly—but rest assured My Darling that you shall hear from me every chance I have—and if you don't have that comfort often I hope it will result in affording a still greater one sooner—Viz that of allowing me to see you sooner—This crisis has to come. We have got to meet it—And for my part the sooner the better.

I believe it is all the better for us—Julius Day[2] called on me this

---

LETTER 53

1. On 27 May McDowell's division had been reported marching south from Fredericksburg, and troops from McClellan's right flank had seized the village of Hanover Court House on the Fredericksburg road. Fearing that the two armies were about to unite, Johnston instructed his division commanders to prepare to move, and designated G.W. Smith to lead an attack on McClellan's right, which was separated from the main body of troops by the rain-swollen Chickahominy River. By the 28th, however, cavalry patrols reported that McDowell had returned to Fredericksburg and appeared to be planning to move even farther north, and the attack was called off. After armed reconnaissance revealed that the Federals were entrenching near Seven Pines, seven miles east of Richmond, Johnston decided to strike a decisive blow against McClellan there on the 31st. Freeman, *Lee's Lieutenants*, 1:220–23; Symonds, *Joseph E. Johnston*, 161–63; Stephen W. Sears, *To the Gates of Richmond: The Peninsula Campaign* (New York: Ticknor and Fields, 1992), 117–24.

2. Julius S. Day, Sr., of Edgefield was probably visiting his son, James S.

morning, I was very glad to see him. I gave him two hundred dollars for you—do the best you can— Do my Darling have little Claude's feet operated on—Give my best love and a sweet kiss to each one of them and, my very kindest regards to all our relatives and my friends. And accept for yourself that love which can only be bestowed on a loving wife by a devoted

Husband

Letter 54   JBG to Leila Griffin

Head Qrs of the Legion
Bivouac in the Woods, June 2nd
1862

My Darling Leila

I telegraphed you yesterday, which I hope you received. I presume you have seen by the papers that we have been in a fight. We had a short, but *terribly* hot fight. I mean my command. Genl Longstreet commenced the attack about 12 oclock and drove the Enemy steadily back, captured his camps &c and a good many of his guns.[1] Genl Smith's command was ordered down on the left to support the right if necessary—We reached the point where we were to halt about 1

Day, of Company B (Gary's Watson Guards). Day's other son, Julius Jr., a private in Company H, Seventh South Carolina Volunteers, had died of congestive fever in September 1861. CSR, M267, roll 216.

LETTER 54

1. The battle of Seven Pines or Fair Oaks was a poorly executed affair: unclear or misunderstood orders resulted in failures to move on schedule and lack of coordination among the attacking units. Longstreet had command of the right wing—his own, D.H. Hill's, and Huger's divisions—and received verbal instructions from Johnston to advance down the Nine Mile road from Richmond and form on the left flank of Hill's Division, which was to hit the Federal center and right. Huger's Division was to assist Hill and form a reserve on the right; when Huger's first brigade reached Rodes's Brigade (Hill's Division), the latter was to go across country from the Charles City road to join the rest of Hill's Division on the Williamsburg road. At Rodes's arrival a gun was to be fired signalling Hill to attack, and the sound of Hill's fire was to send Longstreet into action. The essence of the plan was an early attack by three divisions simultaneously in order to surprise the corps of Erasmus D.

oclock and listened to the thundering war of musketry for several hours—I knew Longstreet was driving everything ahead of him by the sounds of the guns and the shouts of our gallant men. About four oclock Col Hampton recd a message to bring in his brigade—as soon as possible. The Enemy had been reenforced and were moving in strong force against our left with a view to flank Longstreet. A portion of Smith's command was nearer the scene of the engagement than we were & when we got there [we] found them engaged.[2] I had command of the Legion and was in front of the Brigade.[3] As soon as I reached the field I got into the *fight* and the *hottest* kind of one. The Enemy were in a woods behind which was a battery, which was raking our men at a great rate. Col Hampton's first order was to drive the Enemy from the woods and charge that battery—*At it* we went—The Enemy fell back behind the battery—When I got within about 150 yards of

---

Keyes and Samuel P. Heintzelman, isolated on the South bank of the over-flowing Chickahominy River, before they could be reinforced by the three corps on the north. Instead Longstreet moved by the Williamsburg rather than the Nine Mile road, and the advancing divisions got in each other's way. After waiting several hours for Longstreet, Hill finally launched an unsupported attack at 1 p.m. Longstreet did not reach the field until about 2 p.m., disingenuously blaming the delay on Huger's failure to advance, when in fact his own troops had blocked the road. O.R., ser. 1, vol. 11, pt. 1: 939–41; Freeman, *Lee's Lieutenants* 1: 225–37; Clifford Dowdey, *The Seven Days: The Emergence of Robert E. Lee* (1964; rpt., Wilmington, N.C.: Broadfoot Publishing, 1988), 84–105; Sears, *To the Gates of Richmond*, 124–40; Symonds, *Joseph E. Johnston*, 160–72.

2. Hood's, Whiting's, and Pettigrew's brigades preceded Hampton's and Hatton's and were fired on by two artillery batteries supported by infantry. The Legion went into battle on Pettigrew's left. OR ser. 1, 11, pt. 1: 989–90; B&L, 2: 244–46; Freeman, *Lee's Lieutenants*, 1: 238–39.

3. Field reports that Griffin led Hampton's brigade and engaged the enemy in "dense, entangled wood." He quotes from the Charleston *Daily Courier* a report by an anonymous staff officer with the Legion that they "went forward at the double quick, as we got into the woods a most murderous fire of grape, canister and musketry was opened on us. The dead and wounded fell thick around, still we pushed forward; on getting to the woods our little brigade found itself unsupported within fifteen yards of a heavy battery, flanked by fifteen thousand infantry, strongly entrenched" (11 June 1862). Field, *South Carolina Volunteers*, 18.

the battery I—being somewhat protected by the woods, stopped my men for the other regiments to form on me preparatory to the charge—as soon as they came up I gave the order to forward and charge—away went my men—in good line and shouting at the top of their voice. All this time the battery was firing incessantly & very rapidly—but the muskets had stopped—This battery was about 40 yards from the edge of the woods—and a *very large* force of infantry were lying concealed behind it—This of course we found out only by sad experience—when my men reached the edge of the woods—and uncovered themselves—We were met with a most fearful volley, which brought my men to a stand, we returned it and attempted to go on, but not being sustained (I am sorry to say) by the others [*sic*] regiments—and the fire so *terrible*, that we were forced to fall back—I fell back about 150 yards where I reformed, and begged the other men to join me, a few of whom done so, and I made a second charge on it—We went up almost to the battery this time but they were too many for us and we had to fall back again—This time the men wouldnt be rallied until they went farther—I assure you I never felt so bad in my life as I did when I turned my back to the Scoundrels—We had plenty of men there to have taken the battery if they had stood square up to it[4]—

---

4. Fighting in dense woods about 800 yards north of Fair Oaks Station, where the Nine Mile road crossed the Richmond and York River Railroad, Smith's division encountered Maj. Gen. John Sedgwick's division from across the supposedly impassable Chickahominy. Lack of coordination hampered Confederate effectiveness, and both brigades suffered heavy casualties because of the piecemeal attacks. The Richmond *Examiner* described the "gallant charge" of the Hampton Legion, partially supported by the Fourteenth Georgia Infantry Regiment: "The Fourteenth charged up to within forty or fifty yards of the battery, where it received a most galling and destructive fire, and after delivering its own fire, fell back. Afterwards, in conjunction with the other regiments composing the brigade, the Fourteenth made two successive and desperate charges upon the battery, and finally fell back with the brigade." An aide-de-camp to Longstreet wrote: "Very few of Whiting's men had been under fire before, the enemy had a good position, [and] the attack was not made so vigorously as ours. The most of Whiting's men behaved badly and were repulsed with a considerable loss of officers and men." A half-hearted attempt by the Confederates to renew the battle the next day was easily re-

Our loss was fearful—My command was cut up terribly—We suffered by far more than any of the rest—I went into the fight with about
350 men and lost in killed and wounded and missing 154 men—All
this was done within one hour and a half—This will give you an idea
of the kind of fire to which we were exposed—The Legion here in this
short time lost as many men as they lost at the great battle of Manassas—We had 21 men killed dead 118 wounded & 15 missing unac-
counted for.[5] We have lost many of our best men—Jack Tompkins[6]
is missing, Dont know whether he is killed, wounded or taken pris-

---

pulsed by the reinforced Union line. Although the Confederates proclaimed
victory, they gained no permanent ground, their losses were excessive, and
McClellan's army still threatened Richmond. Richmond *Examiner*, 4 June
1862, p. 1 (first quotation); Langston James Goree, ed., *The Thomas Jewett
Goree Letters*, vol. 2: *The Civil War Correspondence* (Bryan, Tex.: Family
History Foundation, 1981), 152 (second quotation); OR ser. 1, 11, pt. 1: 990–
91; B&L, 2: 245–47; Freeman, *Lee's Lieutenants*, 1: 238–44; Allan, *Army of
Northern Virginia*, 47–48. The recriminations and fault-finding that arose out
of the botched battle are fully discussed in Freeman, *Lee's Lieutenants*, 1:
252–61; Dowdey, *The Seven Days*, 84–127; Sears, *To the Gates of Richmond*,
140–49; and Symonds, *Joseph E. Johnston*, 172–74.

5. From the general disaster "on Genl. Whiting's part of the field," Lt.
Thomas Jewett Goree, an aide-de-camp to Longstreet, singled out the Legion
for special praise: "Hampton's Legion, SC troops, in Whiting's Division behaved very gallantly. They lost nearly one half." Hampton, in a letter to the
secretary of war, cited 365 men engaged and 154 killed, wounded, and missing. This was a casualty rate of more than 40 percent, and Hampton asked
Randolph that the infantry be brought up to full strength at once "in justice
to these men, who have always fought well." Griffin's figures are confirmed
in the Richmond *Examiner*, 4 and 7 June 1862. The total Confederate loss
was 6,134 to 5,031 for the Union. B&L, 2: 219; Goree, ed., *The Thomas
Jewett Goree Letters*, 2: 153–54; Hampton to George W. Randolph, 3 June
1862, *Letters Received by the Confederate Secretary of War, 1861–65*, M437,
roll 57, doc. H546, NA.

6. John Warren Tompkins, aged 35, was the brother of Robert and Richard
Augustus (Gus) Tompkins (see letter of 25 April, notes 2 and 4). Tompkins
had been a "planter" and a colonel in the state militia before enlisting in
Confederate service as a member of Gary's Watson Guards, infantry company
B, on 12 June 1861. He was promoted to second corporal on 5 August 1861,
and later demoted. Tompkins was wounded and captured at Seven Pines and
sent to Fort Delaware prison on 5 June. He was exchanged at Aiken's Landing

oner. Yancey Dean[7] was shot in the arm and leg, had to have his arm amputated. Col Hampton was wounded in the foot painfully, but not seriously.[8] Genl Johnson was wounded, not seriously[.][9] Julius Day has just come up and I will get him to take this letter to you—I cant give you all the particulars—When I get quietly back in camp I will write you a long letter[.] I feel very thankful that I was spared and went through without a scratch—Dont know how I escaped for the bullets fell like hail stones[.] I had my mare shot—she was wounded on the inside of the thigh with a large ball—I sent her off to camp & dont know how badly she is hurt—She was very lame—Give my love to all especially the Dear Children.

> Good bye My Darling
> write often to your Jimmie

---

two months later and discharged on a surgeon's certificate on 7 August. Sturkey, Company B, "History and Rolls of the Hampton Legion Infantry"; Edgefield *Advertiser*, 7 May 1862; Heath, "The James S. Tompkins Family."

7. Seventeen-year-old L. Yancey Dean had enlisted in Company B as a private and been promoted to fifth corporal in September or October. At the reorganization on 23 April, he had advanced to fourth sergeant. Dean was wounded in the arm and thigh; his arm was amputated and he was discharged for disability on 1 July. Sturkey, Company B, "History and Rolls of the Hampton Legion Infantry"; Edgefield *Advertiser*, 18 June 1862.

8. Hampton was shot in the foot but refused to dismount or leave the field, and the ball was removed from his foot as he sat on his horse under fire. During his convalescence in a private home he wrote to his sister: "The ball, which was a Minie one, struck the sole of my boot and turned over, driving the . . . large end against the bones in my foot. The ball is mashed up, and the *bones feel pretty much in the same condition.*" OR ser. 1, 11, pt. 1: 991; Cauthen, *Family Letters of the Three Wade Hamptons*, 85. As Hampton remained under fire while undergoing the operation to have the ball removed from his foot, the surgeon performing the procedure, E.S. Gaillard, was shot and killed. Field, *South Carolina Volunteers*, 18.

9. Johnston was wounded slightly in the right shoulder by a musket ball and a few minutes later went down from a shell fragment in the chest and was carried off the field. The following day Lee assumed command of the Army of Northern Virginia. Symonds, *Joseph E. Johnston*, 172, 175.

Letter 55   JBG to Leila Griffin

Head Qrs of the Legion
June 5th 1862

My Darling

I am greatly pressed with business, but knowing your very natural uneasiness of mind, during the present excited times, I will write you very often. Of course you must not expect me to write long letters— Nor you must not get uneasy if you dont get them regularly—For, I may be unable to write regularly. I wrote you in my last that I was acting *Brig Genl*. What do you think of that? does that look like your Husband didnt stand as high as persons would have you to believe— Pay no attention to the many lies you may hear—It is generally the result of envious and ambitious men. And will all work out right after a while—

My being placed in Command of this Brig. while Col Hampton is disabled is a very handsome Compliment to me, and I presume will excite a new the envy of some of my *pretended Friends*. You, know, I never did care much, what People thought of my actions, but I assure you, I care less now than ever—I try to do my duty without regard to whom it pleases or displeases. I am gratified to know that my course has been such as, to at least, satisfy my Superior Officers—I will tell you how I consider that I am complimented by being placed in Command of the Brigade—Of course a man should not, repeat his own praises,[1] but then it is certainly not Criminal for a man to tell these things to his wife—In the first place, you must understand that rank and position, is what *almost* every man in the army (and particularly

---

LETTER 55

1. The Edgefield *Advertiser* lauded Griffin on 11 June when it reported of Seven Pines: "Lieut. Col. J.B. Griffin was in command of the Legion. . . . He sustained fully the reputation of old Edgefield for gallant and chivalrous sons. He bore himself with conspicious courage and ability. He is now in command of the Brigade, Col. Hampton being wounded in the foot." On the 18th it printed a cavalry major's private letter that included praise for Griffin: "The charge was terrific. Col. Griffin conducted himself in the most gallant manner, and has won golden opinions from his men and from all."

the officers) look to. When Col Hampton was wounded the command of the Brigade fell on Col Price[2] of the 14th Ga who between us, is a rather weak stick—Col Davis[3] of the 16th N.C. was killed—and the 19th Ga was commanded by Lt Col Johnson,[4] whose commission is older than mine—Col Price was seperated by some means from his command, and I informed Col Johnson that he was in command in the absence of Price. He declined to take it and asked that I would do so, said he much preferred that I should—Col Price came up after awhile, and of course he took Command—I was unwilling to go in a fight under him, and asked that the Legion might be assigned to some other Brig, until Col H— recovered—

The next thing I heard was that the 14th Ga was assigned to another Brig[5]—and I was placed in Command of this Brig—Col Price was removed because they could not give a Lt Col command of a Colonel—Now wasn't that a compliment. I told you in my last that I had had a talk with Gary—He undertakes to say that he has always been true to me—and even *thinks* or says, I have not been so true to him— This may be so[.] But one thing I know, I have been of great service to him—And all that I know he has done for me, is to have (innocently perhaps) created the impression that I was unpopular with my men. He denies it, but I have heard of his telling different ones that he didn't know why, but the men didnt like me—He has told me this—and I know it was true to a certain extent—but never did believe

---

2. Col. Felix L. Price, a graduate of Georgetown University, had enlisted as captain of Company I of the Fourteenth Georgia and risen rapidly. He was promoted to major on 17 July 1861, to lieutenant colonel on 18 August, and to colonel on 19 December. Price was wounded at Cedar Mountain on 9 August 1862 and resigned from the army on 23 October. Krick, *Lee's Colonels*, 266.

3. Col. Champion Thomas Neal Davis enrolled as captain of Company G of the Sixteenth North Carolina on 9 May 1861 and was promoted to colonel on 26 April 1862. Krick, *Lee's Colonels*, 95.

4. Lt. Col. Thomas Coke Johnson had been commissioned on 8 May 1861. He was subsequently killed in action at Mechanicsville. Krick, *Lee's Colonels*, 180.

5. The Fourteenth Georgia was transferred to Joseph R. Anderson's Third Brigade in A.P. Hill's Division. OR, ser. 1, 11, pt. 3:649.

it was serious—And yesterday I had an opportunity of testing it—- This question of Field Officers has never yet been decided,[6] although applied to twice by Col Hampton and once by a petition from the Company Officers of the Legion—Why he hasnt given his decision I dont know—But yesterday there comes up another petition from the Company Officers, asking for a decision in the matter and requesting me to forward it—

This seeming anxiety for an election of officers, just after we had come out of a very severe battle, and another impending—looked as if the men were unwilling to go into another under their present Field Officers, and if this was the case, I wanted to know it, for now they have seen me tried—I immediately ordered out the battalion & Maj Conner and myself made a short address to them—I asked the men the question—are you willing to serve under your present Field Officers until the Sec decides this question, for in the mean time there may come another fight—and if they were unwilling for us to lead them—we would instantly *resign*. I dismissed the bat— & requested the Capt's to take the vote of their companies on the questions— They did so & every company reported *unanimously—Yes*—perfectly willing— Except Gary's com— & they said they were willing to remain until the 12th of June[;] that after that they thought they ought to have the right to elect—Of course I understood this—I may be mistaken, but as much as you have heard about my unpopularity, I believe I can beat any man in the Legion for my office. I hope it will be decided soon. All is quiet along the lines—I dont think there will be any more fighting of consequence in several days—& I dont reckon we will be in the next one—My love to all—kiss my children.

Do write often to your

Jimmie

---

6. In his letter to the secretary of war only two days earlier asking for an increase in the infantry (see previous letter, note 5), Hampton concluded by calling Randolph's attention again to "the circumstances I laid before you in reference to the Field Officers." It was received on 4 June and the covering memo instructed a war department subordinate to say that the President had determined that the Legion should reorganize by electing its officers. The letter is marked as having been answered on 10 June.

Letter 56   JBG to Leila Griffin

Head Qrs of the Legion
June 7th 1862

My Dearest Leila

I am now on Picket with the whole brigade and let me tell you I am actually living in a *house*. So much for playing *Brig Genl*. I have to be at some convenient place where orders and information from my pickets can reach me. So finding a neat little white deserted cottage, I have taken *possession*. This is the second house I have slept in for the last eight months. I find it very comfortable but for the flies—they are dreadful— My health I am happy to say is still very good—I stand the hardships of camp life first rate—I candidly confess however, that I am getting powerful tired of it—I want to go home and be with my darling wife and children but I cant go, if I would—and to tell you the truth, since So much has been said about me, at home, amongst my *friends*, I am anxious to have this *question* settled. My own private opinion is that I stand very *fair*, especially, since our engagement of last saturday—The Legion has added to its already established reputation—And indeed they are justly entitled to it, for no men on earth, could have stood better, such a fire as they were exposed to—And I flatter myself, if they are entitled to credit, I am entitled to a share— for I was with them through the whole of it—And it really seems miraculous that I wasnt struck, for the balls flew by me in perfect *torrents*. I think, my men, are well pleased with me—some of them have told me since, that they had rather I would lead them into a fight than Col Hampton himself—this is certainly a high compliment—But dont you tell [page torn] he is as gallant a gentleman and as brave one as ever I met—and is entitled to the entire confidence of his men. He is doing very well, his wound was not serious, but painful—he will be out again soon.

He is very much provoked at the scheme that was on foot to throw overboard, the Maj and myself—and I understand says publicly, that if they dont elect both of us, that they neednt elect him, for he will not accept it. I have never, nor will I, electioneer with a man for his vote—and hence, can only conjecture what the feelings of the men are, by their own demonstration. And in this I know a man may be easily decieved—but my impression is, that if a race comes off, that I will beat my *friend*. I think too he begins to believe it, for I hear he has asked for a furlough, on the grounds of ill health—and I know him well enough to know, he would not leave here, if he thought he could be elected—even if it cost him his life. If he goes home, I suspect he will try to make some believe that it is just to keep from being run in opposition to me—And he may succeed with some. My Darling I can give you no news, relative to the army—Both sides are hard at work—The Enemy is trying to approach by a system of fortifications, and we are fortifying so as to be able to resist him—I dont look for any big battle in some time, although the two grand armies are very near together. I will keep you posted. How are you managing about bacon—You will have to sell cotton when you are obliged to raise money— Sorry to hear the wheat is not good—Take good care of it—My love to Sue and the children—Do Darling have Claude's feet examined—My love to your Father & all his family but not a bit to any of those *pretended* friends, who exulted at my reputed [page torn] ition—Let them go by—Accept much love for yourself and [page torn]

Good night
Your Husband

Have you ever heard anything of *Joe*. My Darling I want a tooth brush, send me one if you can a stiff one[.] There isnt one in Richmond[.] G.

Letter 57   JBG to Leila Griffin

Head Qrs of the Legion
June 14th 1862

My Darling Leila

I will take this occasion, to write you a line before the Mail Carrier leaves. My health is very good—Summer is fast coming on us—Last night was the warmest night we have had—The first night that I havent Slept under a couple of blankets—The hot sun will soon dry up the muddy roads, and then McClellan can come ahead if he likes. But I think he dreads it much. The thrashing we gave him on the 31st has served to increase his dread—If he will come out and attack us on our ground, and fight us in an open field, we would whip him *to pieces*—But this he will never do.

I wouldnt be surprised if both Armies spend most of the Summer in digging dirt[1]—I have almost concluded again to go home—Maj Conner has been tendered Command of the 22nd No Ca Regt[2]—This is quite complimentary to the Maj—As he not only didnt seek it—but really knew nothing of it, until he was informed that he was unanimously elected—He is much embarrassed by it—The compliment is so handsome that he doesnt feel at Liberty to decline it, and yet he says his associations here are so pleasant that he doesnt like to break them up—I think he will accept it—and if he does, I think I will decline my election and go home—I couldnt remain pleasantly

---

LETTER 57

1. After Lee assumed command he ordered the army back to the lines in front of Richmond. He set the troops to digging field fortifications and was dubbed the "King of Spades" by disgusted soldiers who resented doing labor customarily performed by slaves, and by impatient civilians who thought the army should be taking the offensive. McClellan's troops were constructing batteries and heavy siege guns were being brought in; he planned to batter his way through the Confederate line, moving forward by increments until he was finally able to shell the city itself. Lee was mounting what artillery he had and planning to post a small defending force in front of Richmond, but he realized that he was both outnumbered—he had 88,000 men to McClellan's 115,000—and outgunned. To keep McClellan from overrunning his defenses, he planned instead to take the offensive by sending three divisions plus Stonewall Jackson's from the Shenandoah Valley against the Union's right flank, the corps of Brig. Gen. FitzJohn Porter. His campaign to drive the Federals away from their fortifications and supply lines, which opened on 25 June 1862, became known as the Seven Days Battles. Douglas Southall Freeman, *Lee* (New York: Scribner's, 1934–35), 2:80–95; Sears, *To the Gates of Richmond*, 154–56.

2. The Twenty-Second North Carolina Infantry Regiment was originally commanded by Col. J. Johnston Pettigrew, who had twice been offered a brigadiership and finally accepted the appointment after the Army of Northern Virginia fell back to Richmond. Lt. Col. Charles E. Lightfoot was promoted to colonel and commanded the regiment at Seven Pines, where he and Pettigrew were both captured. When the regiment reorganized soon afterward, Conner was elected colonel to rank from 14 June 1862. The regiment was then assigned to the brigade of William Dorsey Pender in A.P. Hill's division. Walter Clark, ed., *Histories of the Several Regiments and Battalions from North Carolina in the Great War, 1861–65*, 5 vols. (Goldsboro, N.C.: published by the state, 1901), 2:167–68.

situated. We have had such a pleasant Mess—But now, Col Hampton will be separated from us—Adjt Barker is separated[3]—Dr Darby and Goodwin[4] are now very little with us. And if the Maj leaves—Dr Taylor and myself will be all that is left of our agreeable crowd. And then who is to fill their places—two of the Captains I suppose—Gary will be one of them, and as intimate as, you know we once were, we dont have much now, to do with each other—I dont know yet what we will do, but dont be surprised if you see me at home before long— I think it is but sheer justice to myself to say that the men tell me that I can be elected Col without opposition—so that it is voluntary on my part—In the mean time give my love to all—Kiss my Children.

Good Bye—

Your Jimmie

---

3. See letter of 13 April, note 3.

4. Dr. John Thomas Darby (see letter of 13 April, note 1) was the Legion's head surgeon. Capt. Claudius L. Goodwin, a neighbor of Hampton's in Richland District, was the Legion's quartermaster. *Rolls of South Carolina Volunteers in the Confederate States Provisional Army*, 3: 351, SCDAH.

6 *Tour of Duty Ends*

Letter 58
29 August 1862

Griffin's dilemma over remaining in the Hampton Legion or returning home was resolved when Gary narrowly defeated him in the election. After the letter of 14 June 1862, Griffin's tour of duty ended, and he headed home to the family he longed to see. While away from the Virginia front, Griffin missed a summer of bloody fighting. In the Seven Days Battles of 25 June to 1 July, the Federals lost only one fight, Gaines' Mill, but they were forced to abandon their drive toward Richmond. Elated southerners lauded Lee (who was privately dismayed that McClellan's army had escaped) as a hero, and proclaimed the Seven Days a strategic victory. As James McPherson has pointed out, they were also an ironic one. If McClellan had succeeded in taking Richmond the war might have ended; the Union would probably have been restored without devastating the South or even abolishing slavery, at least for a time. Lee's victory meant that the conflict would go on until the Confederacy was crushed and slavery destroyed.[1]

During the Seven Days, McClellan retreated south from Richmond to the James River and the protection of his gunboats, and he remained there while the forces of John Pope and Robert E. Lee skirmished on the Rappahannock. After McClellan was ordered to

---

1. McPherson, *Battle Cry of Freedom*, 464–71, 490–91; Sears, *To the Gates of Richmond*, 146–358.

*withdraw the Army of the Potomac from the Peninsula and send it
by water to reinforce Pope, Lee took a successful gamble. He split
his army and sent Stonewall Jackson's corps on a wide march to the
left, where it was to flank Pope's rear and hit the Orange and Alexandria Railroad, the Union line of supply. The remainder of the
army, under Longstreet, demonstrated on Pope's front while Jackson
was en route and rejoined him before Pope could be reinforced. On
29–30 August Jackson and Longstreet decisively defeated Pope and
Fitz John Porter at the Second Battle of Manassas.*[2]

*The Hampton Legion was without a colonel that summer, for
Wade Hampton had assumed a brigadier general's command.
While Griffin was at home the companies voted to elect a new colonel, and this time Griffin triumphed over Gary. The files of the
Confederate War Department contain no record of this election,
which can be documented from only a few threads of evidence. On
1 August, John H. A. Wagener, in artillery camp in Virginia, recorded in his diary that the Legion had received an order to hold an
election for colonel the following day. On 2 August, he reported the
results: "Election for Legion Col came off—99 votes were cast for
Col. Griffin by our company, it's said that Col Gary recd a good
vote in the infantry, but that Col Griffin has majority." On 20
August the Edgefield Advertiser announced that the district had
two new colonels: M. C. Butler to command a cavalry regiment in
Hampton's Brigade, which included part of the old Legion Cavalry,
and Griffin to command the Legion Infantry.*[3]

---

2. Freeman, *Lee's Lieutenants*, 2:82–138; John J. Hennessey, *Return to
Bull Run: The Campaign and Battle of Second Manassas* (New York: Simon
and Schuster, 1992).
   3. The OR and CSR say nothing about this election. Robert K. Krick gener-
ously took time to help us pursue the search in the NA through *Unfiled Papers
and Slips Belonging in Confederate Service Records*, M347; *Letters Received by
the Confederate Secretary of War, 1861–65*, M437; *Letters Sent by the Confederate Secretary of War, 1861–65*, M522; *Index to the Letters Received by the
Confederate Adjutant and Inspector General and by the Confederate Quartermaster General, 1861–65*, M410; *Telegrams Received by the Confederate Secretary of War, 1861–65*, M618; and *Letters and Telegrams sent by the Confederate
Adjutant and Inspector General, 1861–65*, M627. John H. A. Wagener Record
Book, SCHS; Edgefield *Advertiser*, 20 Aug. 1862.

Griffin's next letter, dated 29 August, finds him pondering his future. Gratified that the Legion now wanted him to take command, he was in Richmond, on his way to rejoin the Hampton Legion and the Army of Northern Virginia. On his way to Virginia, he had learned that he had also been offered a lieutenant colonel's commission with the South Carolina Reserves. He had to choose between the two offers: prestige and prospective glory with the Hampton Legion or safe reserve duty at home near his family.

Letter 58 JBG to Leila Griffin

Richmond
August 29th 1862

My Dear Leila

After a tedious and tiresome trip, I reached this place on tuesday. I waited a day longer in Columbia than I should in order to come in company with Capt Burris and Lt Talbert,[1] we left Columbia on saturday evening[,] arrived in Charlotte about 3 oClock at night—found no train and had to lie over all day—Started again late in the evening, arrived, in Petersburg monday evening—here we missed connection again and had to stay all night. The next day (tuesday) we came through. I should have written you before this my Darling, but I have been hesitating since I have been here, whether I should not go back home, and if so I thought it would be useless to write as I would get there before the letter would. I found upon arriving in Columbia that "The Hon Governor & Council" had appointed me Lieut Col of the 5th Regt of "Reserves."[2] This I thought would be almost equal to a

---

LETTER 58

1. These men are probably from Company K, Seventh South Carolina Volunteers, an Edgefield company. Burris is probably John L. Burris, the captain elected during the reorganization (see letter of 13 May 1862, note 8), and Talbert may be First Lieutenant J.L. Talbert.

2. The Fifth Regiment, First Corps South Carolina Reserves, was received into Confederate service for 90 days and served from 5 November 1862 until 15 February 1863 on the lower Carolina coast. Griffin and the other field officers were nominated on 15 August and confirmed the following day. CSR, M267, roll 201; *Journals of the South Carolina Executive Councils of 1861 and 1862*, 247.

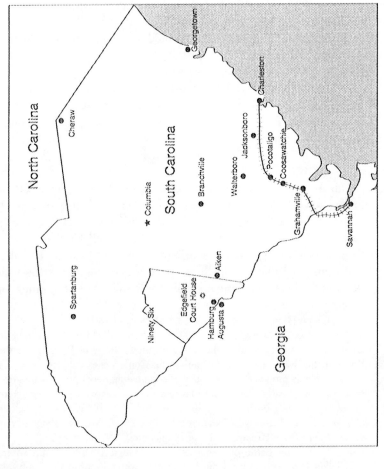

South Carolina

Colonelcy for Bacon[3] was appointed Col and I doubt if his health will allow him to go into the Field again[.] I concluded to come on here and then decide which office I would take. I have concluded to go on and take command of the Legion. I would prefer the other command however, if I was certain I could hold it. But I think Congress will very soon press another "Conscript" law. Which will break up the organization of the State and that would leave me without an office, and [I] would be a conscript myself—This would be an unpleasant position. And so upon the whole I think it best to make sure of what I have. I have met several of my men here who receive me very cordially. Say the whole command are anxious for my return. This is very gratifying. But I assure you I dread the idea of spending another winter in that barren and desolate country, where we were last winter. And from the present indications I wouldnt be surprised if this is the case.

Our Army is pursuing Pope,[4] who seems to be retreating as fast as he can towards Alexandria[.] It is said that McClellan is reinforcing him & it may be that they will halt and make battle. Our Troops have nearly all left Richmond and it is thought we will be able to whip them if they make a stand.[5] I believe if Lee and Jackson can catch and whip Pope that we will have peace before long. I met up with Ben Smith[6] here—he has got his discharge and left, this morning for

3. Thomas Glascock Bacon. See letter of 28 April 1862, note 5.

4. Maj. Gen. John Pope (1822–1892) had been called from Mississippi on 26 June to take command of the newly organized Army of Virginia, all the troops in the East except McClellan's. The Confederates detested Pope, for he immediately proposed a new policy of confiscating Rebel property for army use and harsh treatment for guerrillas and the citizens who protected them. James McPherson, *Battle Cry of Freedom*, 402, 415–16; Wallace J. Schutz and Walter N. Trenerry, *Abandoned by Lincoln: A Military Biography of General John Pope* (Urbana: Univ. of Illinois Press, 1990).

5. The Second Battle of Manassas was in progress while Griffin wrote. McClellan had been ordered on 4 August to withdraw from the Peninsula and reinforce Pope's army in northern Virginia. He had protested the order and was deliberately slow in evacuating. On 24 August his Army of the Potomac troops began to reach Pope on the north bank of the Rappahannock, where he had withdrawn under the pressure of Lee's advance. Hennessey, *Return to Bull Run*, 10, 90–91.

6. Smith was a young poor white from Edgefield.

home. I will leave here in a day or two[.] Write often My Darling, but I fear our mails will be very irregular—Direct your letters to Richmond for the present—I will write you again soon—My love to all—Kiss the children for your absent

Husband

7 On the Carolina Coast: Fifth Regiment South Carolina Reserves

Letters 59 through 73
26 November 1862 through 9 February 1863

Griffin wrote only one letter from Richmond. He found himself unable to follow through his decision to rejoin the Hampton Legion. The separation and reassignment of the units and/or the invalidity of the second election calling him back to command eliminated the choice. Instead, he went back to South Carolina and accepted the commission with the Reserves.

While he was at home, Griffin ventured into politics. He was popular and influential enough in October of 1862 for "kind friends" (prominent and influential gentlemen) to place his name and 16 others, including fellow Hampton Legionnaires Gary and Butler, before the public as candidates for the South Carolina General Assembly. Although Griffin finished only 13th of 17, he was just one vote behind Gary, and 18 ahead of Butler. The men in the field showed some disapproval of all the candidates; soldiers who voted wrote in the names of more candidates than they gave any one of the 17 nominees on the ballot. Griffin's standing was lower with military voters than civilians. Of the 174 army votes, Gary received 57, Butler 58, and Griffin 36. The pattern of precinct voting shows that Griffin was stronger in the towns and Gary was stronger in the countryside.[1]

---

1. Returns for the state legislature, Edgefield *Advertiser*, 22 Oct. 1862, p. 4, c. 2–4. After the election, Gary and Butler in Virginia sent notes to the

Griffin's next set of letters covers 26 November 1862 through 9 February 1863, while he served as lieutenant colonel of the Fifth Regiment, South Carolina Reserves. He wrote these letters from the coast, below Charleston. Here he was no longer homesick and actually seemed to be having a good time. But he found in the Reserves the same tensions between enlisted men and officers that had plagued him in Virginia. Griffin's situation here almost exactly parallels his experience in the Hampton Legion: de facto command of the regiment much of the time, uncertainty over the election of field officers, who were strongly supported by their commander, and lingering indecision over whether or not to go home at the end of his enlistment.

---

newspaper announcing that they would have declined the nominations for the legislature. The editor of the paper editorialized that neither Butler nor Gary were considered candidates, "hence the comparatively small vote." 29 Oct. 1862, p. 4, c. 5; 5 Nov. 1862, p. 4, c. 3.

An analysis by precinct reveals that Griffin did well in the towns of Edgefield, Hamburg, and Graniteville. In his home precinct of Edgefield Court House he came in eighth; nearly a third of the voters supported their neighbor Griffin, and he had substantially more votes than the other candidates, including Gary and Butler, who were also residents of the Edgefield Court House precinct. In the cotton mill town of Graniteville, the least wealthy precinct and the one with the highest voter turnout, Griffin was second with 113 votes out of 155 (73%); he polled substantially more votes than any of the other candidates except John F. Talbert (113), one of the election winners. In contrast, Gary received only 21 Graniteville votes and Butler 14. In Hamburg, where Griffin was 10th of 17, 31 percent of all voters supported him; Butler got only one vote and Gary none. In several of the most remote and rural precincts, Griffin received no votes. And in Norris Township, where Gary was first with 22 of 26 votes and Butler third with 19 votes, Griffin received only one vote. One can only speculate as to why Griffin was more popular in the towns while Gary and Butler had more support in the countryside. But his later business endeavors and antebellum records showing that he rented out slave artisans suggest that he might have been involved in trade and town activities.

Letter 59   JBG to Leila Griffin

Head Qrs 5th Regt Res—
American Hotel Nov. 26th 1862
[Charleston]

My dear Leila

We leave here tomorrow for Jacksonboro, which is 35 miles from this place and about halfway from here to Pocotaligo.[1] We will report to Genl Johnson Hagood.[2] We have about 400 men in Camp and a good many on short furlough—Genl Beauregard[3] says he will not rec-

---

LETTER 59

1. Jacksonboro, roughly thirty miles west of Charleston in Colleton District, was the site of a Charleston and Savannah Railroad bridge over the South Edisto River. Pocotaligo, about twenty-five miles farther southwest along the railroad, was the target of periodic invasion attempts via the Broad and Pocotaligo rivers from the Federal base at Port Royal. It had been the scene of several skirmishes, the most recent on 21–22 October 1862, when Federal gunboats and transports from Hilton Head sailed up Port Royal Sound into Bee's Creek and landed a force. Their aim was to cut communication between Charleston and Savannah by destroying the Charleston and Savannah Railroad and its bridges and to capture the military supplies at Pocotaligo and Coosawahatchie. The invasion was repulsed by state troops under Col. W.S. Walker, commander of the Third Military District. Roman, *Military Operations of General Beauregard*, 2:31–33; CMH, 6:101–6.

2. Brig. Gen. Johnson Hagood (1829–1898) of Barnwell (adjoining Edgefield on the south), a graduate of The Citadel military academy, had been an attorney and a militia brigadier before the war. He entered Confederate service as colonel of the First South Carolina Volunteers and took part in the reduction of Fort Sumter and the battle of First Manassas. Hagood then returned with his regiment to South Carolina, where he fought in the battle of Secessionville in June 1862, and was promoted to brigadier general in July. He commanded the Second Military District, which included Jacksonboro. Hagood was married to Edgefieldian Eloise Brevard Butler, daughter of the late Senator Andrew Pickens Butler and cousin to Matthew Calbraith Butler, both from Edgefield. The Hagoods had a plantation in Edgefield. CMH, 6:400–403; Mrs. Thomas Taylor et al., eds., *South Carolina Women in the Confederacy*, 2 vols. (Columbia, S.C.: State Co., 1903), 2:51.

3. Beauregard had been appointed commander of the Department of South Carolina and Georgia (later expanded to include part of Florida) on 29 August 1862.

ognise the power granted by the "Executive Council" to Col's of Regiments to furlough the men,[4] and that so soon as we report for duty, which we will do tomorrow, he will order every man whose name is on the roll into camp.[5] It is the worst mixed up affair, I have ever seen. I had to go back to Columbia on Sunday night and return yesterday evening. Col Bacon sent me up to see the Executive Council with refference to a confusion which has arisen in refference to the granting of furloughs. I have fixed it up as well as I can. I think our men are getting pretty well satisfied—But the way they curse the council is amusing. Some of the Regiments are exceedingly disaffected and some are in open rebellion. Two whole companies marched off home on monday morning, from Wilson's regiment and another regt (Secrest's) held an election the other day for Field Officers.[6] These regiments are

---

4. On 21 July the Council passed a set of resolutions governing the First Corps of Reserves, those men between 35 and 50. The tenth and last resolution permitted regimental commanders to grant indefinite furloughs without pay "in such cases as in their judgment the public interest will be best promoted by permitting the applicants for furloughs to remain at home until further orders." *Journals of the South Carolina Executive Councils of 1861 and 1862*, 227–29.

5. The commander of the First District had informed Beauregard that 17,000 more men would be necessary to hold Charleston if it were attacked, and the attack on Pocotaligo pointed up the need for increased troop strength in the Third District. Beauregard consequently wanted the eight regiments of state reserves that had been accepted into the Confederate Army for ninety-day service along the coast sent forward at once. On 4 November he urged Governor Pickens that "no time can be prudently lost in securing the services of these troops"; three days later Pickens ordered the regimental commanders to heed Beauregard's "urgent appeal" and report for duty with their commands "at the earliest possible moment." Roman, *Military Operations of General Beauregard*, 2:33–34; OR, ser. 1, 14:665, 15:656, 660–61, 665, 684; *Charleston Mercury*, 14 Nov. 1862.

6. Col. A.J. Secrest and Col. W.B. Wilson commanded the Sixth and Seventh Regiments, respectively, of the First Corps of Reserves. These regiments had not been among the four that the Executive Council had initially offered to the War Department in October for Beauregard. The Sixth and Seventh, along with Bacon's Fifth and the Ninth under Col. J.H. Williams, were not tendered for ninety-day service until 3 November, and the Council informed Beauregard on 5 November. *Journals of the South Carolina Executive Councils of 1861 and 1862*, 289–91.

in camp near Columbia. I am proud to say there is very little feeling of this kind manifested in our regt. I hear no complaint at all of the Field Officers. Upon the whole I think we will get along pretty well. And when we get into camp and get to drilling I think the men will become very well satisfied. Dr Harrington and Sis went home on sunday night, went along with me—We had a very tedious trip—was due in Columbia on Monday morning at five OClock and didnt get there until nearly 12. I transacted my business that evening and returned the next morning. Dr Muse took tea with me last evening and was quite well—He bought some salt for himself and your Father; he asked me to write this and wishes the Capt to send for it but said he would write himself. I bought two sacks of Coast Salt the other day thinking I would let your Father have a Sack if he wanted it—But I presume that Dr has bought as much for him as [he] will need, and he bought it lower than I did—He gave 20 dollars per bushel and I gave 25. If he sends down for his you might get him to carry up ours and if not you had better send down next week for it. Use the Salt you have at home to salt the meat and use this salt in cooking[.] You can let Spradley have some of it if your Father doesnt wish it.

My Darling I have just recieved a letter from you which gives me no little trouble. I hope and pray that Burt[7] may recover. I am surprised that you have received no letter from me. I wrote you last saturday and would have written sooner but was kept so very busy. The truth is, I never worked so hard in my life, I have been playing Quarter Master and have had a deal of trouble. The Qr Master has come at last and I am relieved of that duty. But not from all duty—Col Bacon left this morning for our place of destination and has left me in command of the Regt—This precludes the possibility of my going home as you desire. I hope too that Burt is better by this time. Do write me direct to Charleston[.] I dont know the name of the Post Office near where we will be stationed, but will arrange to have all letters forwarded immediately. And will write you again in a day or two. Maj Noble[8] has gone home for a day or two, So that I am the

---

7. Griffin's son, Moody Burt, age five.

8. Edward E. Noble of Abbeville was the son of former governor Patrick Noble, kinsman of John C. Calhoun; through his mother's family he was related to the Edgefield Pickens clan. A graduate of South Carolina College

only Field Officer with the regt—I am going tonight to see Dr Ogier,[9] Have thus far been unable to see him. I will write you in a day or two what he says. Quilla[10] is quite well but his face gets pretty long sometimes. He is now 1st Lt and Ben Bettis[11] is Capt.

It is now getting quite late and I must go down and see the Dr before he shuts up—My love to all especially Burt. Tell him I hope he will soon be well but if I was him I wouldnt eat any more pinders[?]

Good Night
Your Jimmie

Letter 60   JBG to Leila Griffin

Head Qrs 5th Regt Reserves
Jacksonborough
Nov 29th 1862

My Dear Leila

I am exceedingly anxious to hear again from home—hope I will get a letter to day which will bring me the intelligence of the convalescence of my dear Boy. I sent to the post office and Telegraph office on thursday morning before I left Charleston hoping to hear something but did not. Alfred Hughes[1] arrived here yesterday, said he sent over to our house wednesday and heard no complaint. I hope there-

---

and an attorney, Noble had represented Abbeville in the state legislature in 1848–50 and 1854–56 as well as in the Secession Convention, where he was one of the signers of the ordinance. He had previously served with the Nineteenth South Carolina Volunteers, entering as a first lieutenant and rising to the rank of major. The Noble family was related to the Burts. May and Faunt, *South Carolina Secedes*, 188; CSR, M267, roll 201.

9. This is the surgeon previously referred to as Dr. Osier. See letter of 17 May 1862, note 4.

10. Nickname of Aquilla Miles (see letter of 4 July 1861, note 11), first lieutenant of Company K and Leila's cousin and brother-in-law.

11. Benjamin Bettis was a substantial planter and captain of Company K. CSR, M267, roll 201. The Bettis and Burt families were related.

LETTER 60

1. Alfred J. Hughes of Edgefield was a private in Company K. The muster roll shows that during November and December he was "absent by permission." CSR, M267, roll 201.

fore that Burt was better. Sorry to hear of the death of Mrs Perrin.[2] I saw Pick and Maria[3] at the Charleston Hotel on wednesday night— They spent the night there. I had so much to do that evening, preparing to leave the next morning, that I could remain with them but a short time. They were quite well and gay—Maria says she is spending a very pleasant time—doesnt know when she will leave—was to have gone to her Grandmother's this week but Pick wouldnt let her—We arrived at this place 35 miles from Charleston thursday evening, we will remain at this camp only a few days until our wagons come when we will move about four miles from here and I suppose be permanently located—Our Regt have become very well satisfied and I think will soon be very efficient—we have commenced drilling. This is said to be a very sickly country until frost, after then there is no danger. We have had some tremendous heavy frosts here since we came. This is a great Country for game. Plenty of deer, turkeys, bear and ducks. When you come to Charleston if Dr Burt comes with you and you can do it without too much trouble to yourself and him, I wish you

---

2. Probably Emeline (or Emmala) Elizabeth Butler Perrin, daughter of the late governor Pierce Mason Butler. Elizabeth Butler was the sister of Andrew Pickens Butler and Pierce Mason Butler (see note 3) and the cousin of Matthew Calbraith Butler. She had married Abner Monroe Perrin III, who practiced law in Edgefield and joined the Fourteenth South Carolina Volunteers as a captain; he ultimately became a brigadier general. Perrin was killed at Spotsylvania, Virginia. Watson, *Greenwood County Sketches*, 344; Jervey, "The Butlers of South Carolina," 307. There is some question as to whether Perrin was from Abbeville or Edgefield. *CMH* 6:415, and Warner, *Generals in Gray*, 234, cite Edgefield and give his birthdate as 2 February 1827; *Appleton's Cyclopedia* has him born in Abbeville in 1829.

3. Andrew Pickens Butler and Maria Burt had been married in Edgefield on 2 October. "Pick" Butler was the brother of Lt. Pierce Mason Butler, Jr. (see letters of 11 July 1861 and 28 April 1862) and the son of former governor Pierce Mason Butler. Maria Burt (see 5 Jan. 1862, note 1) was Leila's cousin; sister Annie later became Pierce Butler's second wife. Pick Butler was a lieutenant and subsequently a captain in the Second South Carolina Cavalry commanded by his cousin M. C. Butler. He was captured on 11 October 1864 in a skirmish near Petersburg and not released until the end of the war. McClendon, *Edgefield Marriage Records*, 27; Jervey, "The Butlers of South Carolina," 307–8; Burt Family, roll 6, Leonardo Andrea Genealogical Collection, SCL.

would bring my gun and Joe[,] also my powder flask, caps and all the big shot I have[;] dont bring the bird shot. I want to shoot ducks.

I saw Dr Ogier on wednesday night[;] he says he will go to day to Newberry and return the latter part of next week, so that any time after next week he will be at home and happy to serve us. He says the operation[4] will be simple and not at all dangerous, and that there is no doubt that it will straighten his feet—but it will give you a great deal of trouble—He says he much prefers to attend to it in the City. And now I want you to see Dr Burt and appoint a time, I would prefer week after next, sooner the better, and write me word and I will meet you in Charleston. If I dont meet you at the Depot I will meet you at the Charleston Hotel—Tell Claude I will have something nice for him. If you cant come at the time I indicate, come as soon as you can.

I have an opportunity to send my letter by Alfred Hughes and he is about starting so I will have to close[.] Tell Spradley if it is very cold he had better have more dirt thrown on the potatoes and close them up at top. Direct your letters to
Lt Col J. B. Griffin
5th Regt S. C. Reserves
Jacksonborough
S C
My best love to all[.] Good Bye

Your Jimmie

Letter 61   JBG to Leila Griffin

Jacksonboro
Decr. 6th 1862

My Dear Leila

I recieved a letter from you yesterday which grieved me much— You have really had a hard time in nursing since I came from home. I hope by this time that the Children are better. I am afraid you will not be able to come to Charleston next week. Write me when you think you will be able to come. Did you get the money from Dozier?

---

4. The reference is to the operation to straighten the feet of three-year-old Claude, which had apparently been deferred. See letter of 17 May 1862.

If not you must try to get enough to pay your expenses and your Uncle Williams. I am anxious to see you—Dont: forget to bring my gun. As Joe will be a good deal of trouble to you at least to the Doctr you may leave him—I will have no use for him any way. But I want my gun and ammunition. This is a great Country for game. I went out driving the other day—Dr Glover,[1] one of the citizens invited Col Bacon and myself to join the party in a hunt. We went only two miles from our camp and the dogs soon had a deer going. One of the Standers killed it[,] a very fine young deer. We went then to another drive. They ran out a very large old buck near me, he was a fine one with a fine head of horns. I fired at him both barrels and he still kept on. The standers came up and asked me what I had done. I told them I had shot at a rousing big deer and I was certain I had wounded it. We let the dogs follow it, and they soon crossed a large swamp which we could not cross— The men began to doubt that I had hit him—and when I told them it was the first deer I had ever shot at, they said—"show" then we know you didnt hit it. They laughed at me a plenty all except one old Gentleman who lived in the direction that the dogs were running—He said to me, "Col" I think you must have hit for the dogs run as if they smelt blood" and if so I will find it tomorrow". The day passed and no news of it—The next day however the old Gentleman sent me the horns sure enough, his dogs caught the buck, a very large one, and eat it so the meat was spoilt but I have the horns hanging up near my tent[.] This made them all change their tune. After the hunt was over Dr Glover invited us to his house to dinner—He had a

---

LETTER 61

1. The Glovers were a noted family of low country physicians, descendants of Dr. Joseph Glover of Charleston, who had been state surgeon-general in 1819 and 1824, and his brother, Dr. Henry Glover. The 1860 census shows two men named Dr. Glover in Colleton District, both in St. Barthelomew's Parish. From Griffin's later description of the family (see letter of 11 January 1863), the man referred to here is probably Dr. F.Y. Glover, who in 1869 was a 43-year-old farmer and physician living with his wife Eleanor, an 11-year-old-daughter, and a nine-year-old son. Joseph I. Waring, A *History of Medicine in South Carolina, 1670–1825* (n.p.: South Carolina Medical Association, 1964); 1860 Census of Population, Schedule 1, Free Inhabitants, Colleton District, South Carolina.

magnificent dinner, I have never enjoyed one more and if I had only got my buck I would have spent an exceedingly pleasant day. There is a great deal of wealth in this section of the country, and I think [it] a very desirable Country in the winter. I wish you would make Willie see if he cant buy a *"Bob"* from Mr. Penn to fish with[;] if I had one I could catch plenty of trout[.] We are camped very near the Edisto— And *ducks* there is no end to them.

We will move four miles from here on monday to a very pretty camp—I am going down this morning to lay off the camp. I havent time to write more now as the men are waiting for me[.] I will give you a description of our new camp after I get down there. I am very anxious that you shall bring me a keg of molasses, and as much butter as you can conveniently spare— Give my love to all the Children and my friends—I hope to see you soon

Your Jimmie

Letter 62   JBG to Leila Griffin

Head Qrs 5th Regt Reserves
Camp Griffin 18th Decr. 1862

My Dear Leila

I have only time to write you a few lines. I arrived here safe and well on tuesday about 1 OClock. I found the Regiment moving from the new camp. We have got back near Jacksonboro—The men became very sick at the new camp—Several died very suddenly—This is the cause of moving again. We are now in a very pleasant camp. And the Col has honored me by naming it for me. My Darling I am very uneasy about poor little Callie—I do hope I will get a letter to day, from you saying he is better. I found them all very anxious to see me back. And I have already become very busy[.] I opened my School this morning. And will have to drill directly in battallion drill—Capt Lewis Jones' company[1] has been sent over here[.] They are encamped

---

LETTER 62

1. Lewis Jones was sheriff of Edgefield District from 1852 to 1856 and then was elected to the legislature. During June and July of 1862 he had recruited a militia company in Edgefield called the Partisan Rangers. When the Sixth South Carolina Cavalry, the Dixie Rangers, was organized in 1863 and as-

I suppose you have heard ere this that Col Stevens' Regt[2] has been ordered off and has gone to North Carolina. So tell Minnie that sure enough I brought her box straight through and it is now in my tent[.] I have plenty of butter—I reckon she feels pretty bad over the Dr's going but then if he had not gone I wouldnt have got the butter[.] "It is an ill wind that blows no body good"—I hope you recd the two hundred dollars I sent you by Peter[3]—Pay Spradley as I told you— and use the ballance as you like—I told Peter to buy a few apples and carry up to you for the Children—Do give my love to all the Children especially the poor little sick ones—I must close and go out to drill— Write often to your

Husband

Letter 63   JBG to Leila Griffin

Head Qrs 5th Regt Reserves
Camp Griffin Decr. 21st 1862

My Dear Leila

For the first time since my return to camp, I recd yesterday evening a letter from you. I was exceedingly anxious about poor little Callie— I hope now that he will get well. Your first letter I have not recieved yet. John and Frank Bettis[1] are going to leave for home to day—I will

signed to Butler's Brigade, Jones became captain of Company B. Chapman, *History of Edgefield County*, 378; Edgefield *Advertiser*, 9 July 1862; Brooks, *Butler and His Cavalry*, 544.

2. Col. Clement H. Stevens commanded the Twenty-Fourth South Carolina Volunteers, one of the regiments raised in April 1862 to meet the secretary of war's call for five additional regiments from South Carolina (see 12 February 1862, note 1). Dr. Julius E. Muse, the husband of Leila's sister Minnie, was a private in the regiment. By 30 December the regiment was serving in the Cape Fear District of eastern North Carolina under Brig. Gen. W.H.C. Whiting. *Journals of the Conventions of the People of South Carolina*, 618, 620; OR, ser. 1, 18:809.

3. A slave, earlier referred to as Leila's man Peter.

LETTER 63

1. John and Frank Bettis were the sons of Capt. Benjamin W. Bettis (see letter of 26 Nov. 1862, note 11). In 1862 they would have been about 12 and 13.

get them to take this letter along. The mail has been irregular for the last week, caused by the Government taking charge of all trains to transport Troops to North Carolina.[2]

My Darling I am afraid for Willie & Bobbie to come down here lest they should take this bad disease that is prevailing in camp—I think it is from the effects of cold—But it handles them roughly. We have lost eleven men in the regiment and still have a good many sick. My own health I am happy to say is very good.

Dr Glover invited me to join in another drive yesterday—I went but we got no deer. There were three shots fired at a fawn, and we had a beautiful chase after it—but didnt get it. I didnt get a shot myself. We expect to take another hunt Christmass day. I hope to kill another then. We have had very cold weather for this climate—This is a cold raw windy day—ice aplenty.

We have been living finely on the many good things you put up for me—By the way I wish I had brought down a bag of flour[.] We cant get it at all here. The boys are ready to start and I must close. I will write again in a few days

Your Husband

Letter 64   JBG to Leila Griffin

Head Qrs 5th Regt Reserves
Camp Griffin Decr. 23rd 1862

My Dear Leila

This is the ninth day since I left home and I have had but one letter from you. I know you have written more, but from some cause they

---

2. On 11 December Maj. Gen. John G. Foster and 10,000 Federal infantrymen had left the Union base at New Bern, North Carolina, for Goldsboro. There they planned to destroy the railroad bridge over the Neuse River in an attack timed to coincide with Burnside's on Fredericksburg. Brig. Gen. N.G. "Shanks" Evans, commanding a force of North and South Carolina troops only a little over 2000 strong, had engaged Foster near Kinston on 14 December. Although the Confederate defense was poorly executed and 400 of the Carolinians were captured, Evans refused Foster's demand for surrender. Before Foster could position his men for another attack, Evans ordered a withdrawal. Instead of pursuing, Foster resumed his march toward Goldsboro, while the Confederate government rushed troops to North Carolina. John G.

have failed to come to hand. The letter I received was your second letter, written on thursday after I left. It gave me great satisfaction by telling me that Callie was still improving. I am very anxious to hear again, but in the absence of information all I can hope for is the best. This, you know is my way of doing any way. We are still having some sickness in camp. The Doctrs differ in their opinion about it, some think it is a very severe cold while others think it is a malignant form of typhoid fever.[1] I dont know what it is but I know it is a very severe disease. The men are sometimes taken sick in the morning and are speechless by night[.] We have lost eleven men and have several others very low. James Bean[2] who lives up near Majr. Hughes, was the last one to die—He was a very stout, strong and apparently healthy man. My health is very good, but I have taken a slight cold lately. I have just learned that another poor fellow is dead. I wrote to you in my last that you had better not let Willie and Bobbie come down here. I am afraid they might get sick, tell them I am sorry to disappoint them but I think they had better not come.

We had a little excitement in camp yesterday. Our Cavalry Picket took two Prisoners. They had come out from their vessel in a small

---

Barrett, *The Civil War in North Carolina* (Chapel Hill: Univ. of North Carolina Press, 1963), 139–44.

LETTER 64

1. This diagnosis is less a reflection of physician incompetence than the reality that "the Civil War was fought at the end of the medical Middle Ages," in the words of one historian. Research in bacteriology that would revolutionize medicine within a generation was under way in Europe, but during the Civil War doctors were still ignorant of the connections between contaminated water and typhoid, mosquitoes and malaria. Griffin's letter of 29 November describing the area as "a very sickly country until frost" reflects how little was known about the transmission of pathogens. McPherson, *Battle Cry of Freedom*, 486 (quotation). The standard source on medical care in the Confederacy is H.H. Cunningham, *Doctors in Gray: The Confederate Medical Service* (1958; rpt., Glouchester, Mass.: Peter Smith, 1970), esp. 3–8, 163–83. See also Frank Reed Freemon, "Medical Care during the American Civil War" (Ph.D. dissertation, University of Illinois, 1992).

2. James Bean of Edgefield was a private in Company E. He enrolled on 10 November and died on 22 December at Camp Griffin. CSR, M267, roll 201.

boat in search of oysters, crabs &c. It seems they did not anticipate that we picketed at that point, and so they came close up, when our Boys presented their guns and demanded them to surrender, which they did. To day we took the Regiment down in that direction to reconnoitre. We made no discoveries. On the way back we (I mean the Field Officers) were invited to dine with Mr. Clifford,[3] a wealthy Gentleman in the neighborhood. Col Bacon and Majr. Noble accepted the invitation. I declined and came back to Camp with the Regiment. It was necessary that one of us should come back, and as I had dined out once and the Majr. had not, I insisted on his going. We are all invited to dine with him again on Christmass Day. But I think I will decline again, for I was invited previously to join a deer hunt on that day. We are going to give hollyday that day and that will wind up our Christmas. We are working the men pretty tight,—and I tell you it keeps me very busy. Col Bacon is very often sick[;] I am then in Command. I recd a letter from Sis yesterday, sorry to learn that she has been so very sick. Jim Brooks[4] is in my tent and begs me to say that he is quite well. He is very homesick however. Do My Darling give My love to all the Children as well as my Friends & Relatives[.] Write often to your

Jimmie

Letter 65   JBG to Leila Griffin

Head Qrs 5th Regt Reserves
Camp Griffin Decr 26th 1862

My Dear Leila

What can be the matter[,] only one letter from you since I left home. I hope no one is sick to prevent your writing. I suspect you will be surprised when I tell you that I expect you will see me at home

---

3. Not listed in the 1860 census for Colleton District.

4. James Carroll Brooks was the younger brother of the late Congressman Preston S. Brooks. He enlisted as a private in Company K and was subsequently promoted to sergeant. The Brooks clan was intermarried with the Butlers and Lipscombs and thus were kin to both Griffin and Leila. James Brooks is also listed in the 1860 census as the neighbor of Leila's father, Capt. Eugene Burt. CSR, M267, roll 201; Watson, *Greenwood County Sketches*, 165; Brooks, *Stories of the Confederacy*, 358.

in a week or two. The Legislature have in their wisdom decided that the Regiments of Reserves shall on the 1st day of January elect their Field Officers.[1] I, as I expected am unpopular with some men, and they have already nominated Candidates for the office that I hold— and as I dont feel disposed to scramble for an office which can last only a little more than a month longer, I have declared that I am no Candidate— Some think that the men will elect me any way but I dont think so—I am more obnoxious to the Command than any of the Field Officers— They say I am a *fine Officer*—but too *strict*[2]—

LETTER 65

1. This was as much a political as a military decision. In mobilizing South Carolina for war, the Executive Council (see letter of 20 March 1862, note 6) had inevitably offended the touchy individualism of many in the state, who consequently denounced it as unconstitutional and tyrannical. In Edgefield a mass meeting on 7 April had generated a set of resolutions that criticized the Secession Convention for having created the Council, and called on the Edgefield members of the Convention to exert themselves to end the Council's existence by repealing the enabling ordinance. The Edgefield gathering invited other districts to convene similar protest meetings; although only a dozen did so, most of the state's newspapers pressed the attack unremittingly. The day after the Secession Convention expired on 17 December, the legislature had abolished the Executive Council and declared all of its transactions except contracts illegal. The legislators were especially irritated by the Council's military policies, and resented the offering of the First Corps of Reserves, which included Griffin's regiment, for ninety days of Confederate service. After an investigation, the legislature finally concluded that expediency required the regiments to stifle their grievances and fulfill the commitment, but it passed an act forbidding service beyond the promised ninety days and requiring an election to displace the field officers appointed by the Executive Council. Cauthen, *South Carolina Goes to War*, 152–61; *Statutes at Large of South Carolina* (Columbia: Republican Printing, 1875), 13:111–12.

2. Two days after Griffin wrote this letter, Col. Bacon sent an appeal to Beauregard in Charleston, laying out the situation of the officers:

Genl
    Our Regts are ordered to elect field officers on the first day of Jany next (Thursday). We are in the service of the Confederate States. Our officers hold commissions from the Governor. The Legislature of So. Ca. has lessened the dignity of that body by the act they have passed.

This I take as a compliment and would be so considered by Military men. You would be amused to hear their objections to me—one is that I put a man in the Guard house for smoking his pipe on *Dress Parrade*. Another is that I ordered Silence when two men [were] talking while I was drilling them—&c— Maj Noble is also objected to—and they have started Candidates for his Office— He has also declined to be a candidate— I dont think the Col will serve if they throw us overboard— He has no opposition. He says frankly to the men that I have done more for the regiment than any man in it— And that if it had not been for me, he never could have organized it. And well he may for I have done the larger portion of the work, and besides, I have been in Command of the Regiment nearly half the time on account of the feeble condition of the Col's health. I dont care however a single straw—I have told the men I wouldnt turn on my heel to be elected— And if they dont want me to Command them to elect some one else. If they elect me I will do my duty regardless of consequences and I will make them do theirs. If they elect me (which I dont expect) I will serve, but if they do not I will go home and quit the war— If I am not elected I am ordered to remain in command until my successor is Commissioned which will be, I suppose, in the course of a week after the election.

I went a deer hunting yesterday (Christmass day). One of the party killed a fine buck—and another shot at two but missed— I got no shot— But after the hunt was over—I in the company of Maj Noble went to dine with a Mr. Clifford—a wealthy rice planter in this neighbourhood— The French Vice Consul was a consul—*[sic]* and his Lady— We spent a very pleasant evening— Had an elegant dinner

---

Will you direct us to hold our officers until the expiration of our term. I am to be reelected without opposition but I will lose Lieut. Col. Griffin an able and efficient officer, unless you interpose. Quite probable I will get a Lieut Col not worth one cent.

I am Genl very respectfully yours
Thos G. Bacon
Col 5 Regt Res
Cmdg Post

CSR, M267, roll 201, p. 322.

and plenty of fine old brandy and Maderia—I assure you we did ample justice to all— We were some three hours at dinner and then after the Ladies left, he brought out some fine segars—and we smoked and chatted an hour or so longer— He has no children but one adopted Daughter but she is by no means pretty— And he has two sisters (old maids and as ugly as can be[)]— They are all Irish—but exceedingly clever and cultivated— I will give you a more full account when I see you—

Do give my love to all— Ask Willie if he doesnt intend to write to me at all— And do my Darling write often to your

Husband

Letter 66   JBG to Leila

Head Qrs 5th Regt Res—
Camp Griffin Decr. 28th 1862

My Darling

Sunday as it is, I am busy as a bee. Scarcely time to write to my Darling. But I will write a few lines and send by Jim Brooks. I wrote to you by Rambo[1] and said I only had recd one letter from you— Yesterday I recd three from you and one from Dr Harrington[;] his was dated the 16th inst— I am very uneasy about Sis— Havent heard any thing late from her. I am well—there is a good deal of talk about the election—some think the old Officers will be reelected—but I doubt it. I dont care a cent and so I have told them. If they elect me they must do so without any agency on my part— I will write again in a few days— Tell Minnie to keep Rachel[2] My love to all

Your Jimmie

LETTER 66

1. Probably Cpl. Joseph Rambo, Company D. Private Benajah Rambo of Company K is listed as not reporting until 27 January. CSR, M267, roll 201. Joseph Rambo had no property in 1860.

2. One of Griffin's slaves.

Letter 67   JBG to Leila

Camp Griffin Decr 31st 1862

My Darling

This being the last day of the year, I feel disposed to spend a portion of it in communicating with you. I hope you and all our little Children are well to day. I am sorry that I have not been permitted to spend Christmass with you. I did not ask to go home, for I could not consistently. I have spent a very busy, if not a very pleasant Christmass. We had only one hollyday, which was Christmass day. I believe I gave you a partial account of it. The hunt and the magnificent dinner at Mr. Clifford's. He invited us again yesterday, but we could not go. The citizens are extremely kind to us. We are invited to hunt tomorrow and I think I will go as it is New Year's Day. You know I wrote you that there would be an election on the 1st for Field Officers. As soon as the order came and I heard that a man (Hodges from Abbeville)[1] was a Candidate for my office, I addressed a short communication to the Regiment and had it read at Dress Parade, in which I declined to be a Candidate. Some of my friends came to me and protested. I told them I would not. That I had been long enough with them for them to know me. They all know that I have laboured hard for the Regiment—in fact that I have done by far the larger portion of the work that has been done. Col Bacon told the men that without me he could not have organized the Regt and without my assistance he could not keep it up. The men all say I am a "good Officer—a fine Officer"—but too *strict*. I told them I had done nothing more than discharge my duty, and I would continue to do that regardless of whom it offended. Almost all the Officers were in favour of reelecting the old Officers. *Well* I was no Candidate and for a few days after the election was ordered the men was pretty loud in abusing me. I said not a word but went ahead drilling and attending to my business. They began to come to me and say we are wrong and you are right.

LETTER 67

1. The only Hodges on the roster is Pvt. W. Lud Hodges, Co. A, who was drillmaster of the regiment. His place of enlistment is not given. CSR, M267, roll 201.

You are the best officer we have and we are going to elect you—They softened down greatly without my doing a thing. And it was generally conceded yesterday that there was no doubt that I would be elected. When night before last here comes an order from Genl Beauregard suspending the election, until the War Department shall be heard from.[2] Most of the men say they are glad of it— Some few growl some. So things stand. I will write again soon. My love to all—and my congratulations to Miss Fannie on her birth day[3]— Tell Willie and Bob they are little rascals for not writing to me.

I must close
Your
Husband

Letter 68 JBG to Leila Griffin

Camp Griffin Jany 11th 1863

My Dear Leila

It is now after eleven O Clock, and I have been trying all night to get time to write you a letter but have been kept busy until the present moment—

You have no idea of the vast amount of business that a Commander of a Regiment has on his hands. By the time you are through with one, here comes another. And on account of Col Bacon's feeble health, I have most of the business to attend to. The only leisure I have is when the Col is well and sometimes I steal off on a deer hunt. I killed another fine buck a few days ago, and wounded another, but didnt get it. It ran into the river and got away. I went out yesterday. Three men got shots, and only one killed. And that was a large but very poor buck. The bucks are generally poor this season of the year, but the does are in their prime. Unfortunately almost all we killed are

---

2. The validity of the South Carolina legislation was questionable because the troops had already been mustered into Confederate service. Beauregard criticized it, and at the request of the new governor, Milledge Luke Bonham of Edgefield, a former Confederate general officer, the law was repealed. Cauthen, *South Carolina Goes to War*, 161.

3. Griffin's third child and oldest daughter, Fannie, turned seven on 31 December.

bucks. I have been anxious to kill a nice fat one, so that I could sent you a quarter— But this is generally a bad chance—for the hunters rule is to divide with all the hunters, and there are always so many that each man's share is small. But if I can kill a nice fat one I am determined to send my Darling a quarter. I am sorry to say My Darling that I get your letters very irregularly. I havent heard a word from you since the letter brought me by Jim Brooks. And I have no doubt you have written several. I am still enjoying very good health. And I am happy to say that the health of the whole Command has very much improved. We havent had a case of that horrible disease in over a week. I hope now we will have no more of it. I am going to send this letter by Aquilla[;] he leaves for home tomorrow, on rather an unpleasant business. Viz—to arrest and bring to camp those men who have never reported for duty. I suspect they will create quite a stir in the ranks of these fellows, when they get there. We are ordered to send for them and Court Martial them for not reporting before. What do you think My Darling I had the pleasure of attending a *party* last night. What do you think of that, a sure enough party. A small one tis true but very pleasant. It was Doctr Glover's. He has a very nice and pleasant wife, a daughter some twelve or fourteen years of age, and three young Ladies with him[;] one is a Sister of Mrs Glover, and the other two are Sisters, one of them the Doctr's Governess, the other is I think on a visit to her Sister. The party returned yesterday (Saturday) from a visit to Charleston. And they are going to their home near Walterboro[1] on Monday. So the Doctr came down yesterday evening and invited a few of us to go up and spend the evening with him. We went and had quite a pleasant time. The Ladies were by no means pretty[,] Scarcely passable but still very entertaining. Mr Clifford and his family were there with those horribly ugly old Maids. They come out sometimes to see us drill, and occasionally to hear our Chaplain preach. It is late My Darling and I must bid you good night. I hope you are now sleeping sweetly. My love to all the children

Your husband.

LETTER 68

1. Walterboro, in Colleton County, is fifteen miles northwest of Jacksonboro.

Letter 69 JBG to Leila Griffin

Camp Griffin Jany 19th 1863

My Dear Leila

We have had dreadful weather for the last two or three days. Yesterday morning the ground was hard frozen. I can imagine what it was in the up country. I hope it played havoc with the Yankee Vessels. This hope was the only comfort I had while shivering in my tent. "I never mind the weather so the wind dont blow", for then I can have a good fire in my tent and be comfortable enough—but when the wind blows, and unfortunately my chimney sets right to face all the west winds, the smoke is terrible. I stood it day before yesterday for some time, but finally, put out the fire, thinking it better to stand the cold than the smoke. I am much obliged to you My Darling for your very kind letter received last night. As to the plows. Ask your Uncle William to see how much he can get for them. If he can sell them for ten dollars, let them go, if not keep them until I come home. I have been trying to write this letter for two hours, but can only write a line or two and some one comes in on business. I am now in Command of the Regt— Col Bacon is commanding in Genl Hagood's place who has gone home for a few days. This however doesnt add much to my duties, as I have done a great deal of the business all the time. You would be surprised to see the change in the minds of the men towards me lately. I am told now that I am by far the Strongest man in the Regt— This of course is for your *own ears* alone. I only tell you because I know it will be gratifying to you. Lt [Aquilla] Miles and the ballance of the Officers who were to go home for the defaulters, got as far as Columbia and on account of misunderstanding of the order, they had to return. The whole matter is now submitted to Genl Beauregard who will I hope send an order to send them again. I think the service of this Regt will expire early in Feby, and then I want you to meet me in Charleston with Claude. Make your arrangements to come and I will tell you when, in time. Tell Spradley to push on with his business— How does the Small grain look.

Give my love to all. The Mail Carrier is waiting on me—

Good bye My Dearest
Your Husband

Letter 70   JBG to Leila Griffin

Camp Griffin Jany 20th 1863

My Dear Leila

Having an opportunity to send you a letter direct by George Addison, Jr.[1] I will write if it is only a few lines. We have had a dreadful rainy day to day. We are now paying for some of our good weather. The land is low and flat and in many places under water. My health is very good, and the health of the Regt has very much improved. We however lost another man yesterday, but we have no bad cases now on hand. I think we will get our details off again tomorrow, to arrest the defaulters, but if we do not, dont say any thing about it. I have sent off to night for orders and if I get them I will send off tomorrow, and then Lt Miles will get to see his *dear family,* whom he is so anxious to see. I have heard nothing more of the time when we go out. But think it will be within two or three weeks. Tell Spradley I am not *positive* about going home but I expect to do so. So he can make arrangement accordingly, of course he will make a conditional arrangement, for unless I do go home I will expect him to stay. As soon as I can find out when we are to be disbanded I will inform you. And as I told you before I wish you to meet me in Charleston with dear little Claude. Tell Willie I recd his letter and am obliged to him for it, it is the best letter he has ever written me. Tell Bobbie I am expecting an answer from him[.] My Darling, if Spradley has any Mesquite grass seed left or if you can get any in the neighbourhood, if it is only a quart, I wish you to send it to me. I want to give it to some friends of mine down here. I think it will grow finely in this Climate. And I am anxious to do something for some gentlemen here who have been remarkably kind to me— If you cant send it before you can send it by Quilla when he returns.

My Darling you must excuse me for writing short letters and I suspect disconnected ones, for I cant write but a line or two before I am disturbed[.] Tell the Children to study well at school.

My love to them all and to you

Your Husband

LETTER 70

1. Pvt. George Addison, Company K, enlisted at Edgefield on 10 November 1862. CSR, M267, roll 201.

Letter 71   JBG to Leila Griffin

Camp Griffin
Jany 27th 1863

My Dear Leila

I received yesterday another kind letter from you. Am delighted to hear that you are all well. Let me congratulate you on your industrious habit. Dont do as you used to say I did—"be overly smart for a short time and then get back worse than ever". I have no doubt you spend your time more pleasantly, while you are busily engaged than in any other way. Tell Fannie and Medie I guess they will feel very proud when they get on their homespun dresses. And indeed I will feel quite proud, myself, especially when I think that it was made by their industrious Mother. Allow me My Darling to say that I was very much interested in reading your kind letter, and I join you heartily in the wish that the remnant of our lives "may be as bright as a May Day". I do sincerely hope and pray that the remnant, may be spent agreeably and happily together. If I did not *hope* that it would be so, I would prefer never more to return.

Let me tell you My Darling I am forced to be quite industrious myself. I dont get up so early as you do, for there is no necessity for it, and besides I have no inclination to do so. But then I rise about sun rise, and then I am busy until I go to bed again, which is frequently as late as twelve O Clock. Sometimes, as I have written you before, I steal off and take a deer hunt. I spent last saturday very pleasantly in that way. Genl Hagood and several gentlemen, came over and we had a very nice hunt indeed. We, that is, the party killed two nice deer. Genl Hagood killed one and a Mr. Seabrook killed the other, I didnt get a shot, but nevertheless enjoyed the hunt finely. Of course I couldnt expect to get a shot every time. I have shot at three since I came down here, and believe I killed them all. I am certain as to two and the other was badly wounded and went into the river. It is very fine sport. Genl Hagood has been very kind to me— He told Col Bacon that he would like to build up our Regiment with Conscripts and retain the same Field Officers. But of course this is out of the question.[1] He told me the other day, if I could do no

---

LETTER 71

1. Beauregard had hoped to keep the conscripted reserves after their Confederate service expired and build up the regiments. The secretary of war had

better, to go over and take a place in his Staff. I am very much obliged to him, but have no desire for a Staff office. I would take it however in prefference to the *ranks*. By the way, have you seen that Congress is trying to repeal the exemption act so far as owners and overseers of Slaves are concerned.[2] They may manage to Conscript *me* yet—but I dont believe it. I am expecting every day that we will receive some order respecting the disbanding of our Regt. But we have had nothing yet. There is a rumour in camp this evening that Genl Beauregard has requested the Governor to let him keep the Troops two months longer.[3] I dont think however that this will be done. The Old Fellows are getting very anxious indeed to *go home*. Our details who were sent home after the men who wouldnt come, must have created quite a stir at home. The men are beginning already to pour into Camp. They will all be courtmartialed. We are to have a grand Review of our Regiment on Saturday, I wish you could be here. The Genl is coming over— We will have a fine brass band for the occasion. When it is over I will write you the particulars. Give my love to all the Children— Tell Willie and Bob to write to me, and tell them to take good care of the colts and every thing. My love to Minnie and ask her where she addresses the Doctr[.][4] Good night My Darling

Your Jimmie

---

decided, however, to use the conscripts to fill up old regiments previously in the field. OR, ser. 1, 14:755.

2. (See letter of 13 May 1862, note 5.) The "Twenty Negro Law," under which Griffin could claim exemption either for himself or for his overseer, was significantly amended in May 1863, tightening the restrictions on overseer exemptions. It was never repealed, however, and prompted bitter observations from the common men in the ranks that the rebellion was a rich man's war and a poor man's fight.

3. Beauregard wrote to Governor Bonham on 3 February 1863 that he anticipated an attack on Charleston or Savannah soon and asked that the reserves be kept for an additional thirty days after their time was up. The secretary of war telegraphed also, urging the thirty-day extension or, at the very least, holding the troops for a short while as militia. OR, ser. 1, 14:760, 763–64.

4. On 5 January 1863 Dr. Muse's regiment, the Twenty-Fourth South Carolina Volunteers, had been directed to occupy the vicinity of Island Creek in eastern North Carolina and erect defensive works there. On 30 January it was listed as part of Col. Peyton H. Colquitt's brigade, in the division of Brig. Gen. States Rights Gist, Whiting's command. OR, ser. 1, 18:821, 866.

Letter 72   JBG to Leila Griffin

Camp Griffin Feby 1st 1863

My Dear Leila

This has been a long lonesome Sunday, and now 10 O clock at night it is raining. I intended writing you this evening, but as usual havent been left to myself until this moment. But I am determined to write to My Darling before I go to bed. I am happy to say that I am still enjoying fine health. I certainly have been greatly blessed with good health since I have been in Camps. I wrote to you the other day My Darling that we were to have a grande Review on Saturday (yesterday), and that I would give you an account of it.

Well it came off, and a very nice day we had. The Genl and five of his staff came over, and brought us a fine band of Music (brass band). And now I wish you could only have seen how the Old Fellows marched after the music. They drilled finely— At the close the Genl made us a Speech in which he complimented us, handsomely—the *Field Officers* especially. He expressed himself highly delighted with the Drill and only regretted to loose so fine a Regt. After the drill we invited the Genl and Staff down to dine with us. But stop I haven't told you that the Ladies honoured us with their presence on the occasion. Mrs Genl Hagood and two more officers wives came over from Adam's run, besides several Ladies from this Neighbourhood whom I did not know— Mrs Hagood asked very kindly after you and the Children. She is looking better [than] when I last saw her. Well to go on with the dinner— I invited the Ladies to go down and dine with us, but they declined, said they had dinner with them, and I couldnt persuade them to go. They rode up to Dr Glover's place and took their dinner. But the officers went with us, and we had a very nice dinner indeed. Thanks to your kindness for a part of it. You see Quilla arrived here with my trunk the day before. And besides the good things you sent me, one of the Neighbours of Mr Weitzel had sent us for the occasion a large fine gobler and various other things. And independent of all this we had three large shad. They were caught out of the river near our camp but they sell very high from $1.50, to $2.00 each.

Now dont you think we had a nice dinner—and we enjoyed it too. We had no wine to drink but we had plenty of new Corn Whiskey.

We dined and drank and smoked our pipes, and had a very pleasant evening until after a while the Ladies came along and the party broke up.

We have a good many new customers in Camps within the last few days—The defaulters who had to be invited down *specially*. There is some excitement with them to night as a Court Martial is ordered to convene tomorrow to look into their excuses for not reporting earlier. I wish you could see some of them[.] Old Shimmey Nicholson[1] especially, he is the picture of dispair. He offers five hundred dollars if we will turn him loose and let him go home. George Addison [Sr.],[2] Jim Mims[3] and Butler[4] are all here. I hear Sam Tompkins[5] has got home.

LETTER 72

1. See Chapter 1, note 151, on all these listed as stragglers. Shemuel Wright Nicholson, 47, was a private in Company F. The muster roll lists him as AWOL until 30 January 1863. Shemuel Nicholson was the uncle of John L. Nicholson (letter of 2 Jan. 1861, note 4) and Benjamin E. Nicholson (2 April 1862, note 1). CSR, M267, roll 201; "Genealogy of Nicholson and Allied Families," 37.

2. George A. Addison, Sr., does not appear on the roster. According to the census, he was a 43-year-old farmer with eight children. His son was already serving with the regiment (see letter of 20 Jan. 1863, note 1).

3. James H. Mims does not appear on the roster. The census lists him as a 42-year-old farmer with two children. Among his nearer neighbors were M.C. Butler, Shemuel Nicholson, and former governor Francis Pickens.

4. Cpl. Sampson W. Butler, Company C, appears on the muster roll as a substitute for R.J. Butler. CSR, M267, roll 201.

5. Stephen Samuel Tompkins, a private in Company K, appears on two muster rolls. He is recorded AWOL on the first, and as never having reported to camp on the second. Sam Tompkins was the brother of Robert and Richard Augustus Tompkins (see letter of 25 April 1862, notes 2 and 4), and John Warren Tompkins (2 June 1862, note 7), the oldest of the seven sons of James S. Tompkins. In the 1860 census he was a 40-year-old attorney and a farmer with personal property valued at $60,000. Griffin's plantation accounts for that year also show that he rented slaves to Tompkins. He had served as an aide to Brig. Gen. Milledge L. Bonham, with the rank of major, in 1861, resigning when Bonham did in January 1862. From 23 April until 14 August 1862, he was a member of Company K, Twenty-Fourth South Carolina Volunteers. Tompkins was unable to avoid state service indefinitely: from 1 Au-

He is also invited down. I expect Quilla raised a good deal of excitement around old Edgefield. I wish he could have found Jim Hatcher.[6] I hear he talked very large but he took good care to keep out of the way of Quilla. Strange to say we havent yet received any intelligence when we are to be disbanded. I think it will be some time this week. But dont know— The men are getting very restive and impatient, they are anxious for the order to come. There is a good deal of excitement and commotion among the Conscripts, those under forty— All are ordered to select their Corps at once or they will be assigned to them.[7] I have been Strongly Solicited to get up a Regt—but it will not be allowed[;] if it were, I would find no difficulty in getting up one quick either Cavalry or infantry. Lewis Jones is anxious for me to get up a Cavalry Regt, and try to get him into it. But I dont think it will be permitted—for the act expressly says "no new Commands Shall be formed". I am sorter put about, by Congress repealing or attempting to repeal the exemption act. I have no idea of being a conscript I assure you. And think I will accept Genl Hagood's kind offer. Not until I go home however. Tell Spradley that he can hold on where he is until he hears more from me. Be ready My Darling to meet me in Charleston as I have suggested, I will write you as soon as I can find out the time[.]

It is growing late—Good night—kiss all the dear Children for your
Husband

---

gust through 12 September 1863, he was a private in Company I, Second South Carolina Reserves. Tompkins lived near George Addison and was the immediate neighbor of James Hatcher (see below). CSR, M267, roll 201; "Griffin Scrapbook and Account Book"; O.R, ser. 1, 2:520; Heath, "The James S. Tompkins Family," 2.

6. James Hatcher was recorded in the census as a 42-year-old farmer with five children. He was enrolled as a private in Company K. Muster rolls show Hatcher as "absent, never reported to camp." CSR, M267, roll 201.

7. The second conscription act, passed on 27 September 1862, extended the draft age to 45 but called only for men 35 through 40. When the Confederate service of the ninety-day regiments expired, the men between 35 and 40 were required to remain and the older ones dismissed. Cauthen, *South Carolina Goes to War,* 146.

Letter 73 JBG to Leila Griffin

Camp Griffin 9th Feby 1863

My Dear Leila

Sure enough I did receive your letter to day bringing the unwelcomed intelligence of the exposure of the negroes to the Small Pox. I hope it will turn out to be a false alarm. Where could old man Sib,[1] have contracted the disease? If it is really so, you have made the best arrangement you can. In the mean time have all hands vaxcinated, especially those negroes at the plantation and tell Spradley to be scrupulously particular in not allowing any intercourse between the negroes at home and those at the plantation. I think there is no doubt that this Regt will be mustered out of Service on next Sunday.[2] I cant yet tell you whether I will be able to go home or not. The circumstances are these. Genl Hagood has very kindly offered and invited me to join his Staff. If I am only to be an Aid, as I told you before, it will be to me a very unpleasant post, and I will only accept it in the event that I am Conscripted, and can do no better, that will be infinitely better than the ranks. But he tells me that his Qr Master has been promoted to a Colonelcy, and he expects very soon to loose him, and [in] the event of loosing him he is bound to tender the office to Col Ryan,[3] who commanded one of the Regts of the Reserves, and if he

---

LETTER 73

1. One of Griffin's older slaves.

2. The legislature had refused to extend the service of the eight regiments. After the governor transmitted an urgent message from Brig. Gen. William S. Walker at Pocotaligo that 60 Federal vessels were in sight at the entrance to Port Royal Sound, and that he would need the three regiments of reserves there if he were attacked, the House resolved on February 6 that those three regiments be "requested" to continue in service for an additional thirty days "unless sooner discharged." The attack did not materialize, however, and the Fifth South Carolina Reserves was disbanded on 15 February. OR, ser. 1, 14:768; Charleston *Daily Courier*, 10 Feb. 1863.

3. Col. J.J. Ryan had commanded the Eleventh South Carolina Reserves, one of the first group of four regiments that had been received into Confederate service for ninety days. *Journals of the Conventions of the People of South Carolina, 1860–62*, 259, 289.

does not accept it, then he will give it to me. If he gives me this post, I will accept it, and in that event I shall have to forego, for a little while the pleasure of seeing My dear family. For if I take the Office I shall have to take it at once, So as to receive all the returns of the present incumbent. It is a very responsible and hard working Office (Brigade Qr Master). But if I can keep my health I shall not mind the work. The pay is one hundred and fifty ($150) dollars per month and I will have a good house to live in. And what you would suppose is still better its a very safe Office—for the business of the Office generally keeps its officer out of a fight, except on extraordinary occasions.

I suspect however that the chances are against my getting it and in that case I will go home even if I come back right away. I will know certainly tomorrow or the next day, and will then write you. As to your coming to Charleston, I am not willing for you to come yet. And if I go home, I will then come down with you if it is practicable. Col Bacon is still very feeble, he speaks of going to Charleston day after tomorrow and if he does I presume he will not return before we disband[.] I am getting tired of playing Col. with only rank of Lt Col— And I am still more tired of commanding *Reserves*. I dont think I will be caught in another such scrape again in a hurry. My love to all[.] This is the second letter to day from

Your Husband

8 Fear of Invasion: Colonel of the First South Carolina Militia

Letters 74 through 80
1 December 1864 through 27 February 1865

The last set of letters, dated from 1 December 1864 through 27 February 1865, reveals the first fear of invasion. While the Yankees threatened from without, the home front also had enemies within. Strangers passing through the community were not always trustworthy. One group of about a hundred Confederate deserters pretended to be part of Joseph Wheeler's command en route to join Gen. Nathan Bedford Forrest in Tennessee. The deserters presented to Capt. Benjamin Bettis[1] in Edgefield a government order for precious supplies (forty bushels of corn, fifty pounds of bacon, and ten bushels of potatoes). Tracking these imposters was a company of the Sixth Georgia, which captured more than half of them. Determined to find the remaining stragglers, a group of twenty-five Edgefieldians, "under command of Col Jas. B. Griffin, who had just arrived home on furlough, turned out in pursuit." They chased the deserters most of the night.[2]

Terror also originated closer to home, as opponents of the Confederacy grew bolder. A spate of homes burned down, and rumors of

---

1. See letter of 26 Nov. 1862, note 11.
2. Edgefield *Advertiser*, 28 Dec. 1864.

slave arsonists abounded. On 6 December Griffin's mansion was destroyed by fire. (See letter of 19 December 1864, note 3.)

The optimistic letters of 1861–62 had been filled with nationalism and patriotism; concern for the safety of family and community dominates this last set. Griffin, now colonel of the First South Carolina Militia,[3] wanted to continue the combat and does not appeared discouraged. But in contrast to his earlier willingness that, should he fall in battle, even little Jimmie would continue the fight to the death, he now hoped his eldest son, Willie, would remain at home.

These letters mention the options available to Griffin's slaves now that the Union army was enforcing President Lincoln's Emancipation Proclamation, issued in September 1862 to take effect on 1 January 1863.[4] South Carolina had not given the proclamation much attention when it was announced. The Edgefield Advertiser wrote: "We have expressed our opinion that Lincoln's Proclamation should be met in the South, by Proclamations from the Southern Governors announcing their intention to enforce strictly the existing State laws against negro thieves and insurrectionists."[5]

After the Emancipation Proclamation took effect, the Edgefield Advertiser printed the full text and noted that while some in the North supported the measure, others condemned it. The paper characterized the Proclamation as "unwise, illtimed, impracticable, outside of the Constitution . . . . It will assuredly do no good as a war measure." The editor observed that as long as Jefferson Davis's government in Richmond was secure, such proclamations were useless, "as ridiculous as the Pope's bull against the comet."[6] The whole article took up only half of one column.

Griffin said absolutely nothing about the proclamation. Even after Abram had run off to the Yankees, Griffin continued to trust his slaves. Indeed, after the family mansion burned, the African

---

3. According to CSR, M267, roll 392, "Miscellaneous South Carolina," no rolls exist for the First South Carolina Militia. Only Col. J. Griffin and Lt. Col. [B.Z.] Herndon are noted.

4. The classic account is John Hope Franklin, *The Emancipation Proclamation* (Garden City, N.Y.: Doubleday, 1963). Recent interpretations have stressed that enslaved people freed themselves.

5. Edgefield *Advertiser*, 5 Nov. 1862.

6. Edgefield *Advertiser*, 14 Jan. 1863.

Americans were left in de facto charge of the Griffin plantation,
with a boy not yet sixteen as the only white person in residence.
Although Griffin continued to think of himself as master until Sher-
man drew near, one must question whether these African Americans
were in fact still "enslaved." Certainly the system of slavery had
changed dramatically from the beginning of the war.

Letter 74   JBG to Leila Griffin

Hd Qrs S.C.M. Hamburg
Decr. 1st 1864

My Dear Leila
    It is likely we will soon be moved from this place, and I wish you
to send me my sword, *sword belt* and Sash— You may let Bob[1] come
down with them if he wishes to— Send them tomorrow—I am very
well and doing well— It is thought the Yankee's have passed Augusta
and the Troops are nearly all sent away from here.[2] I dined with Bob
Lamar[3] yesterday evening in company with Col Desaussure,[4] and several other Officers[.] The Col is an elegant Gentleman and very kind in-

---

LETTER 74

1. A slave.
2. As late as 28 November Sherman's cavalry was reported—inaccurately—
to have crossed the Savannah River and entered South Carolina twenty miles
below Augusta, Georgia/Hamburg, South Carolina. It soon became apparent,
however, that his destination was the South Carolina coast, where the Federals were still attempting penetration via the Broad River near Coosawhatchie.
On 29 November Lt. Gen. William Hardee, commanding the Department of
South Carolina, Georgia, and Florida, ordered Georgia militia troops under
Gustavus W. Smith to repulse an invasion force at Grahamville, a few miles
below Pocotaligo and Coosawhatchie. At the battle of Honey Hill the following day, Smith drove the Federals back to their gunboats and preserved the
vital Charleston and Savannah Railroad. He asked that more troops be sent to
him immediately, and at 6 p.m. on 2 December Griffin and 1300 South
Carolina militiamen left for Grahamville to help guard the railroad. OR, ser.
1, 44: 903–14, 923, 927–29.
3. Bob Lamar was an Edgefield farmer.
4. Wilmot G. DeSaussure, former state treasurer and former adjutant and
inspector general of South Carolina, commanded the militia force dispatched
from Hamburg to the coast. O.R., ser 1, 44: 923, 927, and CSR, roll 392.

deed to me— You neednt send me any thing to eat as we have an abun-
dance. A. Glover, Lud Hill and John Bland are messing with me at present[5]— I hear I am to have opposition from Anderson but my friends say
there is no danger. Col Moss[6] will send you this— I enclose some Tithe
receipts which please put in my large leather pocket book—

The Col is waiting for the note and I must close—and besides I
have a great deal of work to do[.]

My love to All and kiss all the darling Children—

Your Jimmie

Letter 75   JBG to Leila Griffin

Hd Qrs 1st Regt S.C.M.[1]
19 Decr 1864

My Dear Wife

One of my discharged men Mr. Johnson[2] is just in the act of leaving for home—and I have begged him to wait until I can write you a
few lines.

My Darling I am almost crazy about your condition—and am not

---

5. All from Edgefield.

6. Two Col. Mosses are listed in the 1860 population census. This is probably the "planter," Col. William H. Moss.

LETTER 75

1. The 403 effectives of the First South Carolina Militia were part of Col.
G.P. Harrison's brigade of five Georgia regiments, the Seventh North Carolina Reserves, and a small force of South Carolina cavalry—2,463 men. Harrison's brigade was one of three under the command of Brig. Gen. Williiam
B. Taliaferro, who on 26 December reported a total effective division strength
of 4,270, about half of it reserves and militia. Headquarters for the brigade
were at Pocotaligo. The First SCM did duty at several different locations during December. On the 9th Griffin took a detachment to Coosawhatchie after
reports of fighting there. The return of 26 December shows the First SCM,
under Lt. Col. Herndon, at the Tullifinney River railroad bridge between
Pocotaligo and Coosawhatchie; on 28 December it was reported at Coosawhatchie OR, ser. 1, 44:946, 992–93, 999–1000.

2. There were numerous Johnson families in Edgefield District, most of
them small farmers. This may possibly be P.D. Johnson, who lived near
Edgefield Court House.

allowed to go to you. I quietly waited nearly a week after hearing of our terrible misfortune[3] before asking for a leave of absence because I thought there was a probability of a fight here and I didnt wish to leave my Boys under those circumstances. I then asked for only 12 days, and Genl Jones[4] said as strong as the case was he was compelled to refuse me because he had recd orders from Hardee[5] to grant no leaves of absence on any grounds whatever.

I have only time to write a few lines as Johnson is waiting.

---

3. On 6 December the Griffin plantation house burned to the ground. The fire was probably set by a slave incendiary; between the end of November and the middle of January, the Edgefield *Advertiser* reported the destruction of another house, a barn full of grain, and a cotton warehouse, all attributed to incendiaries. The paper reported the Griffin fire as follows: "Our whole community has been cast into gloom by the terrible misfortune which has befallen one of its most chivalrous and beloved members. On Tuesday night last—or rather on Wednesday morning, between one and three o'clock—the mansion of Col. James B. Griffin, the largest and most elegant in our vicinity, was entirely consumed by fire. And not only the mansion, but everything in it. Of the costly furniture of ten rooms; of large quantities of handsome china, porcelain, and silver; of stores of valuable provisions and liquors, kept in a room adjoining the main building, not a vestige remains. The sleeping inmates saved not even the clothes they had laid aside upon going to bed. Seldom have we heard of such complete destruction. The fire is supposed to have been the work of an incendiary; it was communicated to the front of the building, which was half consumed before the members of the family, sleeping in the rear, became aware of their danger. Col. Griffin was facing the foe near Grahamville, at the time of this sad disaster, and has not yet reached his family. His wife and children have troops of friends, but their beautiful and happy home is gone. We are confident that Three Hundred Thousand Dollars of the present currency would not replace this house and furniture." Edgefield *Advertiser*, 14 Dec. 1864. Griffin published a reply on 28 December, thanking the community for "the greatest kindness, friendship, and consideration" extended to his homeless family.

4. Maj. Gen. Samuel Jones (1819–1887) commanded the District of South Carolina.

5. Lt. Gen. William Joseph Hardee (1815–1873), known as "Old Reliable," had served throughout the war with the Army of Tennessee and had fought under Johnston in the Atlanta campaign before assuming command of the Department of South Carolina, Georgia, and Florida on 5 October 1864. See Nathaniel C. Hughes, Jr., *General William J. Hardee, Old Reliable* (Baton Rouge: Louisiana State Univ. Press, 1965).

I think you had better get Dr Muse's house & furniture—and live there for the present— If the Dr has rented to any one else tell him he must back out under the circumstances— My Darling you are now thrown upon your own resources and you must do the best you can. I still hope to be able to get off home before long—but it may be they wont let me— How did the house get on fire? Write me very often and very full— Tell Willie and Sue and Maria & Annie and everybody to write me—direct at present to Pocotaligo—I hear nothing from [illegible]. Have they taken your horses[6]— Tell Willie to do his best in the farm. I need some pantaloons[.] Do try to get me some and send them to me if you can—if not I will send Ned for them.

My love to All— My sympathies for Minnie and a kiss for all my darling Children and wife[.]

I will write again soon
Your Jimmie

Letter 76 JBG to Leila Griffin

Head Qrs 1st Regt State Troops
Camp Griffin 25 Jany 1865

My Dear Leila

As Glover[1] leaves this morning for home I will write a few lines although I wrote you only a day or two ago—

I have recd three short letters from you and I think this is my *seventh.*

I do not complain for I know you have had a great deal to do— I am sorry to hear that Willie has been so sick—hope he is entirely well by this time. I am also extremely sorry to learn of Dr Burt's affliction.

---

6. The Confederate Congress had authorized the army to supply its needs by impressment on 23 March 1863. According to Ramsdell, *Behind the Confederate Lines*, 117, "No other one thing, not even conscription, caused so much discontent and produced so much resentment toward the Confederacy." James M. Matthews, ed., *Public Laws of the Confederate States of America Passed at the Third Session of the First Congress, 1863* (Richmond: R.M. Smith, 1863), 102–4.

LETTER 76

1. Arthur Glover.

His family are indeed to be pitied. I sympathize most sincerely with them. Glover recd a letter last night from his wife, saying that all the People had again become alarmed and were expecting to leave. That the Enemy were advancing from Millen to Augusta [2]— This cannot be true; for I was in the City [3] yesterday and no such news as that was heard of there. Dont let those timid, nervous men who are left at home, alarm you unnecessarily. Keep perfectly Cool and Collected. The Enemy cannot come upon you unawares— I see no reason at this time to suppose that they will molest you— But if you find with certainty that they are coming take [line obliterated] place, Newberry if they advance by way of Augusta is more safe than Edgefield. I hear that we are recieving reinforcements from Virginia. Butler's division will soon be here and I have heard that Hampton is looked for. [4] I hope so. Every thing is very quiet here[.] I am still at the same place. Where I have been for two weeks—

---

2. This rumor was not true, but the Federals intended the Confederates to think it was. Sherman had captured Savannah on 21 December, and by late January his army had begun corduroying its way across the rain-swollen rivers and swamps of the Carolina low country. To keep the Confederates from suspecting his true objective, Goldsboro, North Carolina, Sherman directed his right wing to make a feint on Charleston and his left on Augusta, Georgia. Millen, the site of a Confederate prison camp, was approximately fifty miles below Augusta at the junction of the Georgia Central and the Augusta and Savannah railroads. OR, ser. 1, 47, pt. 1: 17–18; John G. Barrett, *Sherman's March through the Carolinas* (Chapel Hill: Univ. of North Carolina Press, 1956), 39–47.

3. Charleston. The Confederates had abandoned Pocotaligo on the night of 14 January and were retreating up the coast.

4. Wade Hampton, by now a major general, had been commander of all Confederate cavalry since 11 August 1864. Griffin's former comrade in arms, Matthew Calbraith Butler, had attained the same rank in September and commanded a division under Hampton; it consisted of his own old brigade, now led by Col. B.H. Rutledge, Young's Brigade, and—temporarily—Dearing's Brigade. Young's Brigade had been detached and Rosser's attached. On 15 January Lee informed Jefferson Davis that he planned to send Butler's division to South Carolina to get fresh mounts and join the forces opposing Sherman, with the understanding that the division was to return to Virginia for the spring campaign. He also decided to release Hampton to accompany Butler, calculating that the esteem in which he was held in South Carolina would be useful not only in securing the horses but in "arousing the spirit and strength of the State." On the 17th President Davis telegraphed Governor McGrath that Butler's Division had been instructed "to proceed as rapidly as possible"

My command is suffering *dreadfully* from Measles—Several have died and more are very ill. I would like to see those old fellows from about the Village, in Camp— I suspect they will conclude it is not so funny as they had imagined. Have you had Willie's detail arranged yet, it ought to be attended to at once—tell him if he has to go into service he will of course report to me [5]— I want him however to take care of you and the Children— The bonded Officers are not allowed to go home yet—they will be after a while— Send my clothes back by Glover—something to eat, and one thousand dollars in money if you can spare it. It takes a great deal of money to live on— Capt Gayer and family beg to be remembered to you— They have been very kind to me. Write me about the cotton[;] how much is sold and what it

[remainder of letter destroyed]

Letter 77   JBG to Leila Griffin

Head Qrs 1st Regt State Troops
Camp Griffin 29 Jany 1865

My Dear Leila

Doctor Gary [1] has just recd a telegram informing him of the severe

---

to South Carolina. The order was officially issued on the 19th and the cavalry arrived in Columbia sometime in late January. On 7 February Hardee assigned Hampton to command the divisions of Butler and Maj. Gen. Pierce Manning Butler Young, and on 16 February Davis telegraphed Hampton that the Senate had confirmed his nomination as lieutenant general the previous day. OR, ser. 1, 42, pt. 3:1191, 1369; 46, pt. 2: 1100–101; 47, pt. 2: 1112; Douglas Southall Freeman, *Lee's Dispatches: Unpublished Letters of General Robert E. Lee, C.S.A., to Jefferson Davis and the War Department of the Confederate States of America, 1862–65*, new ed. (New York: G.P. Putnam's Sons, 1957), 480–81 (first quotation); Dunbar Rowland, *Jefferson Davis, Constitutionalist, His Letters, Papers, and Speeches*, 10 vols. (Jackson: Mississippi Dept. of Archives and History, 1923), 6:480–81 (second quotation); Barrett, *Sherman's March through the Carolinas*, 66.

5. Willie would turn 16 on 8 February and be required to report for militia service.

LETTER 77

1. This may be Dr. Franklin Fincher Gary of Cokesbury (in adjoining Abbeville District), older brother of Gen. Martin W. Gary. Dr. Gary was

illness of his wife. I have approved a leave of absence for him and if he gets off he thinks he will go by way of Edgefield, if he does he will carry this letter through with him, if not he will mail it. I have recd two or three letters from you lately, which have done me a great deal of good. Do continue to write as often as you can as you know I am always glad to hear from you. I am very well, but have an exceedingly sick Regiment. Indeed I have scarcely any command left— Nearly the whole Regt has the measles. I believe, as I have often told you, that it is wrong for Parents to keep their Children away from such diseases, for they must take them sometime and no better time than when they are young— The disease is generally lighter and they can be so much better cared for. I have had near three hundred cases of measles in my Regt and a good many more to have them.[2] I am still at my same Camp. How long I will remain here I cant say. I have no news to write you— No development of Genl Sherman's plans yet that I have heard. There is a good deal of talk of peace movements[3] but I dont

---

chief surgeon of the First Regiment State Troops in 1863–64 and after the war chaired the executive committee of the state board of health and served two terms in the legislature. CSR, M267, roll 392; Margaret Watson, *Greenwood County Sketches* (Greenwood, S.C.: Attic Press, 1970), 235; Atkinson, *Physicians and Surgeons of the United States*, 69; *Transactions of the South Carolina Medical Association 1883*, 27–36. Another possibility is Captain J. Wistar Gary, a graduate of South Carolina Medical College who lived in adjoining Newberry District. J.W. Gary's grandmother was related to Griffin, and his wife was a daughter of Dr. William H. Harrington, whose second marriage was to Griffin's sister. Pope, *History of Newberry County* 1: 221, 259, 264, 268.

2. According to the return of 12 December, there were 612 effectives in the First SCM. The pervasiveness of measles, the camp disease of new recruits, indicates that the majority of these men had no previous military experience; the state was calling out its last reserves of manpower. Roman, *Military Operations of General Beauregard*, 2: 617.

3. After the fall of Fort Fisher, at the mouth of the Cape Fear River in North Carolina, on 15 January, which cut Wilmington off from the Atlantic and made the capture of the Confederacy's last open port only a matter of time, the simmering anti-administration sentiment in the Confederate Congress boiled over. Secretary of State James Seddon resigned, and many Congressmen believed that it was hopeless to carry on the war. The unpopular President Davis, whose government the *Charleston Mercury* described as "a pandemonium of imbecility, laxity, weakness, failure," accepted Lincoln's

believe a word of it. Our only chance for peace *lyes in our rifles,* that will bring it after awhile, if we will only remain true to ourselves.[4] I suppose Glover has reached home before now, and you have my letter that he carried. Tell him that his bonded furlough has not returned, if it comes back approved I will forward it to him immediately— if it does not tell him not to be behind time. What could have become of my Blockade Scrip[5]— It was in that new black pocket book with the red tape tied around it. If it is lost do ask Arthur Glover to try to get me a duplicate or copy— He can get it I suspect in Augusta— I dont wish it sent to me as I have concluded not to sell it. I am anxious to see Glover back as he is company for me and besides I know he will bring something good to eat—which we do not often indulge in except when someone brings a box— The men are very kind to me, frequently sending me some delicacies. As far as I am able to judge I believe the men generally like me very well— Say I am strict but it is all right. I am anxious to get all my Regt together— Have you sent off all the cotton, and what did it bring— Dont sell it down too close. You will need a good deal to spin. If you can muster up enough leather, I suspect there is plenty already tanned sufficiently, Do get London to make a pair of shoes for Ned and a pair for Jackson[6] and send them down by Glover. I am afraid Jackson is taking measles, he is a little complaining to day. Write me what has become of the Boys who were working on the fortifications— Have they returned home

---

suggestion for a peace conference in the hope that humiliating Union demands would stiffen southern resistence. The two governments were arranging for a meeting between three Confederate peace commissioners and Secretary of State William Seward, which would take place at Hampton Roads, Virginia, on 2 February 1865, with Lincoln himself joining on the 3rd. McPherson, *Battle Cry of Freedom,* 821–24; Cauthen, *South Carolina Goes to War,* 228.

4. Years afterward, Griffin's son Bobby bracketed this sentence on the original letter and wrote in the margin: "his sentiments throughout the whole war."

5. Blockade running had been a prosperous but risky business since the beginning of 1862. The South Carolina legislature chartered several blockade-running corporations and in 1864 the state itself purchased a quarter-interest in the thriving Importing and Exporting Company of South Carolina. Ramsdell, *Behind the Confederate Lines,* 80.

6. London was the plantation's slave shoemaker. Jackson replaced Abram, who had run away in Virginia.

and when— Have you sent off any more if so who?[7] How do the negroes behave And how are they getting along with the farm— Has anything developed about the burning of the house— Have you ever been able to find any of the silver. How are you getting along in your new home and what all have you. Write me about every thing and every body— And so Charlie Miles[8] has married[;] well I hope his pain will be eased now. What kind of a Lady is she, and is she rich or poor? Poor I reckon.

How does Dr Muse manage to stay at home so long— I am afraid he will get into a scrape if he doesnt mind. I have not heard a word from Sis since I left Newberry. I suppose she has written but the rail road being broken up, the mails cannot pass.[9] We have had very cold weather for several days and of course it is much worse with you— Give my love to all the dear Children and kiss them every day for

---

7. The procurement of slaves to work on the coastal fortifications was a problem throughout the war and a source of public dissatisfaction with the government. Military commanders complained that they could get only a fraction of the necessary slave labor force to build and repair harbor defenses, while planters resisted complying with calls that drew workers away from the fields during the growing and harvesting seasons. After experimenting with various laws and amendments, the South Carolina legislature finally instituted systematic slave impressment on 23 December 1864. The Confederate bureau of conscription prompted the legislation by making known its intention in the fall of 1864 to impress slaves for twelve months' service with the army in accordance with state laws, where such existed, and targeting 20,000 impressments in South Carolina. The new South Carolina law authorized the impressment for twelve months of one-tenth of all slaves between 18 and 50 ordinarily subject to road repair duty, but permitted the owners to make substitutions every three months. Those who failed to deliver slaves faced having the bondsmen arrested by the sheriff and the term of service doubled. Cauthen, *South Carolina Goes to War*, 178–83; OR, ser. 4, 3: 963–64; *Statutes at Large of South Carolina*, 13: 211–15.

8. Leila's nephew Charlie Miles (see 11 August 1861, note 6) had been wounded at the battle of the Wilderness on 6 May 1864. The Edgefield *Advertiser* did not publish any notice of the marriage.

9. While the mails were already frequently interrupted by changes in railroad schedules due to troop and supply movement, mail service became even more sporadic as the Union army penetrated different areas of the South. The Union armies frequently destroyed railroad tracks and bridges and, on many occasions, intercepted mails. Proctor, *Not Without Honor*, 139–40.

their Papa. Tell Jimmie I am glad to hear he is a good Boy. My kindest regards to all and my purest and best love to My Darling
Tis 12 oClock Good night

Your Jimmie

Letter 78   JBG to Leila Griffin

Head Qrs 1st Regt State Troops[1]
2nd Feby 1865

My Dear Leila

It is now ten oClock and I have just finished a game of Chess with Lieut Prescott and as I do not feel sleepy I will write a few lines to my Darling Wife. I am very well and comfortable for a Soldier. True I would like to see Glover turn up with a box of nice provisions from home. My fare is not very tempting to the appetite—but still it does pretty well. We can get oysters almost any time but they do not eat very well unless we have seasoning for them. My butter has just given out. I have had plenty most of the time since my return. About the time we finished eating that which I brought—I had a present of a large ball, which has lasted me until now. My Mess has grown quite small recently. Glover seceded from the Lt Col. and Majr. during my absence, and since he has been away I have no one with me but my little orderly, Benny Howland, a very nice well behaved and genteel little fellow. Glover[,] Lud Hill, and myself will form my mess. Dr Dozier[2] messes with the Surgeons. As it is more convenient to him. We are close neighbors however, and frequently sit and dine with each other. Dr Taggirt my asst Surgeon has been detailed by Genl Garlington[3] & is therefore exempt from service in my Regt. I will

---

LETTER 78

1. Probably in the vicinity of Bull's Island, in present-day Charleston County.

2. Possibly Dr. Allen Stokes Dozier, the husband of Leila's cousin, Emily Burt. He had been surgeon of the Seventh South Carolina Volunteers until 15 July 1862. CSR, M331, "General and Staff Officers and Non-Regimental Enlisted Men."

3. Albert Cresswell Garlington was one of four brigadier generals appointed by Governor Francis Pickens after secession to command volunteers; he also served in Pickens's cabinet as secretary of the interior. Garlington was later in

have to give the position to Dr Hill. I wish I could give it to Dozier but Hill reported first at Hamburg and applied for a position before Dozier reported. So much for a man being *behind time*. It is always best to be *prompt*. My Regt has dwindled down to almost nothing. I have never known as many cases of measles in one Regt at a time as I have in mine. I have only little more than a hundred men for duty now. It is late and you cant get this letter before monday, so I will bid you good *night* and write more tomorrow and send it to the office on saturday.

Friday 3rd

This is a dark gloomy morning and has rained a little. I have the blues pretty badly—Wish I was at home for a short time, to see you all. But really I am so thoroughly disgusted with men who are resorting to all kinds of pretexts to be exempt from service, now that our *very homes are threatened*. Our *wives* and *children* almost at the mercy of a cruel and heartless enemy—that I dont believe I would go home were it in my power. A man in South Carolina who is really able to bear arms, even for a short time, who is not now found in the front—unless Providentially kept away really does not deserve the name of *Freeman* and should be considered as such for all time to come, by good, honest citizens and more especially by the helpless *women* and *Children*. I hear that nearly all of Capt Frazier's company have been discharged and the Capt amongst the rest.[4] *Short campaign.*

I am badly located to get news—true I get the Charleston papers every day but generally there is very little news in them. It is thought that Sherman is slowly and cautiously moving upon some point of the So Ca rail road near Branchville.[5] While Fos-

---

Confederate service as major of the Holcombe Legion. He was an unsuccessful candidate for governor in 1864, and in 1865 was serving as adjutant and inspector general of South Carolina. *Rolls of South Carolina Volunteers in the Confederate States Provisional Army*, 5: 93, 98, SCDAH; Cauthen, *South Carolina Goes to War*, 81, 115, 183.

4. An Edgefield company. Marshal Frazier was a substantial planter.

5. Branchville, roughly halfway between Augusta and Charleston, was the junction of two branches of the South Carolina Railroad. It lay approximately sixty miles above Charleston, and those who believed that Sherman was

ter[6] is making a demonstration against Charleston. Some think Sherman will attack Augusta, but I doubt it. It seems that I am to be kept here—and the truth is that my command is so reduced that it is scarcely worth moving. I am guarding the approach to the City from the way of Georgetown.[7] I am becoming tired of this location and if I had a Regt would insist on being removed.

I suspect Glover will get notice to day that his additional furlough as a "bonded man" was not granted. So I shall expect in a few days to see him back.

I am beginning to need my clothes particularly my coat as my old one is giving way. I am invited to spend the day on Sunday next with a Mr. Vening four miles from my Camp. There are several Ladies there and one very pretty one. Dont be *jealous*. Mr. Vening has *nine* Children and they are all Daughters. I havent heard a word from Sis yet[.] Strange I get no letters from her. I saw Billy Nance a few days ago who informed me that they were all well.

Have you written yet to your Uncle Moody to ask him if he will take care of you in case Sherman honor's Edgefield with a visit[.] Capt Jack Tompkins says go to his house, that he knows Sherman will never

---

headed for the harbor city expected him to march through Branchville. Instead, the Federal army turned a few miles west of it and went through Orangeburg, fifteen miles to the north. The Seventeenth Corps occupied Orangeburg on 12 February 1865. Barrett, *Sherman's March through the Carolinas*, 58.

6. Maj. Gen. John G. Foster (1834–1903) had served as chief engineer at the Charleston Harbor fortifications before the war. For the last eight months he had been commander of the Department of the South and notably unsuccessful in bringing the siege of Charleston to a successful conclusion for the Union. At Sherman's request, Foster and Rear Admiral John A. Dahlgren had on 26 January 1865 begun new demonstrations before Charleston and along the coast, as a diversion. On 30 January, Maj. Gen. Quincy A. Gillmore was ordered to relieve Foster, who was allowed to save face by announcing that his Mexican War wounds were troubling him. Gillmore took command on 9 February. John Johnson, *The Defense of Charleston Harbor, Including Fort Sumter and the Adjacent Islands, 1863–1865* (Charleston: Walker, Evans, and Cogswell, 1890), 247–48; Burton, *Siege of Charleston*, 314; Madeline Vinton Dahlgren, ed., *Memoir of John A. Dahlgren, Rear-Admiral, United States Navy* (Boston: J.R. Osgood, 1882), 497.

7. Georgetown is sixty miles north of Charleston on Winyah Bay.

get there[.] He has applied for exemption, which I think will be granted— And says if he goes home he will take care of you. Perhaps you will do well to go there[.] It is not far from your Uncle Moody's and much more difficult of access.[8] If you do have to leave—You had better make the negroes hide out the bacon and as much corn and wheat as they can, and take as much with you as you can have hauled— Load both wagons with provisions and take all the Mules and horses— Tell the negroes to drive off from about the house all the cattle and hogs—as they will destroy every thing of the kind. Tell the negroes they can go if they choose, of course— But to remember they will always regret it. They know that I have never deceived them—and the men will be immediately placed in the army—The Women and Children they dont want.

Do give my love to all and kiss all the dear Children for me. Wonder why some of my good Friends and Relatives dont write to me? Good hands to promise but bad to perform. Tell Willie I am obliged to him even for his short letter.

Your Jimmie

Letter 79   JBG to Leila Griffin

Head Qrs Legare Point—Jas.
Island[1]
14 Feb 1865

My dear Leila

Capt Tompkins leaves for home this evening and I must write you a few lines by him. I may have to stop at any moment for I have just recieved orders by telegraph to hold my Regt in readiness to move. It is said that the enemy are landing on the west end of the

---

8. Moody Burt lived across the Savannah River in Columbia County, Georgia. Jack Tompkins (letter of 2 June 1862, note 7) lived in the Dark Corner (see 16 June 1862) section of Edgefield District that bordered Georgia on the west and Abbeville District on the north.

LETTER 79

1. James Island, a neck of land that curved south and east of Charleston into the harbor, was the key to holding the city and had been heavily fortified. Fort Sumter lay directly east of it, in the middle of the harbor.

Island.[2] I have no idea that they will make a fight there, for our lines are exceedingly strong there & I am sure we can repell any attack, they may make. They know this and will therefore will not make an attack. This is my opinion. You will perceive from the heading of my letter that I am at Legare's Point. This is on the East end of James Island.

Last friday at one oclock, while on Battallion drill, I recieved orders to move immediately to James Island which I did, reaching my destination about midnight and was placed in command of a portion of the line, about half a mile long, embracing three Batteries. Here I was kept until sunday evening, and I was then moved to this Point[3]— Here I am now in command of a line a mile long, embracing five batteries. Genl Elliott[4] is in Command of the Island, seems to be a very fine gentleman and is a good Officer.

I am very comfortable quartered in a good home, have a cot to sleep on— My fare since I left camp has been "hard tack" and a little poor beef until to day— Ned managed to get us a good breakfast, and a very good dinner. The Adjutant of the Post is a young Lieutenant from Savannah by name of Symons—quite a nice young man. He and myself and my little orderly, who I keep with me—mess together. Glover has not yet returned and I am sorry for it—If he is still at home

---

2. The following day the *Charleston Courier* reported a "feeble" demonstration on the western end of James Island: three gunboats and an ironclad on the Stono River shelled the batteries. *Charleston Daily Courier*, 15 Feb. 1865.

3. Federal gunboats on the Stono and Folly Rivers began shelling James Island on Friday, 10 February, and two regiments accompanied by two companies of skirmishers landed and made an attempt on the right of the line. Maj. Edward Manigault's Palmetto Battalion lost one-third of its men in a resistance that the Federals finally overcame with a combined frontal and flanking attack. The land forces retreated to Cole's Island that evening, but naval fire continued through the 17th, when the harbor defenses were finally abandoned. *Charleston Daily Courier*, 13 Feb. 1865; Johnson, *Defense of Charleston Harbor*, 248–49.

4. Stephen Elliot, Jr. (1836–1866), formerly colonel of the Holcombe Legion, had been severely wounded in the fighting at the Crater in Petersburg, Virginia, on 30 July 1864 and sent home to South Carolina for convalescence.

tell him he has disappointed me. And that he had better return. I can give you very little news. My impression is that Charleston will very soon have to be evacuated. Branchville has been given up and now our only outlet is by the North Eastern Rail Road. And I dont see why the enemy dont take possession of that. What Gen. Hardee intends to do I do not know [5]—I feel sorta like I might be in a trap which will be difficult to get out of. I hope however it will work out well after awhile.

My judgement is that Charleston should be evacuated at once and all our Troops concentrated at or near Columbia, where I believe we can whip Sherman. If this is done, Capt. Tompkins has promised me to take care of you and the Children. I think if the Yankees come your way you had better go to his house until they pass by Edgefield. Do not be uneasy, my Darling about me. I will try to care for myself, and you take care of yourself and the Children. God bless you and them. If my life is spared we will meet again & I hope not to be separated any more. My love and kisses to all the Children and to my Darling Wife. Remember me to all inquiring friends. No orders to move yet—Hope it may be postponed.

Your Jimmie

---

5. Hardee on 3 February had reported an effective force of only 14,500, of which 3000 were reserves and militia, and estimated that he would need 20–25,000 men to hold Charleston; on the 11th Beauregard ordered him to evacuate the city. Most of the troops were to rendezvous at St. Stephen's on the Northeastern Railroad, where they would be transported to join the forces retreating from Columbia toward North Carolina. Hardee delayed, asking for further guidance, while Governor McGrath voiced his opposition to abandoning the city. Beauregard went to Charleston himself on the 14th and issued detailed orders for the evacuation. The following day he received a telegram from Hardee enclosing one from President Davis, who asked that the city not be given up as long as the enemy could be held in the field. Beauregard wired back testily that his forces were entirely insufficient to hold the Federals and that the evacuation should proceed as directed. Hardee had been taken ill in the meantime, and Lafayette McLaws was brought in to take command, which further delayed the evacuation until the night of 17–18 February. Roman, *Military Operations of General Beauregard* 2: 336–50; OR, ser. 1, vol. 47, pt. 2: 1195, 1202, 1205.

Letter 80 JBG to Leila Griffin

Head Qrs 1st Regt State Troops
Cheraw[1] 27 Feby 1865

My Dear Leila

I wrote you a letter last night, and sent it by a member of the 7th Regt who was going home.[2] I hear to night of another man in the same command who leaves for home tomorrow morning, and knowing that you will be pleased to hear from me as often as possible, I avail myself of the opportunity to write you a few lines again— I hope you will excuse the bad writing as I have to write upon my knee.

I am soldiering it now to the *letter*. And have been for the last ten days at least. But I stand it first rate. I gave you a short sketch of our March from Charleston in my letter last night. We arrived at this place last friday about midday in the rain, it rained on until sunday. I had a fly that protected me somewhat, but it didnt turn the rain very well—My top blankets got wet, but I kept dry. To day my baggage came up, and to night I have my tent up, and am once more quite comfortable. My clothes are getting quite rusty and what is worse nearly worn out. So that you may know that I am anxious to see Glover with my new ones—Do send me another pair of pants if you can get them, as these will not last a great deal longer. I dont know exactly what route these men take to get home, but I know if they can get home Glover and the other men at home can get here if they try. I have heard that the trains run through to Columbia, but I dont know that this is true. I think now there is no doubt that Sherman has

---

LETTER 80

1. Cheraw, eight miles from the North Carolina border, was the last stop on the Northeastern Railroad.

2. This letter has not been found. Since Friday was the 24th, the 130-mile trip from Charleston had taken six days. Hardee had actually been ordered to Chester, forty-five miles north of Columbia on the Charlotte and South Carolina Railroad, but by delaying the evacuation until the 18th he allowed Sherman to cut off the route. Instead, Hardee directed his march some seventy miles farther east, toward Cheraw. Part of the troops and supplies went via Florence on the dilapidated and overloaded Northeastern Railroad, and as Griffin was writing they still had not arrived. OR, ser. 1, 47, pt. 1: 1071–73; vol. 47, pt. 2: 1290; Barrett, *Sherman's March through the Carolinas*, 106.

abandoned the idea of marching through North Carolina by way of Charlotte and is now making for Wilmington or perhaps going back to Charleston or Georgetown. He is reported to day at Lynch's creek about thirty miles from this place, with Butler in his front Skirmishing with his advance guard, and watching his movements.[3] Genl Johnson has, been placed in command of this army, and is anxiously expected here.[4] The army has very little confidence in Hardee. We have about fifteen thousand Troops and when Beauregard, Dick Taylor[5] and D. H. Hill[6] joins us we will have as many men as Sherman has[7] or very near it—and if we can get him to fight, I think we will use him up. But I doubt if we can get him to fight—He is certainly making for the sea coast. I am intensely anxious to hear something definite from Edgefield. I heard to day that the Enemy passed through the District

---

3. Sherman had ordered his left wing to feint toward Charlotte, where Beauregard was headquartered; his actual destination was Fayetteville, North Carolina. The right wing had passed through Camden and was following Hardee. Lynch's Creek, slightly more than thirty miles east of Cheraw, was out of its banks, delaying the Federal crossing for four days. On 2 March the Twentieth Corps, after a skirmish with Butler's cavalry, entered Chesterfield, a dozen miles west of Cheraw. OR, ser. 1, 47, pt. 1: 22; Barrett, *Sherman's March through the Carolinas*, 100, 105–6.

4. Lee had relieved Beauregard, who was in poor health. On 22 February Joseph E. Johnston took command of the demoralized remnants of the Army of Tennessee, with orders to concentrate all forces and push Sherman back. OR, ser. 1, 47, pt. 2:1247.

5. Lt. Gen. Richard Taylor (1826–1879), son of the late President Zachary Taylor, commanded the Department of Alabama and Mississippi. Taylor was not on his way to join Hardee; on 8 May 1865, in Mississippi, he surrendered all of the remaining Confederate troops east of the river.

6. Lt. Gen. Daniel Harvey Hill (1821–1889), after being relieved from his command in the Army of Tennessee for openly criticizing Braxton Bragg as a field commander, had been largely out of active service until January 1865, when he was directed to report to Beauregard at Charleston. He was in Augusta, organizing the troops arriving from the Army of Tennessee.

7. This was an optimistic exaggeration. Desertions were nibbling away at the strength of Hardee's infantry, which was down to fewer than 10,000 men. Johnston's total force, including the reinforcements en route from the Army of Tennessee, was only about 20,000 men, or less than a third of the number marching with Sherman. OR, ser. 1, 47, pt. 1: 1053; Symonds, *Joseph E. Johnston*, 344.

and did a great deal of damage.[8] This I hope is not true and will not believe it until I hear it from a more reliable source. The rumours here are *legend*. And as contradictory as possible. Some says Columbia has been laid in ashes and the most wicked acts perpetrated on its Inhabitants—While others state that the City has been very little injured, and the Citizens treated very courteously.[9] I believe very little that I hear. I hope our communication will soon be opened if it is not already so that we can hear from each other. Write to me at Cheraw until further notice. My love to all and hundreds of kisses to the dear Children and my Darling Wife

from your Jimmie

---

8. Sherman's infantry passed well south of Griffin's home, but on 11 February his cavalry, under Hugh Judson Kilpatrick, rode confidently into Aiken, twenty-one miles southeast of Edgefield Court House. Kilpatrick was unaware that Joseph Wheeler had learned of the Federals' destination in time to gather his own cavalry and conceal it at the rear of the town. Wheeler's troops completely routed Kilpatrick's men, who fled back to the Union pickets. Barrett, *Sherman's March through the Carolinas*, 56–57; D.B. Morgan, "Incidents of the Fighting at Aiken, S.C.," *Confederate Veteran* 32 (Aug. 1924): 300–301.

9. Hampton and Butler evacuated Columbia on the morning of 17 February, with Sherman's infantry on their heels, and that night nearly half of the capital city went up in flames. Sherman claimed that the first fires were started by Confederate cavalry igniting the bales of cotton piled in the streets. Hampton angrily denied this charge, and partisans of both sides have argued endlessly over which side was at fault. The most detailed and dispassionate study is Marion Brunson Lucas, *Sherman and the Burning of Columbia* (College Station: Texas A&M Univ. Press, 1976), which lays some blame on everyone involved: on the Confederates for leaving the cotton in the streets and for failing to destroy the large stores of liquor, on the drunken Federal soldiers, and on their officers who did too little to prevent incendiarism.

9 *Edgefield and Texas: Rebuilding Identities*

> Edgefield and Texas combined makes one stouthearted enough for anything.
>
> —Mary Chesnut. *In* C. Vann Woodward, ed.,
> *Mary Chesnut's Civil War*

In his last extant Civil War letter (27 February 1865), Griffin was optimistic about defeating Sherman. But Sherman marched on undefeated. Colonel Griffin and his troops, their militia having been disbanded, returned to Edgefield by mid-April. The editor of the local paper commented on the return of Griffin and his "fine looking and merry boys." He added, "They have had a hard and rough time journeying from the coast below Charleston to middle North Carolina, but being as hard as lightwood knots, they have returned home again unscathed."[1]

The journal of an upcountry South Carolina woman tells the story of the Confederacy's defeat from her perspective as she recorded her feelings about her brother's return and the end of the war:

24 April 1865: "joy of his arrival was overwhelmed in gloom for he brought to us the awful news of Lee's surrender . . . I have not yet recovered from the stunning effect the news first produced. . . . God forbid if the end is subjugation. Enable us Oh! Father, to be resigned to thy will whatever it may be."

18 May 1865: "We are no longer free but have to bow beneath the Yankee yoke. . . . Our young men have come home and the streets are now filled with familiar faces, still they are not the same[;] a shadow rests over nearly every brow. Regret for the lost is the grief

---

1. Edgefield *Advertiser*, 19 April 1865.

that fills every heart, for the lost in battle, for the lost homes, for the lost Liberty for which we had risked so much. Where on this earth can we ever be happy again? Not in our own Sunnie South."[2]

In September 1865 the editor of the Edgefield *Advertiser* wrote, "All the pomp and circumstance of the war has faded away like the unremembered fantasies of an idle dream."[3] Most white southerners grieved over the passing of the old order. The white South saw itself as the moral region of the nation; it had not calculated the demoralization and humiliation of defeat. Union victory seemed to ensure the northern Republican Party's vision of America and the fulfillment of the Yankee sense of destiny.

Peace between North and South did not produce peace within southern white culture; suspicion and ill-feeling abounded during Reconstruction and afterwards. So too did suspicion and ill-feeling of whites toward the former enslaved people.

Reconstruction in Edgefield

Black South Carolinians did not share the gloom of Confederate defeat. These African Americans, the majority in South Carolina, and in Edgefield, were, in fact, victorious in the Civil War; they wanted freedom and got it. Nevertheless, change, however glorious, requires readjustments. The Civil War abruptly interrupted the slave style of race relations. Slavery was more than a labor system; it was an all-pervasive system of social control. After emancipation, in a tumultuous period of uncertainty, neither race was sure of its role. Relationships were turned upside down, and the web of day-to-day interactions that form the social fabric was unravelled. Turmoil and violence erupted as whites and blacks struggled to define themselves in the new order. Southern whites especially had feelings of anxiety, frustration, and aggression against African Americans.

The entire period of Reconstruction in Edgefield was fraught with unpredictability. Just as race relations were not clearly defined, neither were the role and responsibilities of wealth and aristocracy to the less

---

2. Journal of 1865, pp. 19–21, Watson Papers. See last note of Chapter 1.
3. Edgefield *Advertiser*, 23 Sept. 1865.

well-off white southerner. As if the confusion of daily life were not difficult enough, outlaws and bushwhacker gangs of former Confederates roamed Edgefield District, often attacking African Americans. The postwar years, 1865–1867, were desperate times for all the residents of Edgefield County and South Carolina. Chaos reigned.

Politics were also rife with confusion. On 20 May 1865 President Andrew Johnson granted amnesty to Confederate soldiers who took an oath to support the Constitution of the United States and the presidential proclamations regarding emancipation. On 20 July 1865, provisional South Carolina governor Benjamin Perry declared that all state laws enacted before secession were in effect and all state officials and administrators in power at the time of the Confederacy's surrender were to resume their positions. Prominent former Confederates, including Griffin's old comrade Matthew Calbraith Butler, were elected to the South Carolina General Assembly. In effect, the antebellum government and civil authority were restored, although the Federal military refused to recognize the civil authorities. Until congressional Reconstruction began in 1867 and 1868, opinions varied as to which laws governed South Carolina, those of the state or of the Military District. In 1866, federal military authorities arrested Griffin's former friend Martin Witherspoon Gary and other leading Edgefield white citizens for murdering African Americans. In response to the chaos of the times, and in line with congressional Reconstruction, black and white South Carolinians passed a new state constitution in 1868. With the new constitution, former slaves and their allies came into political power in Edgefield and in South Carolina.[4]

Reconstruction in South Carolina, where it lasted longer than in most southern states and where African Americans outnumbered whites, faced a better chance for success than anywhere in the nation. African Americans served in nearly every office at county and state levels and held a majority in the lower house of the South Carolina General Assembly for six years. Public education, not generally avail-

---

4. Orville Vernon Burton, "Ungrateful Servants? Edgefield's Black Reconstruction: Part I of the Total History of Edgefield County, South Carolina" (Ph.D. dissertation, Princeton University, 1976); "Race and Reconstruction: Edgefield County, South Carolina," *Journal of Social History* 12 (Fall 1978): 31–56.

able to anyone before Reconstruction, was opened to former slave and white children alike, from primary level through college. More land was distributed to former slaves in South Carolina than in any other state. The former bondspeople successfully resisted the reimposition of the gang labor system preferred by many white landowners and forced the compromises of tenantry. Through their families, churches, political and social organizations, their dress and spatial mobility, African Americans defined what freedom meant to them in their daily lives. All of this could occur, however, only because federal troops were enforcing federal laws.[5]

For a man of J.B. Griffin's temperament, a man who loved order and efficiency, a white southerner who lived by the rules, both the written and the unwritten codes of his society, it must have been a time of tremendous strain. Griffin's immediate concern was making a living under the changed labor conditions imposed by emancipation. The crop that his slaves had planted in the early spring of 1865 was still in the field when the laborers were declared free. To cultivate and harvest it, he would have to abide by the rules of the Bureau of Refugees, Freedmen and Abandoned Lands (commonly referred to as the Freedmen's Bureau). Established in 1865 by Congress to deal with problems of the emancipated slaves, "newly placed in society without background, skill, or friendly hand," the bureau required planters to contract with their former slaves to finish out the agricultural season,

---

5. For Reconstruction in Edgefield, see Burton, "Ungrateful Servants? Edgefield's Black Reconstruction," and "Race and Reconstruction." For South Carolina during Reconstruction, see Burton et al., "South Carolina," in *Quiet Revolution in the South: The Impact of the Voting Rights Act, 1965–1990*, ed. Chandler Davidson and Bernard Grofman (Princeton: Princeton Univ. Press, 1994), 193–94; Joel Williamson, *After Slavery: The Negro in South Carolina during Reconstruction* (Chapel Hill: Univ. of North Carolina Press, 1965); Thomas Holt, *Black over White: Negro Political Leadership in South Carolina during Reconstruction* (Urbana: Univ. of Illinois Press, 1977); and Francis Butler Simkins and Robert Hilliard Woody, *South Carolina during Reconstruction* (Chapel Hill: Univ. of North Carolina Press, 1932). For a superb synthesis and the now standard interpretation of Reconstruction in the United States (with substantial attention paid to South Carolina), see Eric Foner, *Reconstruction: America's Unfinished Revolution* (New York: Harper & Row, 1988).

specified how freedmen were to be paid, and defined what responsibilities and privileges they would have. The bureau also mediated disagreements, assisted in transportation, and supervised schools.[6]

Griffin's business-like letter to Capt. Jonathan Bryant, a Union officer in the Freedmen's Bureau at Augusta (printed below), requested clarification of a labor contract. Initially the bureau provided relief measures, but Assistant Commissioner Rufus Saxton's goal was to make the freedmen self-reliant. From Griffin's letter, it would appear that the bureau was attempting to economize by shifting the responsibility for feeding freedmen upon the planter. The number of South Carolina freedmen on government rations per month fell from 8,637 to 3,777 between December 1865 and April 1866. With serious crop failures in 1865–1866, the relief system had to be expanded again. Griffin's method of payment outlined in his letter seemed to be fairly prevalent throughout South Carolina. The problem with this type of crop-lien arrangement was that bad harvests would leave African Americans with a mere pittance. Numerous South Carolina freedmen refused to sign labor contracts for 1866 because they had done so poorly with the sharecrop arrangement.

Griffin, who had owned 61 slaves in 1860, was taxed for 51 slaves in 1863, and reported in his 1865 letter that he had 42 African Americans "on the plantation."[7] Whether these 42 were all that remained

---

6. Williamson, *After Slavery*, 67–69. Lewis C. Chartock, "A History and Analysis of Labor Contracts Administered by the Bureau of Refugees, Freedmen, and Abandoned Lands in Edgefield, Abbeville and Anderson Counties in South Carolina, 1865–1868" (Ph.D. dissertation, Bryn Mawr College, 1974), covers the early period of the bureau in Edgefield County. Griffin's concern was typical of many in Edgefield in 1865. His conditions and concerns about freedmen were more paternalistic and more enlightened than many in the three counties that Chartock studied. Martin Abbott, *The Freedmen's Bureau in South Carolina, 1865–1872* (Chapel Hill: Univ. of North Carolina Press, 1967), esp. 4–5, 23–24, is the standard work on the bureau in South Carolina. Much of the material in Abbott concerns the years after Griffin had already left for Texas. Because of the Union occupation in the Sea Islands, South Carolina was one of the first areas in the South where the question of what to do with former slaves became a problem. Rose, *Rehearsal for Reconstruction*.

7. Tax Record Books, 1863, Box 30, Folder G, Office of the Comptroller General, SCDAH. The letter is written on lined paper, as from a memorandum or note book, and may be a copy.

of his former slaves is not entirely clear. In a wartime letter (9 February 1863) he had distinguished between Negroes "at the plantation" and those "at home," perhaps meaning house servants in addition to the field hands discussed in that letter.[8] Or it may have happened, in a pattern found on larger plantations, that the domestics and craftsmen left after emancipation while the majority of the field workers remained on the land. Only a quarter of Griffin's workers were full hands, and half were non-workers, so the most able or the least encumbered with young children may indeed have left. Most likely some of his former slaves left in the excitement of freedom and because they wanted to own their own land, not because they felt they had been cheated by a sharecropping arrangement. It would have been too early in the season to have been disappointed by a bad harvest.[9]

Griffin asked the bureau specifically if he was required to take back former slaves who had initially left. Southern romanticists have written at length of masters who continued to provide for their former bondsmen, even those too old to labor. Others were less idealistic. Mary Boykin Chesnut in 1866 wanted no responsibility for former slaves: "We are free to desert them now I hope."[10] And in the southeastern section of Edgefield District, James Henry Hammond's widow,

---

8. Leila had put the number at 50 in January 1865. Mrs. J.B. Griffin to Gen. A.C. Garlington, 28 Jan. 1865, Petitions for Exemption, 1864–1865, Administrative Records, Adjutant General, SCDAH.

9. Williamson, *After Slavery*, 34–44; Abbott, *Freedman's Bureau in South Carolina, 1865–1872*, 39, 40–46, 59–62. In one case after the harvest of 1866, a black sharecropper's return was $24.70 for a whole years' worth of work (76). Eventually in 1868, the bureau went to a crop lien system in which it would provide rations for planters to distribute to each worker. A lien would be given to the bureau on the future crop to serve as repayment. Griffin's attitude toward the bureau is difficult to infer from the letter. Abbott reports that critics of the bureau developed a stereotype of the bureau agent as one who encouraged African Americans in delusions pertaining to the procurement of land and who encouraged black political activism (116, 124). Planters resented the bureau when it would set aside labor contracts on the grounds that they were unjust (118–19). Yet, despite criticism, many agents were on good terms with planters and did not earn the respect of the freedmen (126–28).

10. Mary Boykin Chesnut to Virginia Caroline Tunstall Clay, April 1866, Clement Claiborne Clay Papers, Perkins Library, DU, also quoted in Bleser, *The Hammonds of Redcliff*, 136.

Catherine, complained in the aftermath of the Civil War: "We have not lost many negroes . . . [but] I wish we could get clear of many of the useless ones."[11] Griffin's request for information applied to former slaves who had left his plantation, those who felt no obligation to Griffin. He, likewise, felt no reciprocal obligation to them. But Griffin's letter is more typical than the southern romanticist would have it.

Edgefield S.C. 21st June 1865

Capt. J E Bryant

Dear Sir

Jim who has been my *Foreman* desires to visit Augusta, in search of a son of his who left home yesterday morning—said Boy is fourteen or fifteen years of age—I loaned Jim a mule to ride.

I desire to state to you three propositions that I have made to the negroes on my plantation, and request that you will give Jim your views as to the *fairness* of the propositions and any other information relative to the Freedmen that you may deem necessary. There are on the plantation forty two negroes—twenty two (in number) are workers and twenty non workers[;] ten of the workers are half hands—

Proposition 1st I agree to pay at the end of the present year, in provisions, at market price the prices stipulated in your order of the 12th inst. to the workers[,] they to pay me out of that expenses of the Freedmen—

Proposition 2nd, I agree to divide amongst the workers at the end of the year one fourth of the corn, pease, potatoes and sorghum cane raised on the place. They to pay same expenses as stated in 1st Proposition—

Proposition 3—I agree to feed and clothe all the negroes until the close of the year and allow them as much time as the culture of the crop will admit, to burn coal, which before the war was their source of income, I to give them the wood— And what money they make will be clear—

This I am sure is the best proposition of the three, but it may not appear so at first glance— The crop is now nearly made, and a good deal of time may be allowed them— We are very near the village where ready sale is found for all the coal carried there—

Will you take the trouble to state your views in writing and hand it to Jim—One question I desire to submit— I see by your order a person

---

11. Catherine Hammond to M.C.M. Hammond, 3 Sept. 1865 in J.H. Hammond Papers, SCL.

is not allowed to turn off an infirm or helpless [freedman]—at present—
who was on the plantation at the time the order issued— Suppose one
of that class had left of *his own choice, before the date of the order*—
and afterward desires to return—would the person be *required to take
him back?*

Very Respectfully

J B Griffin

Griffin's attention to propositions and details in this letter reflects
his pragmatic concern for making a postwar living. His house had
been burned down; his landholdings were greatly reduced, and the
remainder was mortgaged. In the fall of 1863, two months before he
was called up into the reserves, Griffin had sold 750 acres of land to
Lewis Jones for $13,000. In December 1865 he mortgaged the re-
maining 840 acres. Like so many planters after the war, at least those
who had invested in the Confederacy, he had more debts than assets.[12]
Matthew Calbraith Butler, who said that he came back with $15,000
in debts and $1.75 in his pocket, could still earn a living as a lawyer
or could call upon his father-in-law, wealthy and influential former
Governor Francis Pickens. The richest of all, Hampton, was forced to
declare bankruptcy in 1867, but he had land in other states and, as a
genuine Civil War hero, he, like Butler, would have a political
career.[13]

The war left many of the rich in reduced circumstances and many
of the poor destitute. Within a group of the wealthiest Edgefieldians
in 1860 were 41 persons who are recorded in both the 1860 and 1870
censuses. This group suffered a decline in mean real estate valuation

---

12. Griffin mentions his investment in blockade script. He may also have
invested in Confederate bonds. His plantation journal records show that he
was paid for past debts with Confederate currency during the latter years of
the war, a patriotic move on his part but not sensible economically. See letter
of 29 January 1865.

13. Actually, Hampton had left South Carolina and gone to Mississippi
where his most productive cotton lands were, but he came back at Gary's
request to run for office. Hampton had not been a legal resident of South
Carolina before his election. Gary and Butler both had family in the area,
whereas all of Griffin's immediate family was dead or had moved west. Myrta
L. Avary, *Dixie after the War* (New York: Doubleday, Page, 1906), 161.

of 75 percent and in personal estate valuation of 97 percent. Much of the personal estate which counted as wealth before the war was in the form of slaves. In 1860 per capita wealth for whites in the county was $2,457; for the 41 wealthiest, it was $47,873. In 1870 the per capita wealth was $497; for the same 41 it was $4,460. Wealth declined sharply for all white Edgefieldians. Although the wealthiest remained relatively so, differences in wealth among whites narrowed (in 1860 the 41 were twenty times more wealthy and in 1870 nine times more wealthy than the average Edgefieldian).[14]

James B. Griffin appears to have lost nearly everything of monetary value. At the end of 1865, Griffin was forty years old with nine children to support. The oldest, Willie, was not yet seventeen; the youngest, Minnie Leila, was two and a half. Griffin would want his three daughters, when they grew up, to be comfortably married; his six sons to be financially established. With only a grim future ahead of them in Edgefield, the Griffins, like numerous others, resolved to leave South Carolina.

Even before the Civil War, South Carolina had been a mobile society. In 1860, 41 percent of all free native South Carolinians lived in other states. Only 40 percent of all households present in Edgefield in the 1850 census were still there in 1860. Postbellum hardship caused emigration to soar. Of the wealthiest 136 persons in Edgefield in 1860, only 41 were still listed in the census for the county in 1870. Some, of course, died between 1860 and 1870, but not fighting in the war; not one of the casualties of war were among the prewar wealthiest. Following the Civil War, Edgefield was a center of the emigration movement to Brazil, where slavery still existed. Others moved west. Griffin's sister and brother-in-law, the Harringtons, moved to Mississippi, where they reported themselves in 1869 to be making a good crop. Leila's Uncle Billy relocated his family to Shreveport, Louisiana.[15]

The Griffins departed in 1866, sometime after the 1865 crop was

---

14. Burton, *In My Father's House Are Many Mansions*, 226–27.

15. J.A. Dozier to "My Dear Friend" [J.B. Griffin], 25 Aug. 1869, miscellaneous Griffin papers; Lawrence F. Hill, "The Confederate Exodus to Latin America," *Southwestern Historical Quarterly* 39 (Oct. 1935, Jan. and April 1936): 100–134, 161–99, 309–26.

harvested and sold. They left before the Reconstruction experiment with interracial democracy and white South Carolinians' refusal to tolerate that experiment. By leaving in 1866, Griffin avoided the political aftermath of white terrorism. Between 1867 and 1877 a new civil war was waged between white Democrats and the Republicans, including former slaves. Seven state legislators were murdered between 1868 and 1876.[16]

The officers with whom Griffin had fought during the war turned their attention to this new enemy within. The main force behind the violent overthrow of South Carolina's Reconstruction in 1876 was Griffin's erstwhile friend from Edgefield, Martin Witherspoon Gary. Although Gary's only official position was Democratic chairman for Edgefield County, he was the organizing genius and the author of the state campaign blueprint, the Edgefield Plan, also known as the Straightout Plan. Gary, Hampton, Butler, Conner, Barker, and Hagood opposed Reconstruction with all the gusto they had devoted to fighting Yankees. These so-called "Redeemers" were among the architects of South Carolina post-Reconstruction politics and government.

The Democratic campaign of 1876 was conceived and organized by former officers of the Hampton Legion. Lieutenant General Hampton himself led the ticket; Brigadier General Gary and Major General Butler mapped the campaign. Brigadier General Conner overcame his reservations and accepted the nomination for attorney general, while Brigadier General Johnson Hagood, with Edgefield connections but not a former Legionnaire, was designated for comptroller general. Conner and his assistant, Major Theodore Barker, directed the "troops," white civilians (many of whom had served under these officers) who symbolically donned red shirts and formed themselves

---

16. Orville Vernon Burton, " 'The Black Squint of the Law': Racism in South Carolina," in *The Meaning of South Carolina History: Essays in Honor of George C. Rogers, Jr.*, ed. David R. Chesnutt and Clyde N. Wilson (Columbia: Univ. of South Carolina Press, 1991), 161–85; Reynolds and Faunt, *Biographical Directory of the Senate of the State of South Carolina*, 62; Walter B. Edgar, ed., *Biographical Directory of the South Carolina House of Representatives*, vol. 1: 1692–1973 (Columbia: Univ. of South Carolina Press, 1974), 407, 409, 414, 420–22.

into armed companies called rifle clubs.[17] Ostensibly organized for home protection, the clubs were highly visible during the campaign. The new Democratic legislature promptly elected Matthew Calbraith Butler to the U.S. Senate, an honor that Gary had coveted for himself. Gary counted on the next Senate seat, but that went to Hampton. When Gary hoped to replace Hampton as governor in 1880, Hagood was chosen. Gary's behavior during Reconstruction bears a striking parallel to his actions in the 1862 army reorganization in Virginia.[18]

Only one officer of the Hampton Legion played no part in the Straightout movement: Col. J.B. Griffin. In direct contrast to other South Carolinian leaders, Griffin had already given up on South Carolina, a signal of his disinterest in waging political warfare. Had

---

17. Avary, *Dixie after the War*, 161; Sheppard, *Red Shirts Remembered*, 86–87. Many in the Hampton Legion were provided with red shirts as part of their uniform during the war. Field, *South Carolina Volunteers in the Civil War*, Regimental Uniform of the Hampton Legion, 1861–62, p. 1.

18. The immensely popular Hampton could have been governor as early as 1865 if he had so chosen; he declined the nomination on the entirely correct assumption that it would be impolitic for South Carolina to put a former Confederate lieutenant general in the governor's chair. Many thousands of voters insisted on casting ballots for him anyway, so the declared candidate, James Orr, won by an embarrassingly small margin, fewer than 800 votes. Woody, *South Carolina during Reconstruction*, has some accounts of the Hampton-Gary split, but more information on the Hampton Legion's officers and their specific roles in Reconstruction are found in the generally earlier "tragedy of Reconstruction" school accounts: John S. Reynolds, *Reconstruction in South Carolina* (Columbia, S.C.: State Co., 1905); David D. Wallace, *The History of South Carolina* (New York: American Historical Society, 1932), 3:222–335. Accounts of narrower scope that venerate Hampton are Wells, *Hampton and Reconstruction*, which omits all mention of Gary; Albert B. Williams, *Hampton and His Red Shirts: South Carolina's Deliverance in 1876* (Charleston: Walker, Evans & Cogswell, 1935); and Hampton M. Jarrell, *Wade Hampton and the Negro: The Road Not Taken* (Columbia: Univ. of South Carolina Press, 1949). Gary's only sustained defense has been William Arthur Sheppard's highly polemical *Red Shirts Remembered: Southern Brigadiers of the Reconstruction Period* (Atlanta: Ruralist Press, 1940), which accuses Hampton of depriving Gary of his deserved political rewards. U.R. Brooks reprints complimentary speeches by Gary's political legatees, George and Ben Tillman, in *Stories of the Confederacy*.

he stayed with the regular army for the duration of the war and emerged as a general and a hero, he might have made a different decision.

Why had Griffin rejected vigilante attempts to resuscitate the society of the antebellum planter elite? One reason, perhaps, is that Griffin always valued rules and order. The Confederates had lost, and he was not a man to dress in white sheets and ride with renegade outlaws murdering African Americans, for which Gary had been arrested as early as 1866. Honor also played a role. Griffin's concept of manhood included that of reciprocal responsibility, and others had not kept their end of the bargain. He had given leadership and financial support to the Confederacy, but had not received a proper share of honor in return. In fact, the community honored Gary, a man always looking for his moment, a dishonorable man in Griffin's opinion, despite his status as a popular leader.

Important also were differing temperaments and ambitions. Gary and Butler, both attorneys, thrived on politics; they had farmed only because it was expected of them before the war. Griffin, in contrast, was no lawyer and had believed wholeheartedly in the agrarian planter ideal and the Confederacy as a way of life. His dreams and goals died with the Confederacy.

Griffin had always coupled his devotion to the southern way of life with his commitment to family. He alone in the group of Hampton Legion officers had a large family to support. He had built a good living for his family in the antebellum South, combining agriculture with a certain business acumen in running the plantation. Now his prewar life had disintegrated, and his first consideration had to be to restore the economic well-being of his family.

When Griffin was defeated in the election of officers, he left the battlefield and went home. When his homeland was defeated in war, he left to make a new home. He felt no paternal obligation to former slaves, no burden to return South Carolina to its antebellum grandeur. Griffin also left unmet an obligation he had undertaken in 1853. At that time the brother of his sister Eliza's husband died and left a child, eight-year-old Cornelia. Griffin's brother-in-law, Diomede Hollingsworth, was the administrator of the estate, and Griffin became Cornelia's legal guardian, although the child was no relation to him.

Griffin was meticulous in administering his ward's finances at a time when many other guardians were all too lax. Then, in 1865, because he lacked $20,000 to post a bond, Griffin mortgaged his remaining land, 840 acres valued now at only $2,520, to help pay off the debt. That still left a substantial amount unpaid. He had invested this young woman's money, quite likely with honest motivation, knowing full well that he could easily repay it. But the money was gone when the note became due, the fall of the Confederacy having invalidated Confederate monies and precipitated numerous bank failures. Griffin, as a loyal Confederate, had let others pay their prewar debts in nearly worthless Confederate monies, and he accepted Confederate money for the sale of his land. Yet, after the Griffins had moved to Texas, several of his friends, although unwilling, were forced through litigation to cover the debt because of Griffin's failure to do so.[19] It seems unlikely that Griffin would run out on an obligation and leave his friends to cover for him. He may have thought he could send the money to repay the debt in the future if his financial circumstances improved. He may have reasoned that he had paid all he could and no one would ask for more. The lawsuit was brought many years later, after Cornelia married (it may have been her husband insisting the debt be paid in full). Nevertheless, Griffin freed himself from externally imposed expectations; he crossed off from his duty roster the care of South Carolina and focused instead on James B. Griffin and his immediate family.

Like countless other southerners who scrawled the famous "GTT" (Gone to Texas) on their doors, J.B. Griffin and family joined the great folk movement and headed for the country of longhorned cattle

---

19. James B. Griffin to Lewis Jones, 13 Sept. 1863, Deed Book LLL, 214; J.B. Griffin to J.W. Carwile, Commissioner in Equity, 26 Dec. 1865, Deed Book MMM, 29–30, ECC. Guardian Record Book, vol. G, 1864–68 (incorrectly dated), pp. 267, 268, 384, 385, 519, 520, 521, Office of the Court of Equity; Tax Record Books, 1866, Box 33, Folder G, Office of the Comptroller General, both in SCDAH. On the complicated bond issue for guardianship see *Reports of Cases Heard and Determined by the Supreme Courts of South Carolina* XI, Robert W. Shand, State Reporter (Jersey City, N.J., 1880), 565–88. We are greatly indebted to attorney Kurt McKenzie and historian James Hammond Moore for help in interpreting the bond issue.

and tall cotton. It was as far west as one could go without leaving the South. Texas had suffered the least damage in the war and contained the richest cotton lands to be had.[20] Yet this successful farmer never planted cotton in Texas. Just as he gave up Edgefield, South Carolina, so he gave up his occupation. Griffin's antebellum wealth testified to his skill as a planter, but even then he had been a practical business-man too and perhaps able to see the limitations of cotton as a future. Not a defeatist so much as a pragmatist, Griffin was resigned to the inevitable. He could cope. If Griffin had disappeared in the vast move-ment west, we would be unable to judge his state of mind, but we can follow him to Texas. Griffin was able and willing to break with the past, not just with South Carolina but with the life of a planter. He cast off the old to make a fresh start in a new business on the New South's western frontier.

The Griffins in Texas

Griffin's trek to Texas followed an Edgefieldian tradition. The way to Texas was populated with people from the district. Entire churches and communities from Georgia to Texas reflected Edgefield roots. Past heroes known for political extremism and military leadership had mi-grated to antebellum Texas, the traditional destination of men with a compelling need to avoid their creditors, the law, or just the boredom of settled eastern communities. Griffin's more famous predecessors in-cluded three sons of Edgefield who made names for themselves. Wil-liam Barret Travis, who commanded at the Alamo, distanced himself from an unhappy marriage in Edgefield. At Travis's urging, James Butler Bonham went just for adventure.[21] Another controversial Edge-field émigré, Louis Wigfall, whom Griffin mentions in his letters, fled

---

20. See James L. Watts, *King Cotton: A Historical and Statistical Review, 1790–1908* (New York: James L. Watkins and Sons, 1908), 43, and especially Alfred Glaze Smith, Jr., *Economic Readjustment of an Old Cotton State: South Carolina* (Columbia: Univ. of South Carolina Press, 1958).

21. This daring Edgefield cavalryman, Bonham, brother of Edgefield's sec-ond Civil War governor, slipped through enemy lines, out of the Alamo and back, twice; he wanted to die with his countrymen. From within the mission walls, Commander Travis declared his policy of no surrender in his famous letter to the world.

Edgefield to Texas

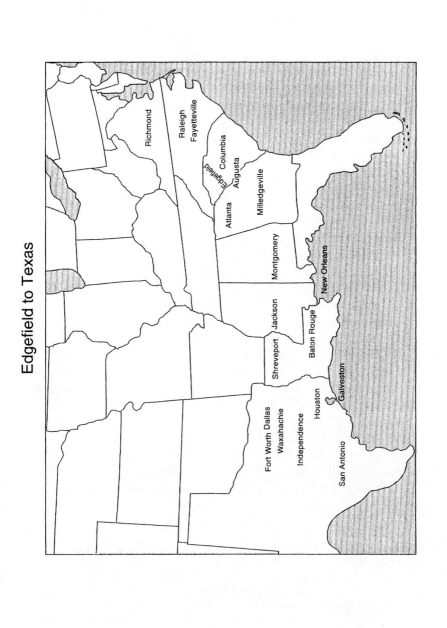

to Texas to avoid his debts and prosecution for a duel. Wigfall became Jefferson Davis's nemesis in the Confederate Congress.[22]

In the popular perception, Texas, the home of the Alamo, the Texas Rangers, and John Bell Hood's celebrated Texas Brigade, stood out in the South as Edgefield did in South Carolina—a bit bolder and more colorful than anything around it. Mary Chesnut captured the idea of how the defiant individualism of the Edgefield community extended beyond its borders. Watching Senator Louis Wigfall's daughters snub Jefferson Davis in a Richmond drawing room, she observed with characteristic insight "It seems incredible—but Edgefield and Texas combined makes one stouthearted enough for anything."[23] This Texas folklore may have been alluring to Griffin, still seeking a little of the glamor and glory that always eluded him.

It is not known when the Griffin family, which still included Leila's sister Sue, arrived in Texas. They went first to Galveston, the traditional entrepot for newcomers. From there they moved to Washington County in the southeast central part of the state, where Stephen F. Austin had brought the first Anglo-American colonists in the early 1820s. The date of the Griffins' arrival in Washington County is unknown, but the Edgefield *Advertiser* reported that Leila's sister, Sue Burt, by then twenty-eight, married William O. Morgan on 11 December 1867 at Griffin's home in Texas.[24] Since Griffin is not listed in the index to the 1870 census (completed in 1869) for Texas, his first occupation is unknown, but whatever he did brought him little remuneration. Griffin first appears on the tax rolls in Washington County in 1871 with no land and only meager taxable assets. He had two horses and two cows; his furniture, merchandise and miscellaneous property were valued at $80. His brother-in-law, William Morgan, owned three cows, two mules, and property worth $140.[25] Griffin, who had been near the top of the wealth pyramid in antebellum

---

22. Alvy L. King, *Louis T. Wigfall: Southern Fireater* (Baton Rouge: Louisiana State Univ. Press, 1970); Burton, *In My Father's House Are Many Mansions*, 70.

23. Woodward, ed., *Mary Chesnut's Civil War*, 433.

24. Griffin lived in or near the little town of Independence. McClendon, *Edgefield Marriage Records*, 109.

25. Washington County Tax Rolls, microfilm roll 897, 1871, 35, 65, TSL.

Edgefield, whose former wealth had brought him so close to the aristocracy, was near the bottom when he first arrived in postbellum Texas.

More members of Leila's clan, the Muse family and her elderly father, migrated to Washington County a few years later, first appearing on the tax rolls in 1875. But by that time the Griffins had moved again, perhaps in search of opportunity. This third move in less than a decade took the family 140 miles farther north to Waxahachie in Ellis County, where Griffin appeared in the tax rolls in 1872. They had left behind the old settlements and were among the thousands of pioneering families who during the next few decades would fill up the abundant northern grasslands. Ellis County grew rapidly, although less spectacularly than Dallas County, which bordered it on the north. Whereas at the end of 1849 the Ellis area had to be scoured for the necessary 100 citizens to sign the petition to the legislature requesting county status, a decade later more than 4000 were residents, and by 1870, over 7500.[26] (Edgefield County, by contrast, had more than 40,000 residents in 1870.)

Although Ellis became one of the heaviest cotton-producing counties in the country, Griffin never planted a crop there. In addition to the fertile black soil that produced such gratifying harvests, Ellis County had substantial resources of clay perfectly suited for brickmaking.[27] Building materials were in high demand as settlers followed the railroad north, but lumber for construction had to be hauled in from eastern Texas because prairie soils did not produce trees. Brickmaking, therefore, was an occupation in which a man could be sure of a livelihood, and Griffin pursued it in both Waxahachie and subsequently in Fort Worth. Washington County also had good brick clay, and it is possible he began his new occupation there. Griffin may have learned brickmaking in Edgefield, which had been an antebellum center of

---

26. *Memorial and Biographical History of Ellis County, Texas* (Chicago: Lewis Publishing, 1892), 104; Margaret Leslie Rowland Felty, "Waxahachie, 1850–1900: A Kaleidoscopic History" (M.A. thesis, University of Texas at Arlington, 1975), 61.

27. Frank Bennett, R.T. Avon Burke, and Clarence Lounsbury, *Soil Survey of Ellis County, Texas, 1910* (Washington, D.C.: U.S. Government Printing Office, 1911), 14. Edward L. Ayers, *The Promise of the New South: Life after Reconstruction* (New York: Oxford Univ. Press, 1992), 107–8.

alkaline-glaze stoneware manufacturers, with both brickyards and pottery establishments near Griffin's home. Lewis Miles, brother of Aquilla, was a prominent potter and also made bricks.[28]

Griffin's accounts in Waxahachie show that he supplied bricks to local builders. Expenditures for powder and fuses, wood, nails, and plaster indicate that he also undertook construction projects on his own.[29] Among those with whom he worked was John Solon, an Irish-born stonemason and builder who had been following the Houston and Texas Central Railroad as it laid track northward from the coast. In 1871 Solon began cutting stone for the new courthouse in the newly incorporated county seat, Waxahachie. For several years Solon had been acquiring contracts for public and commercial buildings as far away as Fort Worth and was on his way to becoming one of the town's most substantial citizens. Again, Griffin had friends among the very top of the wealthy and influential.

On 20 October 1873 Griffin contracted to rent the Waxahachie house of W. J. Coggin and the brickyard that Coggin owned with Robert Carr. Griffin was to pay $150 rent to each man, Coggin agreeing to take his share in burned bricks at eight dollars per thousand as soon as Griffin had made and burned the first kiln.[30]

Griffin's records show that from December 1874 to August 1875 the Catholic Church Committee had an account with Griffin and Solon's associate Peter Cogley for bricks and building materials. Solon had bought a lot near the center of town on which to erect Waxahachie's first Catholic church. On 11 August 1875, a surprising entry occurs:

---

28. Catherine Wilson Horne, *Crossroads of Clay: The Southern Alkaline-Glazed Stoneware Tradition* (Columbia: Univ. of South Carolina McKissick Museum, South Carolina, 1990), see esp. map on 91 of the spread of antebellum Edgefield pottery into Texas. 1850 and 1860 Industrial manuscript census returns for Edgefield District. Griffin's slaves had made money by burning wood to make charcoal, a process less complicated than but similar to making bricks.

29. Griffin Scrapbook, 50–53.

30. Ellis County Deed Records, Microfilm 1034602, Book M (1873–74), 70, TSL, Dallas Regional Depository. Coggin is sometimes referred to as Coggins in the text of the deed.

Griffin, despite his Baptist heritage, himself subscribed $200 to the church.[31]

He had already changed location and occupation; now he decided to change religious affiliation. The conversion from Baptist to Catholic was yet another way that Griffin departed from the antebellum model of the Edgefield community and its aristocracy. Leila was a Baptist, but some of her relatives subscribed to the older faith introduced through the French Giroud branch of the family. Religious diversity seems to have been the norm in the Burt-Miles-Dozier clan.[32] When Claude Marie Dubuis, the Bishop of Galveston, baptized Griffin in Waxahachie on 22 March 1876, four of the children—Bobby, Fannie, Meadie, and Minnie—were received into the Catholic Church with him. Moody was baptized a year later, and Leila joined in 1884.[33]

During the years that he lived in Waxahachie, Griffin slowly im-

---

31. "Sketch of the Life of John Solon," Griffin Scrapbook, 53. Perhaps because he was a convert, Griffin is not listed among the original sponsors of the church. See "History of St. Joseph Catholic Church, Waxahachie, Texas" in D.A.R., Texas, Rebecca Boyce Chapter, *Ellis County Genealogical Records*, typescript, vol. 6, p. 85, TSL.

32. The first Aquilla Miles was an Episcopalian, but his daughter Susannah Burt, Leila's grandmother, was said to have founded a Catholic church at Clearwater Plantation, which in 1854 was moved to Edgefield Court House and rebuilt. Her daughter-in-law, Emily Elizabeth Burt, the second wife of Dr. John Harwood Burt, was also a Catholic, and when Emily Burt died in 1852 the Edgefield *Advertiser* thought it worth mentioning that she had been one of the district's first converts. Harwood had by then been expelled from the Baptist Church, but older brother Eugene, Leila's father, remained a Baptist. Younger brother William was a Catholic. The subject of conversion must have been discussed from time to time, for James Dozier had written from Edgefield in 1869 that Aquilla Miles was "trying to muster religious courage enough" to join the Catholic Church. (According to his obituary, Aquilla finally joined the year before his death in 1881.) Miles Family, 22, Andrea Genealogical Collection, SCL; McClendon, *Edgefield Death Notices*, 96. J.A. Dozier to "My Dear Friend" [J.B. Griffin], 29 Aug. 1869. Obituary of Aquilla Miles, clipping from unidentified South Carolina newspaper, Griffin Scrapbook, page no. obscured.

33. Baptismal records, Immaculate Conception Church, Corsicana, Texas, held at the diocesan archives, Diocese of Dallas; baptism records, 21 July

proved his financial position. His records show that all of his sons except Bobby worked with him at one time or another, and that by 1876 they were operating three kilns.[34] When Griffin first appeared on the Ellis County tax rolls in 1872, his possessions, mostly four horses and nineteen cows, were valued at $390; these assets stayed relatively constant throughout his years there. The large number of cows suggests that Leila and the girls may have been adding to the family funds by selling milk and butter. In 1875, the year that he gave $200 to the Catholic Church, Griffin also made his first land purchase, a ten-acre tract three-quarters of a mile outside town that he bought for $150 in cash and a note for the same amount countersigned by John Solon.[35] The acreage was probably a combination of investment and boosterism, for the seller was the Waxahachie Tap Railroad, the town's passion.

The Griffins made their last move in 1877 to Fort Worth, overlooking the bluffs of the Clear Fork of the Trinity River thirty miles west of Dallas.[36] Griffin's moves reflect an interesting pattern, symbolic of the New South. Each relocation found him in a place where African Americans were a smaller proportion of the population (see table 9-1). African Americans had been an integral part of Griffin's earlier life and had made possible the wealth that he enjoyed in Edgefield. By now, however, Griffin was part of the modern culture of the white entrepreneur in the New South. The 1880 Tarrant County agricultural manuscript census shows neither Griffin nor any of his family operating a farm in the county in 1879. The Edgefield planter/farmer had made a complete break with his pre-Civil War life.[37]

1884, St. Patrick Cathedral Archives, Fort Worth Texas. According to an obituary and a newsclipping for 8 March 1909 in the Butler Papers, SCL, Matthew Calbraith Butler celebrated his 73rd birthday by becoming a Catholic. Jon Wakelyn suggests that Civil War soldiers converted to Catholicism because so many of the battlefield nurses were nuns.

34. Griffin Scrapbook, 62.

35. Ellis County Tax Rolls, microfilm, roll 1920, TSL. Griffin's assessments appear as follows: 1872: 11; 1872: n.p.; 1874: 11; 1875: 14; 1876: 14; Ellis County Deed Records, Microfilm 1034603, Book P (1876–77), 77.

36. Felty, "Waxahachie, 1850–1900: A Kaleidoscopic History," 77–79; *Memorial and Biographical History of Ellis County*, 181–84.

37. Agricultural and Industrial manuscript census rolls held on microfilm at the Rice University library were read from beginning to end for Tarrant County.

Table 9-1. African-American Population in Counties where
Griffin Lived (%)

Year	Edgefield	Washington	Ellis	Tarrant
1860	61	52	21	14
1870	60	53	20	12
1880	65	53	12	9

SOURCE: Published U.S. Censuses of various years.

Griffin undoubtedly made the decision to move to Fort Worth for business reasons. In the immediate postwar years Fort Worth had been a community of between 300 and 500 inhabitants and notable only as the last town where drovers bringing cattle up the Eastern Trail could stock supplies, get drunk, and blow off steam before heading for the Red River and the long, dangerous journey across Indian Territory to Kansas.[38] By July 1876, when the Texas and Pacific Railroad finally reached Fort Worth, a boom was under way. Eleven days before the first train pulled into town, the *Daily Democrat* reported that over fifty buildings were under construction and "dwellings are springing up as if by magic."[39] By 1877 an estimated 1000 people were living in tent camps. The first city directory reported that year that "blocks of brick or stone and iron are being completed . . . while private residences are going up everywhere. Vacant houses are things unknown, tent life or boarding being necessary to the new comer until his residence is

38. Oliver Knight, *Fort Worth, Outpost on the Trinity* (Norman: Univ. of Oklahoma Press, 1953), 40–45, 51–56, 59–56; B.B. Paddock, *History of Texas: Fort Worth and the Texas Northwest Edition*, 4 vols. (New York: Lewis Publishing, 1922), 2:599–603; Randolph Clark, *Reminiscences Biographical and Historical* (Wichita Falls, Tex.: Lee Clark, 1919), 34, 54. Since Fort Worth was not separately enumerated from Tarrant County until the 1880 census, earlier population figures are only estimates. Knight gives the lower figure, Paddock the higher.

39. Paddock, *History of Texas*, 2:611–12; Knight, *Fort Worth, Outpost on the Trinity*, 84–87; Fort Worth *Daily Democrat*, 8 July 1876, quoted in *Fort Worth History Notes*, 5, pt. 1:1621–22.

built."[40] Lumber, of course, was still scarce and expensive, and Griffin saw opportunity in the brisk construction market in a booming new city. He bought his first tract of land in Fort Worth early in 1877 and began making bricks.

In March 1877, Leila Griffin paid a lengthy visit to her relatives in Independence, Texas, and Griffin wrote to her there. Like the war letters, this letter brims with interest in and concern about the extended family. Leila's sister Minnie had died, probably in childbirth or as a consequence of it, and her father's health was poor. Knowing that Leila must be "almost wild with joy" at being reunited with her relatives after so many years, Griffin begged for descriptions of "poor Minnie's" youngest children and expressed his own regret at not being there to help with the care of Captain Burt. About his own financial situation, Griffin wrote, "Say to Dr. Muse and Billy Morgan that I hope they haven't had to struggle as hard as myself to make *buckle* and *tongue* meet (in an old phrase of Dr. Muse). In my own case there is continually a better prospect just ahead—but then it remains *just ahead* and it seems that I will never catch up with it."

Griffin reported that he and Jimmie had already fenced in all their best land and the brickyard with help from Callie, who was in charge of the housekeeping and chickens. (The accounts show that half a dozen young men appeared to be rooming with the family, and perhaps some or all of them worked for Griffin.) Claude was finishing a job hauling brick to John Solon, and twenty-two-year-old Bobby was traveling locally as a sales agent for some unspecified commodity, taking his commissions in trade because his customers had no money. Bobby suffered from rheumatoid arthritis, and Griffin hoped that the young man's earnings would be enough to finance a trip to the hot springs—probably in Arkansas—in the summer. He concluded the letter on an optimistic note: "There is fine prospects for business in my line here this summer. I think there will be a great many brick houses built. I still have most of my brick on hand, but have a prospect of

---

40. Knight, *Fort Worth, Outpost on the Trinity*, 87; Charles J. Swasey and W.M. Melton, *Directory of the City of Fort Worth for the Year 1877* (Fort Worth: *Daily Democrat*, 1877), 11 (quotation).

selling soon and then for my house—and then I will, I hope, be able to get my dear family together."[41]

The opportunity turned out to be good indeed; prospects ceased to stay "just ahead" as Griffin finally caught up financially. By 1879 he owned six and one half acres of city land, the taxable value of his real and personal property in Tarrant County was set at $2,105, and he still owned the ten acres of railroad land in Waxahachie. He had tripled his last assessment of $665 in Ellis County four years earlier and had come a long way from the two horses, two cows, and $80 worth of goods in Washington County in 1871. His wealth in Tarrant County in 1879 placed him among the wealthiest 8.6 percent of people in the county.[42] In antebellum Edgefield, he had been among the top 3 percent of wealthiest household heads and lost it all in the war. Twenty years later, he had reestablished his economic fortune in this Texas county on a scale somewhat comparable to what it had been among his free neighbors in antebellum Edgefield District. In Fort Worth, with his practical nature and entrepeneurial flair unleashed as it never had been in antebellum South Carolina, Griffin climbed successfully into the New South's upper middle class.

The brick house that he built for his family at 704 Penn Street was unpretentious, but the neighborhood was an affluent one. Griffin's friend and neighbor was the foremost citizen of Fort Worth, Major Khleber M. Van Zandt, cofounder and president of the Fort Worth National Bank. Major Van Zandt, who had fought with the Seventh Texas Infantry in Tennessee, and Colonel Griffin probably spent some time exchanging reminiscences of the war. In one of the many flowery poems that she published in the local newspapers, Bobby Griffin's wife

41. Original letter in possession of Jack L. Gunter, Dallas, Texas. A copy was printed in the Fort Worth *Examiner*, 20 Nov. 1964; Griffin Scrapbook, 88–96. For the Muse family, see Tenth Census of Population, 1880, Washington County, Independence Village, p. 3.

42. Tarrant County Tax Rolls, microfilm, roll 580, 1878: 62; 1879: 61; 1880: 60; his total assets were listed as $1,845, TSL; Ellis County Tax Rolls, microfilm, roll 1920, 1876: 14, TSL. There were 5,655 people listed in the 1879 tax records. More than a fifth reported no wealth. The mean wealth reported was $739.63, the median was $150; the standard deviation was 1,910. We use reported wealth from two sources, the Tarrant County 1879 tax rolls and the Edgefield County 1860 census.

Etta sentimentalized her father-in-law as a Confederate war hero. The poem described family evenings around the piano, during the course of which Griffin would always ask one of the girls to play "The Battle of Prague." Etta wrote that the stirring music brought a faraway look to Griffin's face:

> 'Mid the roar of the battle he drifted
> And I knew that his soul was afar
> 'Mid the din and the sword-clashing furor
> Of the battle HE led without fear—

The battle Griffin was remembering, of course, was Eltham's Landing, where he had commanded the Hampton Legion and where John Bell Hood's star first rose. In 1879 Griffin joined the survivors of Hood's Texas Brigade in raising money for the ten Hood children in New Orleans who had been orphaned by their parents' death from yellow fever. Although Griffin himself was barely a member of Hood's Brigade (the Hampton Legion infantry was assigned to it after Seven Pines), he was one of the committee of six veterans appointed to receive the donations, and he signed the newspaper appeal in his official capacity as lieutenant colonel of Hampton's Legion. Griffin had not been with the Texas Brigade during the Seven Days, when it made its reputation at Gaines' Mill, but he and Hood had been under fire together on the Peninsula. Hood's combativeness, and the daring of the Texas scouts who shot their way out of ambush on the Occoquan, were Griffin's ideal; he must have taken pride in the opportunity to identify with "Hood's Texans."[43]

As he had in Waxahachie, Griffin also helped establish the Catholic church in Fort Worth. A missionary priest, Father Vincent Perrier, who had been making spring and fall trips from San Angelo since 1870, increased his visits to once a month in 1876. Several families, including the Griffins, took turns opening their homes for Mass. This

---

43. Etta M. Griffin, "A Winter Night," clipping from unidentified Texas newspaper, Griffin Scrapbook. Fort Worth *Daily Democrat*, 8 Sept. 1879, reprinted in Texas Writers' Project, *Research Data, Fort Worth and Tarrant County, Texas* (n.p., 1941), 30:19–20. See letters of 8 May 1862, esp. note 2, and 2 June 1862.

group of worshippers eventually secured a resident priest and erected a small, frame building, St. Stanislaus Church, which was later replaced by St. Patrick's Cathedral.[44]

When the census taker found the family in 1880, Griffin was fifty-four and settled in his last home. With the notable exception of Willie, who had died in August 1866 of unknown causes, all of the children were still under his roof. Only Bobby, twenty-five, had married. Following the Burt tradition of selecting a spouse from within the family, he had chosen a cousin who still lived in Edgefield, and whom he had not seen since childhood. He married Etta Burt, a daughter of Leila's Uncle Billy Burt and young second wife, Helen Eichelberger of Baltimore.[45]

Griffin did not live to enjoy his grandchildren. In the fall of 1880 he came down with a heavy cold that developed into lingering bronchitis. The following March the newspaper reported him "still quite ill but somewhat improved." Although ill for months, Griffin never made a will. One can imagine his reassuring Leila and his children as they worried over him that he had a strong constitution, reminding them that he had gone without an overcoat during part of the winter at the Virginia front and had come through just fine. His condition, however, did not improve. He died on 15 June 1881, not yet fifty-six years old, and was buried in Oakwood Cemetery, in the plot reserved

44. Texas Writers' Project, *Research Data, Forth Worth and Tarrant County, Texas*, 35:245 (Jimmie Griffin was one of the interviewees), 44:69–70, 46:74, 57:323; Knight, *Fort Worth, Outpost on the Trinity*, 63.

45. The newspaper notices stressed the cousins' romantic reunion; the pair had not seen each other since the groom was twelve and the bride eight; they had carried on their courtship by mail, not meeting until two days before the wedding. Bobby brought home not only his bride, but also her eleven-year-old brother, Eugene Burt, and in 1880 the three of them were living with the rest of the family on Penn Street; Bobby was reported without an occupation due to rheumatism. When Moody married a few years later, he chose another daughter from Uncle Billy's second family, Etta's sister, Sallie. The issue of cousin marriage in the South needs more careful study. On Edgefield see Burton, *In My Father's House Are Many Mansions*, 119–123, 322, 371–72, n. 39. Tenth Census of Population, 1880, Tarrant County, Fort Worth, household #138, manuscript census returns. Clipping from Baltimore *Bulletin*, 28 Aug. 1878, Griffin Scrapbook, 189; Fort Worth *Daily Democrat*, 9 Sept. 1879.

for Confederate soldiers.[46] (In Edgefield, his old nemesis, Martin W. Gary, had died less than three months earlier, on 9 April.) The newspaper made mention of Griffin's health and at his death reported itself "bowed down with grief."[47] Although by this time Fort Worth was a city of some 7000, the paper referred to him only as "Colonel Griffin," as it would have to "Major Van Zandt" or "Major Jarvis," men so well known that no given name was necessary.

Leila Griffin lived another forty-one years on Penn Street. The city directories show that she had a telephone, but not all of the advances of the twentieth century sat well with a woman who had grown up during the 1840s and made homespun clothing for her family during the Civil War. A descendant recalled that an unruly horse did not frighten "Granny," but she did not feel safe in an automobile. In her long-sleeved shirtwaist and black cap with its long veil trailing down her back, she rode apprehensively in a friend's electric runabout, but "she never did like cars."[48] When she died on 5 March 1922, Leila was ninety-two and had outlived most of her children; Fannie, Callie, and Jimmie survived her.[49]

---

46. Obituary for J.B. Griffin by Etta Griffin, unidentified clipping, Griffin Scrapbook. A photograph of his gravestone was published in the Fort Worth *Examiner*, 26 Feb. 1965.

47. Fort Worth *Daily Democrat*, 15 March, 26 June 1881. The Griffin Scrapbook also contains an obituary several columns long, probably from the Edgefield *Advertiser*, that describes Griffin's service with the Hampton Legion and the election of 1862. The year 1881 was a difficult one for the family: there also are obituaries in the scrapbook for Leila's father, Etta's young brother Eugene, and Aquilla Miles at home in Edgefield.

48. Linda Page, interview with Burns Mistrop, 13 Oct. 1979, Dallas, Texas.

49. Texas State Department of Health, Bureau of Vital Statistics, Death Certificate #9540, Lula *[sic]* Burt Griffin, 5 March 1922. The cause of death was listed as senility and the place of burial as Calvary Cemetery. The records of the deaths of Meadie, Minnie, Fannie, Jimmie, Claude, and Cally can be found in the bureau's *An Index to Death Records*, 1903–1940, vol. 20, 1941–45, vol. 5, typescript, TSL. Moody died in 1899 of Bright's (kidney) disease; a copy of his obituary is in the Griffin scrapbook. Bobby does not appear in the city directories after 1904, although some of his children continued to be listed at Leila's address. The state of Texas did not begin to record deaths until 1903, and Bobby's may have been missed.

The Griffin children, born in the Old South to wealth and status, grew up on the western frontier of the New South milking cows and firing bricks. They spent the decade after the Civil War on the move while their father tried to reestablish himself economically, stopping finally in the brash young boom town that billed itself as the city "where the West begins." Along with their parents, they learned to cope with a new urban environment. The children never approached the relative wealth of their father; there were too many for any one to inherit riches, as J.B. had. Instead, they followed occupations that would have been beneath them in antebellum South Carolina. At least one of the daughters, Minnie, worked outside the home as a hat trimmer at Grand Leader Millinery. Antebellum young women had worked in millinery shops—but only those from yeoman or poor families. That a daughter of James B. Griffin did so demonstrates an abrupt change from pre–Civil War days. Minnie Griffin must have shared some of her father's entrepreneurial ambition, as she went into partnership with the Grand Leader's manager and opened the new Fisher and Griffin Millinery.[50] Griffin's sons at various times followed such occupations as dairyman, Wells Fargo express driver, newspaper agent, traveling salesman, and storekeeper. Primarily they became tradesmen and small businessmen. Bobby and Jimmie for a time in the 1880s ran R.H. Griffin and Bro. feed and grain store and livery stable, and Bobby later became vice president of R.H. Griffin and Co., which sold groceries and produce. Callie rose from travel buyer to general manager for Crowdus Brothers, dealers in hides, wool, furs, tallow, and beeswax. Moody was supervisor of the local Singer Sewing Machine outlet.[51]

The North Texas prairie towns, with their expansive young economies and absence of Old South social stratification, welcomed such enterprise, and men and women concentrated on what they could achieve in the future, not what they had been in the past. When Griffin settled in Fort Worth, no distinction divided old and new

---

50. We need more analyses of women in this transitional New South.

51. See city directories for 1878, 1883–84, 1885–86, 1899–1900, 1901–2, and subsequent directories.

money; everyone's money was new, and an "old name" went back a dozen years at most. A man's standing depended on having fought on the right side of the war—preferably at the rank of major or higher—and on his initiative in business or manufacturing. By these standards, which took no account of what a man had been "before the war," Griffin was a solid and successful citizen.

Griffin arrived in Fort Worth a few years too late to become one of the elite; he just missed the initial opportunity to make a great fortune and a great name in land, railroads, or banking. As he had belonged on the second tier of slaveowning gentry, just below the aristocrats, he belonged to the second tier of entrepreneurs and businessmen who literally and figuratively helped build the city. In the process he rebuilt, to an extent, his own fortunes—not to the grandeur of the old order, but sufficiently to give his children a place in a new one, the rising commercial class of the new urban Southwest.

In the Edgefield of 1860, almost all of the white residents would have known of the officer and gentleman James B. Griffin. He was a man of stature and a respected leader. Today in Edgefield no one, not even the most knowledgeable local historian in this history-focused community, knows about Griffin. A visitor to Martin Witherspoon Gary's home, now a "Red Shirt Shrine" of Civil War and Reconstruction memorabilia, will not find mention of Griffin as Gary's friend, sponsor, and militia commander in 1860. Communities, like people, construct and reconstruct memories, and the public memory of Edgefield kept no place for Griffin after his move to Texas.

Nineteenth-century southerners identified themselves simultaneously in multiple communities, defined severally by family, race, class, gender, church, neighborhood, school, hobbies, profession, and voluntary associations like the militia. White Edgefieldians built friendships and networks and established a common culture perpetuated in settlements established by families who migrated out before the Civil War. White émigrés extended their community and maintained a sense of identity with Edgefield through letters, visits, and subscribing to the Edgefield *Advertiser*. The Civil War, however, changed Edgefieldians' perceptions of the roles and meanings of community. In search of opportunity both before and after the Civil War, outmigrants were more rootless after the war. Some, like several who migrated to Brazil, returned to Edgefield, but for many the postbellum move severed the past.[52]

The only discovered postbellum communication between James B. Griffin and someone from Edgefield is a letter from Leila's kinsman James A. Dozier in late 1869.[53] Delighted to hear from Griffin after a "long-long time," Dozier filled his reply with news of family and "our mutual friends" in Edgefield and implored Griffin to return. "I wish you would come back here and go to farming again. I know you could make cotton." Farmers were "making . . . more money than they ever made." Labor was abundant, "plenty of negroes especially around the Village on rail roads and near towns." People were renting plantations, and many "who were common overseers before the war . . . are making 8 to 10000 a year." The opportunities were there at home for his friend, J.B. Griffin, a proven successful cotton farmer.

But Griffin had removed from his old community of Edgefield both physically and psychologically. Although he was still struggling financially in 1869, Griffin preferred his new identity as Texan and businessman rather than that of Edgefieldian planter. The Civil War in some respects freed Griffin from his past, allowing him to rebuild a new and satisfying life in a Texas community. There, James B. Griffin, no longer an Edgefieldian, has become part of the history and historical memory of Fort Worth, Texas.

---

52. See Burton, *In My Father's House Are Many Mansions*; for the extended community, see esp. 117–18.

53. J.A. Dozier to My Dear Friend, 25 Aug. 1869, in possession of Jack L. Gunter. Dozier had written several letters before Griffin replied.

Appendix

THE GRIFFIN FAMILY

The Grandparents

James Griffin (1782–1855), married
Frances Bunting, and after her death, married
Nancy Mims

The Parents

James Benjamin Griffin (1825–1881), son of James Griffin and
Frances Bunting, married
Emma Rebecca Miller (1832–1850), and after her death, married
Eliza "Leila" Harwood Burt (1829–1922)

The Children

James William "Willie" Griffin (b. 8 February 1849)
Robert Henry "Bobby" Burt Griffin (b. 7 September 1854)
Fannie Eugene Griffin (b. 31 December 1855)
Annie Diomede "Meadie" Griffin (b. 23 March 1857)
Moody Burt Griffin (b. 23 May 1858)
Claude Eugene Griffin (b. 30 October 1859)
Francis Calhoun "Cally" Griffin (b. 30 October 1859)
James Hampton "Jimmie" Griffin (b. 19 June 1861)
Minnie Leila Griffin (b. 18 May 1863)

Sis and Dr. Harrington

Eliza Ann Griffin (1823–?), daughter of James Griffin and Frances
Bunting, married
Diomede F. Hollingsworth, and after his death, married
Dr. William H. Harrington

THE BURT FAMILY

The Grandparents

Capt. Eugene Brennan Burt (1797–1881) married
Sarah Ann Dozier (1805–1847)

The Children of Eugene and Sarah Burt

Mary Ann Burt married
  Aquilla "Quilla" Miles
Caroline "Carrie" Burt
Eliza "Leila" Harwood Burt married
  James B. Griffin
Robert Henry Burt (died 1854)
Sarah Eugenia Burt (died 1840)
Harwood Burt (died 1853)
Harriet G. Burt (died 1852)
Minnie Burt married
  Dr. Julius E. Muse
Susan "Sue" Burt married
  William Morgan in 1867

Uncle Moody

Major Moody Burt, brother of Eugene B. Burt

Uncle Billy and Aunt Helen

Dr. William Miles Burt, brother of Eugene B. Burt, married
Mary Atkinson, and after her death, married
Helen M. Eichelberger

The Burt Cousins

Augustus "Gus" Burt,
son of John Harwood and Emily Roper Burt
Emily Elizabeth Burt,
daughter of John Harwood and Emily Roper Burt
William Giroud Burt,
son of William Miles and Mary Atkinson Burt
Maria Burt,
daughter of William Miles and Mary Atkinson Burt, married
Andrew Pickens "Pick" Butler
Mary Ann "Annie" Burt,
daughter of William Miles and Mary Atkinson Burt, married
Pierce Mason Butler
Sallie Burt,
daughter of William Miles and Mary Atkinson Burt, married
Moody Burt Griffin
Henrietta "Etta" Burt,
daughter of William Miles and Helen Eichelberger Burt, married
Robert Henry Burt Griffin
Charles Miles,
son of Aquilla and stepson of Mary Ann Burt Miles
Albert Miles,
son of Aquilla and stepson of Mary Ann Burt Miles

Table A-1. Census Profile

NOTE: When persons mentioned in this book were from Edgefield, we sought out their names in the Edgefield Data Base, a systematic merged data record using the unpublished manuscript census schedules (population, agriculture, slave, mortality, industry, and social statistics). In this data base is socioeconomic information for every individual and farm linked from 1850 to 1880 with details on occupation, age, wealth, slave ownership, and farm ownership.[a] Interested readers are able to place these Edgefieldians in precise socioeconomic status. For comparison purposes, we also include wealth and slave distributions for Edgefield.

Year	Name	Age	Occupation	Relation to Household Head (HH), If Not Head	Number in Household	Real Estate ($)	Personal Estate ($)	Number of Slaves	Farm Acres	Cotton (Bales)
1850	Addison, George	33	planter	head	6	6,000	NA	46	950	30
1860	Addison, George	43	farmer	head	11	37,000	95,000	68	1380	105
1850	Bacon, Thomas G.	38	judge	head	4	3,000	NA	7	365	0
1860	Bacon, Thomas G.	48	judge	head	5	2,000	3,000	9	NA	NA
1850	Barr, John W.	23	farmer	head	6	2,000	NA	7	NA	NA
1860	Barr, John W.	32	farmer	head	3	8,250	13,735	9	550	22
1850	Bates, Andrew, D.	24	none	son						
	(HH = Ann Bates; real estate = $5,000; # slaves = 11)									
1860	Bates, Andrew D.	37	farmer	head	4	11,300	13,270	11	906	43
1850	Bean, James	35	planter	head	3	2,500	NA	13	NA	NA
1860	Bean, James	45	farmer	head	4	4,000	17,200	20	415	17
1850	Bettis, Benjamin	37	farmer	head	5	15,000	NA	56	3,220	0
1860	Bettis, Benjamin	46	farmer	head	8	23,000	75,000	74	2,050	120
1850	Bettis, John	2	none	son	5					
	(HH = Benjamin Bettis; real estate = $15,000; # slaves = 56)									

Year	Name	Age	Occupation	Relationship						
1860	Bettis, John	11	in school	son	8					
	(HH = Benjamin Bettis; total wealth = $98,000; # slaves = 74)									
1860	Bettis, Frank	10	in school	son	8					
	(HH = Benjamin Bettis; total wealth = $98,000; # slaves = 74)									
1850	Bland, Elbert	25	doctor	boarder	17	0	NA	3		
	(HH = H.R. Spann; real estate = $12,000; # slaves = 1)									
1860	Bland, Elbert	37	doctor	head	6	26,000	55,000	11	1,770	30
1860	Bland, John	38	farmer	head	7	37,000	55,000	6		
1860	Boatwright, B.T.	51	farmer	head	5	2,500	7,000			
1860	Bonham, James	7	none	son	9					
	(HH = M.L. Bonham; total wealth = $67,000; # slaves = 60)									
1850	Bonham, Milledge L.	36	lawyer	head	6	13,500	NA	34	180	0
1860	Bonham, Milledge L.	46	lawyer	head	9	17,000	50,000	60	1,250	80
1850	Brooks, James C.	29	farmer	head	4	4,000	NA	25	900	22
1860	Brooks, James C.	39	farmer	head	8	10,000	25,000	25	1,000	65
1850	Brooks, P.S.	31	lawyer	head	5	6,800	NA	18	NA	NA
1860	Burt, Augustus	18	student	son	5					
	(HH = Dr. J.H. Burt; total wealth = $32,000; # slaves = 24)									
1850	Burt, Eugene	50	planter	head	8	4,200	NA	24	500	22
1860	Burt, Eugene	61	farmer	head	6	7,000	25,000	22	700	40
1850	Burt, Francis W.	36	farmer	head	6	0	NA	14		
1860	Burt, Francis W.	45	farmer	head	8	2,500	21,552	28		
1850	Burt, Harwood	47	doctor	head	5	5,000	NA	22	250	30
1860	Burt, Dr. H.	57	farmer	head	5	12,000	20,000	24	3,005	25
1850	Burt, Emily	38	none	wife	5				600	1,095
	(HH = Dr. Harwood Burt; real estate = $5,000; # slaves = 22)									
1860	Burt, Mary A.	54	none	sister	5					
	(HH = Dr. H. Burt; total wealth = $32,000; # slaves = 24)									

continued

Table A-1. (continued)

Year	Name	Age	Occupation	Relation to Household Head (HH), If Not Head	Number in Household	Real Estate ($)	Personal Estate ($)	Number of Slaves	Farm Acres	Cotton (Bales)
1850	Burt, W.G.	7	in school	son	9					
	(HH=Dr. William Burt; real estate=$2,500; # slaves=6)									
1860	Burt, W.G.	17	none	son	12					
	(HH=Dr. William Burt; total wealth=$5,000; # slaves=4)									
1850	Burt, William M.	35	doctor	head	9	2,500	NA	6	NA	NA
1860	Burt, William M.	45	doctor	head	12	0	5,000	4	140	8
1850	Butler, Ann	55	none	head	3	100	NA	0	25	2
1860	Butler, Ann	64	none	head	1	400	300	0	NA	NA
1850	Butler, A.P.	54	planter	head	3	20,000	NA	64	1,000	112
1850	Butler, A.P.	11	in school	son	7					
	(HH=Mrs. M.J. Butler; real estate=$1,500; # slaves=9)									
1860	Butler, A.P.	21	farming	son	5					
	(HH=Julia Butler; total wealth=0; # slaves=5)									
1860	Butler, Matthew C.	24	lawyer	head	2	7,000	17,000	13	106	75
1850	Butler, Pierce M.	13	in school	son	7					
	(HH=Mrs. M.J. Butler; real estate=$1,500; # slaves=9)									
1860	Butler, Pierce M.	23	student	son	5					
	(HH=Julia Butler; total wealth=0; # slaves=5)									
1860	Butler, P.	20	clerk	unknown	15					
	(HH=Lewis Jones; total wealth=$20,000; # slaves=7)									

	Name	Occupation	Age	Relationship		Real estate	Wealth			
1850	Butler, Robert J.	farmer	36	head	10	8,000	NA	28	725	0
1860	Butler, Robert J.	farmer	45	head	8	25,000	32,700	41	1,500	96
1850	Butler, Thomas	farmer	19	unknown	4					
	(HH = J.R. Mobley; real estate = 3,000; # slaves = 21)									
1860	Butler, Thomas	farmer	29	head	5	0	207	0	NA	NA
1850	Butler, William	merchant	35	head	7	4,000	NA	9	NA	NA
1860	Butler, William	merchant	44	head	5	20,760	33,600	9	NA	NA
1850	Carroll, James P.	lawyer	41	head	7	2,500	NA	8	NA	NA
1860	Carroll, James P.	judge	51	head	5	35,000	100,000	22	NA	NA
1850	Carwile, Z.W.	planter	32	head	7	5,000	NA	19	1,450	30
1860	Carwile, Z.W.	judge	41	head	11	10,000	45,000	27	1,375	57
1850	Christie, Simeon	sheriff	50	head	8	13,000	NA	40	2,050	40
1860	Christie, Simeon	merchant	60	head	6	7,000	30,000	13	NA	NA
1850	Clark, T.H.	farmer	21	unknown	6					
	(HH = Isaac Cowards; real estate = $1,500; # slaves = 0)									
1860	Clark, T.H.	lawyer	31	head	2	2,500	2,000	2	1,500	70
1860	Coles, J.S.	farmer	27	head	5	52,500	67,270	58	1,730	66
1850	Crafton, Joseph	farmer	56	head	9	15,000	NA	58	1,250	0
1850	Day, Julius	planter	35	head	6	7,500	NA	14	1,500	38
1860	Day, Julius	farmer	44	head	11	8,000	40,000	30		
1860	Dean, Yancey	clerk	17	unknown	8					
	(HH = E. Penn; total wealth = $40,000; # slaves = 11)									
1850	Dozier, Allen	student	18	son	3					
	(HH = Allen Dozier; real estate = 25,000; # slaves = 74)									
1860	Dozier, Allen S.	doctor	26	head	1	14,000	32,250	33	760	64
1860	Dozier, James	lawyer	28	head	3	18,800	32,715	7	NA	NA
1850	Dunovant, R.	planter	29	head	2	4,500	NA	26	NA	NA
1860	Dunovant, R.	farmer	39	head	4	17,000	49,703	49	NA	NA

continued

Table A-1. (continued)

Year	Name	Age	Occupation	Relation to Household Head (HH), If Not Head	Number in Household	Real Estate ($)	Personal Estate ($)	Number of Slaves	Farm Acres	Cotton (Bales)
1850	Frazier, Marshal	43	planter	head	7	6,000	NA	75	620	0
1860	Frazier, Marshal	53	farmer	head	5	42,700	136,230	50	550	18
1860	Gary, Martin W.	28	lawyer	boarder	28					01
(HH = B.J. Ryan; total wealth = $25,000; # slaves = 14)										
(Gary's mother in Abbeville listed real estate = $10,000 and personal estate = $30,000)										
1850	Glover, Arthur	17	farmer	son	9					
(HH = Wiley Glover; real estate = $15,000; # slaves = 44)										
1860	Glover, Arthur	26	farmer	head	5	12,000	20,000	18	784	58
1850	Griffin, James	67	planter	head	2	8,000	NA	29	1,200	20
1850	Griffin, James B.	24	planter	head	3	3,000	NA	26	340	10
1860	Griffin, James B.	35	farmer	head	10	25,000	56,530	61	1,550	113
1850	Griffin, N.L.	47	lawyer	head	7	27,000	NA	124	1,600	0
1850	Griffin, Nathan L.	7	none	son	7					
(HH = N.L. Griffin; real estate = $27,000; # slaves = 124)										
1860	Griffin, Nathan L.	16	in school	son	5					
(HH = Mrs. N.L. Griffin; total wealth = $20,000; # slaves = 10)										
1850	Griffin, Stanmore	25	planter	head	4	2,000	NA	6		
1860	Griffin, Stanmore	35	lawyer	head	8	2,000	6,000	9		
1860	Hammond, James H.	52	planter	head	7	30,000	40,000	21	460	0
1850	Hatcher, James	33	farmer	son	6					
(HH = Benjamin Hatcher; real estate = $10,000; # slaves = 16)										

Year	Name	Age	Occupation	Relationship						
1860	Hatcher, James	42	farmer	head	7	15,000	13,145	11	1,425	50
1850	Hill, Lud	29	merchant	son	10	0	NA	4		
(HH=Theophilus Hill; real estate=$16,000; # slaves=49)										
1860	Hill, Lud	39	farmer	head	5	20,000	60,000	53	1,000	27
1850	Holland, Daniel	57	planter	head	3	20,000	NA	76	2,100	78
1860	Holland, Daniel	76	farmer	head	1	30,400	65,690	70	NA	NA
1850	Hughes, Alfred J.	29	farmer	head	6	4,000	NA	31	400	48
1860	Hughes, Alfred J.	39	farmer	head	7	5,000	68,925	54	450	85
1860	Hutson, G. W.	19	farming	unknown	7	0	300			
(HH=J.W. Raborn; total wealth=$150; # slaves=0)										
1860	Johnson, P.D.	34	farmer	head	6	400	70	0	106	0
1860	Jones, E.W.	34	farmer	head	8	500	300	15	400	0
1850	Jones, Lewis	37	farmer	head	8	1,200	NA	25	90	0
1860	Jones, Lewis	47	sheriff	head	3	10,000	50,000	19		
1850	Lamar, Robert	21	farmer	unknown		0	NA			
(HH=M. Lamar; real estate=$8,500; # slaves=16)										
1860	Lamar, Robert	28	farmer	head	7	80,000	66,000	9	1,200	31
1850	Lanham, James	23	farmer	son	6	6,900		10		
(HH=Joseph Lanham; real estate=$20,000; # slaves=0)										
1860	Lanham, James	33	farmer	head	6	15,000	46,505	40	1,100	72
1860	Markert, M.A.	29	mechanic	unknown	28	0	2,000			
(HH=B.J. Ryan; total wealth=$25,000; # slaves=14)										
1850	McClintock, Mrs J.	35	none	head	7	2,000	NA	0		
1860	McClintock, Mrs J.	50	teacher	head	4	3,000	4,425	4		
1860	McKie, Robert H.	28	doctor	son	5					
(HH=G.A. McKie; total wealth=$135,150; # slaves=131)										
1850	McKie, Thomas	21	doctor	son	6					
(HH=G.A. McKie; real estate=$12,000; # slaves=112)										
1860	McKie, Thomas	32	doctor	head	4	8,500	38,000	45	0	22

continued

Table A-1. (continued)

Year	Name	Age	Occupation	Relation to Household Head (HH), If Not Head	Number in Household	Real Estate ($)	Personal Estate ($)	Number of Slaves	Farm Acres	Cotton (Bales)
1850	Miles, Albert	10	student	son	7					
	(HH = Aquilla Miles; real estate = $1,600; # slaves = 7)									
1860	Miles, Albert	19	student	son	4					
	(HH = Aquilla Miles; total wealth = $17,925; # slaves = 10)									
1850	Miles, Aquilla	36	farmer	head	7	1,600	NA	7	200	12
1860	Miles, Aquilla	44	farmer	head	4	6,555	11,370	10	437	11
1850	Miles, Charles	12	student	son	7					
	(HH = Aquilla Miles; real estate = $1,600; # slaves = 7)									
1860	Miles, Charles	23	farming	nephew	10					
	(HH = James B. Griffin; total wealth = $81,530; # slaves = 61)									
1850	Miles, Lewis	41	stoneware	head	10	4,000	NA	14	NA	NA
1860	Miles, Lewis	51	stoneware	head	10	10,500	50,000	38	2,100	0
1850	Miller, B.	25	planter	head	3	7,000	NA	14	2,050	45
1860	Miller, B.H.	34	farmer	head	6	16,000	49,170	40	2,000	66
1850	Mims, B.L.	37	planter	head	8	5,000	NA	21	NA	NA
1860	Mims, B.L.	48	farmer	head	9	7,000	33,800	30	700	36
1850	Mims, James	32	planter	head	4	8,000	NA	22	NA	NA
1860	Mims, James	42	farmer	head	8	6,000	10,000	10	1,015	43
1850	Moss, Matthew	18	farmer	brother	5					
	(HH = John Moss; real estate = $1,000; # slaves = 6)									

1860	Moss, Col. M.	28	farmer	head	2	2,000	5,500	3	NA	NA
1850	Moss, William H.	50	planter	head	4	10,000	NA	36	600	10
1860	Moss, William H.	60	planter	head	4	31,500	40,345	41	NA	NA
1860	Muse, J.	32	doctor	son-in-law	6	0	0			
	(HH = E. Burt; total wealth = $32,000; # slaves = 22)									
1850	Nicholson, Ben	9	in school	son	9					
	(HH = J. Nicholson; real estate = $20,000; # slaves = 7)									
1860	Nicholson, Ben	19	student	son	5					
	(HH = Mrs. E. J. Nicholson; total wealth = $80,000; # slaves = 47)									
1850	Nicholson, John	10	in school	son	9					
	(HH = S. Nicholson; real estate = $18,000; # slaves = 71)									
1860	Nicholson, John A.	20	student	son	11					
	(HH = S. Nicholson; total wealth = $110,000; # slaves = 68)									
1850	Nicholson, John	16	student	unknown	9					
	(HH = J. Lake; real estate = $5,000; # slaves = 32)									
1860	Nicholson, J.L.	26	none	unknown	5	0	6,000	2		
	(HH = Mrs. P. Addison; total wealth = $29,000; # slaves = 29)									
1860	Nicholson, J.G.	26	farming	head	13	20,000	68,225	27	900	70
1850	Nicholson, Shemuel	34	planter	head	9	18,000	NA	71	NA	NA
1860	Nicholson, Shemuel	44	farmer	head	11	30,000	80,000	68	2,540	70
1850	Penn, Edmund	15	none	son	13					
	(HH = G. Penn; real estate = 0; # slaves = 8)									
1860	Penn, Edmund	25	none	son	12	0	4,000	0		
	(HH = G. Penn; total wealth = $2,500; # slaves = 11)									
1850	Penn, G.	45	merchant	head	13	0	NA	8		
1860	Penn, G.L.	53	merchant	head	12	0	2,500	11		
	Pickens, Francis W.	44	planter	head	8	90,000	NA	299	NA	NA
	Pickens, Francis W.	55	min Russia	head	3	70,400	313,106	276	NA	NA
	...mbo, Benjamin	37	farmer	head	6	2,500	NA	0		

continued

Table A-1. (continued)

Year	Name	Age	Occupation	Relation to Household Head (HH), If Not Head	Number in Household	Real Estate ($)	Personal Estate ($)	Number of Slaves	Farm Acres	Cotton (Bales)
1860	Rambo, Benjamin	46	farmer	head	5	6,000	14,975	17	407	47
1850	Rambo, Joseph	30	farmer	unknown	2					
(HH = J.F. Adams; real estate = $14,000; # slaves = 11)										
1860	Rambo, Joseph	43	farmer	head	5	0	0	8		
1860	Rutherford, A.	40	driver	boarder	28	0	0	0		
(HH = B.J. Ryan; total wealth = $25,000; # slaves = 14)										
1860	Seibels, E.W.	32	farmer	head	3	5,000	31,500	20	550	40
1860	Seibels, Emmet	35	lawyer	head	1	500	3,000	1		
1850	Smith, Ben	14	none	grandson	3					
(HH = H. Smith; total wealth = 0; # slaves = 0)										
1860	Smith, Ben	24	farming	head	2	0	50	0		
1860	Spradley, B.F.	29	overseer	head	5	0	500			
1850	Sullivan, R.J.	19	merchant	unknown	23	0				
(HH = J.L. Doby; real estate = $1,200; # slaves = 14)										
1860	Sullivan, R.	30	trader	unknown	12	0	15,000	0		
(HH = G.L. Penn; total wealth = $2,500; # slaves = 11)										
1850	Talbert, J.L.	23	farmer	head	4	5,500	NA	10	1,170	18
1860	Talbert, J.L.	33	farmer	head	13	9,500	33,386	30	760	46
1850	Tompkins, J.W.	24	farmer	head	3	2,500	NA	0	NA	NA
1860	Tompkins, J.W.	34	farmer	head	8	0	4,310	26	NA	NA

1850	Tompkins, James	56	planter	head	7	15,000	NA	85	500	0
1860	Tompkins, James	67	farmer	head	4	25,000	120,000	113	0	35
1850	Tompkins, R.W.	15	student	son	7					
	(HH = James Tompkins; real estate = $15,000; # slaves = 85)									
1860	Tompkins, R.W.	25	lawyer	brother	6	1,000	2,000	1		
	(HH = S.S. Tompkins; total wealth = $78,000; # slaves = 44)									
1860	Tompkins, S.S.	40	farmer	head	6	18,000	60,000	44	NA	NA
1860	Wardlaw, Francis H.	59	judge	head	7	6,000	20,000	18	NA	NA
1850	Wilson, William	30	farmer	head	4	0	NA	2	NA	NA
1860	Wilson, William	43	farmer	head	5	0	2,000	0	0	6

[a] See Burton, *In My Father's House Are Many Mansions*, 326–32.

Table A-2. Wealth of Edgefield District Household Heads, 1850 and 1860

Rank	1850 Real Estate	1860 Real Estate	1860 Personal Estate	1860 Real and Personal Estate
90.1 to 100 percent	$5,000 and above	$8,680 and above	$23,294 and above	$32,565 and above
80.1 to 90 percent	$2,500 to $4,999	$4,150 to $8,679	$11,561 to $23,393	$16,000 to $32,564
70.1 to 80 percent	$1,500 to $2,499	$2,500 to $4,149	$6,000 to $11,560	$8,920 to $15,599
60.1 to 70 percent	$900 to $1,499	$1,500 to $2,499	$2,943 to $5,999	$4,500 to $8,919
50.1 to 60 percent	$500 to $899	$800 to $1,499	$1,000 to $2,942	$2,100 to $4,499
40.1 to 50 percent	$1 to $499	$200 to $799	$434 to $9,999	$1,000 to $2,099
30.1 to 40 percent	$0	$1 to $199	$215 to $433	$400 to $999
20.1 to 30 percent	$0	$0	$100 to $214	$150 to $399
10.1 to 20 percent	$0	$0	$50 to $99	$50 to $149
0.1 to 10 percent	$0	$0	$0 to $49	$0 to $49
	N = 3,030	N = 3,001	N = 3,001	N = 3,001

SOURCE: Edgefield Data Base.

Figure A-1. Distribution of Slaves and Slaveownership, 1850 and 1860.

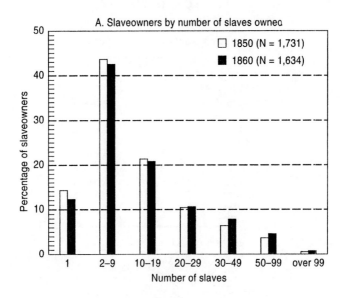

A. Slaveowners by number of slaves owned

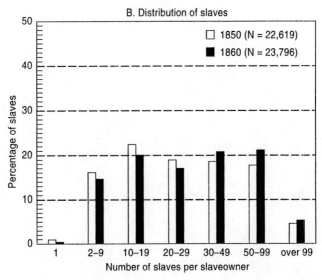

B. Distribution of slaves

SOURCE: Edgefield Data Base.

Table A-3. Total Tax Valuation,
Tarrant County, Texas, 1879

Total Tax Valuation	Rank (%)
$1,841 to 42,510	90.1 to 100
$987 to $1,840	80.1 to 90
$592 to $986	70.1 to 80
$303 to $591	60.1 to 70
$151 to $302	50.1 to 60
$76 to $150	40.1 to 50
$30 to $75	30.1 to 40
$0 to $29	20.1 to 30
$0 to $0	10.1 to 20
$0 to $0	0.1 to 10
N = 5,655	

SOURCE: 1879 Tarrant County Tax Rolls.

Index

343

Printed in the United Kingdom
by Lightning Source UK Ltd.
9768400001B/11